Researching British Probates 1354-1858

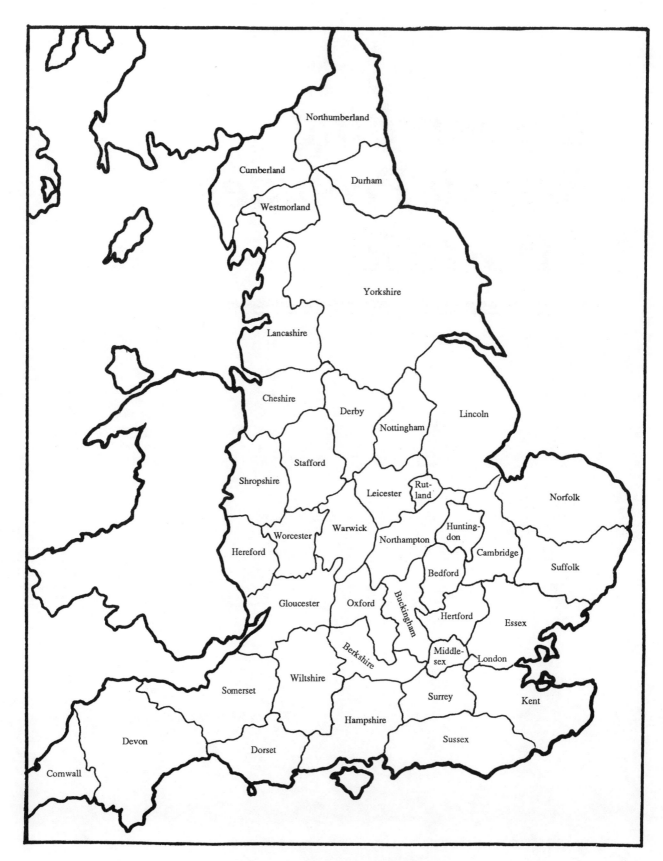

Ancient Counties of England

Researching British Probates 1354-1858

A Guide to the Microfilm Collection of the Family History Library

Volume 1
Northern England/Province of York

David H. Pratt

SR Scholarly Resources Inc.
Wilmington, Delaware

The paper used in this publication meets the minimum requirements of the American National Standard for permanence of paper for printed library materials, Z39.48, 1984.

Scholarly Resources Inc.
104 Greenhill Avenue
Wilmington, DE 19805-1897

The maps for Cumberland, Lancashire, Nottinghamshire, Westmorland, and Yorkshire on pages xxi–xxix are reprinted from *Pre-1858 English Probate Jurisdictions*. Copyright by The Church of Jesus Christ of Latter-day Saints. Used by permission.

Library of Congress Cataloging-in-Publication Data

Pratt, David H.
    Researching British probates, 1354–1858 : a guide to the microfilm collection of the Family History Library / David H. Pratt.
        p. cm.
    Includes bibliographical references and index.
    Contents: v. 1. Northern England/Province of York
    ISBN 0-8420-2420-4 (alk. paper : cloth : v. 1)
    1. Probate records—England—Microform catalogs. 2. England—Genealogy—Sources—Bibliography—Microform catalogs. 3. Church of Jesus Christ of Latter-day Saints. Family History Library—Microform catalogs. I. Church of Jesus Christ of Latter-day Saints. Family History Library. II. Title.
Z5313.G7E57   1992
[CS434]
016.929'341—dc20
                                                                92-18338
                                                                        CIP

To the Memory of Frank Smith

BRITISH PROBATES, 1354–1858

Volume 1   *Northern England/Province of York*: Cheshire, Cumberland, Durham, Lancashire, Northumberland, Nottinghamshire, Westmorland, Yorkshire

Volume 2   *Eastern England/East Midlands*: Bedfordshire, Buckinghamshire, Cambridgeshire, Huntingdonshire, Leicestershire, Lincolnshire, Norfolk, Northamptonshire, Rutland, Suffolk

Volume 3   *Southeastern England/Province of Canterbury*: Essex, Hampshire, Hertfordshire, Kent, London, Middlesex, Surrey, Sussex

Volume 4   *West/Southwestern England*: Berkshire, Cornwall, Derbyshire, Devon, Dorset, Gloucestershire, Herefordshire, Oxfordshire, Shropshire, Somerset, Staffordshire, Warwickshire, Wiltshire, Worcestershire

ABOUT THE AUTHOR

David H. Pratt is an associate professor of history at Brigham Young University. He received an M.A. in medieval history from Brigham Young and a Ph.D. in modern British history from the University of Nebraska. He was trained as a researcher by the Family History Library in Salt Lake City, where he worked from 1960 to 1965. Mr. Pratt is recognized as an Accredited Genealogist of the Family History Library in English research. He is also a Fellow of the Utah Genealogical Association, an international organization. His previous publications include "The Skaggs Saga: A Case Study of a Family Using Genealogy, Family History, and Local History" and *English Quakers and the First Industrial Revolution* (New York, 1985).

CONTENTS

PART 4 Lancashire

PART 5 Northumberland

PART 6 Nottinghamshire

PREFACE

The microfilms of the Family History Library in Salt Lake City, Utah, form a vast, centralized reservoir of primary sources for original research by anyone interested in social data over time. A prime example is British probate records. The actual sources are scattered between forty local archives and two national ones in England, while microfilms of most of these records before 1858 (80 percent to 90 percent) are centrally located in the United States.

The Family History Library was founded in 1894 by The Church of Jesus Christ of Latter-day Saints. In the past it was referred to as the Genealogical Library, and it is still known to many as the Genealogical Society of Utah. The Family History Library, open to the general public, has over seventeen hundred branches, known as Family History Centers, scattered around the world. For a small fee, copies of most of the microfilms in Salt Lake City can be made available for local study in these centers. Copies of the microfilms are also on deposit in the archives where the original records were filmed, as in the case of the various county record offices in England for British probates.

All microfilms housed in Salt Lake City must be examined at the main library or at one of its Family History Centers. To determine the nearest Family History Center or to obtain a list of the addresses and telephone numbers of those in the nearby region, write the Family History Library, Correspondence Section, 35 North West Temple Street, Salt Lake City, UT 84150 or call (801) 240-5267. Provide the Family History Center with the appropriate microfilm call numbers obtained from this reference guide, and their staff will complete the lending procedure in your behalf.

There are thousands of rolls of microfilm for England's wills and related probate documents alone. This collection constitutes a resource of immeasurable value, not only to genealogists but also to demographers and economic and social historians or anyone who has an interest in the social structure, life-styles, and mores of the British people between the Late Middle Ages and the mid-nineteenth century. Yet this filmed resource is virtually untapped.

Few scholars are aware of its existence or the ease with which a microfilm from the collection can be obtained for study relatively close to home. Even those who use the Family History Library for personal research tend to ignore or underutilize the collection. Many indexes exist, but they are scattered throughout the library and are not easily connected to the three hundred or so original court names by which the films are filed. The researcher attempting to find a particular will is faced with the awesome task of knowing which courts are involved and how to coordinate the overall research.

The purpose of this series of volumes is to simplify the complexities of British probate jurisdictions and make the microfilms of the British probate collection more accessible. This and the forthcoming volumes are arranged by county. Some researchers may find the county coverage of each volume a little odd, but the design is to remain faithful to ancient diocesan boundaries as much as possible. Where needed, a county's description is made clear by a colored map depicting the courts of original jurisdiction. Following a brief introduction for each county is a probate decision table of all of the courts to be searched for a particular will, a listing of any known indexes and printed records for each court available in the Family History Library, and an annotated listing of the films by year and court.

The rapidly expanding film collection of the Family History Library requires a six- or seven-digit numbering system to identify each roll of film. The call numbers listed in this guide may actually be preceded by one or two zeros in the library's card catalog. These zeros are not necessary to order a film or to find the correct box of film in the main library and have been omitted here to save space. Continual expansion also means the possible eventual completion of the collection, sufficient to warrant a supplemental volume.

Dividends from the research for Volume 1 can be drawn from the index. They include numerous references to personal migration, both internally and externally; the bishops' transcripts for seven parishes or chapelries, ranging from one to six years in extent; and some bonds from marriage licenses issued by fourteen different jurisdictions.

Volume 1 has been twenty-five years in the making. I designed the overall plan in response to the challenge of my department supervisor, Frank Smith, and completed some of the maps while I was employed as a researcher by the Family History Library in the 1960s. Supervision of the map work continued under Derek F. Metcalfe and later under John H. Stables, who guided the first part through the publication of the maps at the end of that decade.

The second part of the project came under the direction of T. Hoyt Palmer. At any one given time over a two- and one-half-year period, from two to six volunteer aides assisted him in inspecting each roll of film and compiling a handlist of their findings by county and court. Since these handlists were not published and the maps were not widely marketed before going out of print, permission was granted by the Family History Library to review both projects, update them, and combine the best elements of each into one scholarly publication.

A project of this magnitude depends on the efforts and support of many others. I express a deep sense of gratitude to the Family History Library, not only for permission to use its materials but also for its many dedicated workers, past and present, whose guidance and cooperation made the dream a reality. In turn I acknowledge the invaluable role of Anthony J. Camp's *Wills and Their Whereabouts,* 4th ed. (London: The author, 1974), in helping to determine exactly what is and is not encompassed by this collection of microfilms. And finally, I thank those many nameless archivists, filmers, catalogers, and private individuals, including the congenial support of several unsung graduate research assistants, who have cared about and helped to preserve these records.

INTRODUCTION

Hidden away in the indexes of a British probate court far from London is a reference in 1823 to Justino da Silva Cerquinho. The printed index states that he was a merchant of Liverpool. In actuality, Cerquinho was en route to Portugal after conducting business in Brazil and England when he died on board ship near Holyhead. The probate is accompanied by several notarized documents in Portuguese, including his christening certificate.[1] Thus, probate records can aid any student of the past in a variety of ways, particularly if the records are housed in one depository.

The term "probate" refers to any document that deals with the legal disposition of a deceased person's property. The most common probate instrument is the will, whereby a testator declares his intentions before death. Should a property holder die intestate or without a valid will, then a court may decide who has the right to administer the estate. Such grants are known as letters of administration.

In addition to wills and letters of administration, there may be bonds, inventories of property, guardianship papers for the care of minors, accounts of the final distribution, renunciations or refusals to be involved in dispersing the property, caveats or warning notices temporarily halting the legal proceedings, and other records. All such actions are noted by the court in its official proceedings or act books.

To ensure fairness and an accurate accounting, all administrators were bonded (administration bond). Likewise, the executor of a will may have been bonded (probate or testamentary bond). Typically, the amount of the bond was set at twice that of the estimated value of the estate.

In length of time, few British historical records can compete with the span of probates from the thirteenth century to the present. Admittedly, not everyone was involved, nor were all social classes represented equally. A married woman could not leave a will without the permission of her husband until 1882, and no will had to be proven or probated, unless disputed, before 1750. But all social classes were represented, and participation of the lower classes may have been proportionately higher in a society dominated by churchmen who frowned on the idea of dying intestate. Estimates of the total population having their property listed in a probate record at any given time range from 5 to 25 percent.[2]

Probates are especially useful for any study of the Tudor-Stuart period. The lower classes benefited from legislation in 1529 that prohibited court fees in cases where the total worth of the property was £5 or less. Accordingly, detailed inventories became compulsory at the same time. In most courts, inventories continue as a valuable historical source through the late eighteenth century. The middle classes were further encouraged by the *Statute of Wills* in 1540 that permitted the devising of real estate via probate, except land under manorial control (copyhold). The result is that Tudor wills,

---

[1] Consistory Court of Chester, Original Admon for Lancashire, 1823.

[2] For a detailed history and description of the development of the various types of probate records, see Anthony J. Camp's introduction in his *Wills and Their Whereabouts,* 4th ed. (London: The author, 1974).

such as that of Henry Winchcombe (dated 1562) in which he left his best bed and the sealings, portals, and glass of the house to his son, are not uncommon.[3]

Historical research in English probates is further complicated by jurisdictional differences. Prior to 1858 most probates were handled by one of the ecclesiastical courts of the Church of England. The courts were functions of the hierarchical units descending from the province (presided over by an archbishop), to the diocese (presided over by a bishop), to the archdeaconry, to the rural deanery, with the parish at the bottom.

At the height of ecclesiastical dominion over probates, there were two provincial and twenty-seven diocesan courts in England, Wales, and the Isle of Man that always had the right of probate. The archbishops and bishops were assisted by a number of lesser church officials with titles such as chancellor, dean, dean and chapter, and subdean. The bishop's court was known as the episcopal consistory or, simply, consistory court. In a large diocese a commissary court would be commissioned by the bishop to probate in a specified area. In turn, the archdeacons, rural deans (deanery), and parish ministers may have assisted the bishop in matters of probate.

The courts of the archbishops and bishops acted as either original jurisdictions or superior ones restricting lower courts. The lower courts consisted of some archdeaconries, many small church jurisdictions known as peculiars, and civil areas such as manorial and borough courts. The latter are frequently referred to as peculiars also, but a peculiar was an ecclesiastical unit, usually a parish, that was always exempt from the control of the rural dean and archdeacon, and sometimes the bishop and archbishop. Hence, the peculiar tried to assume the rights normally reserved for the jurisdictions from which it was exempt.

Visitations and vacancies further complicated this jurisdictional scheme. Visitations occurred usually in three-year cycles. During a visitation the lower official not only reported to a bishop or archbishop but also the court of the lower official was closed or inhibited for several months. While inhibited, any court business became the prerogative of the higher court responsible for the visitation. In the case of a vacancy in the office of the bishop or archbishop, it was usual for the dean and chapter of either unit to assume all probate business until the new bishop or archbishop was installed.

Altogether there were some three hundred courts scattered among forty ancient counties that might have granted probate before 1858. The result may overwhelm the researcher seeking the probate of a particular person. The section within this introduction entitled "General Instructions for Finding a Specific Probate" is designed to alleviate this problem. The historian wishing to make comparative studies is discouraged by the decentralization of records and repositories and the lack of a national index. The first problem is addressed by this guide to microfilms in one central library that may be more accessible to scholars from around the world than actually going to the sources in England. There is even some hope for the second problem: a national index for the early part of the nineteenth century.

The Inland Revenue Office gathered a tax on probates starting in 1796. The Estate Duty Office was charged with the responsibility of gathering a copy of each will and letter of administration when taxed. The indexes, registers, and some copies have been microfilmed from 1796 to 1811 and from 1812 to 1857. After 1857 probates become a civil matter. Copies of the originals and a national index are located at Somerset House in London. The national index from 1858 to 1957 is already available on microfilm, and the modern probates are now being filmed. See London in Volume 3 of this series for the details of the microfilms on the national level from 1796 onward.

[3]Archdeaconry Court of Berkshire, B. 222, 1563.

Possible Uses of Probates by Economic and Social Historians

Any attempts to study changing family patterns, the status of women, inheritance practices, persistence rates, wealth distribution, capital formation, the development of power elites, and the educational and religious structure of society may be greatly enhanced through the use of probates. It is to be regretted, although understandable, that the technique of family reconstitution developed in the past twenty years did not incorporate or have greater access to probates. Now that they are so readily available, probates must be a part of any further quantitative analyses back into time and are crucial for comparative studies.

The broad outlines of the Industrial Revolution have been vividly sketched, but more needs to be known about the lives of individual entrepreneurs, who did the financing and why, and what were the sources of capital, including the rural contribution. Probates might even shed light on the more difficult question of the standard of living. John West suggests comparing the numerous inventories that exist before 1780 "with the equally detailed contents of farm sale catalogues of the nineteenth and twentieth centuries to show changes in standards of living."[4]

Is there a connection between the rise of industrialization or the emergence of the modern world and the decline of patriarchalism? Mark Friedberger and Janice Webster suggest that the demise or resurgence of patriarchalism can be determined by studying a family over four generations. The keys are child order and age at marriage, the rise or decline of premarital pregnancies, the use of traditional naming patterns or lack of the same, inheritance practices, and an uprise or decline in mobility. (Mobility refers not only to migration but also to the child order and age of the emigrants, who stayed, and which children practiced the father's occupation or departed from it.[5]) Probates are invaluable for answering these kinds of questions.

In turn, probates can aid immigration studies in general. An examination of the probates of all of the early settlers in a given area may provide answers to geographic and social origins, and possibly to religious affiliation. Frequently, entire villages moved together to the new home, or at least the first arrivals would represent several nearby localities within the old homeland, as the leaders sought to persuade friends and neighbors to go with them.[6] The unknown origin of an individual can be resolved by defining the person's network of family, friends, and associates, and their collective origins. The index to this volume may be of further assistance as it concentrates on the names noted in passing in the preparation of this guide to persons and records that were not necessarily where they were supposed to be, either in time or place. (Thus, throughout this volume, it is referred to as the stray-name index.)

An introductory article on the historical use of wills for the Tudor-Stuart period has been published by Michael L. Zell, who points out that the names of the executors and overseers have an important bearing on understanding the system of patronage. The portion set apart for the future marriage of daughters "may act as a rough and ready guide to the wealth of the testator and to the changing value of money."[7] There is evidence for urban investment in land, agricultural techniques, landholding practices, and rural sources of credit. The researcher is cautioned appropriately on how

---

[4]John West, *Village Records* (London: Macmillan and Company, 1962), p. 92.

[5]Mark Friedberger and Janice R. Webster, "Social Structure and State and Local History," *Western Historical Quarterly* 9 (July 1978): 297–314.

[6]For an excellent example of this concept and how to approach it through the integrated use of local records, including probates, see David Grayson Allen's *In English Ways* (New York: W. W. Norton, 1982).

[7]Michael L. Zell, "Fifteenth- and Sixteenth-Century Wills as Historical Sources," *Archives* 14 (Autumn 1979): 67–74.

religious preambles to wills might be used to detect the testator's bias,[8] and how signatures might assist in a study of literacy.

Although some historians have utilized inventories, there is a great need to broaden the use of the entire probate collection. Comparative studies between social classes, different regions, and across national boundaries should be high on the agenda. A step in the right direction is Mark Overton's *A Bibliography of British Probate Inventories* (Department of Geography, University of Newcastle upon Tyne, 1983) that lists inventories in print. The completion of the remaining volumes of *British Probates, 1354–1858* will provide a benchmark for this field. However, scholars need to be more aware of the potential for centralized research in the probates and other local records of the world offered to them by the microfilms of the Family History Library.

General Instructions for Finding a Specific Probate

Normally, probate would have been granted in a court having jurisdiction over the place where the testator resided or possibly where the majority of his property was located. To determine this jurisdiction, proceed as follows:

1) Check the map section in this volume. If there is a map (there are none for Cheshire, Durham, and Northumberland—start with step 2 for these three counties), locate the place of residence or other areas of known affinity. The map will be color coded to the court of original jurisdiction where probate action might first have been considered.

2) Match the color on the map with the color named on the probate decision table at the start of each county section and read horizontally across the top of the table for the appropriate description of the desired court. Then scan vertically down that column to determine the official names of the court of original jurisdiction, the largest nearby court(s) of original jurisdiction, and courts of superior jurisdiction. Each court should be searched in the order of priority indicated by the numbers in that list. There will be a cross-reference to another county if microfilmed records pertaining to those courts are not filed in the sections immediately following the probate decision table.

3) Next, turn to the instructions describing the use of the most reliable indexes or calendars for the pertinent court. If there are no indexes or if they seem incomplete, try using the act books as a substitute index.

4) If the indexes refer to a will or testament of interest, write down the details and refer to the section marked "Original Wills." These were not always filmed. When available, they are more challenging to find than registered copy wills. However, the effort is worth it, as some wills were filed with the originals but not proved and many wills were proved but not registered. Moreover, copying errors may have occurred in the registration process. Finally, the originals frequently are supplemented by additional documents that the registered copies usually do not include, such as inventories, bonds, accounts, and guardianship papers.

The originals usually are filed alphabetically by testator's name, chronologically by date of probate, or in a numerical sequence according to a folio number. Exact systems should not be expected in the first two cases, and in the latter there may be several unnumbered pages before the

---

[8]An interesting phrase used in Lancashire in the sixteenth and seventeenth centuries that helps to identify a Roman Catholic testator is "all my real and personal estate of whatsoever nature or kind and wheresoever it may be." The intent was to hide previously arranged instructions in private to the trustees. B. C. Jones, "Lancashire Probate Records," *Transactions of the Historic Society of Lancashire and Cheshire* 104 (1953): 67.

next folio number appears. Look for the brief identifying statements (idents) that appear either on the back of the folded probate document or along the margins. Should these be missing, then the testator's name can be found in the first few lines of the document. Search either side of the desired document for possible accompanying records. A notation may appear on the identifying statement to indicate if the will also has been registered. If the original cannot be located, recheck the film's description in this volume and the films listed on either side of it. Consider searching through the entire film, but before doing so check the index in this volume, examine the registered copy wills, and determine if a probate bond is available.

The descriptions provided in the card catalog and on the title page of each film may be incorrect or vague, particularly when referring to the type of probate filmed and the years covered. The notation "End" on a film may refer to each item on the film and not to the film itself. A careful check of the listings in this volume and a glance at the amount of film remaining on the spool will prevent omissions.

Registered copy wills may be easier to search, especially if each volume is separately indexed by page number. If only registered copies exist, consult Anthony J. Camp's *Wills and Their Whereabouts,* 4th ed. (London: The author, 1974) for other records that might not have been filmed.

5) Should the indexes indicate that there was an administration or letters of administration-with-will-annexed, then check to see if there is a section marked "Bonds." These will be arranged in a pattern similar to the originals or registered copies. The name of the deceased, however, will appear in the first few lines of the second part of the bond, the "condition." If a will was annexed, it probably will be found with the other wills and only a bond will be located in this group of records.

6) Search the act books, regardless of what is found among the wills or bonds. Frequently, they will provide extra information not listed elsewhere. The act books were written in Latin before 1733.

7) Consider contacting the current archive or county record office in England where the records are stored. The addresses can be obtained from government publications such as *Record Repositories in Great Britain* or Jeremy Gibson and Pamela Peskett's *Record Offices: How to Find Them* (latest ed., Federation of Family History Societies). Such archives may be involved in current indexing projects, willing to locate hard-to-find items, or able to provide assistance in obtaining a more readable copy. The miscellaneous sections of this volume also may lead to an efficient solution. Although valuable, the records in these sections have not been given the same emphasis, as they tend to be edited and incomplete.

Throughout this volume the researcher will find each brief description of records preceded, in bold type, by the time period on the left-hand side and the film or call number on the right. The time period may be further divided into alphabetical units [1699 A–P, 1699 Q–Z] or kinds of records [1660–1680 (Supra), 1650–1660 (Admons)].

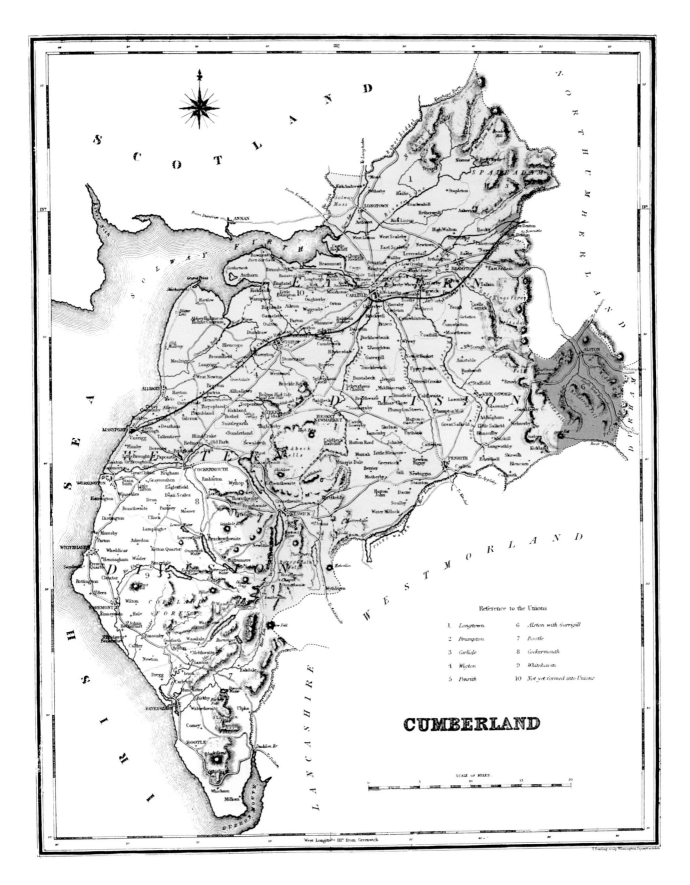

CUMBERLAND

Reference to the Unions

1	Longtown	6	Alston with Garrigill
2	Brampton	7	Bootle
3	Carlisle	8	Cockermouth
4	Wigton	9	Whitehaven
5	Penrith	10	Not yet formed into Unions

SCALE OF MILES

Additions and Corrections to the Map of Lancashire

The township of Bowland with Leagram is north of the River Ribble but comes under the jurisdiction of the Consistory of Chester.

The townships of Aighton with Bailey and Chaigley are also north of the Ribble and are part of the Yorkshire parish of Mitton; hence, they come under the jurisdiction of the Exchequer of York.

The entire parish of Kirkby Ireleth, including its chapelries of Broughton, Dunnerdale, Seathwaite, and Woodland with Heathwaite, belonged to the Dean and Chapter of York.

There were twenty-seven parishes in Lancashire that belonged in their entirety to the Archdeaconry of Richmond. These are listed below by deanery:

Deanery of Amounderness
  Bispham
  Chipping
  Cockerham
  Garstang
  Kirkham
  Lancaster
  Lytham
  Poulton-le-Fylde
  Preston
  Ribchester
  St. Michael-on-Wyre

Deanery of Kendal
(See Westmorland)
  Bolton-le-Sands
  Heysham
  Warton

Deanery of Furness
  Aldingham
  Cartmell
  Colton
  Dalton
  Hawkshead
  Pennington
  Ulverstone
  Urswick

Deanery of Lonsdale
  Claughton
  Melling
  Tatham
  Tunstall
  Whittington

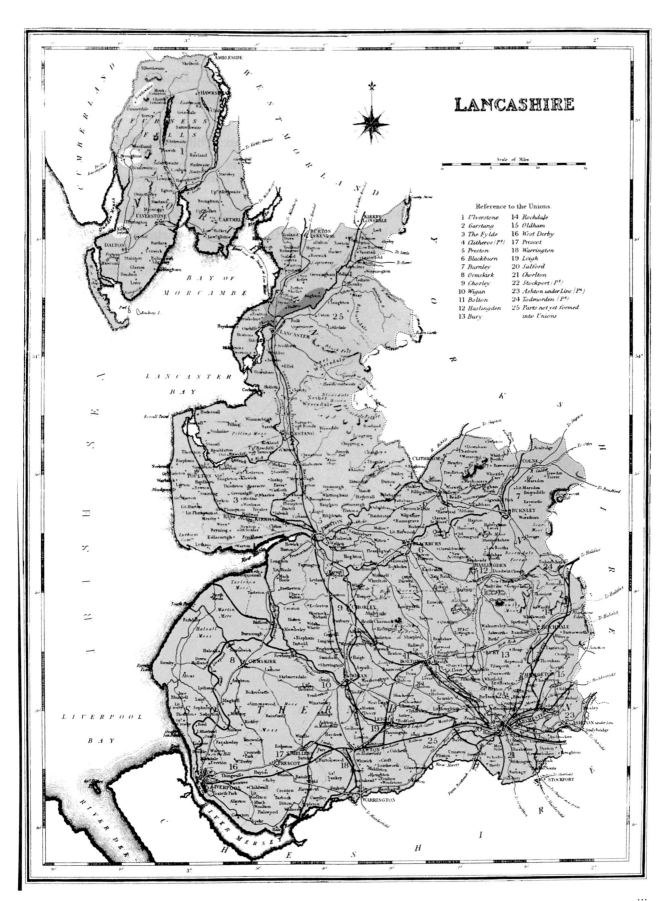

LANCASHIRE

Scale of Miles

Reference to the Unions.

1	Ulverstone	14	Rochdale
2	Garstang	15	Oldham
3	The Fylde	16	West Derby
4	Clitheroe (Pᵗ)	17	Prescot
5	Preston	18	Warrington
6	Blackburn	19	Leigh
7	Burnley	20	Salford
8	Ormskirk	21	Chorlton
9	Chorley	22	Stockport (Pᵗ)
10	Wigan	23	Ashton under Line (Pᵗ)
11	Bolton	24	Todmorden (Pᵗ)
12	Haslingden	25	Parts not yet formed
13	Bury		into Unions

Corrections to the Map of Nottinghamshire

Askham belonged to the Dean and Chapter of York.

Beckingham, for post–1800 also see Gringley-on-the-Hill.

Besthorpe belonged to the Exchequer of York.

Cromwell belonged to the Exchequer of York.

Skegby and Teversal belonged to the manorial court of the same name.

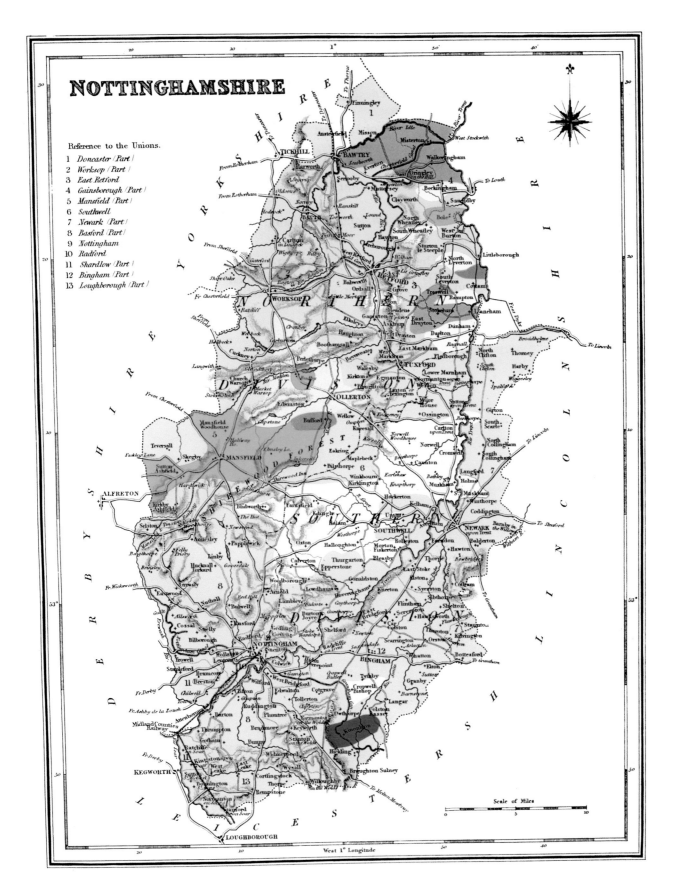

NOTTINGHAMSHIRE

Reference to the Unions.

1 *Doncaster (Part)*
2 *Worksop (Part)*
3 *East Retford*
4 *Gainsborough (Part)*
5 *Mansfield (Part)*
6 *Southwell*
7 *Newark (Part)*
8 *Basford (Part)*
9 *Nottingham*
10 *Radford*
11 *Shardlow (Part)*
12 *Bingham (Part)*
13 *Loughborough (Part)*

Scale of Miles

West 1° Longitude

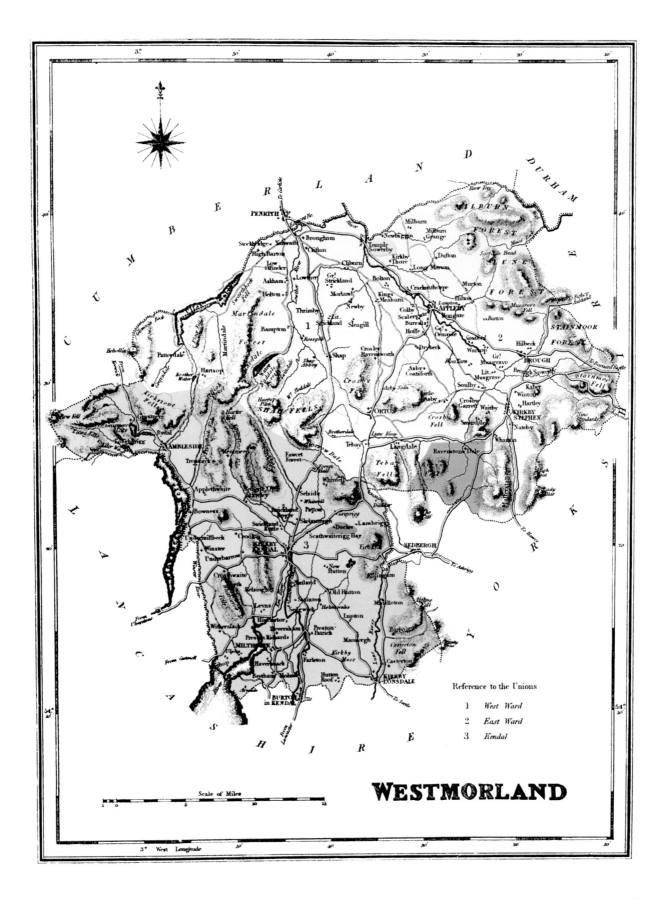

WESTMORLAND

Reference to the Unions

1   *West Ward*
2   *East Ward*
3   *Kendal*

Scale of Miles

Additions and Corrections to the Map of Yorkshire

EAST RIDING

Barlby is shown in Selby but belonged to Howden.
Burnby is shown in the area of the Dean of York but belonged to the Exchequer of York.
Cliff with Lund, see Barlby.
Dunnington (the one circled) belonged to Beeford; the actual prebendary was near the City of York.
Holme on the Wolds is shown in Beverley but belonged to the Exchequer.
Menthorp with Bowthorp, see Barlby.
Osgodby, see Barlby.
South Duffield, see Barlby.
Walkington was claimed by both Beverley and Howden.
Welwick is shown in the Exchequer but belonged to Beverley.
Woodall, see Barlby.

NORTH RIDING

Arrowthorne is shown in Richmond but belonged to the Dean and Chapter of York.
Danby Wisk is shown in Allerton but belonged to Richmond.
High Worsall is shown as a separate peculiar but belonged to Allerton.
Hunton is shown in Richmond but belonged to the Dean and Chapter of York.
Marton is shown in the Exchequer but belonged to Richmond.
West Rouncton is shown in the Exchequer but belonged to Allerton.

WEST RIDING

Barlow is shown in the Exchequer but belonged to Selby.
Handsworth is shown in the Exchequer but belonged to the Chancellor of York.
Hartwith, see Kirkby Malzeard.
Kirkby Malzeard was claimed by both the Dean and Chapter and Masham.
Little Ribston is shown in the Exchequer but belonged to Knaresborough.
Middlesmoor, see Kirkby Malzeard.
Plompton is shown in the Exchequer but belonged to Knaresborough.
Winsley, see Kirkby Malzeard.

Indexes and Calendars for the Consistory Court of Chester

(Some abstracts or extracts of documents relating to Cheshire probates will be found in the miscellaneous section. Searches in these items and the stray-name index to this volume may reveal entries not found in the calendars outlined below. Such materials are usually edited and may still be in Latin for the earlier periods.)

1) The printed indexes are also available on microfilm or microfiche as indicated by the six- or seven-digit number below the call number.

Time Period	Film or Call No.
1545–1620 (Supra)	FHL 942.7 B4Lc vol. 2 823,501 (item 2) & 6,072,908

Vol. 2 of the Lancashire & Cheshire Record Society. The printed index should be more reliable than any known manuscript indexes. It is arranged alphabetically. Match the entries of interest with the corresponding year and alphabet listed in the subsequent section of this volume entitled "Supra Original Wills, Admons, and Inventories." Be sure to search the next item in this list for the infra series. Corrections and additions will be found for these years on pages 222–224 at the end of the printed index.

Search the film for an ident matching the printed entry. Watch for accompanying documents before and after the appropriate item. If not found, reread the film description provided in this volume, scan the entire film for misplaced items, then consider the infra series and the miscellaneous section. Perhaps the missing item will be found with the Lancashire documents (always check the entry against the act books described under Lancashire) or it was never filmed. Consult Anthony J. Camp, *Wills and Their Whereabouts*, 4th ed. (London: The author, 1974), for details of records not filmed.

1590–1665 (Infra)	FHL 942.7 B4Lc vol. 52 823,512 (item 4) & 6,072,958

Vol. 52 of the Lancashire & Cheshire Record Society. The relevant portion of this book will be found on pages 1–59. This is an index to materials at first thought to be lost; hence, the overlap with volume 15 described below. Both should be searched and the likely entries matched against the section entitled "Infra Original Wills, Admons, and Inventories." Note the preceding and subsequent volumes for the supra series in the same general time period. The general instructions in the second paragraph describing the preceding volume will also be of assistance.

1621–1650 (Supra)	FHL 942.7 B4Lc vol. 4 823,502 (item 1) & 6,072,910

Vol. 4 of the Lancashire & Cheshire Record Society. Follow the instructions given above in the two paragraphs under volume 2. Corrections and additions will be found on pages 301–303.

1650–1660 (Wills)	FHL 942.7 B4Lc vol. 4 823,502 (item 1) & 6,072,910

(Continuation of the above) Appendix I on pages 249–280 of volume 4 is an index to Lancashire and Cheshire wills proven at the Prerogative Court of Canterbury (PCC) during the Interregnum and Commonwealth period. (The microfilms of these probate records will be listed under London in a subsequent volume for this series.)

1650–1660 (Admons)	FHL 942.7 B4Lc vol. 4 823,502 (item 1) & 6,072,910

(Continuation of the above) Appendix II on pages 281–300 of volume 4 is an index to Lancashire and Cheshire admons proven at the PCC (see the preceding note).

1660–1680 (Supra & Infra)	FHL 942.7 B4Lc vol. 15 823,504 (item 2) & 6,072,921

Vol. 15 of the Lancashire & Cheshire Record Society. The supra series takes up the majority of this book. The infra series actually appears as an appendix on pages 310–380. Both should be searched. Read the instructions given above under volumes 2 and 52. Note the overlap in the infra series with volume 52. An asterisk is used in this book to indicate documents considered lost or too damaged to produce at that time. Some 169 documents for 1670 were later recovered and are listed in volume 63 below. Corrections to volume 15 will be found just before page 1 and continue on page 380.

1681–1700　　　　　　　　　　**FHL 942.7 B4Lc**
(Supra & Infra)　　　　　　　　　　　　**vol. 18**
　　　　　　　　　　　823,505 (item 1) &
　　　　　　　　　　　　　6,072,924

Vol. 18 of the Lancashire & Cheshire Record Society. The infra series will be found in the appendix on pages 283–365. "A Supplementary Index" to mainly infra admons for 1693, which were discovered at a later date, may be found at the end of the book or in volume 63. Read the instructions given above under volumes 2 and 52. There are some additions to volume 18 preceding page 1.

1701–1720　　　　　　　　　　**FHL 942.7 B4Lc**
(Supra & Infra)　　　　　　　　　　　　**vol. 20**
　　　　　　　　　　　823,505 (item 3) &
　　　　　　　　　　　　　6,072,926

Vol. 20 of the Lancashire & Cheshire Record Society. The infra series will be found in the appendix on pages 233–261. Read the instructions given above under volumes 2 and 52.

1721–1740　　　　　　　　　　**FHL 942.7 B4Lc**
(Supra & Infra)　　　　　　　　　　　　**vol. 22**
　　　　　　　　　　　823,506 (item 1) &
　　　　　　　　　　　　　6,072,928

Vol. 22 of the Lancashire & Cheshire Record Society. The infra series will be found in the appendix on pages 291–343. Read the instructions given above under volumes 2 and 52.

1741–1760　　　　　　　　　　**FHL 942.7 B4Lc**
(Supra & Infra)　　　　　　　　　　　　**vol. 25**
　　　　　　　　　　　823,506 (item 4) &
　　　　　　　　　　　　　6,072,931

Vol. 25 of the Lancashire & Cheshire Record Society. The infra series will be found in the appendix on pages 213–264. The infra documents are missing from 1757–1776. Read the instructions given above under volumes 2 and 52. A page of additions to volume 25 appears at the front of the book.

1761–1780 A–M　　　　　　　　**FHL 942.7 B4Lc**
(Supra)　　　　　　　　　　　　　　**vol. 37**
　　　　　　　　　　　823,509 (item 3) &
　　　　　　　　　　　　　6,072,943

Vol. 37 of the Lancashire & Cheshire Record Society. The infra series 1777–1780 (there are none for 1757–1776) will be found in the next volume. Read the instructions given above under volume 2.

1761–1780 N–Z　　　　　　　　**FHL 942.7 B4Lc**
(Supra)　　　　　　　　　　　　　　**vol. 38**
A–Z (Infra)　　　　　**823,509 (item 4) &**
　　　　　　　　　　　　　6,072,944

Vol. 38 of the Lancashire & Cheshire Record Society. The title page of this book incorrectly shows the cover-

age to be 1741–1760. The infra series (there are none for 1757–1776) will be found in the appendix on pages 113–123. Read the instructions given above under volumes 2 and 52.

1781–1790　　　　　　　　　　**FHL 942.7 B4Lc**
(Supra & Infra)　　　　　　　　　　　　**vol. 44**
　　　　　　　　　　　823,511 (item 1) &
　　　　　　　　　　　443,326 (item 1) &
　　　　　　　　　　　　　6,072,950

Vol. 44 of the Lancashire & Cheshire Record Society. The infra series will be found in the appendix on pages 135–168. Read the instructions given above under volumes 2 and 52.

1791–1800　　　　　　　　　　**FHL 942.7 B4Lc**
(Supra & Infra)　　　　　　　　　　　　**vol. 45**
　　　　　　　　　　　823,511 (item 2) &
　　　　　　　　　　　443,326 (item 2) &
　　　　　　　　　　　　　6,072,951

Vol. 45 of the Lancashire & Cheshire Record Society. The infra series will be found in the appendix on pages 178–242. Read the instructions given above under volumes 2 and 52.

1801–1810 A–L　　　　　　　　**FHL 942.7 B4Lc**
(Supra & Infra)　　　　　　　　　　　　**vol. 62**
　　　　　　　　　　　823,515 (item 2) &
　　　　　　　　　　　443,326 (item 3) &
　　　　　　　　　　　　　6,072,968

Vol. 62 of the Lancashire & Cheshire Record Society. The infra series is interspersed with the supra but printed in italics to emphasize the difference. Read the instructions given above under volumes 2 and 52. The original documents were filed in the nineteenth century by month. This may still be reflected in the microfilms, which are filed initially by year and then roughly alphabetically.

1801–1810 M–Z　　　　　　　　**FHL 942.7 B4Lc**
(Supra & Infra)　　　　　　　　　　　　**vol. 63**
　　　　　　　　　　　823,515 (item 3) &
　　　　　　　　　　　443,326 (item 4) &
　　　　　　　　　　　　　6,072,969

Vol. 63 of the Lancashire & Cheshire Record Society. The infra series is interspersed with the supra but printed in italics to emphasize the difference. Read the instructions given above under volume 62. A supplementary index to documents for 1670 (A–C), thought to be lost earlier, appears on pages 179–187. Another supplementary index to mainly infra admons for 1693, recovered at a later date, will be found on pages 189–199. (Item 4 of film 443,326 does not include the supplements.) The manuscript calendar for the entries from 1693 is also available on microfilm as will be described below. The filmed manuscript calendar does add occupations; otherwise it holds no advantage over the printed index.

1811–1820 A–L   **FHL 942.7 B4Lc**
(Supra & Infra)   **vol. 78**
     823,519 (item 1) &
     6,072,984

Vol. 78 of the Lancashire & Cheshire Record Society. The infra documents are differentiated from the supra by an asterisk at the end of such entries. Read the instructions given above under volumes 2 and 52. The filmed documents are arranged by year, then roughly alphabetically, and perhaps by month. The manuscript calendars are on film from 1815 for the supra and 1819 for the infra, but there seems to be little advantage in searching them until the printed indexes cease.

1811–1820 M–Z   **FHL 942.7 B4Lc**
(Supra & Infra)   **vol. 79**
     823,519 (item 2) &
     6,072,985

Vol. 79 of the Lancashire & Cheshire Record Society. See the above note for volume 78.

1821–1825   **FHL 942.7 B4Lc**
(Supra & Infra)   **vol. 107**
     823,525 (item 4) &
     6,073,013

Vol. 107 of the Lancashire & Cheshire Record Society. See the above note for volume 78. The Cheshire documents are indexed separately on pages 159–205. There is a typescript index for 1821–1827 on film 165,324. This may have been the basis for the printed index; however, the typescript also contains the occupation, date the will was written, and the testator's death date. The infra series is on the left-hand page and the supra on the right side of the typescript.

1826–1830   **FHL 942.7 B4Lc**
(Supra & Infra)   **vol. 113**

Vol. 113 of the Lancashire & Cheshire Record Society. See the notes given above under volumes 78 and 107. The Cheshire documents are indexed separately on pages 143–186. Missing documents are listed in italics. Additions to volume 113 appear on page vii.

1831–1833   **FHL 942.7 B4Lc**
(Supra & Infra)   **vol. 118**

Vol. 118 of the Lancashire & Cheshire Record Society. See the notes given above under volume 78. The Cheshire documents are indexed separately on pages 110–140. Missing documents are listed in italics. Additions and corrections appear on page 145.

1834–1837   **FHL 942.7 B4Lc**
(Supra & Infra)   **vol. 120**

Vol. 120 of the Lancashire & Cheshire Record Society. See the notes given above under volume 78. The Cheshire documents are indexed separately on pages 145–187. Missing documents are listed in italics. There are separate indexes by occupation and place.

2) The filmed calendars are arranged as follows:

1815–1823   **90,072**
(Supra)   **(item 1)**

Vol. 401 of a manuscript index to supra wills and admons. Use the printed indexes described above under volumes 78, 79, and 107. Infra calendars are described below.

1824–1830   **90,072**
(Supra)   **(item 2)**

Vol. 402 of a manuscript index to supra wills and admons. Use the printed indexes described above under volumes 107 and 113. Infra calendars are described below.

1831–1838   **90,073**
(Supra)   **(item 1)**

Vol. 403 of a manuscript index to supra wills and admons. For 1831–1837, use the printed index described above for volumes 118 and 120. For 1838, turn to Lancashire and check the section entitled "Supra Registered Copy Wills." The manuscript index will provide the name, place, occupation, type of probate, and the month and day of the grant. For registered copy wills, the index adds the volume and page number. Infra calendars are described below.

1839–1844   **90,073**
(Supra)   **(item 2)**

Vol. 404 of a manuscript index to supra wills and admons. Read the above note for 1831–1838. Unfortunately, the original wills, 1838–1858, were not filmed. Turn to Lancashire and check the section entitled "Supra Registered Copy Wills." Further instructions will be found there, if the will has not been copied.

1845–1849   **90,074**
(Supra)   **(item 1)**

Vol. 405 of a manuscript index to supra wills and admons. Read the above notes for 1831–1838 and 1839–1844. Infra calendars are described below.

1850–1853   **90,074**
(Supra)   **(item 2)**

Vol. 406 of a manuscript index. Read the above notes for 1831–1838 and 1839–1844. Infra calendars are described below.

1854–1858   **90,074**
(Supra)   **(item 3)**

Vol. 407 of a manuscript index. Read the above notes for 1831–1838 and 1839–1844. Infra calendars are described below.

1693   **90,123**
(Infra)   **(item 1)**

Vol. 491 of a manuscript index to mainly infra admons, which were found at a later date. Use the printed index described above under volume 63.

1819–1858   **90,123**
(Infra)   **(item 2)**
Vol. 492 of a manuscript index to infra wills and admons.
For 1819–1837, use the printed indexes described above
under volumes 78, 79, 107, 113, 118, and 120. For
1838–1858, match the entries from this manuscript index
with the following section entitled "Infra Original Wills,
Admons, and Inventories." The index is arranged the
same way as the supra calendars described above.

1858–1867   **395,533**
This is an index to the modern wills proven at the
District Probate Registry of Chester. The distinction
between supra and infra is no longer made. The index
will provide a page number that can be matched with the
appropriate year in the section entitled "Modern Copied
Wills" to locate quickly an official copy of any will. No
other types of probate documents were filmed for the
modern period. If the death date is not given in this
index, it will be found in the national index mentioned in
the introduction, which is on microfilm from 1858–1957.

It is not the intent of this study to go into the modern
period, but as long as the records for this district had
been filmed, it was thought advisable to at least add an
outline to them here. Further information about the modern districts and the Principal Probate Registry will be
found in the introductory chapter to this volume.

1868–1887   **395,534**
(A continuation of the above; see the note for 1858–1867.)

1888–1911   **395,535**
(A continuation of the above; see the note for 1858–
1867.)

1912–1921   **395,536**
(A continuation of the above; see the note for 1858–
1867. The copy wills continue on film through 1940. For
an index to 1922–1940, see the calendar of the Principal
Probate Registry described in the note for 1858–1867.)

Supra Original Wills, Admons, and Inventories for the Consistory Court of Chester

---

1541–1546
Missing; apparently no original probates survived for
Cheshire unless they were incorrectly filed with those for
Lancashire. See the miscellaneous section for references
to abstracts referring to the fifteenth through eighteenth
centuries.

1547–1562   **89,906**
                                                                (item 1)
Box 1 contains just a few scattered documents for these
years as follows: 1547, S; 1552, an ident only for C;

1553, B, C, K; 1554, E; 1555, A, C, L; 1556, D, G; 1557,
B, M, T, S; 1558, R, H, L, R; 1560, B, R, E; 1561, A, C,
F; and 1562, H. There are no documents for 1548–1551
and 1559. See the preceding note for 1541–1546.

1563–1572   **89,906**
                                                                (item 2)
Box 2 contains scattered documents for: 1563, an ident
only for L; 1564, C, G, M; 1565, D; 1566, B; 1567, S;
1568, W; 1571, A, Y; and 1572, A, B, H, T, W. There are
no documents for 1569–1570. See the above note for
1541–1546.

1573 A–W   **89,906**
1574 A–D,S–W   **(item 3)**
Box 3

1575 A–W   **89,906**
1576 A–W   **(item 4)**
1577 A–S
Box 4 contains a will for William Higson filed among
the Gs for 1576.

1578–1580   **89,907**
                                                                (item 1)
Box 5. The documents are filed chronologically and then
roughly alphabetically in each box.

1581–1582   **89,907**
                                                                (item 2)
Box 6

1583–1585   **89,908**
                                                                (item 1)
Box 7

1586–1587   **89,908**
                                                                (item 2)
Box 8. The alphabetical sequence for 1587 begins B, A,
B, and then proceeds normally.

1588–1589   **89,909**
                                                                (item 1)
Box 9

1590   **89,909**
                                                                (item 2)
Box 10. The documents are filed chronologically and
then roughly alphabetically in each box.

1591   **89,909**
                                                                (item 3)
Box 11

1592   **89,910**
                                                                (item 1)
Box 12. The documents are filed chronologically and
then roughly alphabetically in each box.

1593 A–G	**89,910** **(item 2)**

Box 13

1593 H–Y	**89,910** **(item 3)**

Box 14

1594 B–W **1595 A–D**	**89,911** **(item 1)**

Box 15 contains some idents without any matching documents. It begins with sixteen items for 1594, which are intermingled from B–M, and then proceeds normally for N–W.

1595 E–W	**89,911** **(item 2)**

Box 16. There is an ident for John Orme among the Ms.

1596 B–L,R–W	**89,911** **(item 3)**

Box 17. (There is some confusion on the film as to whether this is Box 16 or 17.)

1597 B–C	**89,911** **(item 4)**

Box 18. (There is some confusion on the film as to whether this is Box 16 or 18.) There is a D in the middle of the Cs.

1597 E–Y Box 18	**89,912**

1598 A–S	**89,913** **(item 1)**

Box 19. The will of John Robinson is filed with the Ps and another for Hugh Okell appears among the Ss.

1598 T–Y	**89,913** **(item 2)**

Box 20

1599 A–W	**89,913** **(item 3)**

Box 20 continued. The will of John Ridding is filed with the Ps.

1600 C,H,M,O	**89,914** **(item 1)**

Box 21 contains documents only for the letters listed. From here on the boxes are not numbered.

1601 A–W	**89,914** **(item 2)**

1602 A–W	**89,914** **(item 3)**

1603 A–W The Ys precede the Ws.	**89,915**
1604 A–W	**89,916**
1605 A–W	**89,917**
1606 A–W	**89,918**
1607 A–Y	**89,919**
1608 A–M	**89,920**
1608 M–Y	**89,921**
1609 A–Z	**89,922**
1610 A–L	**89,923**
1610 L–W	**89,924**
1611 A–D	**89,925**
1611 D–Z	**89,926**
1612 A–L	**89,927**
1612 L–Y	**89,928**
1613 A–H	**89,929**
1613 I–Y	**89,930**
1614 A–H	**89,931**
1614 I–Y	**89,932**
1615 A–H	**89,933**
1615 I–Y	**89,934**
1616 A–I	**89,935**
1616 I–Y	**89,936**
1617 A–E	**89,937**
1617 F–H	**89,938**
1617 I–R	**89,939**
1617 R–Y	**89,940**
1618 A–H	**89,941**
1618 I–Y	**89,942**
1619 A–H	**89,943**

1619 I–Y   89,944
The film begins with K, reverts to J, then goes back to K and on through the alphabet.

1620 A–H   89,945
Four Cs appear in the middle of the Bs. Also filed with the Bs is the will of Elizabeth Birkenhead, widow of Manley, proven in 1622.

1620 I–Y   89,946

1621 A–H   89,947

1621 I–Y   89,948

1622 A–H   89,949
Note the entry for 1622 filed with 1620 above.

1622 I–Y   89,950

1623 A–H   89,951

1623 I–Z   89,952
A will of Alexander Young is the first document on this film, but the alphabetical sequence follows from there on.

1624 A–H   89,953

1624 I–Z   89,954

1625 A–H   89,955

1625 I–Z   89,956

1626 A–H   89,957

1626 I–Z   89,958

1627 A–H   89,959

1627 I–Z   89,960

1628 A–H   89,961

1628 I–Z   89,962

1629 A–H   89,963

1629 I–Z   89,964

1630 A–H   89,965

1630 I–Y   89,966

1631 A–H   89,967

1631 I–Y   89,968

1632 A–H   89,969

1632 I–Y   89,970

1633 A–B   89,971

1633 B–H   89,972

1633 I–Y   89,973

1634 A–H   89,974

1634 I–Y   89,975

1635 A–H   89,976
The will of Gwenne Fisher is included in the Hs.

1635 I–Y   89,977

1636 A–H   89,978

1636 I–Y   89,979

1637 A–H   89,980

1637 I–Y   89,981

1638 A–H   89,982

1638 I–Y   89,983
An inventory for Richard Newhall dated 1636 is included.

1639 A–H   89,984

1639 I–Y   89,985

1640 A–H   89,986

1640 I–S   89,987

1640 S–Y   89,988

1641 A–H   89,989

1641 I–Y   89,990

1642 A–H   89,991

1642 K–Y   89,992
The will of Margery Thomley is filed with the Ms.

1643 B–W   89,993
                                            (item 1)

1644 B–W   89,993
                                            (item 2)

1645 B–W   89,994

1646 A–B	89,995	1663 M–Y	90,021
1646 B–H	89,996	1664 A–H	90,022
1646 I–M	89,997	1664 I–Z	90,023
1646 M–Y	89,998	1665 A–H	90,024
1647 A–F	89,999	1665 I–Z	90,025
1647 G–H	90,000	1666 A–H	90,026
1647 I–O,S	90,001	1666 I–Z	90,027

1647 I–O,S — See the next film for P–R.

1667 A–H — 90,028
The inventory and will of Richard Clough, yeoman, of Bunnsley Bank in the township of Audlem was dated and proven in December 1677 and is incorrectly filed here. The printed index compounds the error by referring to the same probate twice, as though two different persons were involved.

1647 S,R,P,T–Y	90,002		
1648 A–H	90,003		
1648 I–L	90,004	1667 I–Z	90,029
1648 L–Y	90,005	1668 A–H	90,030
1649 A–H	90,006	1668 I–Z	90,031
1649 I–W	90,007	1669 A–D	90,032
1649 W	90,008	1669 E–H	90,033
1650 A–M	90,009		

1669 E–H — A C appears among the Hs.

1650 N–Z	90,010	1669 J–R	90,034

1651–1659
Missing, due to the Interregnum and Commonwealth. See the probate decision table for further instructions.

		1669 R–Z	90,035
1660 A–W	90,011	1670 A–B,G–H	90,036

1670 A–B,G–H — The documents for C–F are lost.

1661 A–H	90,012	1670 I–Z	90,037
1661 I–P	90,013	1671 A–B	90,038
1661 P–Y	90,014	1671 B–H	90,039

1661 P–Y — The will of Richard Maddocks is included with the Ws.

1662 A–H	90,015	1671 I–S	90,040
1662 I–T	90,016	1671 T–Z	90,041

1662 I–T — A J appears in the Ms.

1662 T–Y	90,017	1672 A–B	90,042
1663 A–C	90,018	1672 B–H	90,043
1663 C–H	90,019	1672 I–T	90,044
1663 I–M	90,020	1672 T–Y	90,045

1673 A–H	**90,046**	**1681 I–V**	**164,821**
1673 I–Z	**90,047**	**1681 V–Z**	**164,822**

The Ps come before the Ls.

		1682 A–H	**164,823**
1674 A–H	**90,048**	**1682 I–R**	**164,824**
1674 I–O	**90,049**	**1682 R–Y**	**164,825**
1674 P–Z	**90,050**	**1683 A–B**	**164,826**
1675 A–H	**90,051**	**1683 B–H**	**164,827**
1675 H	**90,052**	**1683 I–T**	**164,828**
1675 I–R	**90,053**	**1683 T–W**	**164,829**

A J appears among the Ts. There are four Os between the Vs and the Ws.

1675 R–Z	**90,054**		
1676 A–C	**90,055**	**1684 A–C**	**164,830**
1676 C–H	**90,056**	**1684 C–H**	**164,831**
1676 I–W	**90,057**	**1684 I–Z**	**164,832**

Camp, in *Wills and Their Whereabouts*, reports that I–Q are lost and the documents for T and W were damaged.

1676 W	**90,058**		
1677 A–C	**90,059**	**1685 A–H**	**164,833**

The inventory and will of Richard Clough proven in this year was actually filed with 1667. See film 90,028.

		1685 H	**164,834**
1677 C–H	**90,060**	**1685 I–R**	**164,835**
1677 I–U	**90,061**	**1685 R–Z**	**164,836**
1677 U–Z	**90,062**	**1686 A–B**	**164,837**
1678 A–H	**90,063**	**1686 B–H**	**164,838**
1678 I–Z	**90,064**	**1686 I–R**	**164,839**
1679 A–H	**90,065**	**1686 R–Z**	**164,840**

At the beginning of the film is the note: "1679 wills are in very poor state, I am filming what I can." Pages are torn, worn, and stained.

		1687 A–H	**164,841**
1679 I–Z	**90,066**	**1687 I–Z**	**164,842**

See the preceding note.

1680 A–F	**90,067**	**1688 A–H**	**164,843**
1680 F–H	**90,068**	**1688 I–Z**	**164,844**
1680 I–P	**90,069**	**1689 A–H**	**164,845**
1680 P–Z	**90,070**	**1689 I–Z**	**164,846**
1681 A–H	**164,820**	**1690 A–H**	**164,847**

1690 I–Z	164,848	1703 I–Z	164,877
1691 A–H	164,849	1704 A–H	164,878
1691 I–Z	164,850	1704 I–Z	164,879
1692 A–H	164,851	1705 A–H	164,880
1692 I–Z	164,852	1705 I–Z	164,881
1693 A–H	164,853	1706 A–H	164,882
1693 I–Z	164,854	1706 I–Y	164,883
1694 A–H	164,855	The will of George Venables is misplaced among the Ws.	
1694 I–Z	164,856	1707 A–H	164,884
1695 A–H	164,857	1707 I–Z	164,885
1695 I–Z	164,858	1708 A–B	164,886
1696 A–H	164,859	1708 B–H	164,887
1696 I–Z	164,860	1708 I–Z	164,888
1697 A–H	164,861	1709 A–G	164,889
1697 I–Z	164,862	1709 G–H	164,890
1698 A–H	164,863	A number of F entries appear between G and H.	
1698 I–Z	164,864	1709 I–R	164,891
1699 A–F	164,865	1709 R–Z	164,892
1699 F–H	164,866	1710 A–H	164,893
1699 I–O	164,867	1710 I–Z	164,894
1699 O–Y	164,868	1711 A–H	164,895
1700 A–B	164,869	1711 I–Z	164,896
1700 B–H	164,870	1712 A–H	164,897
1700 I–Z	164,871	1712 I–Z	164,898
1701 A–H	164,872	1713 A–B	164,899
1701 I–Z	164,873	1713 B–H	164,900
1702 A–H	164,874	1713 I–Z	164,901
1702 I–Z	164,875	1714 A–H	164,902
1703 A–H	164,876	1714 I–Z	164,903
		1715 A–H	164,904

1715 I–Z	**164,905**	1724 I–S	**164,932**
1716 A–H	**164,906**	1724 S–Z	**164,933**
1716 I–Z	**164,907**	1725 A–H	**164,934**
1717 A–H	**164,908**	1725 I–P	**164,935**
1717 I–Z	**164,909**	1725 P–Z	**164,936**
1718 A–H	**164,910**	1726 A–B	**164,937**
1718 I–T	**164,911**	1726 B–H	**164,938**
1718 T–Z	**164,912**	1726 I–Y	**164,939**

1719 A–H   **164,913**
A J will is filed at the end of this roll.

1726 I–Y   **164,939**
The U/Vs appear between the Ws and the Ys.

1727 A–D   **164,940**

1719 I–S   **164,914**
See the preceding note.

		1727 D–H	**164,941**
1719 S–Z	**164,915**	1727 I–R	**164,942**
1720 A–H	**164,916**	1727 R–Z	**164,943**
1720 I–Z	**164,917**	1728 A–D	**164,944**
1721 A–B	**164,918**	1728 D–H	**164,945**
1721 B–H	**164,919**	1728 I–P	**164,946**
1721 I–S	**164,920**	1728 P–W	**164,947**
1721 S–Z	**164,921**	1728 W–Z	**164,948**
1722 A–C	**164,922**	1729 A–B	**164,949**
1722 C–H	**164,923**	1729 B–G	**164,950**
1722 I–Z	**164,924**	1729 G–H	**164,951**
1723 A–B	**164,925**	1729 I–M	**164,952**
1723 B–H	**164,926**	1729 M–S	**164,953**
1723 H	**164,927**	1729 S–Z	**164,954**
1723 I–R	**164,928**	1730 A–B	**164,955**

1723 I–R   **164,928**
The will of Anne Henry of Chelsea, Middlesex, is filed
with the Ls.

		1730 B–H	**164,956**
1723 R–Z	**164,929**	1730 I–W	**164,957**
1724 A–B	**164,930**	1730 W–Z	**164,958**
1724 B–H	**164,931**	1731 A–H	**164,959**
		1731 I–Y	**164,960**

1732 A–H	**164,961**
1732 I–Z	**164,962**
1733 A–H	**164,963**
1733 I–Z	**164,964**
1734 A–H	**164,965**
1734 I–Z	**164,966**
1735 A–H	**164,967**
1735 I–Z	**164,968**
1736 A–H	**164,969**
1736 I–Z	**164,970**
1737 A–H	**164,971**
1737 I–Z	**164,972**
1738 A–H	**164,973**
1738 I–Z	**164,974**
1739 A–H	**164,975**
1739 I–W	**164,976**
1740 A–H	**164,977**
1740 I–Z	**164,978**
1741 A–H	**164,979**
1741 I–Z	**164,980**
1742 A–B	**164,981**
1742 B–H	**164,982**
1742 I–Z	**164,983**
1743 A–H	**164,984**
1743 I–Z	**164,985**
1744 A–H	**164,986**
1744 I–Z	**164,987**
1745 A–H	**164,988**
1745 I–Z	**164,989**

The Js and Ls are intermingled.

1746 A–H	**164,990**
1746 I–Y	**164,991**
1747 A–H	**164,992**
1747 I–Z	**164,993**
1748 A–H	**164,994**
1748 I–Z	**164,995**
1749 A–H	**164,996**
1749 I–Z	**164,997**
1750 A–H	**164,998**
1750 I–Z	**164,999**
1751 A–Z	**165,000**
1752 A–H	**165,001**
1752 I–Z	**165,002**
1753 A–H	**165,003**
1753 I–Y	**165,004**
1754 A–H	**165,005**
1754 I–Z	**165,006**
1755 A–H	**165,007**
1755 I–Z	**165,008**
1756 A–H	**165,009**
1756 I–W	**165,010**

This film contains the will of Caleb Ransted, gentleman of the city of Chester, who previously resided in the city of Philadelphia, Pennsylvania. There is also a renunciation with other documents for Margery Dudley, the wife of Thomas Dudley, gentleman of New Cross near Deptford, Kent, concerning the estate of her father, Abner Scoles the elder, upholsterer of the city of Chester. The Vs come after the Ws.

1757 A–H	**165,011**
1757 I–Z	**165,012**
1758 A–H	**165,013**
1758 I–Z	**165,014**

1759 A–H	**165,015**
1759 I–Z	**165,016**
1760 A–H	**165,017**
1760 I–Z	**165,018**
1761 A–H	**165,019**
1761 I–Z	**165,020**
1762 A–H	**165,021**
1762 I–Z	**165,022**
1763 A–H	**165,023**
1763 I–Z	**165,024**
1764 A–H	**165,025**
1764 I–Z	**165,026**
1765 A–H	**165,027**
1765 I–Z	**165,028**
1766 A–H	**165,029**
1766 I–Z	**165,030**
1767 A–H	**165,031**
1767 I–W	**165,032**
1768 A–H	**165,033**
1768 I–Z	**165,034**
1769 A–H	**165,035**
1769 I–Z	**165,036**
1770 A–H	**165,037**
1770 I–Z	**165,038**
1771 A–H	**165,039**
1771 I–Z	**165,040**
1772 A–H	**165,041**
1772 I–Z	**165,042**
1773 A–H	**165,043**

1773 I–Z	**165,044**
1774 A–H	**165,045**
1774 I–Z	**165,046**
1775 A–H	**165,047**
1775 I–W	**165,048**

An admon for William Jackson is filed with the Ps.

1776 A–H	**165,049**
1776 I–Z	**165,050**
1777 A–H	**165,051**
1777 I–Z	**165,052**
1778 A–H	**165,053**
1778 I–Z	**165,054**
1779 A–H	**165,055**
1779 I–Z	**165,056**
1780 A–H	**165,057**
1780 I–Z	**165,058**
1781 A–H	**165,059**
1781 I–Z	**165,060**
1782 A–H	**165,061**
1782 I–Z	**165,062**
1783 A–H	**165,063**
1783 I–Z	**165,064**
1784 A–H	**165,065**
1784 I–Z	**165,066**
1785 A–H	**165,067**
1785 I–Z	**165,068**
1786 A–H	**165,069**
1786 I–Z	**165,070**
1787 A–H	**165,071**
1787 I–Z	**165,072**

1788 A–H	165,073	1800 P–Z	165,102
1788 I–Z	165,074	1801 A–F	165,103
1789 A–H	165,075	1801 F–H	165,104
1789 I–Z	165,076	1801 I–M	165,105
1790 A–H	165,077	1801 M–Z	165,106
1790 I–Z	165,078	1802 A–C	165,107
1791 A–H	165,079	1802 C–H	165,108
1791 I–Z	165,080	1802 I–R	165,109
1792 A–H	165,081	1802 R–Z	165,110
1792 I–Z	165,082	1803 A–B	165,111
1793 A–H	165,083	1803 B–H	165,112
1793 I–Z	165,084	1803 I–S	165,113
1794 A–H	165,085	1803 S–Z	165,114
1794 I–Z	165,086	1804 A–B	165,115
1795 A–H	165,087	1804 B–H	165,116
1795 I–Z	165,088	1804 I–T	165,117
1796 A–H	165,089	1804 T–Z	165,118

(From 1805–1837, death dates are given for many of the testators.)

1796 I–Z	165,090		
1797 A–H	165,091	1805 A–C	165,119
1797 I–Z	165,092	1805 C–H	165,120
1798 A–H	165,093	1805 I–Z	165,121
1798 I–Y	165,094	1806 A–H	165,122
1799 A–H	165,095	1806 I–O	165,123
1799 H	165,096	1806 P–Z	165,124
1799 I–N	165,097	1807 A–G	165,125

A B appears on the next film.

1799 N–Z	165,098	1807 G–H	165,126

The will of Peggy Butler of Witton is filed with the Hs. Also in the Hs is the will of Ann Roylance of Little Warford.

1800 A–D	165,099		
1800 D–H	165,100		
1800 I–P	165,101	1807 I–M	165,127

1807 M–Z	**165,128**	1814 L–T	**165,157**
An R entry is listed with the Hs for this year.		**1814 T–Z**	**165,158**
1808 A–G	**165,129**	**1815 A–B**	**165,159**
1808 G–H	**165,130**	**1815 B–H**	**165,160**
1808 I–O	**165,131**	**1815 I–P**	**165,161**
1808 O–Z	**165,132**	**1815 P–W**	**165,162**
1809 A–D	**165,133**	**1815 W–Z**	**165,163**
1809 D–H	**165,134**	**1816 A–B**	**165,164**
1809 I–M	**165,135**	**1816 B–H**	**165,165**
1809 M–Z	**165,136**	**1816 I–R**	**165,166**
1810 A–E	**165,137**	**1816 R–Z**	**165,167**
1810 E–H	**165,138**	**1817 A–D**	**165,168**
1810 I–T	**165,139**	**1817 D–H**	**165,169**
1810 T–Z	**165,140**	**1817 I–R**	**165,170**
1811 A–B	**165,141**	**1817 R–Z**	**165,171**
1811 B–H	**165,142**	**1818 A–D**	**165,172**
1811 I–R	**165,143**	**1818 D–H**	**165,173**
1811 R–Z	**165,144**	**1818 I–P**	**165,174**
1812 A–G	**165,145**	**1818 P–Z**	**165,175**
1812 G–H	**165,146**	**1819 A–D**	**165,176**
1812 I–M	**165,147**	**1819 D–H**	**165,177**
1812 M–Z	**165,148**	**1819 I–S**	**165,178**
1813 A–C	**165,149**	**1819 S–Z**	**165,179**
1813 C–H	**165,150**	**1820 A–F**	**165,180**
1813 I–T	**165,151**	**1820 F–H**	**165,181**
1813 T–Z	**165,152**	**1820 I–M**	**165,182**
1814 A–B	**165,153**	**1820 M–T**	**165,183**
1814 B–G	**165,154**	**1820 U–Z**	**165,184**
1814 G–H	**165,155**	**1821 A–B**	**165,185**
1814 I–L	**165,156**		

1821 B–H	165,186	1828 A–B	165,217
1821 I–R	165,187	1828 B–H	165,218
1821 R–Z	165,188	1828 H	165,219
1822 A–G	165,189	1828 I–N	165,220
1822 G–H	165,190	1828 N–T	165,221
1822 I–L	165,191	1828 T–Z	165,222
1822 L–S	165,192	1829 A–B	165,223
1822 S–Z	165,193	1829 B–G	165,224
1823 A–G	165,194	1829 G–H	165,225
1823 G–H	165,195	1829 I–L	165,226
1823 I–N	165,196	1829 L–S	165,227
1823 N–Y	165,197	1829 S–Z	165,228
1824 A–C	165,198	1830 A–F	165,229
1824 C–H A will is included for John Elliott of Barbados.	165,199	1830 F–H	165,230
1824 I–R	165,200	1830 I–P	165,231
1824 R–W	165,201	1830 P–Z	165,232
1824 W–Z	165,202	1831 A–F	165,233
1825 A–C	165,203	1831 F–H	165,234
1825 C–H	165,204	1831 I–S	165,235
1825 H	165,205	1831 S–Z	165,236
1825 I–P	165,206	1832 A–D	165,237
1825 P–Z	165,207	1832 E–H	165,238
1826 A–C	165,208	1832 I–L	165,239
1826 C–H	165,209	1832 L–R	165,240
1826 I–S	165,210	1832 R–Z	165,241
1826 S–Z	165,211	1833 A–B	165,242
1827 A–B	165,212	1833 B–G	165,243
1827 B–H	165,213	1833 G–H	165,244
1827 I–M	165,214	1833 I–M	165,245
1827 M–W	165,215	1833 M–W	165,246
1827 W–Z	165,216	1833 W–Z	165,247

1834 A–D	**165,248**
1834 D–H	**165,249**
1834 I–R	**165,250**
1834 R–Z	**165,251**
1835 A–D	**165,252**

For further information concerning other possible Cheshire documents, see the note under this year in the section entitled "Supra Original Wills" for Lancashire.

1835 D–H	**165,253**
1835 I–S	**165,254**
1835 S–Z	**165,255**
1836 A–D	**165,256**
1836 D–H	**165,257**
1836 I–S	**165,258**
1836 S–Z	**165,259**
1837 A–B	**165,260**
1837 B–G	**165,261**

Office copy of the will of Davies Davenport, Esq., extracted from the Prerogative Court of Canterbury.

1837 G–H	**165,262**
1837 I–M	**165,263**
1837 M–S	**165,264**
1837 S–Z	**165,265**

1838–1858
Not filmed, see the registered copy wills under Lancashire. To contact the repository holding the original wills and admons for this time period, consult Camp, *Wills and Their Whereabouts.*

Infra Original Wills, Admons, and Inventories for the Consistory Court of Chester

---

1541–1589
Missing. Apparently infra probates were not a practice in this court until 1590 or none of the original records has survived. Check the supra probates described in the preceding section.

1590–1599
Missing. Either they never existed, are now lost, or they may have been filed incorrectly with the infra series for Lancashire or with the supra series for Cheshire or Lancashire. Perhaps the act books (filed under Lancashire) or the repository where the originals are kept may have further information. See Camp, *Wills and Their Whereabouts.*

1600 A–Y	**165,266**

1601
Missing. See the note for 1590–1599.

1602 A–Y	**165,267**

1603
Missing. See the note for 1590–1599.

1604 A–Y	**165,268**

1605 G
The only document for 1605 is an inventory for John Green of Stapeley in Wybunbury. See the note for 1590–1599.

1606–1607
Missing. See the note for 1590–1599.

1608 B–S	**165,269** **(item 1)**
1609 B–W	**165,269** **(item 2)**
1610 A–W	**165,269** **(item 3)**
1611 M	**165,270** **(item 1)**

There is one admon for Alice Massy of Aldford. See the note for 1590–1599.

1612 A–W	**165,270** **(item 2)**
1613 A–W	**165,270** **(item 3)**
1614 H	**165,270** **(last item)**

There is one will for Henry Hughson of Woodhouse. See the note for 1590–1599.

1615
Missing. See the note for 1590–1599.

1616 A–W	**165,271**

1617
Missing. See the note for 1590–1599.

1618 B 165,272
There is one will and inventory for James Bateman of Old Withington. See the note for 1590–1599.

1619 B–W 165,272
(item 2)

1620 O–P 165,272
(item 3)
There are just two inventories. The first is for Ellen Proudlove of Hankelow in Audlem and the other is for Margaret Oulton of Barthomley, Staffs. See the note for 1590–1599.

1621 A–W 165,272
(item 4)

1622–1626
Missing. See the note for 1590–1599.

1627 A–W 165,273
(item 1)

A K appears after the Ws.

1628 B–W 165,273
(item 2)

1629
Missing. See the note for 1590–1599.

1630 B–W 165,274

1631–1632
Missing. See the note for 1590–1599.

1633 D–R 165,275
(item 1)

1634–1635
Missing. See the note for 1590–1599.

1636 H–Y 165,275
(item 2)

1637 B–W 165,275
(item 3)

1638–1640
Missing. See the note for 1590–1599.

1641 A–W 165,275
(item 4)

1642–1659
Missing, due to the Civil War and Commonwealth. See the probate decision table for further instructions. Some infra records for 1642–1650 may have been filed with the supra series.

1660 A–W 165,275
(item 5)

See the next film for another H document.

1661 A–W 165,276
There is an admon and inventory dated 1660 for Joane Howe.

1662
Missing. See the note for 1590–1599.

1663 A–W 165,277

1664–1665 165,278
Filed chronologically and then roughly alphabetically.

1666 165,279

1667 165,280

1668 A–W 165,281
(item 1)

1669 O 165,281
(last item)
There is one will for Thomas Oldham of Strands in Brinnington. See the note for 1590–1599.

1670–1673
Missing. See the note for 1590–1599.

1674 E 165,282
(item 1)
There is one admon for John Ecches of Wigthington. See the note for 1590–1599.

1675
Missing. See the note for 1590–1599.

1676 F–T 165,282
(item 2)

1677
Missing. See the note for 1590–1599.

1678 W 165,282
(item 3)
There is just a will for Richard Willobee of Whitby and an inventory for George Warburton of Elton. See the note for 1590–1599.

1679 B 165,282
(item 4)
There is one admon for John Bollington of Buglawton. See the note for 1590–1599.

1680 B   **165,282**
                                              (item 5)

There is an admon and inventory for Roger Bolton of Hulme. See the note for 1590–1599.

1681 H   **165,282**
                                              (item 6)

There is one will for Elizabeth Hurst of Godley. See the note for 1590–1599.

1682 B,L   **165,282**
                                              (last item)

There are only two admons. The first is for Mary Bromfield of Audlem and the other is for Anne Lingard of Mottram Andrew. See the note for 1590–1599.

1683
Missing. See the note for 1590–1599.

1684 H   **165,283**
                                              (item 1)

There is one inventory for John Higginson of Bostock. See the note for 1590–1599.

1685 B,H   **165,283**
                                              (item 2)

There are two wills: Mary Brundrett of Smallwood and Ann Hatton of Crowley. See the note for 1590–1599.

1686 A–W   **165,283**
                                              (item 3)

1687 A–W   **165,283**
                                              (item 4)

1688–1689   **165,284**
Filed chronologically and then roughly alphabetically.

1690–1691   **165,285**
Filed chronologically and then roughly alphabetically. Included on this film is the will of Margrett Ashton dated 10 August 1692.

1692–1693   **165,286**
Filed chronologically and then roughly alphabetically. A letter, dated 21 June 1882, explains the whereabouts of the will of Anne Bostock dated 2 April 1691. See the preceding film for another A for 1692.

1694–1695   **165,287**
Filed chronologically and then roughly alphabetically.

1696 A–W   **165,288**
                                              (item 1)

1697–1698   **165,288**
                                              (item 2)

There are three wills: Ann Burgess of Northenden, proved in 1697, and John Ryle of Etchells in Northenden

and George Beswick of Stayley in Mottram, both proved 1n 1698. See the note for 1590–1599.

1699
Missing. See the note for 1590–1599.

1700 B–W   **165,288**
                                              (item 3)

1701 C–T   **165,288**
                                              (item 4)

1702   **165,288**
                                              (item 5)

There are just two inventories for William Massies of Northenden and Alice Ward of Baddiley. See the note for 1590–1599.

1703 C–W   **165,288**
                                              (item 6)

1704 B–L   **165,288**
                                              (item 7)

1705   **165,288**
                                              (item 8)

There are two inventories for Robert Dodge of Offerton and Sarah Wright of Aston. See the note for 1590–1599.

1706 D–S   **165,288**
                                              (item 9)

1707 B–W   **165,288**
                                              (item 10)

1708   **165,288**
                                              (item 11)

There is only an inventory for Thomas Phillips of Aston in Acton. See the note for 1590–1599.

1709   **165,288**
                                              (item 12)

There is an admon for Solomon Steele of Moldsworth. See the note for 1590–1599.

1710   **165,288**
                                              (item 13)

There is an inventory for Dorothy Jennyon of Newton. See the note for 1590–1599.

1711   **165,288**
                                              (item 14)

There is just a will and inventory for Edward Coppock of Northenden. See the note for 1590–1599.

1712   **165,288**
                                              (item 15)

There is an inventory for Joseph Shepley of Hyde. See the note for 1590–1599.

1713–1715
Missing. See the note for 1590–1599.

1716   **165,289**
                                                          (item 1)
There is only a will for Richard Bentlie of Cumberbach.
See the note for 1590–1599.

1717   **165,289**
                                                          (item 2)
There are two inventories for Samuel Haward of
Macclesfield and William Smallwood of the same place.
See the note for 1590–1599.

1718   **165,289**
                                                          (item 3)
There is an inventory for George Andrew of Matley in
Mottram. See the note for 1590–1599.

1719–1720
Missing. See the note for 1590–1599.

1721   **165,289**
                                                          (item 4)
There is only an admon for Mary Bennion of Ince and a
will and inventory for Peter Kinsey of Nether Peover.
See the note for 1590–1599.

1722–1728
Missing. See the note for 1590–1599.

1729 A–W   **165,290**
Two Bs are filed with the As.

1730   **165,291**

1731–1732   **165,292**
Filed chronologically and then roughly alphabetically.

1733 B–W   **165,293**
                                                          (item 1)

1734 A–L   **165,293**
                                                          (item 2)

1735 A–W   **165,294**
                                                          (item 1)

1736 A–Y   **165,294**
                                                          (item 2)

1737 A–W   **165,294**
                                                          (item 3)

1738 C–W   **165,294**
                                                          (item 4)
The Ds precede the Cs.

1739–1741   **165,295**
Filed chronologically and then roughly alphabetically.
The will of John Littler was proven in both 1741 and
1742 and is filed here under 1741.

1742–1744   **165,296**
Filed chronologically and then roughly alphabetically.

1745 B–W
The sixteen wills for this year are mixed with the alphabetical sequence for 1746.

1746 A–W   **165,297**
                                                          (item 1)
The Gs are intermingled with the Hs. The documents for
1745 are mixed together with those for this year.

1747 A–W   **165,297**
                                                          (item 2)

1748 A–W   **165,297**
                                                          (item 3)
The J comes after the Ks. The Ws include one document
for 1749.

1749 A–Y   **165,297**
                                                          (item 4)
See the preceding entry for another W.

1750–1753   **165,298**

1754–1757   **165,299**

1758–1775
Missing. See the note for 1590–1599.

1776–1784   **165,300**
There are no 1778 documents on this film. See the note
for 1590–1599.

1785–1790   **165,301**

1791–1795   **165,302**

1796–1800   **165,303**

1801–1803   **165,304**

1804–1806   **165,305**
The will of Jonathan Whitley, surgeon and apothecary of
Ollerton, which was proven 7 September 1805, appears
with a miscellaneous collection of supra and infra documents on film 166,083, which is listed at the end of the
section entitled "Supra Original Wills" for Lancashire.

1807–1809   **165,306**

1810–1811   **165,307**

1812–1814   **165,308**
The will of Richard Mutchell of Buglawton, proved in 1815, is filed with 1814.

1815–1818   **165,309**
See 1814 for another M for 1815.

1819–1821   **165,310**

1822–1824   **165,311**
See film 165,319 for a B will proven in 1824 which went through a second grant.

1825–1828   **165,312**

1829–1831   **165,313**

1832–1835   **165,314**
See film 165,317 for a B will proven in 1834 which went through a second grant.

1836–1838   **165,315**

1839–1841   **165,316**
The will and admon of James Seddon, weaver of Chester, which was proven 10 October 1839, appears with a miscellaneous collection of supra and infra documents on film 166,083 which is listed at the end of the supra original wills for Lancashire. See the next film for two wills proven in 1841 which received a second grant.

1842–1844   **165,317**
The wills of Ann Bennett of Tranmere, proven in both 1834 and 1842; James Hough of Middlewich, proven in 1841 and 1842; and Samuel Smith of West Kirby, 1841 and 1843, are located on this film. The wills are filed chronologically and then roughly alphabetically.

1845–1846   **165,318**
The wills are filed chronologically and then alphabetically.

1847 B–W   **165,319**
                                                 (item 1)
The will of Nathaniel Booth of Marthall was proven in both 1824 and 1847.

1848 B–W   **165,319**
                                                 (item 2)
A T appears among the Ds. Listed among the Ss is the will for Margaret Upcraft of Chorlton upon Medlock in Manchester, Lancs.

1849 A–W   **165,319**
                                                 (item 3)

1850–1851   **165,320**
Three documents pertaining to church upkeep and a notice of visitation are about the only readable docu-

ments on this film. The act books filed under Lancashire will help. Contact the County Record Office to have the originals read where the film is unreadable.

1852–1853   **165,321**

1854–1855   **165,322**
Filed chronologically and then roughly alphabetically. A codicil to the will of Samuel Hulse precedes the actual will.

1856 A–W   **165,323**
                                                 (item 1)

1857 A–Y   **165,323**
                                                 (item 2)
The Ms and Ns are intermingled. There is a will proven 24 December 1858 for Andrew Plant of Hulme among the Ps for this year.

Modern Copied Wills for the District Probate Registry of Chester

---

1858–1859 A–K   **395,443**

1858–1860 L–Z   **395,444**

1859–1861 A–J   **395,445**

1860–1861 K–Z   **395,446**

1862   **395,447**

1863   **395,450**

1864   **395,448**

1864   **395,449**

1865   **395,451**

1866   **395,452**

1867   **395,453**

1867   **395,454**

1868   **395,455**

1869   **395,456**

1870   **395,457**

1871   **395,458**

1872	395,459	1890	395,489
1873	395,460	1891	395,488
1873–1874	395,461	1892	395,490
1874–1875	395,462	1893	395,491
1874–1875	395,463	1894	395,492
1876	395,464	1895	395,493
1876	395,465	1896	395,494
1876–1877	395,466	1897	395,495
1877–1878	395,467	1898	395,496
1878–1879	395,468	1899–1900	395,497
1878–1879	395,469	1901	395,498
1879–1880	395,470	1902	395,499
1879–1880	395,471	1903	395,500
1880–1881	395,472	1904	395,501
1882–1883	395,473	1905	395,502
1882–1883	395,474	1906	395,503
1883–1884	395,475	1907	395,504
1883–1884	395,476	1908	395,505
1883–1884	395,477	1909	395,506
1883–1884	395,478	1910	395,507
1884–1885	395,479	1911	395,508
1884–1885	395,480	1912	395,509
1885–1886	395,481	1913	395,510
1885–1886	395,482	1914	395,511
1886–1887	395,483	1915	395,512
1886–1887	395,484	1916	395,513
1887–1888	395,485	1917	395,514
1887–1888	395,486	1918	395,515
1888–1889	395,487	1919	395,516

1920	**395,517**
1921	**395,518**
1922	**395,519**
1923	**395,520**
1924	**395,521**
1925	**395,522**
1926	**395,523**
1927–1928	**395,524**
1929–1930	**395,525**
1931–1932	**395,526**
1933–1934	**395,527**
1935–1936	**395,528**
1937–1938	**395,529**
1939	**395,530**
1939–1940	**395,531**
1940	**395,532**

Miscellaneous: Abstracts, Documents, and Select Indexes for Probates Related to Cheshire

---

Some information from the Consistory Court of Chester has been compiled and partially published. Although not complete, searches in this material may accelerate research or supplement previous findings. It is presumed that the researcher would compare any discoveries in printed abstracts with the original records for other details and possible transcription errors.

1) 14th–18th   **FHL 942.7 B4Lc**
centuries
Publications of the Lancashire & Cheshire Record Society. Certain volumes of the printed indexes, which see for further details, contain indexes to wills copied into the bishop's "Enrollment Books," 1512–1740. These indexes provide references to wills now missing from the originals for 1512–1635 (vol. 2, pp. xi–xix), 1621–1650 (vol. 4, p. viii), 1660–1680 (vol. 15, pp. vii–viii), and 1681–1700 (vol. 18, pp. vi–vii).

Abstracts have been printed for those listed with an asterisk in volume 2 and all those indicated as missing in volume 4 in volumes 33, 51, and 54 of the Chetham Society. Other abstracts from the "Enrollment Books" will be found in volume 30 of the Lancashire & Cheshire Record Society described below.

Page xxxii of volume 2 also gives a short list of some wills, 1423–1644, preserved at the British Museum in the Harleian Manuscripts, 1991. An asterisk in this list means that the will is no longer with the originals. Manuscript 1991 is not available at the Family History Library.

Volume 30 (also on film 823,508—item 1 and fiche 6,072,936) is a collection of abstracts for 123 wills, 1301–1752, not presently in any registry. Thirty-two of these wills are from the "Enrollment Books" for 1411–1579.

Volume 76 (also on film 823,518—item 3 and fiche 6,072,982) adds, on pages 173–225, a "Calendar of Abstracts of Wills, Administrations, etc., Contained in Books Relating to Lancashire and Cheshire."

2) 1487–1800
Probate Documents Used In Testamentary Suits. This is a large filmed collection of various documents gathered together as evidence in several thousand cases. It may contain some wills no longer found with the originals. The documents are filed alphabetically by the first two letters of the testator's surname.

The Lancashire & Cheshire Record Society published an index to this collection as follows: 1487–1620 (FHL 942.7 B4Lc vol. 33, 3d part, also on film 823,508—item 4 and fiche 6,072,939), 1621–1700 (vol. 43, also on film 823,510—item 4 and fiche 6,072,949), and 1701–1800 (vol. 52, 2d part, also on film 823,512—item 4). The filmed collection is outlined below.

1572–1620 A	**166,106**
Pre–1620 B–Bird	**166,107**
Pre–1620 Bird–Bux	**166,108**
Pre–1620 C	**166,109**
Pre–1620 D	**166,110**
Pre–1620 E–F	**166,111**
Pre–1620 G	**166,112**
Pre–1620 H	**166,113**
Pre–1620 I–L	**166,114**

Pre–1620 M	166,115	**1701–1800 C–F**	166,142
Pre–1620 N–P	166,116	**1701–1800 G–H**	166,143
Pre–1620 R	166,117	**1701–1800 I–L**	166,144
Pre–1620 S	166,118	**1701–1800 M–N**	166,145
Pre–1620 T–V	166,119	**1701–1800 O–P**	166,146
Pre–1620 W–Z	166,120	**1701–1800 R–V**	166,147
1621–1700 A	166,121	**1701–1800 W–Z**	166,148

1621–1700 B–Ben 166,122

1621–1700 Ben–Bro 166,123
See the next film for another Bo.

1621–1700 Bro–But 166,124
There is an allegation for Bo on this film.

1621–1700 C 166,125

1621–1700 D 166,126

1621–1700 E–F 166,127

1621–1700 G 166,129

1621–1700 Ha–He 166,128

1621–1700 He–Hy 166,130

1621–1700 I–K 166,131

1621–1700 L 166,132

1621–1700 M 166,133

1621–1700 N–O 166,134

1621–1700 P 166,135

1621–1700 R 166,136

1621–1700 S 166,137

1621–1700 T 166,138

1621–1700 W–Z 166,139

1701–1800 A 166,140
This film is mostly filled with documents concerning a
suit challenging a pretended marriage.

1701–1800 B 166,141

3) 1477–1746   **FHL 942.7 B4c**
Publications of the Chetham Society. In the Old Series,
there are some will abstracts for 1525–1554 in volume
33 (also on fiche 6,023,801–6,023,803), 1483–1589 in
volume 51 (also on fiche 6,023,865–6,023,868), and
1596–1639 in volume 54 (also on fiche 6,023,875–
6,023,877). There is an index to all three volumes in volume 54, as well as in volume 2 of the Publications of the
Lancashire & Cheshire Record Society.

Volume 3 of the New Series covers 1477–1746 and contains abstracts from a wide selection of wills, including
many "now lost or destroyed" between 1545–1650, from
the Piccope Manuscripts. (This same volume is on film
824,015—item 5 and fiche 6,072,708.) Another index to
this material for 1477–1650 will be found in volume 2,
pages xxviii–xxxii, and volume 4, pages ix–x, of the
Lancashire & Cheshire Record Society.

Volume 28 of the New Series adds more abstracts for
wills proven between 1572–1696, with an appendix to
Cheshire and Lancashire wills proved at York or
Richmond, 1542–1649. (This same volume is on film
824,020—item 3 and fiche 6,072,733.)

Volume 37 of the New Series adds further abstracts for
1563–1807 on microfiche 6,072,742.

4) 1383–1616   **FHL 942 B4s**
Publications of the Surtees Society. The Society began
publishing materials concerning the northern counties in
1834. Research on any of the counties that make up the
Province of York could benefit from examining the contents of this series. A master index will be found in volume 150.

Abstracts of some wills from the PCC concerning the
northern counties were published in volume 116
(1383–1558) and volume 121 (1555–1616). These two
volumes have been microfilmed as items 5 and 6 of film
990,300. Likewise there may be something of interest
for Cheshire and Lancashire in the volumes of this
series, which are abstracts of some wills registered at
York, especially the Prerogative Court of York (PCY).

These include volume 4 (1316–1430), volume 30 (1426–1467), volume 45 (1395–1491), volume 53 (1484–1509), volume 79 (1509–1531), and volume 106 (1531–1551).

5) Area Wills

Stockport. Transcripts and abstracts of all known probates, 1578–1619, for this township are in volume 124 of the Publications of the Lancashire & Cheshire Record Society (FHL 942.7 B4Lc).

Sandbach. Will books from solicitors' offices held by the Nantwich branch of the Cheshire Family History Society have been microfilmed. They are principally for Sandbach in the nineteenth and twentieth centuries but include items from Crew, Middlewich, and Stockport as well.

Part 1 of item 1 on film 1,278,550 is a typescript index to the six books that are items 2–7 of the same film covering 1831–1939. Part 2 indexes the draft and copy wills that are items 1 and 2 of film 1,278,551. It is not clear if the next three films are indexed, but they are in alphabetical order for the late nineteenth to twentieth centuries as follows: A–F on 1,278,552; G–S on 1,278,553; and S–Y on 1,278,554. A few additional probates for the Sandbach collection appear on items 5–6 of film 1,278,615.

6) Individual Wills

Many copies and abstracts of wills from the medieval period through the twentieth century appear in Alan Dale's collection entitled, "Records of Local Cheshire Persons." Of greatest interest are volumes 8–12. Each volume is indexed and arranged as follows: A–C on film 886,624; D–H on 886,625; H–N on 886,626; N–S on 886,627; and T–Y on 886,628.

Abstracts for two Cheshire wills proved at York are published in volume 1 of *The Northern Genealogist* (FHL 942 B2ng) for Francis Fytton, Esq. of Gawseworth (1608—p. 228) and Thomas Malbon, Clerk of Congleton (1779—p. 232).

Part 2 Cumberland
Probate Jurisdictions and Microfilmed Records

Introduction

Two of the parishes of Cumberland—Alston and Upper or Over Denton—came under the jurisdiction of the Consistory Court of Durham. (See Durham for a full description of that court's records.) Around 1777, Upper or Over Denton was transferred to the Consistory Court of Carlisle, whose records are described below.

Most of County Cumberland was in the jurisdiction of the Consistory Court of Carlisle. The earliest wills for this court date from 1353 to 1386 and have been printed in full. There are no other known wills until 1558, at which point the microfilms commence. However, there are only seventeen documents for the period 1558–1563, and the items before 1563 are not included in the manuscript index. Other than the obvious damage that time has wreaked on the earlier records, some apparently were destroyed during the Civil War. The index contains references to documents that no longer exist. A list of nearly eighty testators with Cumberland connections in the eighteenth and nineteenth centuries who served in the military or who died in the West Indies, East Indies, the Americas, Scotland, Ireland, and the Channel Isles was compiled by Mrs. A. N. V. Turner and printed in *The Genealogists' Magazine* 15 (September 1967): 420–421. These names are included in the index in this volume.

The registered copy wills do not begin until 1727. No act books were filmed for this court. Inventories are numerous; frequently, they are the only available probate document through the first quarter of the seventeenth century. After 1621 through the early part of the eighteenth century, the probate inventories are often missing or misfiled; they may have been filed with the administration inventories from 1662 to 1716. However, from 1717 to 1726 almost every will is accompanied by both an inventory and a probate bond. References to administrations are found among the original wills up to 1661 but are not always listed as such in the index. Administration bonds were rarely filed before 1700. Before that time, references to administrations appear mainly on lone inventories. Nuncupative wills will be found among these administration inventories from 1662 to around 1692.

Nearly one third of the county, located in its southwestern portion, came under the jurisdiction of the Archdeaconry Court of Richmond. Part of the Diocese of York until 1541, Richmond thereafter came under the Diocese of Chester. Apparently, the Diocese of Chester never exercised superior jurisdiction over Richmond in probate matters; rather, such business continued to be handled by the Prerogative Court of York. The probates granted by the Archdeaconry Court of Richmond were filed under the name of the deanery in which the testator resided. Since the Deanery of Copeland was limited to County Cumberland and no other Richmond deaneries pertained to that county, any microfilms relevant to the Deanery of Copeland will be outlined in the sections following Carlisle.

The earliest original will for the Deanery of Copeland was proven in 1466. Some of the originals were lost (probably when the records were moved to a new repository in 1748) or misfiled, but two of the lost ones for the Deanery of Copeland were recovered. The information for these two wills, which were proven in 1588 and 1592, has been published,[1] and the names are included in the index in this volume. Abstracts of these records were preserved by the British Museum along with the more numerous entries for the Deanery of Amounderness. (See Lancashire for further details.) References to "Calendar W" usually mean that the original has been lost or possibly filed with the Eastern Deaneries, which were in Yorkshire and are described under that county's section of this volume.

The registered copy wills for Copeland are sparse, and the act books are confined to the eighteenth and nineteenth centuries. Inventories rarely appear with the administration bonds after 1750 but still will be found frequently with the wills as late as 1770.

Probate Decision Table for Cumberland

If the Research Subject Lived in One of These Jurisdictions:	Archdeaconry of Richmond	Episcopal Consistory of Durham	Episcopal Consistory of Carlisle	Anywhere in the County, 1645–1660
Search the probate records of these courts in the order shown below:	BLUE	ROSE	GREEN	
Archdeaconry Court of Richmond (Copeland Deanery)	1			
Archdeaconry Court of Richmond (Eastern Deaneries— see Yorkshire)	2			
Consistory Court of Durham (see Durham)		1		
Consistory Court of Carlisle	4	3	1	
Prerogative Court of the Archbishop of York (see Yorkshire)	3	2	2	
Court of the Dean and Chapter of York (see Yorkshire for vacancy jurisdiction)	5	4	3	
Chancery Court of the Archbishop of York (see Yorkshire)	6	5	4	
Prerogative Court of the Archbishop of Canterbury (see London)	7	6	5	1
Court of Delegates, 1643–1857 (see London)	8	7	6	

[1]Henry Fishwick, ed., *A List of the Lancashire Wills Proved within the Archdeaconry of Richmond, from A.D. 1457 to 1680; and of Abstracts of Lancashire Wills, from A.D. 1531 to 1652,* Lancashire & Cheshire Record Society, Vol. 10 (The Record Society, 1884), pp. viii–ix. See page 40 of this volume for Robinson and Benn.

look first for the idents. When the appropriate document is found, watch for possible accompanying documents just before or after it. Before 1662 the admons and any supplementary documents are intermingled with the wills. If the document is not found, scan the entire film for misplaced items before turning to step B.

B) Miscellaneous. The abstracts and select indexes found in this section will be of value mainly for pre–1668 research.

C) Anthony J. Camp, *Wills and Their Whereabouts*, 4th ed. (London: The author, 1974). This reference work should be consulted to determine what was not filmed. Records not filmed for Carlisle include the original wills, supplementary documents, and admons from 1727–1858, as well as all of the act books.

Indexes and Calendars for the Consistory Court of Carlisle

(Some abstracts or extracts of documents relating to Carlisle probates will be found in the miscellaneous section. Searches in these items and the stray-name index to this volume may reveal entries not found or easily found in the filmed calendars outlined below. Such materials are usually edited and may still be in Latin for the earlier periods.)

1) The indexes are as follows:

R. S. Ferguson, ed., *Testamenta Karleolensia: The Series of Wills from the Pre-Reformation Register of the Bishop of Carlisle, 1353–1386* (Cumberland & Westmorland Antiquarian & Archaeological Society, Extra Series, vol. 9, 1893). FHL 942.8 B4cwc, vol. 9, and also on film 823,681, item 2. This offering represents all of the known wills before 1558. The wills are printed in full.

Jim Richardson and Ron Shaw, *Index and Extracts of Cumbrians in Wills Proved at the Prerogative Court of Canterbury* (Cumbria Family History Society, 1984). FHL 942.8 P2.

2) The filmed calendars are arranged as follows:

Time Period	Film or Call No.

1563–1599   **90,284**
Vol. 1 of a nineteenth-century Manuscript Index to Wills, Inventories, and Admons. The names are arranged roughly alphabetically by the year of probate. The wills for a given letter in any year are listed first, followed by unattached inventories or admons. The few surviving records for 1558–1562 were not indexed. All of the individual documents for this court are filed alphabetically by the initial letter in the person's surname as outlined herein. To find a particular will, turn to:

A) Original Wills. Match the year located in the index with the appropriate film call number. Within that film

1600–1644   **90,284**
Vol. 2 of the Manuscript Index. This portion of the index is arranged the same and should be treated as the above, with two exceptions. First, only three admons are listed in the index after 1608. It is assumed that the index is imperfect and that many of the admons or their inventories survive. The researcher looking for a specific person during this time period is advised to search the desired alphabetical sequence of the original wills in the suspected years regardless of the index. Second, the index indicates that there are no records at all between 1645–1660. This is not quite the case, as will be determined by consulting film 90,396 for the original wills.

1661–1699   **90,284**
(Continuation of the above) The indexes do not include admons until 1729 and the act books are not available on film as a substitute, but from 1662 onward the admons and their inventories were grouped separately from the original wills. The microfilm collection reflects that fact. Mixed with these records, which were mainly inventories in the last half of the seventeenth century, are nuncupative wills, probate inventories, and other miscellaneous documents ordinarily filed with the wills. Thus, the researcher interested in the period from 1661–1726 should scan the films listed under "Administration Bonds and Inventories" besides using the indexes listed here and the stray-name index.

1700–1800 A–K   **90,285**
Vol. 3 of the Manuscript Index. Note the reference above for pre–1729 information. From 1727 forward the microfilms in this collection are of registered copy wills only. The index provides the residence of the testator and a page number for registered copy wills. The page numbers are listed faithfully from 1727–1752, then there are no listings until 1800–1858. Approach the original wills from 1700–1726 as described above for the other parts of the index. After 1726 turn to the section marked "Registered Copy Wills" and note whether each volume

was separately indexed. Finally, consider step C listed under the first film for this index.

1700–1800 L–Z   **90,286**
Vol. 4 of the Manuscript Index. Consult the note above.

1800–1858 A–J   **90,287**
Vol. 5 of the Manuscript Index. Consult the note above.

1800–1858 K–Z   **90,287**
Vol. 6 of the Manuscript Index. Consult the note above.

Original Wills and Inventories for the Consistory Court of Carlisle

---

1558–1564   **90,288**
The first entries on this film are seventeen individual probate documents scattered over 1558–1563 in no particular order. The ones before 1563 are not listed in the manuscript index to this court. Then comes 1564 in the following alphabetical groupings: C, A, B, D, P, K, R, M, T, M, J, H, E, G.

1565 A–P   **90,289**
See the next film for E.

1565 P–W   **90,290**
An R is filed toward the end of the Ps, and a U near the end of the Ws, followed by an unreadable inventory that seems to be out of place. The Es are located at the end of the film.

1566 B   **90,291**
See the next film for B also.

1566 A–Y   **90,292**
Starts with a B document followed by an A, then it is fairly consistent in its arrangement from C–W except for a Y which appears with the Vs. The rest of the Bs are on the preceding film.

1567 A–W   **90,293**
The alphabetical arrangement is: A–L, U–W, S, R, P, N, M, T.

1568 A–W   **90,294**

1569 A–G   **90,294**
                                                         (item 2)

1569 G–Y   **90,295**
An H appears between T and W.

1570 A–H   **90,296**

1570 H–W   **90,297**

1571 A–M   **90,297**
                                                         (item 2)
See the next film for K also.

1571 M–T   **90,298**
A K is filed in the middle of the Ss.

1572 A–L   **90,299**

1572 L–W   **90,300**

1573 A–L   **90,300**
                                                         (item 2)

1573 L–V   **90,301**

1574 A–J   **90,302**

1574 J–Y   **90,303**

1575 A–T   **90,304**
See the next film for T, J, and C also.

1575 T,J,C   **90,305**

1576 A–J   **90,306**

1576 J–Y   **90,307**

1577 A–M   **90,308**

1577 M–W   **90,309**

1578 A–B   **90,310**

1578 B–M   **90,311**

1578 M–T   **90,312**

1578 T–Y   **90,313**

1579 A–H   **90,314**
See the next film for C also.

1579 H–T   **90,315**
A C is mixed with S.

1579 T–Y   **90,316**

1580 A–H   **90,317**

1580 H–S   **90,318**
See the next film for K also.

1580 S–W   **90,319**
Two Ks appear at the end of the film.

1581 A–G   **90,320**

1581 G–U 90,321

1581 V–W 90,322

1582
Missing. See step C under item 2 of the preceding section entitled "Indexes and Calendars."

1583 A–R 90,323

1583 R–Y 90,324

1584 A–S 90,325

1584 S–W 90,326

1585 A–J 90,327

1585 J–W 90,328
An L will be found on film 90,331 below.

1586 A–P,V 90,329

1587 A–D 90,330

1587 D–M 90,331
Includes an inventory dated 1589 for John Emerson of Lazonby, which is incorrectly entered under 1587 in the manuscript index as John Easton; and an inventory dated 1585 for Hew Langhbourne of Dufton, which is also listed incorrectly under 1587 in the index as John Langhorne.

1587 N–S 90,332
Includes some documents for 1588.

1587 S–Y 90,333

1588 A–K 90,334

1588 K–T 90,335
See the note above for film 90,332.

1588 T–W 90,336

1589 A–Y 90,337
An E appears on film 90,331 above. Other Es and a J will be found at the end of this film.

1590 A–E 90,338

1590 E–W 90,339

1591 B–W 90,340
A W appears between S and V; otherwise the alphabetical sequence ends with V, including an inventory for Thomas Vearie or Vayray of Moreland, which is incorrectly listed in the manuscript index under Wayray. A list of his debts dated 1592 follows.

1592 B–R 90,340
(item 2)

1592 R–Y 90,341

1593 A–H 90,342

1593 H–W 90,343

1594 A–V 90,344
A P is filed in the middle of the Ss.

1595 A–W 90,345

1596 A–M 90,346

1596 M–W 90,347

1597 B–M 90,348

1597 M–W 90,349

1598 A–P 90,350

1598 R–Y 90,351

1599 A–W 90,352
The alphabetical sequence is: A–H, N, J, M, P–W, U.

1600 A–W 90,353

1601 A–H 90,354

1601 H–Y 90,355

1602 A–P 90,355
(item 2)

1602 P–W 90,356

1603 A–R 90,357
See the note for item 2 of film 90,358.

1603 R–Y 90,358

1604 A–P 90,358
(item 2)
Some 1603 entries may appear between B and C.

1604 P–Y 90,359

1605 A–R 90,360

1605 R–Y 90,361

1606 A–W 90,361
(item 2)

1607 A–W	90,362
1608 A–C	90,363
1608 C–W	90,364
1609 A–W	90,365
1610 A–L	90,366
1610 L–W	90,367
1611 A–W	90,367 **(item 2)**
1612 A–W	90,368
1613 A–P	90,369
1613 P–Y	90,370
1614 A–C	90,371

1614 C–W 90,372
The alphabetical arrangement is: C–K, W, P–T, N, V, Y, O.

1615 A–W	90,373
1616 A–H	90,374

1616 H–W 90,375
The Js appear at the end of the film.

1617 A–N 90,376
An L is filed with the Bs.

1617 N–W	90,377
1618 A–B	90,378
1618 B–T	90,379
1618 T–Y	90,380
1619 A–W	90,381
1620 A–Y	90,382

1621 A–W 90,383
The alphabetical arrangement is: A–C, F–K, M, P–W. A V is filed with the Ws. After the Ws there is an irregular series as follows: C, T, S, J, S, B, H, G, C, S, B, D, B.

1622 A–Y 90,383 **(item 2)**

1623 A–D,R–Y 90,384
The alphabetical arrangement is: R–T, Y, T, W, T, A–D. Between the last T and A is an index to missing wills for this year. See the next film for D–R.

1623 D–R 90,385

1624 A–W 90,385 **(item 2)**
The alphabetical arrangement is an A followed in reverse order by W–M, K, L, J–A. The As continue on the next film.

1624 A 90,386

1625 B–W 90,386 **(item 2)**
The alphabetical arrangement, in reverse order, is: W, T–P, U, P–H, K, H–B, M.

1626 A–W 90,387
The alphabetical arrangement, in reverse order, is: O, W, S, T, S, P, O, M, L, K, I, J, M, B, G–A.

1627 A–E 90,388
The alphabetical arrangement is in reverse order. A B appears in the middle of the Cs.

1627 E–W 90,387 **(item 2)**
The alphabetical arrangement is in reverse order.

1628 A–W 90,388 **(item 2)**
The alphabetical arrangement is in reverse order.

1629 A–W 90,388 **(item 3)**

1630 A–M,Y,W 90,389
Further entries are found on the next film for the Ws.

1630 N–W 90,390
The alphabetical arrangement is in reverse order as follows: W, T–S, W, S–N. A Y and more Ws are on the preceding film.

1631 A–W 90,390 **(item 2)**

1632 A–W 90,390 **(item 3)**
F and G are intermingled.

1633 A–P 90,390 **(item 4)**

1633 P–W 90,391

1634 A–W 90,392

1635 A–W 90,392
(item 2)

1636 H,B,D 90,392
(item 3)

Further entries are found on the next film.

1636 A–W 90,393
The alphabetical arrangement is: D–W followed by A, B, W. Some entries also appear on the preceding film.

1637 A–Y 90,394

1638 A–W
1639 D 90,395
The alphabetical arrangement is in reverse order, followed by the Ds for 1639, which continue on the next film.

1639 A–Y 90,395
(item 2)
This film continues with more Ds as were started on the last film. The alphabetical arrangement, in reverse order, goes Y–J, F, H, G, I, H–G, H, F–E, C–A.

1640 A–W 90,396

1641 A–W 90,396
(item 2)

1642 A–W 90,396
(item 3)

1643 A–W 90,396
(item 4)
See the next entry for more Ts.

1644 A–W 90,396
(item 5)
W is followed by T for 1643.

1645–1660 90,396
(end of film)
Due to the Commonwealth and Interregnum, there are few entries for this period. See the probate decision table for further instructions. The existing documents for this court are mixed together as follows: 1648, B; 1658, L; 1659, R; 1657, W; 1656, P; 1648, R; 1647, T; 1648, W, N, B; 1647, B; and 1646, B.

1661 A–T 90,397
The alphabetical arrangement is somewhat irregular but in fair order. At the beginning of the film is an original ident, but no documents, for Thomas Studholme. His will was proven 23 April 1670.

1661 T–Y 90,398

1662 A–Y 90,401

1663 A–D 90,402

1663 D–Y 90,403

1664 A–R 90,403
(item 2)

1664 R–W 90,404

1665 A–J 90,406
The alphabetical arrangement, in reverse order, is: J, H, G, H, G, F–A. Four more As will be found on film 90,408.

1665 A,K–Y 90,408
The film starts with four As, then jumps to K–Y. The rest of the alphabetical sequence for this year is on film 90,406.

1666 A–Y 90,408
(item 2)

1667 A–H 90,408
(item 3)

1667 H–W 90,409

1668 A–G 90,412

1668 G–W 90,413
Some Ss and Ts follow the Ws.

1669 A–S 90,413
(item 2)
Includes a renunciation to administer the goods of Richard Routeledge.

1669 S–W 90,414

1670 A–Y 90,420

1671 A,T–Y 90,420
(item 2)
The alphabetical arrangement is: W, Y, W, T, followed by the start of the As, which continue on the next film.

1671 A–T 90,421
The rest of the alphabetical sequence for this year is found on the preceding film, including some more As.

1672 A–S 90,422

1672 S–Y 90,423

1673 A–W	90,423 (item 2)	1688 A–M	90,452

Some of the entries between A–D are out of order.

1688 M–Y — 90,453

1674 A–W — 90,427

1689 A–W — 90,453 (item 2)

1675 A–C — 90,427 (item 2)

1690 A–O — 90,453 (item 3)

1675 C–Y — 90,428

1690 O–W — 90,454

1676 A–W — 90,433

1691 A–H — 90,458

1677 A–P — 90,433 (item 2)

1691 H–W — 90,459

1677 N–W — 90,434

1692 A–Y — 90,459 (item 2)

1678 A–Y — 90,434 (item 2)

1693 A–Y — 90,460

1679 A–S — 90,435

The alphabetical arrangement is somewhat irregular but in fair order.

1694 A–S — 90,460 (item 2)

1679 S–W — 90,436

1694 S–Y — 90,461

1680 B–Y — 90,436 (item 2)

1695 A–Y — 90,462

A P appears in the Ns.

1696 A–J — 90,462 (item 2)

1681 A–R — 90,436 (item 3)

1696 J–W — 90,463

1681 R–Y — 90,437

1697 A–W — 90,464

Includes an admon bond dated 1694 for Francis Grainger.

1682 A–W — 90,440

The alphabetical arrangement begins irregularly as follows: A, B, A, B, C, S, C, D, H, F, G, H.

1698 A–C — 90,464 (item 2)

Includes a bond dated 1774 of Joshua Nicholson concerning the will of Thomas Brown proven in 1698.

1683 A–P — 90,440 (item 2)

1698 C–W — 90,465

1683 P–Y — 90,441

1699 A–Y — 90,465 (item 2)

1684 A–W — 90,442

Starts with the Ws, then continues in proper alphabetical sequence.

1685 A–H — 90,442 (item 2)

1700 A–W — 90,466

1685 H–Y — 90,443

1701 A–T — 90,466 (item 2)

1686 A–W — 90,447

A T appears in the middle of the Ss.

1687 A–H — 90,447 (item 2)

1701 T–Y — 90,467

1687 H–Y — 90,448

1702 A–Y — 90,468

Two As appear in the middle of the Bs.

1703 A–S   **90,468**
                                      (item 2)

1703 S–Z   **90,469**

1704 A–W   **90,470**
Continues on the next film.

1705 A–W   **90,471**
Starts with Ws from 1704.

1706 A–R   **90,472**

1706 R–W   **90,473**
Includes an admon bond in the Ws.

1707 A–W   **90,473**
                                      (item 2)
Two of the F wills proven in this year were actually filed with 1708.

1708 A–W   **90,473**
                                      (item 3)
See the notes for 1707 and 1709 about stray documents.

1709 A–B   **90,473**
                                      (item 4)
A D will proven in this year was filed with 1708.

1709 B–W   **90,474**

1710 A–Y   **90,475**
The alphabetical arrangement, in reverse order, is: Y, K–A. This is followed by L–W.

1711 A–L   **90,475**
                                      (item 2)

1711 L–W   **90,476**

1712 A–M   **90,477**

1712 N–W   **90,478**

1713 A–W   **90,478**
                                      (item 2)

1714 A–H   **90,478**
                                      (item 3)

1714 J–W   **90,479**

1715 A–W   **90,480**
A T appears at the end of the Ws.

1716 A–B   **90,480**
                                      (item 2)

1716 B–Z   **90,481**

1717–1726
During this time period, each will is usually accompanied by a probate bond and inventory.

1717 A–Y   **90,483**

1718 A–Y   **90,484**
The alphabetical arrangement is: A–C, L, D–G, T, H–J, N–P, M, R–S, W–Y.

1719 A–Y   **90,485**
T and S are intermingled.

1720 A–T   **90,486**

1720 T–Y   **90,487**

1721 A–K   **90,490**
The alphabetical arrangement is: A, B, A–E, G, F, G, H, L, K.

1721 K–W   **90,492**
The alphabetical arrangement is: K, J, M–N, P, O, T, W, T–W, R–S.

1722 A–C   **90,491**

1722 C–W   **90,493**
The alphabetical arrangement is: C–M, T–W, S, R, S, N, P.

1723 A–L,T   **90,495**
The rest of the alphabet, including further entries of T, will be found on the next film.

1723 M–Y   **90,496**
The alphabetical arrangement is: T–Y, M–P, R, S, R–S. Further entries of T will be found on the preceding film. There is an admon bond filed with the Ps, and another in the Rs. An N will may be found in item 2 on this film among the admon bonds for 1723; see the section entitled "Administration Bonds and Inventories" for filing details.

1724 A–B   **90,497**

1724 B–R   **90,498**
The alphabetical arrangement is: B–J, M, J–R. An admon bond was filed with the Ps.

1724 R–W   **90,499**

1725 A–M   **90,500**
An I appears in the middle of the Hs.

1725 M–Y   **90,501**

1726 A–F   **90,504**

1726 F–Y   **90,505**
The alphabetical arrangement is: F–J, T, W, Y, and L–S.
An admon bond was filed with the Ns.

1727–1858
Not filmed. See the registered copy wills, which follow,
and step C under item 2 of the section entitled "Indexes
and Calendars."

Registered Copy Wills for the Consistory Court of Carlisle

1558–1726
Do not exist; see the section entitled "Original Wills and
Inventories."

1727–1731   **90,506**
1727 covers pages 1–86 and is not in any alphabetical
sequence, but there is an index at the end of the film
arranged by year. 1728 covers pages 87–181 and is filed
alphabetically A–W, as are the remaining years. 1729
covers pages 181–395 for A–Y. 1730 covers pages 396–
544 for A–W. 1731 covers pages 545–628 for A–O, with
the remainder for this year appearing on the next film.

1731–1734   **90,507**
The index at the beginning of the film is arranged alphabetically, with each letter subdivided chronologically for
all of the years treated. 1731 covers pages 1–80 for P–Y
but is not included in the index on this film. It may have
been treated in the index on the preceding film. NOTE:
This index description applies to the subsequent films in
this section unless noted otherwise.

1735–1738   **90,508**

1739–1742   **90,508**
                                                (item 2)

1743–1745   **90,509**

1746–1748   **90,509**
                                                (item 2)

1749–1752   **90,510**

1753–1756   **90,510**
                                                (item 2)

1757–1760   **90,511**
Dashes are used like ditto marks in the index.

1761–1763   **90,511**
                                                (item 2)

1764–1766   **90,512**

1767–1769   **90,513**

1770–1772   **90,514**

1773–1775   **90,515**
The index at the beginning of the film is arranged alphabetically, with each letter subdivided chronologically for
all of the years treated. NOTE: This applies to the subsequent films unless stated otherwise.

1776–1778   **90,516**

1779–1781   **90,517**

1782–1784   **90,518**

1785–1788   **90,518**
                                                (item 2)

1789–1792   **90,519**

1793–1796   **90,519**
                                                (item 2)

1797–1799   **90,520**

1800–1801   **90,521**

1802–1804   **90,522**
Indexed at the beginning, but the entire alphabet for one
year is treated before going on to the next year.

1805–1807   **90,523**
Indexed at the beginning, with each letter subdivided
chronologically for all of the years treated.

1808–1810   **90,524**
Reverts to an annual index for the entire alphabet.

1811–1812   **90,525**
Annual index for the entire alphabet.

1813–1814   **90,526**
Annual index for the entire alphabet.

1815–1816   **90,527**
Index has R–W 1815 first, then A–F 1816, then A–P
1815, then G–W 1816.

1817–1818   **90,528**
Annual index for the entire alphabet.

1819–1821   **90,529**
Annual index for the entire alphabet.

1822–1823   **90,530**
Annual index for the entire alphabet. At the end of the ledger are inserted some E, G, and R entries.

1824–1825   **90,531**
Annual index for the entire alphabet. At the end of the ledger is a codicil to one will and an admon that was annexed to another. Both are cross-referenced to their respective wills.

1826–1827   **90,532**
Annual index for the entire alphabet. One admon is at the beginning of the ledger.

1828–1829   **90,533**
Annual index for the entire alphabet. NOTE: This applies to the subsequent films unless stated otherwise.

1830–1831   **90,534**

1832–1833   **90,535**

1834–1835   **90,536**

1836–1837   **90,537**

1838–1839   **90,538**
Three admons that were annexed to wills come at the beginning. They are cross-referenced to their respective wills. Then follows the annual index for the entire alphabet.

1840–1841   **90,539**
The index at the beginning of the film is arranged alphabetically with each letter subdivided chronologically for all of the years treated. There is an appendix concerning three admons that were annexed to wills. Only the third admon is cross-referenced to a will within this ledger. The three wills referred to are: George Thornwaite, whose will is copied on page 732; Matthew Brunskill, page 118; and William Ion, page 431.

1842–1843   **90,540**
Annual index at the beginning. One admon follows the index.

1844–1845   **90,541**
Index at the beginning. One admon follows the index. The admon is cross-referenced by page number to the will to which it was annexed.

1846–1847   **90,542**
Indexed, with mention of admon as per the preceding entry.

1848–1849   **90,543**
Indexed, with two admons included.

1850–1851   **90,544**
Indexed.

1852–1853   **90,545**
Indexed.

1854–1855   **90,546**
Indexed, with one admon included.

1856–10 Jan 1858   **90,547**
Indexed.

Administration Bonds and Inventories for the Consistory Court of Carlisle

1558–1661
Any surviving documents for this time period were filed with the original wills. Note the instructions for 1600–1644 in the section entitled "Indexes and Calendars."

1662–1726
Note the instructions for 1661–1699 in the section entitled "Indexes and Calendars" before proceeding. Missing items may have been filed with the original wills.

1662 A–S   **90,399**
The alphabetical arrangement is: A, R, K, R, A–D, B, D, C, G, F, E, D, H, J, H, C, K, J, M, L, M, N, P, O, N, P, R, S, R, S.

1662 S–Y   **90,400**
Irregularly filed. These are all inventories, about one half of which mention the process of administration. At least one half are not listed in the manuscript index.

1663 C–W   **90,400**
                   (item 2)
The percentage of admon inventories seems higher than noted in the preceding entry. Wills filed here (most of which were not listed in the manuscript index) include: Henry Fisher, Leonard Matchell, Robert Twentyman, Thomas Ward, William Wheelwright, John Wait, and Christopher Whitlock.

1664 A–Y   **90,405**
Mainly inventories, most of which mention the act of administration. Nuncupative wills were filed for William Judson of Hilton; William Jack; John James of Knells; William Harrison, the younger; and John Lawson.

1665 A   **90,405**
                   (last item)

1665 A–W   **90,407**
Only one admon bond was noted. It was filed with the Ss.

1666 C–Y   **90,410**
Seems to be about half-and-half administration and probate inventories. Wills were noted for William Fearon, William Harryson, John Hudson, John Milborne, William Richmond, and Agnes Sanderson.

1667 A   **90,410**
                                              (last item)

1667 A–W   **90,411**
The As start on the preceding film. This film is again about half-and-half administration and probate inventories. The alphabetical arrangement is: A, B, S, B–H, W, H–N, P, R–W. The will of Reginald Hobson was included.

1668
Missing. See step C under item 2 of the section entitled "Indexes and Calendars." These may be filed with the original wills.

1669 B–W   **90,415**
Includes a will for William Barwick.

1670 T–Y   **90,415**
                                                 (item 2)
The alphabetical arrangement is: W, Y, V, T. Apparently, there were no other entries for this year, but note the instructions above for 1668.

1671 A–L   **90,416**
                                                 90,417
Probably about half-and-half administration and probate inventories, some of which are not listed in the manuscript index. The alphabetical arrangement is: A, B, A, B, A, B–G, A, G, H–L. The following wills, mostly nuncupative, were noted: Margaret Crozier, Robert Dalton, Thomas Elwood, Richard Green, Thomas Greenapp, John Hugginson, Robert Hodgson, Ellinor Hodgeson, Fridswith Hodgson, Henry Judson, Richard Jackson, and John Lister. The second film is an exact duplicate of the first.

1671 L–Y   **90,418**

1672 A–R   **90,418**
                                                 (item 2)
The following wills, mostly nuncupative, were noted: Hugh Bayly, John Beachem, Jane Bowman, Christopher Hodgson, and John Ireland. At the start of the Ls is part of a memo, undated, concerning a contested probate. The only name given in full in it is for an Edward Fallyday.

1672 R–Z   **90,419**

1673 A–H   **90,424**

1673 H–Z   **90,425**

1674 A–P   **90,425**
                                                 (item 2)

1674 P–Z   **90,426**

1675 A–H   **90,429**
Note the next film for a B reference.

1675 H–Y   **90,430**
A B appears among the Ts. Nuncupative wills were noted for Margeratt Mitchell, Allan Pattinson, Margaret Shearman, Janett Tiffin, William Wilson, Christopher Westray, Robert Wilson, and Henry Wharton.

1676
Missing. See step C under item 2 of the section entitled "Indexes and Calendars." These may be filed with the original wills.

1677 B–C   **90,430**
                                                 (item 2)

1677 C–W   **90,431**
After L come three M entries for 1692, then an M for 1677 followed by five more for 1692 before reverting to M for 1677. Two more M entries for 1692 appear between N and P. There are no further entries for 1692. R and T are intermixed. Some wills were noted in passing.

1678 A–S   **90,431**
                                                 (item 2)
The alphabetical arrangement is: A–H, L–P, J–K, and R–S.

1678 S–Z   **90,432**

1679 A–Z   **90,438**

1680 A–H   **90,438**
                                                 (item 2)

1680 H–W   **90,439**

1681 A–Z   **90,439**
                                                 (item 2)

1682 A–W   **90,444**
Starts with an O, otherwise the alphabetical sequence is in order.

1683 A–B   **90,444**
                                                 (item 2)

1683 B–Z   **90,445**

1684 A–R   **90,445**
                                                 (item 2)
Some A entries appear after B. Intermingled with K and L are items for 1693–1694. An A appears on the next film.

1684 R–Z   **90,446**
An A appears in the middle of the Ws.

1685 A–D   **90,449**
A P appears in the middle of the Bs. The nuncupative
will of Elizabeth Alexander of Smardale and an assignation to the will of Edmond Bell of Denton were included.

1685 D–Y   **90,450**
The alphabetical arrangement is: D, H, E–G, J–W, U, Y,
and W. Note the P entry on the preceding film and the
ones on the next item of this film. Included are nuncupa-
tive wills for William Dargue, Margaret Hewetson, Jane
Ellison, Reginald Graham, William Grainger, Isabell
Ion, John Nickell, John Stamper, William Sowerby,
Thomas Wood, John William, and John Winskell.

1686 A–T   **90,450**
                                                     (item 2)
The alphabetical arrangement first goes in reverse: E–A
followed by F–T. Some of the Ps for 1685 are included
with the Ps for 1686. One admon bond will be found in
the Ls. Nuncupative wills were noted for George
Dobinson, Ann Glaisters, James Pearson, Arthur
Pattinson, and Mabell Rashell.

1686 T–Z   **90,451**

1687 A–T   **90,448**
                                                     (item 2)
Probate inventories are found as well as admon invento-
ries. A G appears in the middle of the Bs. There is an
admon bond in the Js. Included are nuncupative wills for
Thomas Bird, George Dixon, Robert Rea, and George
Stockbridge.

1688 A–Z   **90,451**
                                                     (item 2)
Some As appear in the Ws.

1689 A–Z   **90,455**

1690 A–C   **90,455**
                                                     (item 2)

1690 C–Z   **90,456**
T comes before R.

1691 A–W   **90,456**
                                                     (item 2)

1691 W   **90,457**

1692 A–W   **90,457**
                                                     (item 2)
Some Rs follow the Ws. Some Ms were filed with 1677
on film 90,431.

1693–1702
Missing, except for a few scattered entries observed
elsewhere. Some K and L items for 1693–1694 were
filed with the admon inventories for 1684; see film
90,445 (item 2). Others for 1694, 1697–1698 were filed
with the original wills for 1697–1698; see film 90,464.
Others might also be found among the original wills. See
step C under item 2 of the section entitled "Indexes and
Calendars."

1703 A–Z   **90,469**
                                                     (item 2)

1704 C–T   **90,471**
                                                     (item 3)
Contains admon bonds and inventories.

1705
Missing. See step C under item 2 of the section entitled
"Indexes and Calendars." These may be filed with the
original wills.

1706 W
One admon bond was noted among the original wills for
this year on film 90,473. See the preceding notation.

1707–1709
Missing. See the note above for 1705.

1710 B–W   **90,476**
                                                     (item 2)
Admon bonds and inventories.

1711 H,P–W   **90,476**
                                                     (item 3)
Apparently, the rest of the first half of the alphabet is
missing. See the note above for 1705.

1712
Missing. See the note above for 1705.

1713 B   **90,479**
                                                     (item 2)
Probate and administration bonds as well as inventories.
Apparently, the rest is missing. See the note above for
1705.

1714
Missing. See the note for 1705.

1715 A–Z   **90,481**
                                                     (item 2)

1716 A–Z   **90,482**

1717
Missing. See step C under item 2 of the section entitled
"Indexes and Calendars." These may be filed with the
original wills.

1718 A–Z 90,482
(item 2)

1719
Missing. See the note for 1717.

1720 A–Y 90,488
Admon bonds and inventories. The alphabetical arrangement is: A, B, L, B, A, H, F, D, H, G, H, L, M, P, O, N, M, and P–Y.

1721 A–W 90,488
(item 2)

1722 A 90,493
(item 2)

1722 A–W 90,494

1723 A–W 90,496
(item 2)
A D precedes the Cs. There is a will in the Ns. One P entry and one R were filed among the wills for the same year, which are on film 90,496.

1724 B,F,D 90,488
(item 3)
Further entries appear on the next film.

1724 B–W 90,489
The alphabetical arrangement is: D, C, B, G, F, H–W.

1725 A–W 90,502
The alphabetical arrangement is: A–C, W, V, T, S, R, P, N, M, L. Further entries appear on the next film.

1725 A–L 90,503
The alphabetical arrangement is: L, J, H, G, F, E, D, C, B, C, A, B, C, B, A. Other entries are on the preceding film.

1726 A–W 90,503
(item 2)
One admon bond was noted among the original wills for this year on film 90,473.

1727–1858
Not filmed. See step C under item 2 of the section entitled "Indexes and Calendars."

Miscellaneous: Abstracts and Select Indexes for Probates Relating to Cumberland

---

(Some information from the Consistory Court of Carlisle and its superior jurisdictions has been compiled and partially published. Although not complete, searches in this material may accelerate research or supplement previous findings. It is presumed that the researcher would compare any discoveries here with the original records for other details and possible transcription errors.)

1) 1383–1616 **FHL 942 B4s**
The Publications of the Surtees Society. The Society began publishing materials concerning the northern counties in 1834. Research on any of the counties that make up the Province of York could benefit from examining the contents of this series. A master index will be found in volume 150.

Abstracts of some wills from the PCC concerning the northern counties, including Cumberland, were published in volume 116 (1383–1558) and volume 121 (1555–1616). These two volumes have been microfilmed as items 5 and 6 of film 990,300. Likewise, there may be something of interest for Cumberland in the volumes of this series that are abstracts of some wills registered at York, especially the PCY. These include volume 4 (1316–1430), volume 30 (1426–1467), volume 45 (1395–1491), volume 53 (1484–1509), volume 79 (1509–1531), and volume 106 (1531–1551).

2) 1457–1680 **FHL 942.7 B4Lc**
vol. 10, p. viii
also 823,526
(item 3)
Vol. 10 of the Lancashire & Cheshire Record Society mentions two probates housed at the British Museum for persons from Cumberland: Elizabeth Benn of St. Bees (1592), Ellen Robinson of Lowswater (1588).

3) 1564–1668 **252,674**
Testamenta Carliolensia. This is a handwritten, indexed collection of wills and admons referring to Carlisle. In format it has the appearance of similar compilations done by Raines. If so, the researcher will probably wish to consult items 5 and 6 of Special Collections in the miscellaneous section of Durham.

The same index is at both the beginning and the end of this short collection. After the last index there are two entries for later dates. The first is dated 1676 for John Peacoke of Caldbeck, and the second is dated 1697 for Hugh Peacocke of Mosedale.

4) 1609–1795 **FHL 942 B2ng**
The Northern Genealogist. There are a few scattered references in this publication to wills of Cumberland residents proven at York.

The extracts in volume 1 are for John Hudson of Bowtherbeck in 1609, Sir Edward Musgrave of Hatton Castle in 1673, and James Adderton of Penreth in 1726.

The extracts in volume 3 are for Sir Timothy Fetherstonhaugh of Kirk Ouswould in 1661/2, Patricius Senhouse of Bridekirk in 1682, William Ferryes of Whitehaven in 1711, Thomas Benson of Stanwix in 1727, George Brownrigg of Wigton in 1727, Sir George Fleming of Carlisle in 1747, Barbara Relffe of Cockermouth in 1727, William Pearson of Bridekirk in 1777, Henry Fletcher Partis of Tallentire Hall in 1777, John Langton of Cockermouth in 1777, Mary Grayburne of Whitehaven in 1795, John Dodgson of Bridekirk in 1779, and Thomas Irwen of Aldston in 1779.

5) Varies   **FHL 942.8 C4c**

Transactions of the Cumberland & Westmorland Antiquarian & Archaeological Society. An occasional probate will be found printed in both the lst Series and the more numerous New Series of this publication. There are master indexes to volumes 1–12 and 13–25 of the New Series, which would be worth consulting for research on a particular person.

FHL 942.8 P2i

Index and Extracts of Cumbrians in Wills Proved at the Prerogative Court of Canterbury (1984). Compiled by Jim Richardson and Ron Shaw and published by the Cumbria Family History Society. Only some of the items indexed have accompanying extracts.

Calendars and Indexes and Act Books for the Archdeaconry Court of Richmond, Copeland Deanery

---

(A few abstracts of documents relating to Richmond probates will be found in the miscellaneous section. The researcher should also check the miscellaneous section for Carlisle and note the warning provided there.)

1) The filmed calendars stop in 1720. Hence, the act books will be outlined next as a substitute index for 1720–1857. The filmed calendars are arranged as follows:

1540–1720 A   **98,557**
                                                  (item 3)

This nineteenth-century manuscript begins with maps and a gazetteer for the eight deaneries. Next come the calendars, arranged alphabetically by the names of the five Western Deaneries, for the letter A. Copeland will be the second deanery indexed in each case. Watch for C or Co in the right margin to be certain that it is the Deanery of Copeland.

The entries are listed in chronological order, except for a few listed out of sequence after 1720 or on a supplement to be found either at the beginning or the end of that alphabetical portion for each deanery.

An indication to the types of probate is given first, followed by the date of probate, and person's name and residence. If a will has been registered, the index will give the name of the register and page number. Cross references to documents filed with the Eastern Deaneries are also provided. References to Calendar W usually refer to an item now lost.

All of the original records, regardless of type, were filed together in boxes after the pattern of this calendar. Match the index entry with the years and letters listed under the section entitled "Original Wills, Probate Bonds, Admons, and Inventories" to determine the microfilm call number. Wills not located between 1697–1731 might be found among the registered copy wills. Items not filmed can be identified by consulting Camp's *Wills and Their Whereabouts*.

1570–1720 B	**98,558** (item 2)
1530–1720 C	**98,559** (item 2)
1573–1720 D	**98,559** (item 7)
1587–1720 E	**98,560** (item 2)
1570–1720 F	**98,560** (item 7)
1562–1720 G	**98,560** (item 12)
1540–1720 H	**98,561** (item 2)
1476–1720 I/J	**98,562** (item 2)
1469–1720 K	**98,562** (item 7)
1570–1720 L	**98,562** (item 12)
1476–1720 M	**98,563** (item 2)
1567–1720 N	**98,563** (item 7)
1691–1720 O	**98,563** (item 12)
1533–1720 P	**98,563** (item 17)

1577 Q   **98,563**
                                                  (item 22)
One entry.

1466–1720 R   **98,564**
                                                  (item 2)

1560–1720 S   **98,565**
                                                  (item 2)

1567–1720 T   **98,566**
                                                  (item 2)

1587–1720 U/V   **98,566**
                                                  (item 7)

1544–1720 W   **98,567**
                                                  (item 2)

1605–1720 Y   **98,567**
                                                  (item 7)

2) All of the act books for Copeland were filmed and can be used in lieu of any further indexes as well as a source of additional information.

1712–1718   **99,950**
                                                  (item 2)
The acts for Copeland, Furness, Kendal, and Lonsdale deaneries are mixed together without an index, but they are in chronological order. Personal and place names, including an indication of deanery, appear in the left margin. The acts are in Latin. They include references to some marriage license bonds for 1705 and 1712–1715.

At the beginning of this group of act entries are two pages from an act book for 1705 containing three items for Copeland. There are also references to caveats that refer to contested estates, and sequestrations that involve property where there was no heir or claimant.

1719–1726   **99,950**
                                                  (item 3)
                                                  166,279
The acts for Copeland, Furness, Kendal, and Lonsdale are in turn rather than mixed. There is a master index at the beginning. The actual entries for Copeland appear on pages 45–81. The acts are in Latin, but the index is sufficiently clear that one can find the original document without reading the act itself. (The second film is an exact duplicate of the first, but it may be more readable.)

1727–1748   **99,950**
                                                  (item 5)
Copeland Act Book. The acts are in Latin until 1733. The index at the end continues on to 1751. The letters U and V come after Y in the index. (One could go directly from the index to the original probate; however, the act may provide additional information.)

1748–1798   **100,062**
Copeland Act Book. The acts are divided into three sections, each with its own index. First comes an index for 1748–1751 arranged alphabetically, with each letter subdivided chronologically for all of the years treated. This is followed by the act entries. The second section treats 1752–1783 in the same fashion, and the third does the same for 1784–1798.

1798–1838
                                                  100,063
Copeland Act Book. The acts are divided into two sections in the same manner as the preceding film. The first group covers 1798–1819, and the second is for 1819–1838. At the end of the film is a list of parishes for which "registers and terriers" were missing. The dates given are for the seventeenth and eighteenth centuries. There is no indication as to what types of registers are meant.

1838–1857   **100,064**
Copeland Act Book. The acts for 1838–1856 are arranged like the two preceding rolls of film. The entries for 1857 are listed separately.

Original Wills, Probate Bonds, Admons, and Inventories for the Archdeaconry Court of Richmond, Copeland Deanery

---

1540–1679 A   **98,745**
Box 92 was arranged in rough chronological order with some out of sequence between 1613–1628, and many out of sequence between 1661–1679.

1679–1720 A   **98,746**
Box 92 (cont.)

1721–1748 A   **98,747**
Box 93

1570–1613 B   **98,748**
Box 94

1613–1660 B   **98,749**
Box 94 (cont.)

1661–1670 B   **98,750**
Box 95

1671–1680 B   **98,751**
Box 96

1681–1690 B   **98,752**
Box 97

1691–1700 B   **98,753**
Box 98

1701–1705 B	**98,753** (item 2)	**1681–1700 F** Box 113	**98,768**
Box 99		**1701–1730 F** Box 114	**98,769**
1705–1710 B Box 99 (cont.)	**98,754**	**1731–1748 F** Box 115	**98,770**
1711–1720 B	**98,754** (item 2)	**1562–1666 G** Box 116	**98,771**
Box 100		**1666–1700 G** Box 116 (cont.)	**98,772**
1721–1730 B Box 101	**98,755**	**1701–1748 G** Box 117	**98,773**
1731–1740 B Box 102	**98,756**	**1540–1646 H** Box 118	**98,774**
1741–1748 B Box 103	**98,757**	**1646–1670 H** Box 118 (cont.)	**98,775**
1530–1681 C Box 104	**98,758**	**1671–1690 H** Box 119	**98,776**
1681–1700 C Box 105	**98,759**	**1691–1699 H** Box 120	**98,777**
1701–1720 C Box 106	**98,760**	**1699–1720 H** Box 120 (cont.)	**98,778**
1721–1748 C Box 107	**98,761**	**1721–1742 H** Box 121	**98,779**
1573–1661 D Box 108	**98,762**	**1742–1748 H** Box 121 (cont.)	**98,780**
1661–1680 D Box 108 (cont.)	**98,763**	**1476–1643 I/J** Box 122	**98,781**
1681–1720 D Box 109	**98,764**	**1643–1680 I/J** Box 122 (cont.)	**98,782**
1721–1748 D Box 110	**98,765**	**1681–1720 I/J** Box 123	**98,783**
1587–1693 E Box 110 (cont.)	**98,765** (item 2)	**1721–1748 I/J** Box 124	**98,784**
1693–1748 E Box 110 (cont.)	**98,766**	**1469–1748 K** Box 125	**98,785**
1570–1660 F Box 111	**98,766** (item 2)	**1570–1690 L** Box 126	**98,786**
1661–1680 F Box 112	**98,767**	**1691–1748 L** Box 127	**98,787**

1476–1665 M   **98,788**
Box 128

1665–1680 M   **98,789**
Box 128 (cont.)

1681–1720 M   **98,790**
Box 129

1721–1748 M   **98,791**
Box 130

1567–1700 N   **98,792**
Box 131

1701–1748 N   **98,793**
Box 132 is arranged in rough chronological order, with some out of sequence between 1715–1719, 1731–1737, and 1741–1742.

1691–1748 O   **98,793**
                                  (item 2)
Box 132 (cont.)

1533–1660 P/Q   **98,794**
Box 133 starts with the only Q entry, which is dated 1577 but actually is a cross-reference to William Whytsyd. The Ps are not in consistent chronological order.

1661–1680 P   **98,795**
Box 134

1681–1710 P   **98,796**
Box 135

1711–1730 P   **98,797**
Box 136

1731–1748 P   **98,798**
Box 137

1466–1661 R   **98,799**
Box 138

1661–1680 R   **98,800**
Box 138 (cont.)

1681–1720 R   **98,801**
Box 139

1721–1748 R   **98,802**
Box 140

1560–1660 S   **98,803**
Box 141

1661–1680 S   **98,804**
Box 142

1681–1700 S   **98,805**
Box 143 starts with three documents for 1688, 1689, 1682. It is then consistent from 1681–1690, when three more occur out of sequence for 1696, 1694, and 1692. The next entry is 1691, from which point the rest are in proper order.

1701–1720 S   **98,806**
Box 144

1721–1730 S   **98,807**
Box 145

1731–1748 S   **98,808**
Box 146

1567–1661 T   **98,809**
Box 147 has one entry for 1589 filed with 1588.

1661–1680 T   **98,810**
Box 147 (cont.) has one entry for 1678 and one for 1677 filed with 1676.

1681–1720 T   **98,811**
Box 148

1721–1726 T   **98,812**
Box 149

1727–1748 T   **98,813**
Box 149 (cont.)

1587–1746 U/V   **98,813**
                                  (item 2)
Box 149 (cont.) has the first item, the will of John Vicars dated 1692, out of place. It is refilmed later in the proper chronological sequence.

1544–1662 W   **98,814**
Box 150

1662–1670 W   **98,815**
Box 150 (cont.)

1671–1690 W   **98,816**
Box 151

1691–1710 W   **98,817**
Box 152

1711–1730 W   **98,818**
Box 153

1731–1748 W   **98,819**
Box 154

1605–1748 Y	**98,819** **(item 2)**

Box 154 (cont.) starts with three documents for 1677 and 1680, before going to 1605. Then it continues in correct chronological order.

1748–1760 A–C	**99,162**

See film 99,163 for D–F.

1748–1750 G	**99,162** **(last item)**
1750–1760 G	**99,163**
1748–1760 D–F	**99,163** **(items 2–4)**

See the above film for the start of the Gs.

1748 H	**99,163** **(last item)**
1748–1760 H	**99,164**
1748–1760 J–L	**99,165**
1748–1750 M	**99,165** **(last item)**
1750–1760 M	**99,166**
1748–1760 N–P	**99,166**
1748–1760 R–T	**99,167**

The last entry on this film is one W for 1748.

1748–1760 W–Y	**99,168**

One W appears on the preceding film.

1761–1770 A–B	**99,169**
1761–1770 B–F	**99,170**
1761–1770 F–G	**99,171**
1761–1770 H–L	**99,172**
1761–1770 M–P	**99,173**
1761–1770 R–S	**99,174**
1761–1770 S–Y	**99,175**
1771–1780 A–E	**99,176**
1771–1780 F–O	**99,177**
1771–1780 P–R	**99,178**

1771–1779 S	**99,178** **(last item)**
1780 S	**99,179**
1771–1780 T–Y	**99,179**
1781–1790 A–B	**99,180**
1781–1790 B–H	**99,181**
1781–1790 J–S	**99,182**
1781–1790 T–Y	**99,183**
1791–1800 A–D	**99,184**
1791–1800 E–J	**99,185**
1791–1800 K–R	**99,186**
1791–1800 S–Y	**99,187**
1801–1810 A–C	**99,188**
1801–1810 D–G	**99,189**
1801–1807 H	**99,189** **(last item)**
1807–1810 H	**99,190**

The first will entered is for Jonathan Harris, merchant of Fredericksburg, Virginia. The next of kin was his sister, Isabella Williamson of Parton.

1801–1810 J–O	**99,191**
1801–1810 P–S	**99,192**
1801–1810 T–Y	**99,193**
1811–1820 A–B	**99,194**
1811–1820 B–D	**99,195**
1811–1820 D–F	**99,196**
1811–1820 G–H	**99,197**
1811–1820 H–L	**99,198**
1811–1820 M–P	**99,199**
1811–1820 R–S	**99,200**
1811–1820 S–Y	**99,201**
1821–1830 A–B	**99,202**

1821–1830 B–E	**99,203**	1841–1850 Q	**99,228** (item 2)
1821–1830 F–H	**99,204**	1841–1850 R	**99,228** (item 3)
1821–1830 H–L	**99,205**	1841–1845 S	**99,228** (last item)
1821–1830 M–P	**99,206**		
1821–1830 Q–R	**99,207**	1845–1850 S	**99,229**
1821–1829 S	**99,207** (last item)	1841–1850 T	**99,230**
		The Us and Vs are on film 99,231.	
1829–1830 S	**99,208**	1841–1844 W	**99,230** (last item)
1821–1830 T–W	**99,208**		
1821–1830 W–Y	**99,209**	1844–1850 W	**99,231**
1831–1840 A–B	**99,210**	1841–1850 U/V,Y	**99,231**
1831–1840 B–D	**99,211**	1851–1858 A	**99,232**
1831–1840 D–F	**99,212**	1851–1853 B	**99,232**
1831–1840 G–H	**99,213**	1853–1858 B	**99,233**
1831–1840 H–J	**99,214**	1851–1857 C–E	**99,233**
1831–1840 K–M	**99,215**	1851–1858 F–H	**99,234**
1831–1840 N–Q	**99,216**	1851–1858 I–J	**99,235**
1831–1840 R–S	**99,217**	1851–1858 K–O	**99,236**
1831–1840 S–T	**99,218**	1851–1857 P	**99,236** (last item)

1831–1840 T–Y   **99,219**
This film starts with the Ts for 1838–1840, followed by the Ws, and then the U/Vs.

1841–1850 A	**99,220**	1857 P	**99,237**
1841–1850 B–C	**99,221**	1851–1857 Q–R	**99,237**
1841–1850 C–F	**99,222**	1851–1858 S–Y	**99,238**

1841–1850 G–H	**99,223**
1841–1850 H–J	**99,224**
1841–1850 K–M	**99,225**
1841–1850 M–O	**99,226**
1841–1847 P	**99,227**
1847–1850 P	**99,228**

Registered Copy Wills for the Archdeaconry Court of Richmond, Copeland Deanery

1466–1696
Do not exist; see the original wills in the preceding section.

1697–1706   **166,277**
The "Carr" register for the deaneries of Copeland, Kendal, Lonsdale, and Furness. The wills for the various deaneries are mixed together in fair chronological order.

There is an index at the end arranged alphabetically, with each letter subdivided chronologically for all of the years treated. The index does not indicate the deanery; however, this information is provided in the manuscript index mentioned at the start of the description of Copeland's records. See the section entitled "Calendars and Indexes and Act Books." Further entries for 1697–1698 will be found on the next film.

1705–1731   **166,278**
The "Todd" register covering 1716–1717 for the same deaneries as the above entry comes first. Its index appears at the back of the next register, which follows it.

The "Preston" register starts with some entries for 1697–1698, but it mainly goes from 1705 through the first half of the 1720s with a few entries continuing on to 1731. Apparently there is no overlap between the three registers. The index starts out like the one on the preceding film by first covering the As for 1705–1723. It then refers to a rider that indexes the As for the "Todd" register before moving on to do the same for the Bs.

1731–1809
Do not exist; see the original wills.

1810–1811
See Camp's *Wills and Their Whereabouts*.

1812–1858
Do not exist; see the original wills.

Miscellaneous: Abstracts of Probates Relating to Richmond

(The material listed here may or may not refer to the Deanery of Copeland. Such entries as might be found should be compared with the original documents.)

Volume 26 of the Publications of the Surtees Society contains copies of some 208 Richmond wills and inventories, proven between 1442–1579. Volume 26 appears as item 7 on film 994,031 and fiche 6,073,308. See the miscellaneous section of Carlisle for further details about these publications.

Volume 3 of *The Northern Genealogist* provides information on a few more Richmond wills. Again, consult the miscellaneous section of Carlisle for further details. Volume 6 contains an abstract of the will of John Curwen of Workington (1530).

Part 3   Durham
Probate Jurisdictions and Microfilmed Records

Introduction

No map has been prepared, as all of this county belonged to the probate jurisdiction of the Consistory Court of Durham. The bishop of Durham also presided over the peculiar courts of Allerton and Allertonshire as well as Howden and Howdenshire, which had jurisdiction over parishes located in Yorkshire. All of the microfilms listed for these two peculiar courts are filed under Yorkshire.

The earliest original wills for Durham date from 1540, but there are some registered copy wills for 1526 and 1534. There are earlier records filed with the superior courts, and, according to J. W. Robinson, "there are wills dating back to 1311" in the bishop's general series of act books.[1] There are obviously gaps in the records for the earlier periods, while many other records are in poor condition. Those that were torn, faded, or water damaged have been filmed more than once in an attempt to obtain greater legibility.

Inventories are prevalent from the earliest period through the first quarter of the eighteenth century. They may be filed with the administration bonds as well as with the original wills. The registered copies are usually indexed and arranged chronologically. Page numbers appear in the upper right corner, and testators' names are frequently written in the margins. There may be an inventory written at the end of the copy will, and almost always there will be a probate act in Latin indicating when the will was proven.

Probate Decision Table for Durham

If the Research Subject Lived in One of These Jurisdictions:	Anywhere in the County	Anywhere in the County, 1651–1660	Anywhere in the County before 1540
Search the probate records of these courts in the order shown below:			
Consistory Court of Durham	1		
Prerogative Court of the Archbishop of York (see Yorkshire)	2		1
Court of the Dean and Chapter of York (see Yorkshire for vacancy jurisdiction)	3		2
Chancery Court of the Archbishop of York (see Yorkshire)	4		3
Prerogative Court of the Archbishop of Canterbury (see London)	5	1	4
Court of Delegates, 1643–1857 (see London)	6		

[1]"Durham Wills by John Walton Robinson," Vol. 1, A–B (film 574,952).

residence and occupation are added, but there is little information given in this first volume as to the type of probate. The reference number given refers to a folio or document number, which will be of little value when searching the original wills as they were rearranged either chronologically or alphabetically within a given year.

The reference numbers for probate and administration bonds in the calendar refer to the number that usually appears on the left margin of the documents. There may be two separate documents for each bond, plus additional documents such as inventories and renunciations.

1600–1660   **90,802**
(item 2)
Vol. 2 of the Manuscript Index. This section provides an indication of the type of document involved by using "T" for a will, "I" or "inv." for an inventory, "A" or "adm." for an administration, and "comp." for account. The administrations will be listed separately on a page facing the wills for the same time period.

1661–1786   **90,803**
Vol. 3 of the Original Calendar. Starting in 1739, the calendar lists the wills first, followed by the administrations for each year. Residences are rarely given before 1770. The clerks ran out of space in this volume for some letters of the alphabet. The continuation from 1770–1786 for these letters will be found at the end of the film. There, one will also find the signatures of the various clerks, their dates of appointment, and death information from the 1750s forward.

1787–1831   **90,804**
(Continuation of the above) A reference number is provided only for the administrations after 1790.

1832–1839   **90,804**
(item 2)
(Continuation of the above)

1832–1858   **90,804**
(item 3)
(Repeat and continuation) Apparently everything in the second item of this film was duplicated here.

Indexes and Calendars for the Consistory Court of Durham

(Other indexes, thought to be less reliable, and abstracts of documents relating to Durham probates will be found under the miscellaneous section. Searches in these items and the stray-name index to this volume may reveal entries not found or easily found in the typescript index and filmed calendars outlined below. The abstracts are edited and may still be in Latin for the earlier periods.)

1) The indexes are as follows:

Index of Wills, etc., in the Probate Registry, Durham and from Other Sources, 1540–1599. (FHL 942.82/N1 B4nt, vol. 8; item 2 on film 962,690; and also on fiche 6,024,197–6,024,199.) This volume was edited by H. M. Wood and published by the Newcastle-upon-Tyne Records Committee in 1928. It may be incomplete, but it does serve as a master index to the first three volumes of Durham wills published by the Surtees Society.

"Calendar to the Episcopal Consistory Court of Durham, 1650–1786." (FHL 942.8 P2d index and also on film 990,061 item 1.) This is a manuscript compiled under the auspices of the Family History Library from its microfilms. Arranged alphabetically, it provides residence, date of probate, type of probate, film number, and sometimes a page or folio number. Apparently the data were extracted from films 90,856–90,917, covering mainly original wills and inventories; it would appear that the bonds were not indexed. Check the filmed calendars for other types of documents and the periods before 1650 and after 1786.

2) The filmed calendars are arranged as follows:

Time Period	Film or Call No.

1540–1599   **90,802**
Vol. 1 of a nineteenth-century Manuscript Index to Wills, Inventories, and Admons. The names are arranged roughly alphabetically by the year of probate. Usually

Original Wills and Inventories for the Consistory Court of Durham

Before 1540
A few documents dated before 1540 will be found among the registered copy wills that follow this section.

1540–1550   **90,805**
Chronological order.

1551–1557   **90,805**
     (item 2)

1558–1560   **90,806**
Alphabetical order within each year.

1561–1580
Missing. See the registered copy wills and the General Instructions in the Introduction to this volume.

1581–1582   **90,809**
     (item 2)

Chronological order by year.

1583–1584
Missing. See the note for 1561–1580 above.

1585 A–W   **90,810**
     (item 2)

Documents start with W, then proceed alphabetically from A to W.

1586 A–Y   **90,811**
1587 A–B

1587 C–W   **90,812**
Two documents for R are filed under S.

1588 A–M,R–W   **90,813**
1589 A–D
One U document is filed under S in 1588. The 1589 group begins with F, then proceeds from A alphabetically. Two G documents are filed under B.

1589 F–Y   **90,814**
1590 A–N,R–W
1589 begins with F and then is very erratic. 1590 has one M will at the beginning.

1591 A–R   **90,815**
1592 A–W
1593 A–E,H–N,P–W
1591 is in alphabetical order for the most part, but there are some documents out of place both by year and letter. 1592 is not in alphabetical order. In 1593, P wills are mixed with R. There are no S wills.

1594–1595 A–W   **90,816**
1596 A–H
1595 starts with T and skips around erratically. There are a few 1596 A wills out of place by letter, and one or two are out of place by year.

1596 J–Y   **90,817**
1597 A–R

1597 S–Y   **90,818**
1598 A–W
1599 A–P

1599 R–W   **90,819**
1600 A–W
1601 A–W
1602 A–W
The documents for 1600 are in alphabetical order to H, then skip to P and then to W. The 1601 segment is not in alphabetical order. In 1602 there is a copy of a proclamation by King George III dated 3 December 1800, concerning the use of all grains. The documents are in alphabetical order to R; then there are a few out of place, and they resume in order from S.

1603 A–W   **90,820**
1604 A–D
The As and Bs are intermixed for 1603 with an L and a B at the end of W.

1604 D–Y   **90,821**
The documents skip from D–O and then proceed alphabetically. There are a few W wills after Y. One W is typewritten. The missing ones for D–O follow Y but are not in order.

1605 A–W   **90,822**
1606 A–D
A few are out of order for 1605 following W.

1606 E–Y   **90,823**
1607 A–N

1607 O–Y   **90,824**
One O will is out of place between S and T.

1608 A–Y   **90,825**
Alphabetical order to H, then erratic to P, and then proceeds in order.

1609 A–Y   **90,826**
1610 C–M
This film begins with a "Prayer of Thanksgiving" issued by the king to be used in all churches, dated 1832.

1610 O–Y   **90,827**
1611 A–H
Not in alphabetical order for 1611.

1611 H–Y   **90,828**
1612 A–H
Not in alphabetical order for 1611.

1612 I–Y   **90,829**
1613 A–K
Some H wills follow J in 1613.

1613 L–Y   **90,830**
1614 A–P
A 1613 T will is filed under S.

1614 R–W   **90,831**
1615 A–K

1615 L–Y   **90,832**
1616 A–G
A 1615 P will is filed under M. Y wills appear before and after W.

1616 H–Y   **90,833**
1617 A–F

1617 G–Y   **90,834**
1618 A–O
1617 is very erratic from H to P. 1618 R will is filed after O.

1618 P–Y   **90,835**
1619 A–S
U and some W wills are filed under T for 1618.

1619 T–W   **90,836**
1620 A–W
1621 A–W
1620 is in order to D, then it is very erratic.

1622 A–W   **90,837**
1623 A–F
Some G and H wills for 1623 are at end of film.

1623 F–Y   **90,838**
1624 A–G
See above note. 1623 Y will is filed under T.

1624 H–W   **90,839**
1625 A–Y
1624 Ks are intermixed with H.

1626 A–W   **90,840**
1627 A–W
1627 is not in alphabetical order.

1628 A–Y   **90,841**
1629 A–Q
An S will for 1629 is filed under D.

1629 S–Y   **90,842**
1630 A–W
1631 A–G
1630 and 1631 are not in alphabetical order.

1631 H–Y   **90,843**
1632 A–W
1632 is in order except for a C in B and an L in M.

1633 A–W   **90,844**
1634 A–J
Both years are in order, except for some G wills intermixed with H.

1634 L–Y   **90,845**
1635 A–S
1635 C will is filed under B.

1635 T–Y   **90,846**
1636 A–W
A group of W wills and a Y will dated 1635 appear at the end of the film.

1637 A–Y   **90,847**
1638 A–E

1638 F–Y   **90,848**
1639 A–S
1639 is in order, except L, M, and O are between P and R.

1639 T–Y   **90,849**
1640 A–W
1641 A–Y
Y is before W in 1639. 1640 is in alphabetical order from A to C, then it is erratic.

1642 A–Y   **90,850**
1643 A–L
1642 is in order to T, then it is erratic, with some R and S documents in the W section.

1643 L–T   **90,851**
1644 A–W

1645 A–S   **90,852**
An L is out of place between H and J.

1645 S–W   **90,853**
1646 A–W

1647 A–Y   **90,854**
1648 A–W
1648 is not in alphabetical order.

1649 A–W   **90,855**
1650 A–Y
1649 B will is filed under C. E and F are intermingled. 1650 includes both probate and administration bonds. C and F are intermingled, an N is filed under J and a J under P. H and I documents appear between P and R.

1651–1659   **90,856**
Due to the Interregnum, there are few entries for this period. See the probate decision table and the miscellaneous section for further instructions. The existing documents are intermixed both as to date and alphabetical sequence. No entries were noted for 1657, but there are two filed here that were proven in 1759. They are for Robert Rayne (dated 1757), yeoman of Stockton, and Thomas Redman (dated 1759), yeoman of Bishopton.

1660 **90,857**
1661 A–G
1660 is not in alphabetical order.

1661 H–Y **90,858**
1662 A–C
1661 includes a document for Christopher Hopper dated 1665.

1662 D–W **90,859**

1663 A–W **90,860**
Includes documents dated 1654 and 1668.

1664 A–Y **90,861**
Y is intermixed with W.

1665–1684
One will dated 1665 is located on film 90,858, and one dated 1668 on 90,860. The rest are missing; see the registered copy wills.

1685 A–W **90,863**
The Us follow the Ws.

1686 A–Y **90,864**

1687 A–W **90,865**
P is intermixed with R.

1688 A–W **90,866**
In alphabetical order to P, then erratic.

1689 A–Y **90,867**
H and J are intermixed.

1690 A–W **90,868**
In alphabetical order to D, then skips to H; F follows H, then proceeds in order to R; erratic after R.

1691 A–Y **90,869**
In alphabetical order to J, then erratic through S. Continues in order to end of film.

1692 A–W **90,870**
In alphabetical order to L, then mixed and very erratic from R.

1693 A–W **90,871**
An extract from the Prerogative Court in the name of Sir John Heron of Chipcase, Northumberland, is included. In alphabetical order to P, then erratic.

1694 A–W **90,872**
In order to H, then from there they are mixed up in spots. C out of place in P; J, K, L follow W. There is a J listed in W.

1695 A–W **90,873**
In order to J, then erratic.

1696 A–W **90,874**
1697 A–G
1696 is in order to J, then erratic.

1697 H–Y **90,875**
1698 A–P
1697 is in order to J, then erratic.

1698 R–W **90,876**
1699 A–T

1699 U–W **90,877**
1700 A–Y
A 1700 F will is filed under B, an M will under H, and several Ss between V and W.

1701 A–G **90,878**

1701 H–Y **90,879**
1702 A–Z
O and P are intermixed for 1701. 1702 is in alphabetical order, except a B will is filed under A.

1703 A–Z **90,880**
1704 A–E
Some A wills are mixed with W for 1703.

1704 M–R,F–L,S–W **90,881**
An R will is filed under P.

1705 A–S **90,881**
(item 2)
A C will is filed under A.

1705 T–Y **90,882**
1706 A–Y
A J will is filed under E; otherwise, 1706 is in alphabetical order to J, then erratic to P, and then proceeds in order.

1707 A–Y **90,883**

1708 A–S **90,884**

1709 A–Y **90,885**
1710 A–K
1709 is in order to J; then there is a group of F, G, and H documents after J, and R and S are intermixed. A B will is filed under E for 1710.

1710 L–Y **90,886**
1711 A–Y
1710 is in order, except the S follows V, and V and W are intermixed.

1712 A–Y	**90,887**
1713 A–J	

1713 L–Y	**90,888**
1714 A–Y	

1715 A–Y	**90,889**
1716 A–Y	

1717 R–W,A–P   **90,890**
1718 A–E
The 1717 will of Nicholas Newton includes a note on the deaths and marriages of his family.

1718 F–W   **90,891**
1719 A–Y
G and H are intermixed, and an M is filed under N in 1718.

1720 A–W	**90,892**
1721 A–Y	

1722 A–Y   **90,893**
An S is filed under R.

1723 A–Y   **90,894**
B and A are intermixed.

1724–1752
Missing. See the registered copy wills.

1753 H–Y   **90,900**
1754 A–W

1755 A–W   **90,901**
1756 A–W

1757 A–W   **90,902**
Document for Ann Batwell extracted from the Prerogative Court of Ireland.

1758 A–W   **90,903**

1759–1762
Two wills for R are filed with the 1650s on film 90,856. The rest of the documents for 1759–1762 seem to be missing; see the registered copy wills.

1763 A–Y   **90,905**

1764 A–Y   **90,906**
The idents note if the wills are also registered.

1765 A–W   **90,907**
A document for James Huntley dated 1737 is included.

1766 A–Y   **90,908**
Some inventories and probate bonds. The idents note if the will is registered.

1767 A–W   **90,909**
Some inventories.

1768 A–Y   **90,910**
In alphabetical order to F, then erratic. The idents note if the will is registered.

1769 A–W   **90,911**
The idents note if the will is registered.

1770 A–W   **90,912**
The idents note if the will is registered.

1771–1796
Missing. See the registered copy wills.

1797 A–Y   **90,920**

1798 A–M   **90,921**
1798 N–R entries are at the end of the next film.

1798 S–W   **90,922**
1799 A–F
1798 N–R

1799 G–Y   **90,923**

1800 A–G   **90,924**
The Cs are followed by the F, E, D, and G wills in that order. One A is at the end of the Bs. An H is located toward the end of the Gs.

1800 H,L,K,J,M–W   **90,925**
An L is at the end of the Js, and a W appears in the middle of the Ts.

1801 A–R,S–Y   **90,926**
See the next film.

1802 A–E   **90,927**
1801 S–Y

1802 H,G,F,J–Y   **90,928**

1803 A–N   **90,929**

1803 O–Y   **90,930**
1804 A–G

1804 H–Y   **90,931**
Two Ts and Vs are filed under W.

1805 A–S   **90,932**

1805 T–Y   **90,933**
1806 A–G

1806 H–Y   90,934

1807 A–R   90,935
1807 S–Y entries are at the end of the next film.

1808 A–D   90,936
1807 S–Y

1808 E–Y   90,937

1809 A–N   90,938

1809 O–Y   90,939
1810 A–C

1810 D–P   90,940

1810 R–Y   90,941
1811 A–H

1811 J–Y   90,942

1812 A–L   90,943

1812 M–Y   90,944

1813 A–H   90,945

1813 I–Y   90,946
The will of Adam Sibbet is accompanied by a map of property and value of same.

1814 A–H   90,947

1814 I–Y   90,948

1815 A–P   90,949

1815 R–Y   90,950
1816 A–B

1816 C–R   90,951
An E appears between C and D.

1816 S–Y   90,952
1817 A–D

1817 E–P   90,953
A G will is filed under H. One or two wills are extracted from the PCC.

1817 R–Y   90,954
1818 A–H
Some extractions from the PCC for 1817, and one W follows Y.

1818 I–Y   90,955
Some extractions from the PCC.

1819 A–L   90,956
An extraction from the PCC is included.

1819 M–Y   90,957
1820 A–G
One E will for 1820 is located at the end of G.

1820 H–R   90,958
There are a few H wills for 1821 among the wills for 1820.

1820 S–Y   90,959
A V, U, and T follow Y. There are one or two extractions from the PCC.

1821–1858
Missing. See the registered copy wills.

Registered Copy Wills for the Consistory Court of Durham

1526,1534,   90,982
1543,1546,
1550–1553,
1556–1574
The majority of these wills are for 1560–1572. Some inventories are included. An index appears at the end, but the page numbers to which it refers are often impossible to find. The original page numbers were in the top center position on every other page, but a later clerk sometimes rewrote them in the left corner or on the bottom of the page. The testators' names might appear in the margins or at the top of each entry. The information on this film partially overlaps that which follows on the next three films.

However, the latter are more complete, contain more inventories, and are written in a larger hand. Despite this, comparisons between the overlapping entries are advised to produce a more readable document. Toward the end of this film is a probate act for Peter Riddell dated 1618, which was apparently written on a smaller stray page.

NOTE: This film as well as the next four films may also overlap film 90,810.

1561–1567   90,806
                                                (item 2)
Includes inventories. Index for this volume is on the next film.

1567–1571   90,807
Most wills have inventories. Indexed at end.

1571–1582   **90,808**
Note that this film overlaps with the next film. Some of
the documents may have been duplicated.

1577–1580   **90,809**
Also see the preceding film for documents from 1577–
1582.

1552,1568,   **90,810**
1575,1577,
1579–1591,
1594,1596,
1597,1599,
1601,1605,
1607,
1609–1614
The title of the microfilm indicates that these are registered copies for 1581–1584, 1614. Actually there are
scattered entries for the years itemized, with the majority
of the entries occurring between 1580–1591. This film
may overlap with the preceding five films. An index is
located at the end of the film. The series of inventories
between pages 147–153 refers to 1588 followed by the
registered copy wills for 1585. Otherwise the inventories
accompany the wills they pertain to.

This film actually begins with four notarized documents
in Latin, which are apparently commissions or certificates of office. Just before the last one is a probate bond
in English for Edward Turner of York, gent. Since it is
undated and does not appear in the index, this was
probably a sample for the clerks and is presumed to be
fictitious. Then follow the wills for 1582.

1592–1664
Missing, except for the scattered entries itemized on film
90,810 above. Try the original wills in the preceding
section.

1665–1669   **90,862**
Volume 7 of the copied wills. There is an index after
page 232.

1665–1684   **90,862**
                                                               (item 2)
Volume 8 of the copied wills. This volume is preceded
by an index. There is a separate index for the year 1674.
Since this volume was numbered in the upper right-hand
corner only on every other page and the page numbers
listed in the 1674 index are often higher, it would appear
at first glance that this index is useless. However, it
refers to the actual pages, not every other page, and will
be roughly accurate if one divides the 1674 reference
number by 2.

1685–1723
Missing. See the original wills. There are a few wills
dated 1702, 1706–1707 on film 90,898 item 2.

1724–1770
This time period seems to be covered completely, but the
situation on film is somewhat confusing. Read through
the descriptions of the following seven films (90,895–
90,899 and 90,903–90,904) carefully, before conducting
further research. Also note that the original wills are on
film for 1753–1758 and 1763–1770.

1724   **90,895**
There is an alphabetical index at the beginning, followed
by another index listing entries chronologically by page
number. In the body of the film the pages are numbered
in upper corners beginning with 143, but they are dark
and almost impossible to read. Names of the testators
appear in the margin at the side of each will.

1725–1729   **90,895**
                                                               (item 2)
Pages misnumbered in some places. The index for this
volume is at the end, alphabetically by surname. Note
that further entries for 1728–1729 will be found on film
90,899, and for 1729 on 90,898 item 2.

1729–1733,   **90,896**
1735
Alphabetical index at end in yearly chronological order.
Following this index is a chronological index in poor
condition. Note that further entries for 1735 will be
found on films 90,898 item 2 and 90,897.

1733–1734,   **90,896**
1750,1752   **(item 2)**
Indexed at front, and names of testators are in the mar-
gins by the will. Note that 1735 is included with the first
item on this film, and that 1736 will be found on film
90,899.

1735,   **90,898**
1742–1746,   **(item 2)**
1763
Title page says 1742–1753, but this is incorrect. The
years are intermingled to an unusual degree. The film
starts with pages 884–890 of 1735, followed by two or
three wills proven in 1743, and then reverts to pages
872–873 of 1735. Next comes a series of wills from the
1760s but without an indication of when they were
proven, perhaps in 1763.

They are roughly alphabetically arranged starting with
the last part of the H wills, then J, M–S, and back to H
and P. Following this are several pages from wills
proven in 1743, and then more appear for the 1760s for
M, O, M. Following this are wills for 1744; a few dated
1706, 1702, 1707, 1742, 1735 for pages 880–883, and
1744. Then comes a large section of wills proven in
1742, followed by a few more for 1743, 1735 (p. 875),
and 1742 again. Next appears a large section without any
indication of when they were proven, but probably in

1745–1746, followed by a small group for 1743 and 1745–1746 again. There is then a section for 1742–1744 too intermingled to describe, except for pages 515–531 of 1742. After this are small groups for the 1760s, 1743, 1742, 1735 (pp. 876–879), and 1743. Note that this film may overlap or be a continuation of 90,896 item 1, and that the period from 1735–1741 continues on the next film.

1735–1741   90,897
Title page says 1735–1742, but this is incorrect. This film is a continuation of the above film starting with pages 896–966 of 1735, followed by a series without page numbers or indication of dates proven, which appear to be for 1736. If so, note also the entries for 1736 on the next film. Following this are the wills proven in 1737, pages 1–146; 1738, pages 1–170; 1739, pages 172–282; 1740, pages 282–410; and 1741, pages 411–495. An extract from the PCC for Francis Clavering of Whitehouse, Durham, is included with 1738.

1736   90,899
Title page gives incorrectly 1750. These are the wills proven in 1736, which may overlap or be a continuation of the entries listed on the film above. The pages are numbered 1–207. Index at end.

1737–1746
See films 90,897 and 90,898 item 2.

1747–1749
Missing.

1750–1752
See film 90,896 item 2.

1753–1758
Missing, although there are some wills dated 1757–1758 on film 90,898 item 1. Try the original wills.

1759   90,903
     (item 2)
Names of testators in margin. Alphabetical index at end. Note that further entries for this year may be covered on film 90,898 item 1.

1760
Missing. There are entries for the 1760s on film 90,898 items 1–2.

1761–1762   90,904
Pages numbered at bottom. In alphabetical order. Index at end of 1761. The second section is titled "Fragment Enrollments." Pages numbered at bottom. A few 1767 and 1766 documents included. Not in alphabetical order. This series ends with S. Note that further entries for these two years may be covered by film 90,898 items 1–2.

1763
See film 90,898 items 1–2, and note that the originals for this year have been filmed.

1764–1769
Probably missing, but see the notes for 90,898 items 1–2, and 90,904. Try the original wills.

1770   90,898
     (item 1)
Title page says 1736, but this film covers wills dated between 1757–1770. The dates when proven are not provided; however, these were probably proven in 1770. Not in order by year. No index for this series. Note that this film covers some of the same years as films 90,898 item 2, 90,903, and 90,904.

1771   90,913
In alphabetical order through G, then erratic to P, then follows in order again.

1772   90,914
Not in alphabetical order. No index.

1773   90,914
     (item 2)
This series begins with a document for G. Thereafter, the wills are in alphabetical sequence except at the first, where A–C are intermixed. The wills then begin again at A and are consistent from this point onward, except for a D, an R, and an S entry found at the beginning. The third item on this film includes an A–B sequence of wills for 1800.

1774–1775   90,915
In alphabetical order for the most part with a few out of place. See the next entry also for 1775. Indexed at the end.

1776–1777,   90,915
1778 A–K   (item 2)
Arranged alphabetically by year. An E and F for 1775 were noted. An L is located between J and K, the M and N are mixed for 1776. The section for 1778 has some extractions from the PCC. Alphabetical index at the end, by years.

1778 L–Y   90,916
Index at the beginning.

1779   90,916
     (item 2)
In alphabetical order to C, then erratic to P, and then continues in order. Index at the end of item 4 on this film.

1780   90,916
     (item 3)
Alphabetically arranged. A few extractions from the PCC. T and W are intermixed. Index at the end of item 4 on this film.

1781 A–W   **90,916**
                                               (item 4)
An N and S will be found at the end of this section. Alphabetical index at the end from L, 1778, by years.

1781 W–Y   **90,916**
                                               (item 5)
Index at the end of item 8 on this film.

1782   **90,916**
                                               (item 6)
M and N are mixed. Index at the end of item 8 on this film.

1783   **90,916**
                                               (item 7)
Index at the end of item 8 on this film.

1784 A–P   **90,916**
                                               (item 8)
In alphabetical order. An E is filed under F. Index at the end of this film listed alphabetically for entire series from W–1781 to 1784.

1784 R–Y   **90,917**
Index at the end of item 4 on this film.

1785   **90,917**
                                               (item 2)
A J is filed under K, otherwise in alphabetical order. Index at the end of item 4 on this film.

1786   **90,917**
                                               (item 3)
An extraction from the PCC is included. W and Y are intermixed, otherwise in alphabetical order. Index at the end of item 4 on this film.

1787 A–K   **90,917**
                                               (item 4)
Index at the end of this section, listed alphabetically and by year, for 1784 R–Y through 1787 A–K. A few wills are out of alphabetical order, but they are listed correctly in the index.

1787 L–W   **90,917**
                                               (item 5)
Not in alphabetical order. Partial index at the end of this film.

1788   **90,917**
                                               (item 6)
In alphabetical order. Index at the end of this film.

1789   **90,917**
                                               (item 7)
In alphabetical order. Index at the end of this film.

1790 A–J   **90,917**
                                               (item 8)
In alphabetical order. Index at the end, beginning with L in 1787 through J 1790.

1790 K–Y   **90,918**
In alphabetical order. Index at the end of item 4 on this film.

1791   **90,918**
                                               (item 2)
1791 starts on page 116. Index at the end of item 4 on this film. In alphabetical order. Some entries are extracted from the PCC.

1792   **90,918**
                                               (item 3)
1792 starts on page 316. Index at the end of item 4 on this film.

1793 A–Y   **90,918**
                                               (item 4)
1794 A–Y
1795 A–H
In alphabetical order. An index at the end of this film is in alphabetical order and arranged by year. 1794 starts on page 148, 1795 starts on page 424.

1795 I–Y   **90,919**

1796 A–W   **90,919**
                                               (item 2)

1797 A–D   **90,919**
                                               (item 3)

1797–1819
Except for the few entries noted above for 1797 and below for 1800, this period is missing. Try the original wills.

1800 A–B   **90,914**
                                               (item 3)
See the above note. Names in left margin.

1820–1822   **90,960**
Arranged chronologically by the month and year of probate.

1822–1823   **90,960**
                                               (item 2)
Arranged chronologically by the month and year of probate. Names in left margin.

1824
1825 A–D   **90,961**
The year 1825 is not in order by month. Index at end, listing entries alphabetically and also by year.

1825 E–Y   **90,962**
In alphabetical order.

1826 M–R, A–M, R–Y   **90,962 (item 2)**

In alphabetical order.

1827   **90,963**
Some wills are extracted from the PCC.

1828   **90,963 (item 2)**
In alphabetical order. Some extractions from the PCC.

1829   **90,964**
Index at the beginning. Wills listed alphabetically.

1830   **90,964 (item 2)**

Indexed and filed alphabetically.

1831   **90,965**
Alphabetical index at the beginning. Wills also in alphabetical order. Some extracts from the PCC.

1832   **90,966**
Filed by date of probate. Alphabetical index at the end. Names in margin.

1833   **90,967**
Index at the beginning. Wills not in alphabetical order.

1833–1834   **90,967 (item 2)**

Index at the beginning.

1835–1836   **90,968**
Index at the beginning. Filed in chronological order. Names in margin for some.

1837–1838   **90,969**
Film begins with two pages of probate and administration entries from an act book of September (no year given). They are written in Latin and appear to be from the time period of 1663–1723. The names are not included in the index at the end of this film.

1838–1839   **90,970**
Not in alphabetical order. Some extractions from the PCC.

1839–1840   **90,970 (item 2)**

Index at the beginning.

1840–1841   **90,971**
Index at the beginning.

1842   **90,971 (item 2)**
Index at the beginning. Some extractions from the PCC.

1843–1844   **90,972**
Index at the beginning.

1845   **90,973**
Index at the beginning.

1846   **90,973 (item 2)**

Wills in alphabetical order.

1847   **90,974**
Index at the beginning.

1848   **90,975**
1849 A–C
In alphabetical order by year. Page numbering begins over for 1849. The year 1849 ends with "Clarke" on this film.

1849 C–Y   **90,976**
1850 A–P
1849 begins with "Cookson." Numbering starts again for 1850. In alphabetical order for each year.

1850 R–Y   **90,977**
1851
1852
Begins with R. In alphabetical order for each year. Page numbering begins over for each year.

1852–1853   **90,978**
Page numbering continued from previous film. This part, however, is not in alphabetical order. In order by month with a few for April out of place in May for 1852. Some extractions from the PCC.

1854–1855   **90,979**
Entries in chronological order. Some extractions from the PCC.

1856   **90,980**

1856–1858   **90,981**
Continuation of pages from previous film. Numbered in upper center of page. Film ends 9 January 1858.

Probate and Administration Bonds for the Consistory Court of Durham

---

1565–1566,   **90,983**
1569, 1578,
1589
There will be two documents per bond. Usually the first is the obligation, written in Latin. This will be followed

by another document written in English, which is the condition of the obligation. These documents may be in reverse order. Many are numbered, typically at the bottom of the document, but there is no numerical sequence nor does the obligation number necessarily match the one on the condition.

1570–1577
Missing.

1578–1694   **91,034**
Torn, dark documents that are difficult to read but arranged like the preceding film. The obligations are frequently numbered in the upper left corner. Further entries for 1578 and 1589 may be found on the above film. Further entries from 1637 onward will be found on the films that follow this one. The majority of the items on this film seem to be for 1578, 1589, 1616, 1618, 1625, 1639, 1667, and 1685. Apparently, there are no entries on this film for 1579–1581, 1584–1588, 1590–1591, 1594, 1596–1615, 1617, 1620–1624, 1627–1628, 1630–1634, 1636–1637, 1641–1660, 1662–1666, 1668–1670, 1672–1674, 1676–1677, 1679–1684, 1686–1692. The documents for 1589 include three marriage license bonds.

1637   **90,994**
This film covers approximately one half of the year. The obligation may come either before or after the condition. The obligations are numbered in the upper left corner but are not in sequence until about one fourth of the way into the film, when they start in the 20s and go up to 146. There is an index at the end.

1637   **90,995**
This film starts with document 147 for June 1637 and is in sequence to 200, followed by an erratic mix numbered 535–560, low 500s to 527, low 200s to 271, and finally 300–430 in that order.

1638–1640
Mostly missing, but see film 91,034 for scattered entries under 1578–1694.

1641–1660
Missing, except for 1650. See the probate decision table for 1653–1660. The bonds for 1650 are filed with the original wills on film 90,855.

1661
There is at least one document, number 245, on film 91,034; see 1578–1694.

1662–1666
Missing.

1667
Scattered entries available on film 91,034; see 1578–1694.

1668–1669
Missing.

1670   **90,998**
                                                       (item 2)

1671   **90,999**
There is also at least one document for this year on film 91,034; see 1578–1694.

1672
Missing.

1673   **91,001**
Film begins with bond dated 1677, then goes to 1673. In order by month. Documents numbered in upper left-hand corner. See the next two films.

1673   **91,002**
(Continued) In order by month, from July to March. Documents are numbered in upper left-hand corner. Index at the end.

1674   **91,003**
In order by month. A bond for January 1673 is included. Continued on next film.

1674   **91,004**

1675   **91,005**
Documents numbered in upper left corner. Continued on next film.

1675   **91,006**
Numbered in order but backward; for example, from 300s to 85, then skips to 53 and is erratic from then on. Includes a group of documents pertaining to Roger and Jane Fawcett dated 1683. Document 194 for this series will be found on film 91,034; see 1578–1694.

1676   **91,008**

1676   **91,009**

1677   **91,010**
Contains months of January, December, and November. Also see film 91,001.

1677   **91,011**
Contains months of November, October etc., backward through March. Documents are numbered, but very few numbers can be seen as the pages are dark and blurred.

1677–1679   **91,007**
Not in order by year. A few inventories are included. A bond for 1678, number 26, is on film 91,034; see 1578–1694.

| 1680 | 91,013 |

| 1680 | 91,014 |

Documents are in order by month.

| 1680 | 91,015 |

Contains only months of January, February, and December.

| 1681 | 91,016 |

Documents in order by month from April to June.

| 1681 | 91,017 |

In order by month from June through December.

| 1681 | 91,018 |

Index at the end.

1682–1684

Missing, except for one item for 1683 on film 91,006.

| 1685 | 91,020 |

In order by month from April through February, then erratic from there on. There are also scattered entries for bonds in 1685 on film 91,034; see 1578–1694.

| 1686 | 91,021 |

In order by month beginning with March through September, then skips around some. One document for December is out of place in May. One found dated June 1692.

| 1686 | 91,022 |

| 1687 | 91,023 |

A document for W dated 1692. In order by month. Two or three documents for March are filed under June.

| 1688 | 91,024 |

Months somewhat mixed.

| 1688 | 91,025 |

Not in order by month.

1689

Missing.

| 1690 | 91,026 |

In order by month from March to July.

| 1690 | 91,027 |

Fairly chronological by months, beginning in July. A document for W, dated 1691, is included. Pages numbered in upper left-hand corner.

| 1691 | 91,028 |

In order by months from March through March, with one or two December and October documents out of place. See the preceding entry. Index at the end.

| 1692 | 91,029 |

Admon for Ellenora Hall dated 1695, very informative. Also see films 91,021 and 91,023.

| 1692 | 91,030 |

| 1693 | 91,031 |

In numerical order from 1–172, the numbers appearing in the upper left corner. Also in fairly good monthly order. Between documents 38 and 39 is a probate bond dated 1716 for the estate of Joan Dawson of Bishop Auckland. The administrator of her estate was William Slater.

| 1693 | 91,032 |

There is also at least one document, number 256, for this year on film 91,034; see 1578–1694. A document for S, dated 1694, is included on this film.

| 1694 | 91,033 |

Fairly good monthly order, with some entries out of place. See the preceding entry.

| 1695–1699 | 91,035 |

| 1695 | 91,036 |

In consecutive order by month, with a few documents out of place. Also numbered 1–311. See films 91,029 and 91,035.

| 1696 | 91,036 (item 2) |

Documents for December 1695 and October 1697 included. In consecutive order April–February by month, and consecutively numbered 1–247.

| 1697 | 91,037 |

In fairly good order by months. Index at the end. Also see films 91,035, 91,036, and 91,038.

| 1698 | 91,038 |

Document for Richard Hyatt of New Castle-on-Tyne dated 1697 is included. Also see film 91,035.

| 1699 | 91,039 |

Document for Elizabeth Maxwell of Kirkconnell, Scotland, is included. Also see film 91,035.

| 1700 | 91,040 (item 2) |

Documents generally in order by months. Index at the end. Numbered 1–308.

| 1701–1702 | 91,035 (item 2) |

1703–1735

Missing, except for one dated 1716 on film 91,031.

1736 **91,042**
In order by months and numbered 4–231.

1737 **91,042**
(item 2)
Inventories and letters accompany a few admons. There are some guardianship papers. The documents are numbered 5–260.

1738 **91,043**
Index at the beginning. Numbers in left margin.

1739 **91,043**
(item 2)
Index at the beginning. The index entries are alphabetically arranged and numbered in reverse order from 90–1. Then comes a series of documents not referenced by this index but by another index that follows these documents. After this second index come the documents referred to in the first index. See 1749 for another entry of R.

1740 **91,044**
Index at the beginning. Numbered in left margin. Not in order by month. This section is followed by another index and series of documents.

1741 **91,044**
(item 2)
Index at the beginning. Document for B, dated 1742, included. Numbered to 117, then starts over with 1. No index for last section of documents.

1742 **91,045**
Index. Admons in order by month with a few out of place. Another index precedes another section. See the preceding entry.

1743 **91,046**
Index at the beginning. Numbers go backward from 143 to 1 with some out of sequence. Another index at end of film is in fair condition and pertains to administrations preceding it.

1744 **91,047**
Index at the beginning. The first few pages are not numbered, but then they begin with 1 and go consecutively to 120. Then the numbers change from the left-hand margin to the upper right-hand corner and begin with 129 and go down. Thereafter is an erratic section covering the numbers 1 through 116.

1745 **91,047**
(item 2)
Index at the beginning. There are two sets of documents. The first series is numbered in the upper right corner, 1–134, and also arranged alphabetically, A–Y. The second series is numbered 1–109 and arranged alphabetically, A–H, M–Y. At the end of the film are six documents, one dated 1744 and the rest for 1745, that refer to oaths concerning church wardens and guardianship.

1746 **91,048**
Index at the beginning. The pages are numbered consecutively to 130, then proceed from 155 backward to 68. Another index references administrations following it.

1747 **91,049**
Index at the beginning. Documents are numbered 1–119, then start over from 1–135. Another index follows this section and apparently refers to the documents preceding it. Some 1747 documents may be found intermixed with 1748.

1748 **91,048**
(item 2)
Index at the beginning. Documents are numbered 1–131 at which point some 1747 bonds will be found intermixed with these. The numbering goes from 1–112 and then starts over again from 1–130.

1749 **91,049**
(item 2)
An index begins this section. There is also a checklist of names not in alphabetical order. Another index follows, referencing the rest of the film. A document for R for 1739 is included.

1750 **91,050**
A list of names (not an index) for admons and wills follows the first section.

1751 **91,050**
(item 2)
Index at the beginning. Pages are numbered in upper left corner but are mostly torn or blurred; numbers go backward from 91–1. Another index pertaining to the admons follows. These page numbers also go backward.

1752 **91,051**
Documents are numbered backward from 81–1, then start over at 1 and go to 127. Document 48 in the first series is a curation bond granted to Mary Massam over the estate left to her children, Catherine and George Dent, by their uncle, William Dent. Copies of certificates are provided to prove when she married her first husband, George Dent, in Chester-le-Street; when their children were christened; and when she was buried at St. Paul Shadwell in Middlesex. Between the two sequences is a renunciation to administer the goods of Henry Brearly, dated 1623.

1753 **91,052**
Documents are numbered in left-hand margin. They begin with 96 and go backward. An inventory for Thomas Birkbeck of Barnard Castle is included.

1754   **91,053**
Documents are numbered in left-hand margin. They proceed backward from 124 to 1, then the numbering begins with 91 and goes to 1.

1755   **91,053**
                                                        (item 2)
An index at the beginning. There are two sections; the last section begins with 1 and goes forward. Another index at the end pertains to admons preceding it.

1756   **91,054**
Begins with 154 and goes backward to 1. Then it begins over from 111–1.

1757   **91,055**
Documents are numbered in left-hand corner. Numbers go backward to 7, then begin again at 1–6, and are erratic thereon with short sections in consecutive order.

1758   **91,056**
Numbering in left-hand margin begins with 114 and goes backward to 1. Then the documents begin with 139 and go in order for a few pages, then return to 2 and proceed consecutively to 120; then the numbering is very erratic to the end.

1759   **91,057**
Numbers are very erratic.

1760   **91,058**
Numbering goes backward but is erratic. Small sections are consecutive. Some guardianship bonds and renunciations are included. There are also some oaths of performance dated 1759.

1761   **91,059**
Numbering as above. See 1763 for another W.

1762   **91,060**
Both numbers and months go backward for part of the film, and then reverse. See the next item.

1763   **91,061**
Documents for H, A, P, F, and M are all dated 1762; W for 1761, and B for 1768 were noted. The numbers go backward in short consecutive sections. See the next item.

1764   **91,062**
Some folios at the beginning are not numbered. Other sections are numbered irregularly. Not in alphabetical order. Mixed by month. Documents for H, S, B, W, R, W, S, B, all dated 1763, were noted.

1765   **91,063**
Numbers are irregular. See the next item.

1766   **91,064**
Document for T, dated 1765, is included.

1767   **91,065**
Folios numbered in left margin. Numbering is forward from 1 to 77 for first section. After 77 the numbering begins with 207 and goes backward.

1768   **91,066**
This film starts and ends with a page showing the marriages for the first part and the last half of the year 1748 for the parish of St. John in Newcastle-upon-Tyne. It is presumed that these pages were from the bishop's transcripts and used here as wrappers. Index at beginning. Bonds are numbered on the left margin. The first series of documents is arranged in reverse order from 136–1. Then comes another index and a series of documents labeled the same way from 203–1. Noted in the second section was number 25 for Thomas Allen of Stanhope Bridge, dated 1767, and number 29 for Robert Bramwell of Wheelbarrow Hall, dated 1766. See 1763 for another entry of B.

1769   **91,067**
Index at the beginning. Folios numbered backward. Second section documents are numbered consecutively from 1–208. An index for this group follows it. Another group of documents follows, unindexed.

1770   **91,068**
Folios numbered consecutively from 1–231. After 231 another section begins, 1–130. Documents for John Turner of Aldston dated 1768; James Vickers of Knarsdale, Jacob Moor of Black Cleugh, John Armstrong of Garragil in Gateshead, all dated 1769; Jane Henderson of Netherwarden dated 1766; Thomas Hall of Elsdon dated 1769 were noted. See 1772 for another entry of D.

1771   **91,069**
Folios numbered backward from 206 to 1, then the next section starts with 1 and goes consecutively through. Documents for Thomas Lumley of Corbridge and James Donaldson of Berwick, both dated 1770, were noted.

1772   **91,070**
Folios numbered consecutively from 1 to 125. Next section is numbered backward from 214 to 1. Document for D, dated 1770, is included.

1773   **91,070**
                                                        (item 2)
Folios numbered 1 to 106, then begin again with 185 and go backward.

1774   **91,071**
Folios numbered backward from 114. After 1 the numbering begins again with 211.

1775   **91,072**
Includes renunciations and guardianship bonds.
Numbered backward from 111. Numbering begins again
with 200 and goes backward. There may be a correlation
of first arranging the administration bonds in reverse
order by month from December through January and
then repeating this arrangement for the probate bonds.

1776–1778
Missing.

1779   **91,073**

1780–1800
Missing.

1801   **91,074**

1802   **91,074**
                                                      (item 2)

1803   **91,074**
                                                      (item 3)
Document for Amos Barnes of St. John, New Castle-on-
Tyne, dated 1802, is included.

1804   **91,075**

1805   **91,075**
                                                      (item 2)

1806   **91,075**
                                                      (item 3)

1807   **91,076**
The first series is for administration bonds and is numbered 1–117. This is followed by a series numbered 1–20
for administrations where a will was annexed. The wills
are not included here, but there may be renunciations or
other explanatory documents as to why a will was
annexed. The will should be filed with the originals or
appear in the registered copies.

1808   **91,076**
                                                      (item 2)
Similar to the above with the administrations numbered
1–116, followed by administrations where a will was
annexed that are numbered 1–21.

1809   **91,076**
                                                      (item 3)
The administrations are numbered 1–112, then 124–113,
followed by administrations where a will was annexed
that are numbered 1–16, 23–22, 17–21. The documents
are also arranged by month and reverse their order with
the numbering. Document 114 concerns the estate of
John Gilbert Ironside of Houghton le Spring, late of
Jamaica, dated 1806.

1810–1857
Missing. See the original wills for 1810–1820.

Act Books for the Consistory Court of Durham

1571–1576   **90,986**
Probate acts in Latin until 1733; recorded in order by
year. Name in margin. Pages numbered in upper left corner of right-hand page to page 37, then resume again at
page 40. Will of William Wynterskett in 1571 is
included. One probate act dated 1573 is found with 1574.
Index after year 1576.

1577–1582   **90,986**
                                                      (item 2)
Index after 1582.

1582–1584   **90,987**

1585–1587   **90,987**
                                                      (item 2)
Index at the end of 1587.

1587–1591
Act Book 5 was not filmed.

1591–1594   **90,987**
                                                      (item 3)
At the beginning of the film there are six pages with documents dated 1591 to 1594 followed by an index. The
entries then begin again from 1591.

1595–1598   **90,988**
Index following page 94. See also film 90,990.

1599–1606   **90,989**
Index at the beginning.

1598,   **90,990**
1624–1629,
1633–1636,
1634,
1639–1646,
1662
Numbering begins with page 218 and stops with 270.
Entries begin with 1598, then jump to 1624, proceed in
order by year through 1629, then jump to 1633, and proceed in order through 1636; then four pages of 1634 follow, and the film resumes with 1639. There is a gap from
1647 to 1661. Film ends with 1662.

1607–1614   **90,991**
Index at the beginning. First few pages are dated 1609 to
1613 but are badly torn and difficult to read, followed by
1607. The year 1614 is continued on next film.

1614–1625   **90,992**
Film begins with four pages dated 1614 to 1620, then begins with 1614 on page 1. 1624–1625 may overlap or be in addition to film 90,990.

1619–1624   **90,993**
Index covering four-year period (1621–1624) at the beginning of second section of film. The first part of this film may overlap or be in addition to the preceding film.

1625–1629
See films 90,990 and 90,992.

1629–1633   **90,993**
                                                (item 2)
Index at the beginning. Documents are in order by year. Names in margin. Some 1631–1632 documents out of place in 1633.

1633–1636
See film 90,990.

1635–1637   **90,996**
                                                (item 2)
1635–1636 may overlap or be in addition to film 90,990.

1638–1644   **90,996**
Index after 1644. Pages of index are in alphabetical order except for H, which follows Y. 1639–1644 may overlap or be in addition to film 90,990.

1645–1650   **90,997**
1660–1665
Film begins with an index, but it is in poor condition and contains only part of the alphabet. Pages are numbered in upper left corner of right-hand page. Two or three 1649 entries are out of place in 1647, otherwise documents are in order by year through 1650. They then continue in order from 1660 through 1665. 1645–1646, 1662 may overlap or be in addition to film 90,990.

1646–1652   **90,997**
                                                (item 2)
Note the overlap with the first item on this film. One 1657 entry at end of 1652.

1652–1660
Missing due to the Interregnum. See the probate decision table.

1660–1668   **90,997**
                                                (item 3)
1662 may overlap or be in addition to the first item on this film and film 90,990. See the next entry.

1669–1723
Missing. Some entries for 1663–1723 will be found among the copy wills on film 90,969.

1724–1735   **91,041**

1736–1775
Missing.

1776–1778   **91,072**
                                                (item 2)
This section is arranged chronologically from January 1776 through 1778.

1778–1779
Missing.

1780–1790   **91,072**
                                                (item 3)

1791–1800   **91,072**
                                                (item 4)

1801–1809
Missing.

1809–1813   **91,077**
This film starts with November 1809.

1814–1821   **91,077**
                                                (item 2)
In order by month for each year.

1822–1832   **91,077**
                                                (item 3)
In order by month.

1833–1842   **91,078**
See also item 2 on this film.

1843–1853   **91,078**
                                                (item 3)
In order by month. See also the next entry.

1835–1845   **91,078**
                                                (item 2)
This appears to be a general act book that leans heavily to matters of guardianship. Some references to wills and administrations-with-wills-annexed, which seemed to have no reference to minors, were noted. Possibly, there is an overlap with the preceding two items listed for this film. There is a reference on page 10 to a document for William Robinson of Blyth, dated January 1834.

Miscellaneous: Notes, Abstracts, and Their Indexes from Probates Relating to Durham

---

(From time to time, various compilers have gathered information from the Consistory Court of Durham or its superior jurisdictions. Some of this material has been printed. None of the collections is complete; however, the use of such information might enable the researcher to find a particular item more quickly or supplement previous findings. It is presumed that the researcher would want to check this material against the actual court records whenever possible.)

GENERAL INDEXES

1) 1540–1812   **90,795**
                                                     574,951

J. W. Robinson's Index of Durham Wills. Transcript of an incomplete index to wills and administrations, typed in 1915. Surnames are first grouped together alphabetically and then arranged chronologically by date of probate. Following this is a second index that references the special collections referred to later on in this handlist and Durham wills proved in other courts.

This index has been filmed twice. The first sixty pages of the second part mentioned above are easier to read on film 90,795. However, film 574,951 contains interlined entries to material added after 1915, including an index to J. C. Hodgson's wills for Northumberland from the late eighteenth through the early nineteenth centuries. There is yet a third filming of this index, a reduction of 574,951, that is item 2 on 1,040,217 but stops at J. It continues as item 1 on 1,040,218.

Robinson's index included smaller compilations by Sir Cuthbert Sharp, H. R. Leighton, and others as well as the following collections, which are filmed and outlined below under "Special Collections": his own collection; at least some of George Neasham's collection; volumes 2, 38, and 112 of the Surtees Society; and probably all of J. Raine's unpublished material.

2) 16th–19th   **207,622**
   centuries

Card Index to wills in the Newcastle City Archives. An incomplete index handprinted on 4×6 cards, which refer to the box and bundle where the document will be found, including items at the Public Library. Brief abstracts of the probate and sometimes other information are provided. However, when the information continues on another card, it is not always clear on microfilm which card refers to which probate.

3) 1540–1599   **FHL 942.82/N1**
                                                     B4nt vol. 8
                                                     962,690 (item 2)

Index of Wills, etc., in the Probate Registry, Durham and from Other Sources, 1540–1599. This volume was edited by H. M. Wood and published by the Newcastle-upon-Tyne Records Committee in 1928. It is probably incomplete but does serve also as a master index to the first three volumes of Durham wills published by the Surtees Society. It collates the pre–1599 material described in Raine's Dunelmensia below. This book is now available on microfiche: 6,024,197–6,024,199.

4) 1649–1660   **1,564,756**
                                                     (item 7)

Commonwealth Wills, 1649–1660: for the counties of Northumberland and Durham, extracted from the index at Somerset House, London (1909).

SPECIAL COLLECTIONS

1) 1540–1800   **574,952 &**
   A–B   **1,040,219**
                                                     (item 1)

Robinson's Collection, in nine volumes. Volume 1, A–B, indexed at the beginning. It is followed by brief extracts from the wills, which are arranged alphabetically and include a notation as to their source.

   C–F   **574,953 &**
                                                     1,040,220
                                                     (items 1 & 2)

Volume 2. Some entries are complete abstracts and some are accompanied by pedigree information.

   G–J   **574,954**

Volume 3. It is partly on item 2 of 1,040,220 and continues as item 1 on 1,040,221.

   K–P   **574,955 &**
                                                     1,040,221
                                                     (item 2)

Volume 4.

   R   **574,956 &**
                                                     1,040,222
                                                     (item 1)

Volume 5. The entries are not arranged strictly alphabetically by given name.

   S–W   **574,957**

Volumes 6–7. Volume 6 is partly on item 2 of 1,040,222 and continues as item 1 of 1,040,223. Volume 7 is item 2 of 1,040,223. Volume 8 is item 3 of 1,040,223.

   W–Y   **574,958 &**
                                                     1,040,224

Volumes 8–9.

2) 1540–1800

Neasham's Collection. Two volumes of probate abstracts made by George Neasham were purchased in 1916 by J. W. Robinson. These films represent Robinson's brief extracts from Neasham's work. They are arranged like Robinson's Collection described above. Some of the extracts include coats of arms. It has been filmed twice.

   A–F   **574,977 &**
                                                     1,040,216
                                                     (item 2)

The index at the end of this film goes from A–Y but refers to Neasham's volume I, which has not been filmed. The page numbers refer to it and not this film. This is followed by another index to Neasham's volume II. These two indexes are repeated two times on the second filming. They are item 1 on 1,040,216 and appear at the end of item 2 of the same film. After the indexes come seventeen pages of Robinson's interpretations of brief extracts made by Neasham from parish registers and deeds, including the parish of Stranton, 1583–1692.

G–Y   **574,978**
The second filming gives G–He as item 3 of 1,040,216. He–Y is item 1 of 1,040,217.

3) 1576–1735   **90,796**
Howe's Collection. The six volumes of J. J. Howe have been preserved on one roll of film. All of the volumes are indexed. They include entries for Northumberland and some nonprobate items as summarized below.

Volume 1 starts with two sections of extracts from wills and administrations covering 1629–1636 and 1637–1640, respectively. Included are offenses of various individuals as judged by the Consistory Court of Durham. This is followed by a section of "Presentations" (installations of ministers, licenses to teach, etc.) for 1662–1725. The next section for 1665–1674 is like the first two. Then come three sections of extracts from act books for 1665–1677, 1608–1610, and 1619–1622. Finally, there is a volume of visitation extracts concerning Northumberland for 1609–1618.

Volume 2 contains extracts from probate and administration bonds for the sixteenth and seventeenth centuries, and a few marriage license bonds, 1732–1735. Howe thought that many of these bonds had not been indexed.

Volume 3 has extracts from probate and administration bonds for 1576–1577, 1583, 1585–1587, 1603, and 1618. Again, Howe believed that one half of these were never indexed.

Volume 4 continues volume 3 for the years 1624–1625, 1629–1630, 1632, 1637–1638, 1640, 1642, and 1644.

Volume 5 is a continuation of the last three, plus extracts from visitation act books and marriage license bonds.

Volume 6 contains probate information from the oaths of performance taken by executors for 1671–1734.

4) Medieval–1650   **FHL 942 B4s**
The Publications of the Surtees Society. The Society began publishing materials concerning the northern counties in 1834. Research on any of the counties that make up the Province of York could benefit from examining the contents of this series. A master index will be found in volume 150.

Abstracts of some wills from the Consistory Court of Durham and pre-1540 ones from the Dean and Chapter of York are in volume 2 (1259–1580/1) on fiche 6,073,284; volume 38 (1563–1599) on fiche 6,073,320;

volume 112 (1543–1602) on fiche 6,073,394; and volume 142 (1603/4–1649) on fiche 6,073,424. The first three volumes are indexed in the work by H. M. Wood described as item 3 above under "General Indexes." Volume 38 contains a master index to all persons mentioned in every document in both it and volume 2. There is a similar index format in volumes 112 and 142. In addition to these, volume 22 contains abstracts for the wills of some Durham clergy of the sixteenth century.

Other volumes of interest in this series are 116 (1383–1558) and 121 (1555–1616), which are abstracts of some wills from the PCC concerning the northern counties, including Durham and Northumberland. These two volumes have been microfilmed as items 5 and 6 of film 990,300.

Likewise, there may be something of interest for these two counties in the volumes of this series that are abstracts of some wills registered at York, especially the PCY. These include volume 4 (1316–1430), volume 30 (1426–1467), volume 45 (1395–1491), volume 53 (1484–1509), volume 79 (1509–1531), and volume 106 (1531–1551).

5) 1540–1806
Raine's Dunelmensia (Durham). This collection of Raine's consists of manuscript volumes of various probate extracts, often entire wills, arranged in chronological order. The right-hand page, containing the abstracts, is divided into thirds or halves with each grouping numbered. On the opposite page will appear burial dates, coats of arms, pedigrees, or other notations referring to the testator.

Volumes A–F may have been published. All of the entries in Raine's Dunelmensia were indexed by J. W. Robinson (see item 1 above), and the pre-1599 entries would also appear in the volume edited by H. M. Wood (see item 3 above under "General Indexes."). Portions of this collection were filmed twice as outlined below.

1540–1746   **98,555**
                                                          252,668
Volume A covers 1540–1578, volume B is 1569–1613, and volume C is 1582–1586 and 1575–1746. Film 252,668 has handwritten notes that may contain more information than film 98,555. The index at the start of 252,668 refers to volumes I–VII below. The index at the end of 252,668 may refer to volume C or volumes A-C.

1556–1708   **98,555**
                                                          252,669
Volume D

1580–1694   **98,555**
                                                          252,669
Volume E. This volume starts with abstracts of wills, 1580–1586, on pages 1–47; followed by guardianship

bonds, 1592–1638, on pages 51–57; wills, 1630–1633, on page 58; administration bonds from the Dean and Chapter of York, 1558–1640, on pages 59–60; inventories, 1512–1685, on pages 61–68; an index on page 69; and then miscellaneous wills to 1694.

1567–1582   **98,555**
                                                                252,669
Volume F

1571–1623   **98,555**
Volume I. The emphasis of volumes F and I is administrations. A note says that volume I was drawn from Act Books 67, 70–71. Following volume I is more of volume F, and then either a continuation or duplication of I, or another volume I.

1629–1757   **98,555**
Volume II. This was drawn from Act Book 51.

1544–1806   **98,555**
Volumes I–VII. These are abstracts of wills and some inventories. Volume I covers 1544–1615, volume II 1580–1631, volume III 1612–1763, volume IV 1646–1717, volume V 1719–1806, volume VI 1410–1720, and volume VII 1574–1712. They are indexed as outlined below.

                                                                98,555
                                                                252,668
Index. An index for volumes I–VII appears at the end of 98,555, as the first index listed. It also appears at the start of 252,668 but is mislabeled as an index to volumes A–F. The index on film 252,668 may be easier to read.

6) 1554–1801
Raine's Eboracensia (York). This collection concerns wills and some administrations extracted from the various courts of York that refer to Durham and Northumberland. The format is similar to Raine's Dunelmensia described above.

All of the volumes in Raine's Eboracensia were indexed by J. W. Robinson (see item 1 above). Portions of this collection were filmed twice as outlined below.

1554–1691   **98,554**
                                                                252,670
Volume 1. This volume ends with 1691, but random entries were noted dated 1722, 1769, and 1772. There is an index at the end of this volume on film 252,670.

1598–1686   **98,554**
                                                                252,670
Volume 3. These are entries taken from the PCY act books. The spine of this volume is mislabeled "Hexhamshire."

1687–1727   **98,554**
Volume 4. These are entries taken from the Dean and Chapter of York act books. Entries are included for Hexhamshire, which is also the case for the remaining volumes in this series.

1727–1772   **98,554**
Volume 5

1773–1801   **98,554**
                                                                252,670
Volume 6. These entries are from the PCY act books.

1692–1721   **98,554**
                                                                252,671
Volume 7. These entries are from the PCY registered copy wills, volumes 63–76.

1731–1739   **98,554**
                                                                252,671
Volume 8. These entries are from the PCY registered copy wills, volumes 82–86.

1721–1731   **98,554**
                                                                252,671
Volume 9. These entries are from the PCY registered copy wills, volumes 76–81.

1740–1750   **98,554**
                                                                252,672
Volume 10. These entries are from the PCY registered copy wills, volumes 87–94.

1751–1770   **98,554**
                                                                252,672
Volume 11. These entries are from the PCY registered copy wills, volumes 94–114.

1771–1793   **98,554**
                                                                252,672
Volume 12. These entries are from the PCY registered copy wills, volumes 115–137.

                                                                98,555
                                                                252,673
Index Volumes 1, 3–12. This index is the last item listed on film 98,555

7) 1595–1597   **FHL 942 B2m 5s**
                                                          vol. 7, pp. 199–205
Extracts from Durham administration and probate grants.

8)   **1,595,120**
                                                                (item 6)
Wills and Deeds of Hartlepool and Vicinity. This book was edited by W. Boagey and published in 1975.

Part 4 Lancashire
Probate Jurisdictions and Microfilmed Records

Introduction

The majority of the population in Lancashire lived south of the River Ribble, which area came under the probate jurisdiction of the Consistory Court of Chester. The lone exception, the parish of Flixton, was under peculiar jurisdiction, but it is likely that any probates for this parish were also filed with those of Chester. Before 1541, Lancashire south of the Ribble belonged to the jurisdiction of the Consistory Court of Lichfield, but it is unlikely that any Lancashire probates survive there.

The earliest original will on film for Lancashire in the Consistory Court of Chester is for 1533. Abstracts of some pre–1545 probates and others for later dates, noted as missing from the originals, are described in the miscellaneous section for Chester (see Cheshire for further details).

From the late sixteenth century onward, the probate records of the Consistory Court of Chester were filed in two separate divisions. The estates of clergymen, esquires, and those of anyone else worth £40 or over were proven in the bishop's court. Such grants are frequently referred to as "supra." When the estates of the remainder of the testators were valued at less than £40, the grant was made by the rural dean. The records were then sent to Chester where they were categorized as "infra." It was possible for a will to be moved from the infra to the supra series if the accumulated value of the estate so merited before the final probate action. It is possible that the records from one series may have been mistakenly filed with the other, and vice versa. Accordingly, both series always should be searched to gain an accurate picture of the probate situation in Lancashire.

The inventories and administration bonds for this court are filed with the original wills. Rarely do the inventories extend much later into the modern period beyond the first quarter of the eighteenth century. There are no registered copy wills for the infra series, and those for the supra series begin in 1838. However, it is obvious that registered copy wills for the supra series were once available for earlier periods, as 105 registered copy wills for the period from 1701 to 1769 will be found at the start of the act books for 1811–1814 (see film 90,105). These copies may relate to those entered in the "Enrollment Books" as described in the miscellaneous section under Cheshire. The registered copy wills were not always registered in order; hence, the indexes should be thoroughly searched and any page numbers and their appropriate volumes noted carefully. Unfortunately, not all wills were registered, and the microfilms of the supra original wills stop at the end of 1837.

The situation concerning act books is confusing. The researcher should also check the miscellaneous section for a small group of caveats and bill books. Similarly, the same section contains references to probate documents used in testamentary suits and grants known as "Limited Administrations." The latter refer to specific instructions limiting the authority of the executors or narrowing their supervision to a certain part of the estate. They cover the period between 1824 and 1857, and frequently the will or copy of the same is attached.

The area north of the River Ribble belonged mainly to the jurisdiction of the Archdeaconry Court of Richmond. Three townships adjacent to the Ribble on the eastern border of the county came under the Consistory Court of Chester and the Exchequer Court of York. The township of

Bowland with Leagram belonged to Chester, and Aighton with Bailey and Chaigley to York. In the north there were several manorial courts with probate jurisdiction; and one parish, Kirkby Ireleth, came under the peculiar jurisdiction of the Dean and Chapter of York.

Richmond was part of the Diocese of York until 1541 and thereafter the Diocese of Chester. Apparently, Chester never exercised superior jurisdiction over Richmond in probate matters; rather, such business continued to be handled by the Prerogative Court of York. The probates granted by the Archdeaconry Court of Richmond usually were filed under the name of the deanery in which the testator resided. Any printed indexes and miscellaneous data for Richmond, as well as the microfilms for the deaneries of Amounderness, Furness, and Lonsdale, are outlined after the descriptions of the records for the Consistory Court of Chester in the Lancashire section. Since most of the Deanery of Kendal was in the County of Westmorland, its records (other than the printed calendars) will be described and listed under that county.

The earliest original wills for the deaneries of Amounderness, Furness, and Lonsdale are 1530, 1528, and 1480, respectively. Many of the orginal records for Amounderness were lost (probably when the records were moved to a new repository in 1748) or misfiled. Abstracts of these records were preserved by the British Museum. References to "Calendar W" usually mean that the original has been lost or possibly filed with the Eastern Deaneries, which were in Yorkshire and are described under that county's section of this volume.

There are no registered copy wills for Amounderness. Remnants remain for Furness and Lonsdale. Outside of three years in the seventeenth century for Amounderness, the act books for all three deaneries are confined to the eighteenth and nineteenth centuries. Inventories rarely appear with the administration bonds after 1750, but they still will be found frequently with the wills as late as 1770.

See Yorkshire for the records of the area covered by the Peculiar Court of the Dean and Chapter of York. Of the four manorial courts, Halton is the only one at present known to have surviving records. However, it would be wise to search the indexes to the deaneries of Richmond for residents of any of these four manors.

The original wills, administrations, and inventories for Halton, 1615–1814, are all mixed together in rough chronological order by the initial letter of the surnames involved. There is a matching printed index.

Probate Decision Table for Lancashire

If the Research Subject Lived in One of These Jurisdictions:	Manor of Halton	Any of the Other Manors	Archdeaconry of Richmond	Episcopal Consistory of Chester plus Flixton and Bowland with Leagram	Prebendal of Flixton prior to 1541	Episcopal Consistory of Chester prior to 1541	Parish of Kirkby Ireleth	Townships of Aighton with Bailey and Chaigley	Anywhere in the County, 1651–1659
Search the probate records of these courts in the order shown below:	BROWN	BLUE ROSE PURPLE	GREEN	TAN			YELLOW		
Manor Court of Halton	1								
Manor Court Records (NO FILMS)		1							
Archdeaconry Court of Richmond by deanery (see Westmorland for Kendal Deanery)	2	2	1				2	3	
Archdeaconry Court of Richmond (Eastern Deaneries—see Yorkshire)	3	3	2				3		
Consistory Court of Lichfield (see Staffordshire)					2	1			
Court of the Dean and Chapter of Lichfield (see Staffordshire)					1				
Consistory Court of Chester			4	1				2	
Prerogative Court of the Archbishop of York (see Yorkshire)	4	4	3	2			4	1	
Court of the Dean and Chapter of York (see Yorkshire for vacancy jurisdiction)	5	5	5	3			(not vacancy) 1	4	
Chancery Court of the Archbishop of York (see Yorkshire)	6	6	6	4			5	5	
Prerogative Court of the Archbishop of Canterbury (see London)	7	7	7	5	3	2	6	6	1
Court of Delegates, 1643–1857 (see London)	8	8	8	6			7	7	

*Indexes and Calendars for the
Consistory Court of Chester*

(Some abstracts or extracts of documents relating to Lancashire probates will be found in the miscellaneous section. Searches in these items and the stray-name index to this volume may reveal entries not found in the calendars outlined below. Such materials are usually edited and may still be in Latin for the earlier periods.)

1) The printed indexes are also available on microfilm or microfiche as indicated by the six- or seven-digit number below the call number.

Time Period	Film or Call No.

1359–1858   **FHL 942.7 B4Lc
                                                        vol. 105
                                                 823,525 (item 2)**

Vol. 105 of the Lancashire & Cheshire Record Society. The appendix of this volume (pp. 126–143) is an index to Lancashire wills for both the Consistory of Chester and the Archdeaconry of Richmond that were not recorded in any printed index as of 1953. The documents came from family records, Roman Catholic wills as required by the act of 1717, and others that surfaced after several sortings at different record offices. They are all housed at the Lancashire Record Office. More of these types of records may yet appear; hence, the value of including the act books in one's research in addition to the printed indexes. The following volume may also contain some pre–1545 information.

1545–1620   **FHL 942.7 B4Lc
(Supra)   vol. 2
                                                 823,501 (item 2) &
                                                      6,072,908**

Vol. 2 of the Lancashire & Cheshire Record Society. The printed index should be more reliable than any known manuscript indexes. It is arranged alphabetically. Match the entries of interest with the corresponding year and alphabet listed in the subsequent section of this volume entitled "Supra Original Wills, Admons, and

Inventories." Be sure to search the next item in this list for the infra series. Corrections and additions will be found for these years on pages 222–224 at the end of the printed index.

Search the film for an ident matching the printed entry. Watch for accompanying documents before and after the appropriate item. If not found, reread the film description provided in this volume, scan the entire film for misplaced items, and then consider the infra series and the miscellaneous section. Perhaps the missing item will be found in the act books or was never filmed. Consult Anthony J. Camp, *Wills and Their Whereabouts*, 4th ed. (London, The author, 1974), for details of records not filmed.

1590–1665   **FHL 942.7 B4Lc
(Infra)   vol. 52
                                                 823,512 (item 4) &
                                                      6,072,958**

Vol. 52 of the Lancashire & Cheshire Record Society. The relevant portion of this book will be found on pages 1–59. This is an index to materials at first thought to be lost; hence, the overlap with volume 15 described below. Both should be searched and the likely entries matched against the section entitled "Infra Original Wills, Admons, and Inventories." Note the preceding and subsequent volumes for the supra series in the same general time period. The general instructions in the second paragraph describing the preceding volume will also be of assistance.

1621–1650   **FHL 942.7 B4Lc
(Supra)   vol. 4
                                                 823,502 (item 1) &
                                                      6,072,910**

Vol. 4 of the Lancashire & Cheshire Record Society. Follow the instructions given above in the two paragraphs under volume 2. Corrections and additions will be found on pages 301–303.

1650–1660   **FHL 942.7 B4Lc
(Wills)   vol. 4
                                                 823,502 (item 1) &
                                                      6,072,910**

(Continuation of the above) Appendix I on pages 249–280 of volume 4 is an index to Lancashire and Cheshire wills proven at the Prerogative Court of Canterbury during the Interregnum and Commonwealth period. (The microfilms of these probate records will be listed under London in a subsequent volume for this series.)

1650–1660   **FHL 942.7 B4Lc
(Admons)   vol. 4
                                                 823,502 (item 1) &
                                                      6,072,910**

(Continuation of the above) Appendix II on pages 281–300 of volume 4 is an index to Lancashire and Cheshire admons proven at the PCC (see the preceding note).

1660–1680
(Supra & Infra)

FHL 942.7 B4Lc
vol. 15
823,504 (item 2) &
6,072,921

Vol. 15 of the Lancashire & Cheshire Record Society. The supra series takes up the majority of this book. The infra series actually appears as an appendix on pages 310–380. Both should be searched. Read the instructions given above under volumes 2 and 52. Note the overlap in the infra series with volume 52. An asterisk is used in this book to indicate documents considered lost or too damaged to produce at that time. Some 169 documents for 1670 were later recovered and are listed in volume 63 below. Corrections to volume 15 will be found just before page 1 and continue on page 380.

1681–1700
(Supra & Infra)

FHL 942.7 B4Lc
vol. 18
823,505 (item 1) &
6,072,924

Vol. 18 of the Lancashire & Cheshire Record Society. The infra series will be found in the appendix on pages 283–365. "A Supplementary Index" to mainly infra admons for 1693, which were discovered at a later date, may be found at the end of the book or in volume 63. Read the instructions given above under volumes 2 and 52. There are some additions to volume 18 preceding page 1.

1701–1720
(Supra & Infra)

FHL 942.7 B4Lc
vol. 20
823,505 (item 3) &
6,072,926

Vol. 20 of the Lancashire & Cheshire Record Society. The infra series will be found in the appendix on pages 233–261. Read the instructions given above under volumes 2 and 52.

1721–1740
(Supra & Infra)

FHL 942. 7 B4Lc
vol. 22
823,506 (item 1) &
6,072,928

Vol. 22 of the Lancashire & Cheshire Record Society. The infra series will be found in the appendix on pages 291–343. Read the instructions given above under volumes 2 and 52.

1741–1760
(Supra & Infra)

FHL 942.7 B4Lc
vol. 25
823,506 (item 4) &
6,072,931

Vol. 25 of the Lancashire & Cheshire Record Society. The infra series will be found in the appendix on pages 213–264. The infra documents are missing from 1757–1776. Read the instructions given above under volumes 2 and 52. A page of additions to volume 25 appears at the front of the book.

1761–1780 A–M
(Supra)

FHL 942.7 B4Lc
vol. 37
823,509 (item 3) &
6,072,943

Vol. 37 of the Lancashire & Cheshire Record Society. The infra series 1777–1780 (there is none for 1757–1776) will be found in the next volume. Read the instructions given above under volume 2.

1761–1780 N–Z
(Supra)
A–Z (Infra)

FHL 942.7 B4Lc
vol. 38
823,509 (item 4) &
6,072,944

Vol. 38 of the Lancashire & Cheshire Record Society. The title page of this book incorrectly shows the coverage to be 1741–1760. The infra series (there is none for 1757–1776) will be found in the appendix on pages 113–123. Read the instructions given above under volumes 2 and 52.

1781–1790
(Supra & Infra)

FHL 942.7 B4Lc
vol. 44
823,511 (item 1) &
443,326 (item 1) &
6,072,950

Vol. 44 of the Lancashire & Cheshire Record Society. The infra series will be found in the appendix on pages 135–168. Read the instructions given above under volumes 2 and 52.

1791–1800
(Supra & Infra)

FHL 942.7 B4Lc
vol. 45
823,511 (item 2) &
443,326 (item 2) &
6,072,951

Vol. 45 of the Lancashire & Cheshire Record Society. The infra series will be found in the appendix on pages 178–242. Read the instructions given above under volumes 2 and 52.

1801–1810 A–L
(Supra & Infra)

FHL 942.7 B4Lc
vol. 62
823,515 (item 2) &
443,326 (item 3) &
6,072,968

Vol. 62 of the Lancashire & Cheshire Record Society. The infra series is interspersed with the supra but printed in italics to emphasize the difference. Read the instructions given above under volumes 2 and 52. The original documents were filed in the nineteenth century by month. This may still be reflected in the microfilms, which are filed initially by year and then roughly alphabetically.

1801–1810 M–Z
(Supra & Infra)

FHL 942.7 B4Lc
vol. 63
823,515 (item 3) &
443,326 (item 4) &
6,072,969

Vol. 63 of the Lancashire & Cheshire Record Society. The infra series is interspersed with the supra but printed in italics to emphasize the difference. Read the instructions given above under volume 62. A supplementary index to documents for 1670 (A–C), thought to be lost earlier, appears on pages 179–187. Another supplementary index to mainly infra admons for 1693, recovered at a later date, will be found on pages 189–199. (Item 4 of film 443,326 does not include the supplements.) The manuscript calendar for the entries from 1693 is also available on microfilm as will be described below. The filmed manuscript calendar does add occupations; otherwise, it holds no advantage over the printed index.

1811–1820 A–L   FHL 942.7 B4Lc
  (Supra & Infra)   **vol. 78**
                                        823,519 (item 1) &
                                               6,072,984
Vol. 78 of the Lancashire & Cheshire Record Society. The infra documents are differentiated from the supra by an asterisk at the end of such entries. Read the instructions given above under volumes 2 and 52. The filmed documents are arranged by year, then roughly alphabetically, and perhaps by month. The manuscript calendars are on film from 1815 for the supra and 1819 for the infra series, but there seems to be little advantage in searching them until the printed indexes cease.

1811–1820 M–Z   FHL 942.7 B4Lc
  (Supra & Infra)   **vol. 79**
                                        823,519 (item 2) &
                                               6,072,985
Vol. 79 of the Lancashire & Cheshire Record Society. See the above note for volume 78.

1821–1825   FHL 942.7 B4Lc
  (Supra & Infra)   **vol. 107**
                                        823,525 (item 4) &
                                               6,073,013
Vol. 107 of the Lancashire & Cheshire Record Society. See the above note for volume 78. The Lancashire documents are indexed separately on pages 1–157. There is a typescript index for 1821–1827 on film 165,324. This may have been the basis for the printed index; however, the typescript also contains the occupation, date the will was written, and the testator's death date. The infra series is on the left-hand page and the supra on the right side of the typescript.

1826–1830   FHL 942.7 B4Lc
  (Supra & Infra)   **vol. 113**
Vol. 113 of the Lancashire & Cheshire Record Society. See the notes given above under volumes 78 and 107. The Lancashire documents are indexed separately on pages 1–141. Missing documents are listed in italics. Additions to volume 113 appear on page vii.

1831–1833   FHL 942.7 B4Lc
  (Supra & Infra)   **vol. 118**
Vol. 118 of the Lancashire & Cheshire Record Society. See the notes given above under volume 78. The Lancashire documents are indexed separately on pages 5–109. Missing documents are listed in italics. Additions and corrections to volume 118 appear on page 145.

1834–1837   FHL 942.7 B4Lc
  (Supra & Infra)   **vol. 120**
Vol. 120 of the Lancashire & Cheshire Record Society. See the notes given above under volume 78. The Lancashire documents are indexed separately on pages 1–144. Missing documents are listed in italics. There are separate indexes by occupation and place.

2) The filmed calendars are arranged as follows:

1815–1823   **90,072**
  (Supra)   **(item 1)**
Vol. 401 of a manuscript index to supra wills and admons. Use the printed indexes described above under volumes 78, 79, and 107. Infra calendars are described below.

1824–1830   **90,072**
  (Supra)   **(item 2)**
Vol. 402 of a manuscript index to supra wills and admons. Use the printed indexes described above under volumes 107 and 113. Infra calendars are described below.

1831–1838   **90,073**
  (Supra)   **(item 1)**
Vol. 403 of a manuscript index to supra wills and admons. For 1831–1837, use the printed index described above for volumes 118 and 120. For 1838, match the entries from this manuscript index with the following section entitled "Supra Registered Copy Wills." The manuscript index will provide the name, place, occupation, type of probate, and the month and day of the grant. For registered copy wills, the index adds the volume and page number. Infra calendars are described below.

1839–1844   **90,073**
  (Supra)   **(item 2)**
Vol. 404 of a manuscript index to supra wills and admons. Read the above note for 1831–1838. Unfortunately, the original supra wills, 1838–1858, were not filmed. Not all wills were registered. For unregistered wills, check the act books and then consult Camp's *Wills and Their Whereabouts* for details of records not filmed.

1845–1849   **90,074**
  (Supra)   **(item 1)**

Vol. 405 of a manuscript index to supra wills and admons. Read the above notes for 1831–1838 and 1839–1844. Infra calendars are described below.

1850–1853   **90,074**
  (Supra)   **(item 2)**

Vol. 406 of a manuscript index. Read the above notes for 1831–1838 and 1839–1844. Infra calendars are described below.

1854–1858   **90,074**
  (Supra)   **(item 3)**

Vol. 407 of a manuscript index. Read the above notes for 1831–1838 and 1839–1844. Infra calendars are described below.

1693   **90,123**
  (Infra)   **(item 1)**

Vol. 491 of a manuscript index to mainly infra admons, which were found at a later date. Use the printed index described above under volume 63.

1819–1858   **90,123**
  (Infra)   **(item 2)**

Vol. 492 of a manuscript index to infra wills and admons. For 1819–1837, use the printed indexes described above under volumes 78, 79, 107, 113, 118 and 120. For 1838–1858, match the entries from this manuscript index with the following section entitled "Infra Original Wills, Admons, and Inventories." The index is arranged the same way as the supra calendars described above.

Supra Original Wills, Admons, and Inventories for the Consistory Court of Chester

1533–1600

The original records for this time period are filed roughly alphabetically by year as per the descriptions in the following entries. For missing documents, including those for periods earlier than the starting dates listed below, see the miscellaneous sections for both Cheshire and Lancashire and the first entry under the section entitled "Indexes and Calendars" for Lancashire.

1558–1599 A   **89,436**

1546–1589 B   **89,437**

In fair chronological order with the following exceptions: an entry for 1562 follows those for 1565, one for 1574 is at the end of 1575, one for 1576 is at the end of 1577; there is an entry for 1580 about halfway through the 1581s; similarly, there is one for 1582 in the 1583s

and a 1583 in the 1584s. The entries for 1587 and 1588 are intermingled, and in the midst of these entries is a will for Miles Baldwin of Foldridgehey proven in 1597. There are also two entries for 1588 about halfway through 1589.

1590–1600 B   **89,438**

See the preceding entry for a will proven in 1597.

1551–1600 C   **89,439**

In fair chronological order through 1589. The entries for 1590–1600 are frequently filed chronologically but in reverse order, that is, from 1600–1590.

1553–1600 D   **89,440**

1574–1600 E–G   **89,441**

1547–1590 H   **89,442**

1591–1599 H   **89,443**

See film 89,455 for any entries of H for 1600.

1585–1600 I/J   **89,444**
1553–1600 K

1560–1600 L   **89,445**

Poor chronological order as follows: starts with an entry for 1600, then jumps back to 1560. There is an entry for 1578 about halfway through 1579, the entries for 1580 and 1581 are intermingled and include one for 1579, there are two entries for 1582 at the end of 1583, and after several entries for 1584 there is a jump to 1587 with one entry for 1585 about halfway through this mixture. Several entries for 1589–1591 appear at the end of 1593, including the will of Agnes Leigh, widow of Ashton in Winwick, who was incorrectly recorded in the printed index as Agnes Wright. The entries then jump to 1598 and work roughly backward to 1587–1588 with several wills filmed earlier repeated, including what looks like a more complete one for Agnes Leigh. The final entries build from 1593–1592 through 1594, jump to 1598–1599, add one for 1600, and then end with three for 1599.

1563–1600 M   **89,446**

Fair chronological order. See film 89,455 for another entry for 1600.

1562–1600 N   **89,447**
1572–1600 O

Fair chronological order.

1558–1600 P   **89,448**

Poor chronological order as follows: starts with an entry for 1561, reverts to 1558, and then jumps to 1571–1581. Between 1581 and 1582 is an unindexed will for John Pennington of Billinge for 1580. There is an entry for

1581 in the middle of 1582 and one for 1583 in the middle of 1584. Some intermingling occurs between 1590–1593. There is an entry for 1593 in the middle of 1594, one for 1596 in 1595, one for 1598 in 1597, two for 1597 in 1598, and 1598 is followed by an entry for 1600, whereupon the film ends with one for 1599. See film 89,455 for another entry for 1600.

1554–1600 R   **89,449**
See film 89,455 for another entry for 1600.

1549–1600 S   **89,450**
See film 89,455 for two more entries for 1600.

1533–1600 T   **89,451**
1590–1600 U
1550–1600 V
1582–1600 Y

1550–1587 W   **89,452**
The first three documents are repeated after 1584. There may be further repetitions.

1588–1593 W   **89,453**

1594–1600 W   **89,454**
See film 89,455 for another entry for 1600.

1582–1600 Y
See film 89,451 above.

1601   **89,455**
A short film that is not arranged alphabetically, plus it includes some entries for 1600 and one for 1602. The sequence is as follows: L, W, H, M, P, P, W for 1600, S, I, and H for 1600. All of the entries up to this point are then repeated in exactly the same order followed by: P for 1600; L, M for 1600; W, H for 1600; L, W for 1602; R for 1600; two S entries for 1600; C, T, G, I, T, F, H, H, T, W, G, B, and H. For missing documents, check the infra series, the act books, the miscellaneous section, and the first entry under the section entitled "Indexes and Calendars." Consult Camp's *Wills and Their Whereabouts* for details of records not filmed.

1602 A–W   **89,456**
Fair alphabetical sequence as follows: A–E (there is an M in the Bs), H, F–G, J–L (there is an E in the Ks), and M–W. Included are an inventory for Henry Ashcroft of Preston for 1607 and an unindexed inventory for Anne Tarleton, wife of John Tarleton. See film 89,455 above for another W.

1603   **89,457**
The alphabetical sequence is as follows: L, three As, four Bs, C, two Ds, four Es, F, G, ten Hs, G, J, three Ls, H, two Ls, P, two Ms, seven Ps, three Rs, T, S, two Ts, two Ss, W, Y, L, G, L, W, H, R, L, R, H, and A. See the note for 1601.

1604 A–Y   **89,458**

1605 A–W   **89,459**
Fair alphabetical sequence, except that G follows H, there is one L between R and S, and the only Y precedes W.

1606 A–Y   **89,460**

1607 A–Y   **89,461**
See film 89,456 above for another A.

1608 A–C   **89,462**

1608 C–H   **89,463**

1608 I–Y   **89,464**

1609 A–Y   **89,465**

1610 A–M   **89,466**

1610 M–W   **89,467**

1611 A–H   **89,468**

1611 I–W   **89,469**

1612 A–W   **89,470**

1613 A–P   **89,471**

1613 R–Y   **89,472**

1614 A–G   **89,473**

1614 H–O   **89,474**

1614 P–W   **89,475**

1615 A–K   **89,476**

1615 L–W   **89,477**

1616 A–G   **89,478**

1616 H–P   **89,479**
See film 89,480 for another P.

1616 R–Y   **89,480**
The Ws include the will and inventory of Nicholas Whitehead of Lymm, Ches., for 1617. The last entry on this film is actually the will and inventory of Thomas Piccop of Wolfenden.

1617 A–F   **89,481**

1617 G–M   **89,482**

1617 N–Y 89,483
See film 89,480 for another W.

1618 A–F 89,484

1618 G–M 89,485

1618 N–W 89,486

1619 A–G 89,487

1619 H–N 89,488

1619 P–Y 89,489

1620 A–G 89,490

1620 H–O 89,491

1620 P–Y 89,492

1621 A–G 89,493

1621 H–O 89,494

1621 P–Y 89,495

1622 A–G 89,496

1622 H–O 89,497
There is a U among the Hs.

1622 P–Y 89,498
See the preceding film for another U.

1623 A–E 89,499

1623 F–L 89,500

1623 M–R 89,501

1623 S–W 89,502

1624 A–F 89,503

1624 G–H 89,504
Good alphabetical sequence except for the first entry, which is an H.

1624 H–O 89,505

1624 P–Y 89,506

1625 A–K 89,507

1625 L–Y 89,508

1626 A–H 89,509

1626 I–Y 89,510

1627 A–H 89,511

1627 I–Y 89,512

1628 A–H 89,513

1628 I–Y 89,514

1629 A–H 89,515

1629 I–Y 89,516

1630 A–H 89,517
An E appears among the Bs.

1630 I–W 89,518

1631 A–H 89,519

1631 I–Y 89,520

1632 A–G 89,521

1632 H–P 89,522

1632 R–Y 89,523

1633 A–E 89,524

1633 F–L 89,525
See film 89,527 below for another H.

1633 M–N 89,526

1633 N–Y 89,527
An H appears between T and U/V.

1634 A–G 89,528

1634 H–P 89,529

1634 R–W 89,530

1635 A–H 89,531

1635 I–Y 89,532

1636 A–H 89,533

1636 I–Y 89,534
A Y appears among the Ws.

1637 A–E 89,535

1637 F–P 89,536

1637 R–Y	**89,537**	**1647 P–Y**	**89,558**
1638 A–G	**89,538**	**1648 A–H**	**89,559**
1638 H–M	**89,539**	**1648 I–Y**	**89,560**
1638 N–Y	**89,540**	**1649 A–G**	**89,561**

1649 A–G   **89,561**
See film 89,563 for another A.

1639 A–G   89,541   **1649 H–Y**   **89,562**

1639 H–R   89,542

1650   **89,563**
Fair chronological order as follows: it begins with an A
for 1649, the will and inventory of John Tarleton of
Liverpool is found at the start of the Cs, there is an H in
the Gs, an L in the Ms, and an M in the Ws.

1639 S–Y   89,543

1640 A–E   89,544

1640 F–N   89,545
This film starts with six entries of F for 1641, then an E
for 1641 followed by six more entries of F and five of G
for 1641. The remainder of the film is F–N for 1640.

1651–1659
Missing due to the Interregnum and Commonwealth. See
the probate decision table for further instructions.

1640 O–Y   89,546   **1660 A–Y**   **89,564**

1641 A–E   89,547   **1661 A–F**   **89,565**
See film 89,545 for another E.

1661 G–O   **89,566**

1641 F–N   89,548
See film 89,545 for more entries of F and G.

1661 P–Y   **89,567**

1641 O–Y   89,549   **1662 A–G**   **89,568**

1662 H–P   **89,569**

1642 A–H   89,550

1662 R–Y   **89,570**

1642 I–Y   89,551
The first entry is for Allard Vanwicke, merchant of
Dublin, who is listed in the printed index as Vanwyke
Allarti Rafen. Then follow entries for P, L, and K, after
which the alphabetical sequence returns to good order.

1663 A–C   **89,571**

1663 C–G   **89,572**

1663 H–L   **89,573**

1663 M–R   **89,574**

1643–1645   89,552
In alphabetical order by year. For missing documents
check the act books, the miscellaneous section, and the
first entry under the section entitled "Indexes and
Calendars." Consult Camp's *Wills and Their Whereabouts* for further details.

1663 S–Y   **89,575**

1664 A–H   **89,576**

1664 I–R   **89,577**

1646 A–H   89,553   **1664 S–Y**   **89,578**

1646 I–P   89,554   **1665 A–F**   **89,579**

1646 R–Y   89,555   **1665 F–M**   **89,580**

1647 A–G   89,556   **1665 N–Y**   **89,581**

1647 H–O   89,557   **1666 A–G**   **89,582**

1666 H–P	**89,583**	**1671 A–E**	**89,602**
1666 R–W	**89,584**	**1671 F–H**	**89,603**

1666 R–W   **89,584**
U/V comes before T.

1671 I–M   **89,604**

1667 A–G   **89,585**

1671 M–R   **89,605**

1667 H–O   **89,586**

1671 S–Y   **89,606**

1667 P–Y   **89,587**
There is a long list of creditors with the will of Arthur Scholfield that may be of value.

1672 A–B   **89,607**

1672 B–E   **89,608**

1668 A–G   **89,588**

1672 F–L   **89,609**

1668 H–P   **89,589**

1672 M–R   **89,610**

1668 R–Y   **89,590**
Y comes before W.

1672 S–Y   **89,611**

1673 A–E   **89,612**

1669 A–C   **89,591**

1673 F–L   **89,613**

1669 C–E   **89,592**

1673 M–Y   **89,614**

1669 F–H   **89,593**

1674 A–E   **89,615**

1669 H–L   **89,594**

1674 F–L   **89,616**

1669 M–R   **89,595**

1674 M–R   **89,617**

1669 S–Y   **89,596**

1674 S–Y   **89,618**
Y comes before W.

1670 A,G–H   **89,597**
The Bs and one C are on the next film. The entries for the rest of the Cs and D–F are missing, which is probably the case for many of the other entries for this year. For missing documents check the act books, the miscellaneous section, and the first entry under the section entitled "Indexes and Calendars." Consult Camp's *Wills and Their Whereabouts* for further details.

1675 A–H   **89,619**

1675 I–S   **89,620**
At least one R appears in the Ms.

1675 S–Y   **89,621**

1670 B–C   **89,598**
There is only one entry for C. See the note above for film 89,597.

1676 A–C   **89,622**

1676 D–E   **89,623**

1670 I–O   **89,599**
See film 89,597 for G–H and the note about D–F. The Ls on this film are followed by one N, then four Ps, another N, two Ps, two more Ns, and it ends with seven Os. The Ps continue on the next film. The inventory for Jane Langford of Withington appears with a miscellaneous collection of supra and infra documents on film 166,083, which is listed at the end of these supra original wills.

1676 E–H   **89,624**

1676 I–O   **89,625**

1676 P–S   **89,626**

1676 T–Y   **89,627**

1677 A–C   **89,628**

1670 P–S   **89,600**

1670 T–Y   **89,601**
Y comes before W.

1677 D–H   **89,629**

1677 I–S	**89,630**	**1684 I–O**	**89,655**
1677 T–Y	**89,631**	**1684 P–S,W**	**89,656**
The will of Ellen Young comes before the Ws and an inventory for Ellen Young follows the Ws.		For missing documents see the note under film 89,597.	
1678 A–H	**89,632**	**1685 A–F**	**89,657**
1678 I–Q	**89,633**	**1685 G–H**	**89,658**
The will of Henry Prescott of Eccleston, Ches., is filed here.		**1685 I–O**	**89,659**
1678 R–Y	**89,634**	**1685 P–S**	**89,660**
1679 A–H	**89,635**	**1685 S–Y**	**89,661**
1679 I–Y	**89,636**	**1686 A–E**	**89,662**
For missing documents see the note under film 89,597.		**1686 F–H**	**89,663**
1680 A–D	**89,637**	**1686 I–Q**	**89,664**
1680 E–H	**89,638**	**1686 R–Y**	**89,665**
1680 I–N	**89,639**	**1687 A–H**	**89,666**
1680 O–Y	**89,640**	**1687 I–Y**	**89,667**
See the note under film 89,636.		**1688 A–H**	**89,668**
1681 A–D	**89,641**	Some of the Gs are mixed in with the Fs.	
1681 E–H	**89,642**	**1688 I–Y**	**89,669**
1681 I–P	**89,643**	The Ks and Ls are intermixed.	
1681 R–Y	**89,644**	**1689 A–H**	**89,670**
1682 A–G	**89,645**	**1689 I–Y**	**89,671**
1682 H–P	**89,646**	**1690 A–H**	**89,672**
1682 R	**89,647**	**1690 I–N**	**89,673**
1682 S–Y	**89,648**	**1690 M–Y**	**89,674**
1683 A–F	**89,649**	**1691 A–G**	**89,675**
1683 G–M	**89,650**	**1691 H–Q**	**89,676**
1683 N–S	**89,651**	**1691 R–W**	**89,677**
1683 S–Y	**89,652**	There are entries for S before and after T.	
The second item is actually an infra admon for John Carter, mariner of Liverpool, dated 26 July 1809.		**1692 A–H**	**89,678**
1684 A–D	**89,653**	**1692 I–M**	**89,679**
1684 E–H	**89,654**	**1692 M–Y**	**89,680**
		1693 A–H	**89,681**

1693 I–S	89,682
1693 S–Y	89,683
1694 A–H	89,684
1694 I–S	89,685
1694 S–W	89,686
1695 A–H	89,687
1695 I–Y	89,688
1696 A–B	89,689
1696 B–H	89,690
1696 I–R	89,691
1696 R–Y	89,692

The admon of Jonathan Willoughby of Horwich appears with a miscellaneous collection of supra and infra documents on film 166,083, which is listed at the end of these supra original wills.

1697 A–H	89,693
1697 I–T	89,694
1697 T–Y	89,695
1698 A–B	89,696
1698 B–G	89,697
1698 H–O	89,698

One H comes after I.

1698 P–Y	89,699
1699 A–E	89,700
1699 F–K	89,701
1699 L–Y	89,702
1700 A–G	88,608

One M appears in the As.

1700 H–R	88,609

H not in order; some entries follow L with others after M. See film 88,608 for another M.

1700 S–Y	88,610

1701–1720
Some twenty registered copy wills for this period will be found at the front of the act books for 1811–1814 on film

90,105. They will be of value if the original cannot be found.

1701 A–G	88,611
1701 H–P	88,612
1701 R–Y	88,613
1702 A–H	88,614

A D appears about halfway through the As.

1702 I–Y	88,615
1703 A–G	88,616

The Hs are missing. They may have been filed incorrectly with the infra series or perhaps with either the supra or infra series for Cheshire. If not, contact the repository where the originals are kept. See Camp's *Wills and Their Whereabouts*.

1703 I–Y	88,617
1704 A–G	88,618
1704 H–M	88,619
1704 N–Y	88,620
1705 A–G	88,621
1705 H–R	88,622
1705 S–Y	88,623
1706 A–G	88,624
1706 H–Y	88,625
1707 A–G	88,626
1707 H–P	88,627
1707 R–Y	88,628
1708 A–H	88,629
1708 J–Y	88,630
1709 A–H	88,631

See film 88,633 for another G.

1709 I–R	88,632
1709 R–Y	88,633

An entry for Thomas Garnett, yeoman of Torbuck, appears in the Ws.

1710 A–F	88,634		
1710 G–M	88,635		
1710 N–Y	88,636		
1711 A–H	88,637		
1711 I–Y	88,638		
1712 A–H	88,639		
1712 I–Y	88,640		
1713 A–H	88,641		

ter were not found in the printed indexes. They are for Barbara Dod, spinster of London (will dated 22 May 1703 and proved 7 September 1721); Jane Allcock, spinster of Wilmslow, Ches. (will dated 2 May 1733); and Sarah Mather, widow of Tongue in Bolton, Lancs. (will dated 2 October 1738).

Intermingled with this set of wills are copies for: John Gardiner of Lancaster (will dated 21 June 1472) on page 113; Edward Russell, advocate in the ecclesiastical court of Chester (will dated 7 June 1665) on page 195; John Hutton, yeoman of Hindon in the parish of Crookfield, Durham (will dated 16 July 1657) on page 92; and James Arderne, Dean of Chester (will proved in 1691) on page 155.

1713 I–Y	88,642	1721 A–G	88,660
1714 A–H	88,643	1721 H–P	88,661
1714 I–Y	88,644	1721 R–Y	88,662
1715 A–H	88,645	1722 A–F	88,663
1715 I–Y	88,646	1722 G–L	88,664
1716 A–G	88,647	1722 M–R	88,665
1716 H–Y	88,648	1722 S–Y	88,666
1717 A–G	88,649	1723 A–E	88,667
1717 H–Y	88,650	1723 F–K	88,668
1718 A–G	88,651	1723 L–P	88,669
1718 H–L	88,652	1723 R–Y	88,670
1718 M–Y	88,653	1724 A–D	88,671
1719 A–H	88,654	1724 E–H	88,672
1719 I–Q	88,655	1724 I–P	88,673
1719 R–Y	88,656	1724 R–Y	88,674

1720 A–G   88,657
A B appears among the Gs and a C among the Ds.

		1725 A–E	88,675
1720 H–N	88,658	1725 F–L	88,676
1720 O–W	88,659	1725 M–R	88,677

1721–1740
Some fifty-five registered copy wills for this period will be found at the front of the act books for 1811–1814 on film 90,105. They will be of value if the original cannot be found. In fact, three of the wills copied into the regis-

		1725 S–Y	88,678
		1726 A–E	88,679
		1726 F–H	88,680

1726 I–P	**88,681**
1726 R–Y	**88,682**
1727 A–B	**88,683**

The will and inventory of Abram Bate, carpenter of Leyland, appears with a miscellaneous collection of supra and infra documents on film 166,083, which is listed at the end of these supra original wills.

1727 C–G	**88,684**
1727 H–K	**88,685**
1727 L–P	**88,686**
1727 R–T	**88,687**
1727 U/V–Y	**88,688**
1728 A–B	**88,689**
1728 C–F	**88,690**
1728 G–H	**88,691**
1728 I–O	**88,692**
1728 P–S	**88,693**
1728 T–Y	**88,694**
1729 A–B	**88,695**
1729 C–F	**88,696**
1729 G–H	**88,697**
1729 I–M	**88,698**
1729 N–S	**88,699**
1729 T–Y	**88,700**
1730 A–G	**88,701**
1730 H–O	**88,702**
1730 P–W	**88,703**
1731 A–G	**88,704**
1731 H–Y	**88,705**
1732 A–H	**88,706**
1732 I–Y	**88,707**

1733 A–H	**88,708**
1733 I–P	**88,709**
1733 R–Y	**88,710**
1734 A–H	**88,711**
1734 I–Y	**88,712**

An S appears among the Ts.

1735 A–G	**88,713**
1735 H–P	**88,714**
1735 R–Y	**88,715**
1736 A–H	**88,716**
1736 I–Y	**88,717**
1737 A–G	**88,718**
1737 H–Y	**88,719**
1738 A–G	**88,720**
1738 H–P	**88,721**
1738 Q–Y	**88,722**
1739 A–H	**88,723**
1739 I–Y	**88,724**
1740 A–H	**88,725**
1740 I–Y	**88,726**

1741–1760
Some eighteen registered copy wills for this period will be found at the front of the act books for 1811–1814 on film 90,105. They will be of value if the original cannot be found.

1741 A–G	**88,727**
1741 H–P	**88,728**
1741 R–W	**88,729**
1742 A–G	**88,730**
1742 H–P	**88,731**
1742 R–Y	**88,732**

A V follows W.

1743 A–G	88,733
1743 H–Y	88,734
1744 A–H	88,735
1744 I–Y	88,736
1745 A–O	88,737
1745 P–Y	88,738
1746 A–G	88,739
1746 H–R	88,740
1746 S–Y	88,741
1747 A–G	88,742
1747 H–P	88,743
1747 R–Y	88,744
1748 A–G	88,745
1748 H–Y	88,746
1749 A–H	88,747
1749 I–P	88,748
1749 R–Y	88,749
1750 A–G	88,750
1750 H–Y	88,751
1751 A–H	88,752
1751 I–Y	88,753
1752 A–G	88,754
1752 H–P	88,755
1752 R–W	88,756
1753 A–F	88,757
1753 G–O	88,758
1753 P–Y	88,759

1754 A–G   88,760
This film includes the will of John Butterworth, husbandman of Rochdale, for 1769. An H appears among the Gs.

1754 H–P   88,761
See the preceding film for another H.

1754 Q–W   88,762
See the next film for another W.

1755 A–G   88,763
The admon of Robert Wall of Manchester, son of Mary Wall, for 1754 appears at the end of the Gs.

1755 H–O	88,764
1755 P–Y	88,765
1756 A–G	88,766
1756 H–W	88,767
1757 A–G	88,768
1757 H–O	88,769
1757 P–W	88,770
1758 A–G	88,771
1758 H–P	88,772
1758 R–Y	88,773
1759 A–G	88,774
1759 H–O	88,775
1759 P–W	88,776
1760 A–F	88,777
1760 G–O	88,778
1760 P–Y	88,779

1761–1769
Some twelve registered copy wills for this period will be found at the front of the act books for 1811–1814 on film 90,105. They will be of value if the original cannot be found. In fact, two of the wills copied into the register were not found in the printed indexes. They are for Roger Parry, yeoman of Ridley, Ches. (will dated 3 April 1766), and John Wawn, yeoman of Mawdesley and Rufford, Lancs. (will dated 10 July 1768).

1761 A–F	88,780
1761 G–M	88,781
1761 N–Y	88,782

1762 A–E	**88,783**	**1768 P–Y**	**88,804**

1762 F–K   **88,784**

1769 A–F   **88,805**
See film 88,760 for another B.

1762 L–R   **88,785**

1769 G–P   **88,806**

1762 S–Y   **88,786**
The admon of James Sharrock, mariner of Liverpool, appears with a miscellaneous collection of supra and infra documents on film 166,083, which is listed at the end of these supra original wills.

1769 R–Y   **88,807**
U/V entries come between W and Y.

1770 A–G   **88,808**
The admon of Richard Bulkeley, mariner of Liverpool, appears in the same miscellaneous collection on film 166,083 as described above.

1763 A–G   **88,787**

1763 H–O   **88,788**

1770 H–O   **88,809**

1763 P–Y   **88,789**
A Q appears among the Ts.

1770 P–Y   **88,810**

1764 A–E   **88,790**

1771 A–G   **88,811**

1764 F–L   **88,791**

1771 H–O   **88,812**

1764 M–Y   **88,792**

1771 P–Y   **88,813**

1765 A–F   **88,793**

1772 A–G   **88,814**

1765 G–M   **88,794**

1772 H–O   **88,815**

1765 N–Y   **88,795**

1772 P–S   **88,816**

1766 A–F   **88,796**

1772 T–Y   **88,817**

1766 G–P   **88,797**
The admon of John McClumphy (not McClumpley as entered in the printed index), sailor of Liverpool, appears with a miscellaneous collection of supra and infra documents on film 166,083, which is listed at the end of these supra original wills.

1773 A–E   **88,818**

1773 F–L   **88,819**

1773 M–R   **88,820**

1773 S–Y   **88,821**

1766 R–Y   **88,798**

1774 A–E   **88,822**

1767 A–F   **88,799**

1774 F–K   **88,823**

1767 G–P   **88,800**
The admon of Elizabeth Gaskell, widow of Winstanley in Wigan, appears in the same miscellaneous collection on film 166,083 as described above.

1774 L–R   **88,824**

1774 S–W   **88,825**

1775 A–C   **88,826**

1767 R–Y   **88,801**

1775 D–H   **88,827**

1768 A–F   **88,802**
The will of Elizabeth Diggle, widow of Prestwich, appears in the same miscellaneous collection on film 166,083 as described above.

1775 I–P   **88,828**

1775 R–Y   **88,829**

1768 G–O   **88,803**

1776 A–D   **88,830**

1776 E–J	**88,831**	1783 L–P	**88,854**
1776 K–P	**88,832**	1783 R–Y	**88,855**
1776 R–Y	**88,833**	1784 A–G	**88,856**
1777 A–G	**88,834**	1784 H–Q	**88,857**

1777 A–G — A C appears among the Fs.

1777 H–O — **88,835**

1777 P–Y — **88,836**
The will of Henry Wilcock, dealer and chapman of Walton-in-the-Dale, appears with a miscellaneous collection of supra and infra documents on film 166,083, which is listed at the end of these supra original wills.

		1784 R–W	**88,858**
		1785 A–G	**88,859**
1778 A–G	**88,837**	1785 H–P	**88,860**
1778 H–P	**88,838**	1785 R–W	**88,861**
1778 R–Y	**88,839**	1786 A–G	**88,862**
1779 A–G	**88,840**	1786 H–O	**88,863**
1779 H–P	**88,841**	1786 P–Y	**88,864**
1779 R–Y	**88,842**	1787 A–F	**88,865**
1780 A–G	**88,843**	1787 G–O	**88,866**
1780 H–O	**88,844**	1787 P–Y	**88,867**
1780 P–Y	**88,845**		

1787 P–Y — An S appears among the Ts.

1781 A–F — **88,846**
A G appears among the Bs.

1781 G–O — **88,847**
See the preceding film for another G.

		1788 A–F	**88,868**
		1788 G–M	**88,869**
		1788 N–Y	**88,870**
		1789 A–B	**88,871**
1781 P–Y	**88,848**	1789 C–H	**88,872**
1782 A–G	**88,849**	1789 I–Q	**88,873**
1782 H–P	**88,850**	1789 R–Y	**88,874**
1782 R–Y	**88,851**	1790 A–G	**88,875**

1782 R–Y — A V appears before the Rs.

1783 A–F — **88,852**
The will of James Ashcroft, yeoman of Aughton, appears with a miscellaneous collection of supra and infra documents on film 166,083, which is listed at the end of these supra original wills.

		1790 H–O	**88,876**
		1790 P–Y	**88,877**
		1791 A–G	**88,878**
		1791 H–N	**88,879**
		1791 O–Y	**88,880**
		1792 A–E	**88,881**
1783 G–K	**88,853**	1792 F–H	**88,882**

1792 I–P	88,883	1798 T–Y	88,911
1792 R–Y	88,884	1799 A–B	88,912
1793 A–G	88,885	1799 B–C	88,913
1793 H–P	88,886	1799 D–F	88,914
1793 Q–Y	88,887	1799 G–H	88,915
1794 A–E	88,888	1799 I–K	88,916
1794 F–M	88,889	1799 L–O	88,917

1799 L–O: This film includes the will of Peter Le Cocq, native of Guernsey and merchant of Liverpool, written in Boston, Massachusetts, in 1797 and proven at this court in 1799. Also among the Ls will be found an admon for Thomas McKivett, mariner of ship *Sally*, of Liverpool, granted to his mother, Judith McKivett, widow of Carlingford, Louth, Ireland.

1794 M–Q	88,890		
1794 R–Y	88,891		

1794 R–Y: V comes after W.

1795 A–C	88,892	1799 P–R	88,918
1795 D–H	88,893	1799 S–V	88,919
1795 I–Q	88,894	1799 W–Y	88,920

1795 I–Q: A Q appears among the Ls.

		1800 A	88,921
1795 R–Y	88,895	1800 B	88,922
1796 A–E	88,896	1800 C–D	88,923
1796 F–H	88,897	1800 E–G	88,924
1796 I–P	88,898	1800 H–J	88,925
1796 R–Y	88,899	1800 K–L	88,926
1797 A–B	88,900	1800 M–O	88,927
1797 C–G	88,901	1800 P–S	88,928
1797 H	88,902	1800 T–Y	88,929
1797 I–P	88,903	1801 A	88,930
1797 R–S	88,904	1801 B	88,931

1801 B: The will of John Barlow, weaver of Little Hulton, appears with a miscellaneous collection of supra and infra documents on film 166,083, which is listed at the end of these supra original wills.

1797 T–Y	88,905		
1798 A–C	88,906	1801 C	88,932
1798 D–G	88,907	1801 D	88,933
1798 H–K	88,908	1801 E–H	88,934
1798 L–P	88,909		
1798 Q–S	88,910		

1801 H–L	88,935	1804 G–H	88,964
An L and a J appear among the Ks.			
		1804 H–K	88,965
1801 L–N	88,936		
		1804 L–P	88,966
1801 O–R	88,937		
		1804 R	88,967
1801 R–W	88,938		
		1804 R–T	88,968
1801 W–Y	88,939		
		1804 T–Z	88,969
1802 A–B	88,940		
		1805 A–B	88,970
1802 B–D	88,941		
		1805 B–D	88,971
1802 D	88,942		
		1805 D–E	88,972
1802 E–H	88,943		
		1805 F–H	88,973
1802 H	88,944		
		1805 H–K	88,974
1802 I–M	88,945		
		1805 L–P	88,975
1802 M–P	88,946		
		1805 P–R	88,976
1802 R–S	88,947	See film 88,978 for a Q.	
1802 S–W	88,948	1805 S–T	88,977
1802 W–Z	88,949	1805 T–Y	88,978
		A Q follows the Ys.	
1803 A–B	88,950		
		1806 A–C	88,979
1803 B–C	88,951		
		1806 C–E	88,980
1803 C–E	88,952		
		1806 F–G	88,981
1803 F–H	88,953		
		1806 G–H	88,982
1803 H–J	88,954		
		1806 H–K	88,983
1803 K–L	88,955		
		1806 L–M	88,984
1803 L–O	88,956		
		1806 M–P	88,985
1803 O–P	88,957		
		1806 Q–R	88,986
1803 R–S	88,958		
		1806 R–V	88,987
1803 S–T	88,959	A Y appears among the Ts.	
1803 T–Y	88,960		
		1806 V–Y	88,988
1804 A–B	88,961	See the preceding film for another Y.	
1804 C–E	88,962	1807 A	88,989
1804 F	88,963	1807 A–C	88,990

1807 C–E	88,991		1810 B–D	89,018
1807 F–H	88,992		1810 D–E	89,019
1807 H	88,993		1810 F–G	89,020
1807 I–M	88,994		1810 G–J	89,021
1807 M–P	88,995		1810 J–L	89,022
1807 P–R	88,996		1810 M	89,023
1807 R–W	88,997		1810 M–R	89,024
1807 W–Y	88,998		1810 S	89,025
1808 A–B	88,999		1810 S–W	89,026
1808 B–D	89,000		1810 W–Y	89,027
1808 D–F	89,001		1811 A–B	89,028
1808 G–H	89,002		1811 B–C	89,029
1808 H	89,003		1811 D–G	89,030

1811 D–G: E and F are intermixed.

1811 G–H — 89,031
The wills of Mrs. Dorothy Hoyle (formerly married to Worsley) of Haslingden and John Heywood, gentleman of Bury, appear with a miscellaneous collection of supra and infra documents on film 166,083, which is listed at the end of these supra original wills.

1808 I–K — 89,004

1808 K–O — 89,005

1808 O–P — 89,006

1808 R–S — 89,007

1808 S–Z — 89,008

1811 I–M — 89,032
Some Ps will be found with the Ms.

1809 A–B — 89,009

1809 B–D — 89,010

1811 M–R — 89,033
Some Rs will be found with the Ps. More Ps will be found on the preceding film.

1809 E–H — 89,011

1809 H–M — 89,012

1811 S–W — 89,034

1809 M — 89,013

1811 W–Y — 89,035

1809 N–S — 89,014
The letters of guardianship granted Silvester Robinson of the City of New York for the minor Samuel M. Neill are included on this film.

1812 A–B — 89,036

1812 B–C — 89,037

1812 C–E — 89,038

1812 F–H — 89,039

1809 S–W — 89,015
A V appears before T.

1812 H — 89,040

1809 W–Y — 89,016

1812 I–K — 89,041

1810 A–B — 89,017

1812 K–M — 89,042

1812 M–P	**89,043**	**1815 C–F**	**89,071**
1812 R–S	**89,044**	**1815 F**	**89,072**
1812 S–W See the next film for the Us.	**89,045**	**1815 G–H**	**89,073**
		1815 H–L	**89,074**
1812 W–Y U follows Y.	**89,046**	**1815 L**	**89,075**
1813 A–B	**89,047**	**1815 M–P**	**89,076**
1813 B–C	**89,048**	**1815 Q–S**	**89,077**
1813 C–D	**89,049**	**1815 S–W** See the next film for another T.	**89,078**
1813 E–G	**89,050**		
1813 G–H	**89,051**	**1815 W–Y** A T appears among the Ws.	**89,079**
1813 H–L	**89,052**	**1816 A**	**89,080**
1813 M–P	**89,053**	**1816 A–B**	**89,081**
1813 Q–R	**89,054**	**1816 B–E**	**89,082**
1813 R–W	**89,055**	**1816 E–F**	**89,083**
1813 W–Y	**89,056**	**1816 G–H**	**89,084**
1814 A–B	**89,057**	**1816 H**	**89,085**
1814 B–C	**89,058**	**1816 I–K**	**89,086**
1814 C–E	**89,059**	**1816 K–N**	**89,087**
1814 F–G	**89,060**	**1816 N–R** See the next film for a Q.	**89,088**
1814 G–H	**89,061**		
1814 H–K	**89,062**	**1816 S–T** A Q comes before S.	**89,089**
1814 L	**89,063**	**1816 T–Y**	**89,090**
1814 L–P	**89,064**	**1817 A–B**	**89,091**
1814 P–R	**89,065**	There are documents for William Ashton, translated from the Danish, consisting of about 100 pages. These are followed by the documents in Danish. William Ashton, merchant, resided in the Island of St. Croix in the West Indies but died in London, England.	
1814 S	**89,066**		
1814 S–W	**89,067**	**1817 B–C**	**89,092**
1814 W–Y	**89,068**	**1817 C**	**89,093**
1815 A	**89,069**	**1817 D–G**	**89,094**
1815 A–C	**89,070**	**1817 G–H**	**89,095**

1817 H–K	**89,096**
1817 L	**89,097**
1817 L–P	**89,098**
1817 P–R	**89,099**
1817 S	**89,100**
1817 S–W	**89,101**
1817 W–Y	**89,102**
1818 A–B	**89,103**

1818 B–C   **89,104**
Ends in the middle of a document. The next film picks up the remainder of that document.

1818 C–D   **89,105**
See the previous film for the beginning document.

1818 E–G	**89,106**
1818 G–H	**89,107**
1818 H	**89,108**
1818 I–L	**89,109**
1818 L–N	**89,110**
1818 N–P	**89,111**
1818 R–S	**89,112**
1818 S–T	**89,113**
1818 T–Y	**89,114**
1819 A–B	**89,115**
1819 B–D	**89,116**
1819 D–F	**89,117**
1819 G–H	**89,118**
1819 H–K	**89,119**
1819 L–N	**89,120**
1819 O–S	**89,121**
1819 S	**89,122**
1819 T–Y	**89,123**

1820 A–B	**89,124**

1820 B–C   **89,125**
See the next film for the rest of the last document.

1820 C–E   **89,126**
Begins with page 3 of a will continued from the previous film.

1820 E–F	**89,127**
1820 G–H	**89,128**
1820 H–J	**89,129**
1820 J–L	**89,130**
1820 M	**89,131**

1820 M–P   **89,132**
Some Ms are mixed with Os. See the next film for the rest of the last document.

1820 P–R   **89,133**
Begins with page 4 of the will of James Perry.

1820 S	**89,134**
1820 S–W	**89,135**
1820 W–Y	**89,136**
1821 A	**89,137**
1821 A–B	**89,138**
1821 B–E	**89,139**
1821 F–G	**89,140**
1821 G–H	**89,141**
1821 H–L	**89,142**
1821 M	**89,143**
1821 M–R	**89,144**
1821 S–T	**89,145**
1821 T–W	**89,146**
1821 W–Y	**89,147**
1822 A–B	**89,148**
1822 B–D	**89,149**

1822 D	89,150	1824 B–C	89,175

See the next film for the rest of the last will.

1822 E–G	89,151	1824 C–E	89,176

Begins with page 4 of the last will on the previous film.

1822 G–H	89,152		
1822 H	89,153	1824 F–H	89,177
1822 I–L	89,154	1824 H	89,178
1822 L–P	89,155	1824 I–K	89,179
1822 P	89,156	1824 L–M	89,180
1822 R–S	89,157	1824 M–P	89,181
1822 S–W	89,158	1824 P–Q	89,182
1822 W–Y	89,159	1824 R–S	89,183
1823 A	89,160	1824 S–T	89,184
1823 A–B	89,161	1824 U–Y	89,185
1823 B–C	89,162	1825 A–B	89,186

This film contains several pages of notarized documents, including a christening and a death certificate in Portuguese with an English translation, accompanying the admon of Justino da Silva Cerquinho. The printed index states that he was a merchant of Liverpool; actually, he was en route to Portugal after conducting business in Brazil and England when he died on board ship near Holyhead.

		1825 B	89,187
		1825 C	89,188
		1825 C–E	89,189
		1825 F–G	89,190
1823 D–E	89,163	1825 H	89,191
1823 F–G	89,164	1825 H–K	89,192
1823 G–H	89,165	1825 L	89,193
1823 H	89,166	1825 L–P	89,194
1823 I–K	89,167	1825 P–Q	89,195
1823 K–M	89,168	1825 R	89,196
1823 M–O	89,169	1825 R–S	89,197
1823 P–R	89,170	1825 T–W	89,198
1823 R–S	89,171	1825 W–Y	89,199
1823 T–W	89,172	1826 A–B	89,200
1823 W–Y	89,173	1826 B	89,201
1824 A–B	89,174	1826 C	89,202

1826 D	89,203	1828 H	89,232
1826 D–G	89,204	1828 H	89,233
1826 H	89,205	1828 I–L	89,234
1826 H–K	89,206	1828 L	89,235
1826 L	89,207	1828 M–O	89,236
1826 L–M	89,208	1828 P	89,237
1826 M–O	89,209	1828 P–R	89,238
1826 P–R	89,210	1828 S	89,239
1826 R–S	89,211	1828 T–W	89,240
1826 S–T	89,212	1828 W–Y	89,241
1826 U–Y	89,213	1829 A	89,242
1827 A–B	89,214	1829 A–B	89,243
1827 B–C	89,215	1829 B	89,244
1827 D–G	89,216	1829 C	89,245
1827 H	89,217	1829 C–E	89,246
1827 H	89,218	1829 F–G	89,247
1827 I–L	89,219	1829 H	89,248
1827 L	89,220	1829 H	89,249
1827 M	89,221	1829 H	89,250
1827 M–P	89,222	1829 I–K	89,251
1827 R	89,223	1829 K–M	89,252
1827 S	89,224	1829 M–N	89,253
1827 T	89,225	1829 O–S	89,254
1827 T–Z	89,226	1829 S	89,255
1828 A–B	89,227	1829 T–W	89,256
1828 B–C	89,228	1829 W–Y	89,257
1828 D–G	89,229	1830 A–B	89,258
1828 G	89,230	1830 B	89,259
1828 H	89,231	1830 B–C	89,260

1830 D–G	89,261	1832 H	89,290
1830 G	89,262	1832 H	89,291
1830 H	89,263	1832 I–K	89,292
1830 I–L	89,264	1832 K–L	89,293
1830 L–M	89,265	1832 M	89,294
1830 N–R	89,266	1832 N–P	89,295
1830 R	89,267	1832 R	89,296
1830 S	89,268	1832 S	89,297
1830 S–U	89,269	1832 T–W	89,298
1830 W–Z	89,270	1832 W	89,299
1831 A–B	89,271	1832 W–Y	89,300
1831 B	89,272	1833 A	89,301
1831 C–D	89,273	1833 B	89,302
1831 D–E	89,274	1833 B	89,303
1831 F–G	89,275	1833 C	89,304
1831 H	89,276	1833 D	89,305
1831 H	89,277	1833 D–F	89,306
1831 I–L	89,278	1833 G–H	89,307
1831 M–O	89,279	1833 H	89,308
1831 P	89,280	1833 I–L	89,309
1831 Q–S	89,281	1833 M	89,310
1831 S	89,282	1833 N–Q	89,311
1831 T–W	89,283	1833 R	89,312
1831 W–Y	89,284	1833 S	89,313
1832 A–B	89,285	1833 T	89,314
1832 B	89,286	1833 U–Y	89,315
1832 C	89,287	1834 A	89,316
1832 D	89,288	1834 B	89,317
1832 D–G	89,289	1834 B	89,318

1834 C	89,319	1836 A	89,344
1834 C–D	89,320	1836 B	89,345
1834 E–G	89,321	1836 B–C	89,346
1834 H	89,322	1836 C–F	89,347
1834 H	89,323	1836 G–H	89,348
1834 I–L	89,324	1836 H–J	89,349
1834 M–O	89,325	1836 J–M	89,350
1834 O–Q	89,326	1836 M–O	89,351
1834 R	89,327	1836 P–S	89,352
1834 S	89,328	1836 S–W	89,353
1834 T–V	89,329	1836 W–Y	89,354
1834 W–Y	89,330	1837 A–B	89,355
1835 A–B	89,331	1837 B–C	89,356

1835 A–B   89,331
The Bs continue on the next film, but it should also be noted here that film 90,124 supposedly contains A–B entries omitted in the "first take" on both films 89,331 and 89,332. There are also entries for Cheshire on film 90,124. A search of this film should be made for items missing from the other two or where the entries are unreadable.

1837 C   89,357
This film includes the will of Thomas Coward, gentleman of Chorley, which was not probated until 1841.

1835 B	89,332	1837 D–G	89,358
1835 C–D	89,333	1837 G	89,359
1835 D–E	89,334	1837 H	89,360
1835 F–G	89,335	1837 H–J	89,361
1835 G–H	89,336	1837 J–K	89,362
1835 H–K	89,337	1837 L	89,363
1835 L–M	89,338	1837 L–M	89,364

1835 L–M   89,338
See the next film for another L.

1835 M–P	89,339	1837 M–N	89,365
		1837 O–R	89,366

1835 M–P   89,339
An L will be found among the Ms.

1835 P–R	89,340	1837 R	89,367
1835 S	89,341	1837 S	89,368
1835 S–W	89,342	1837 S	89,369
1835 W–Y	89,343	1837 T	89,370
		1837 T–W	89,371

1837 W–Y   **89,372**

1838–1858
Not filmed; see the registered copy wills that follow this section. To contact the repository holding the original wills and admons for this time period, consult Camp's *Wills and Their Whereabouts*.

                                                166,083
This film is a miscellaneous collection of thirteen supra documents probated between 1670–1811 and forty-six infra documents probated between 1800–1855. The majority appear in the printed indexes but apparently were not filmed in their proper order. Each is listed in the stray-name index to this volume.

Supra Registered Copy Wills
for the Consistory Court of Chester

Apparently copy wills were never made for the infra series, and there are few for the supra series before 1838. In both cases, see the original wills. The supra registered copy wills for 1838–1845 were filmed twice over a six-year interval. The call numbers of the other filming are given below in parentheses.

1838   **89,373**
                                                (90,075)
Volume A

1838   **89,374**
                                                (90,075)
Volume 2

1838   **89,375**
                                                (90,076)
Volume 3

1838   **89,376**
                                                (90,076)
Volume 4

1838–1839   **89,377**
                                                (90,077)
Volume 5

1839   **89,378**
                                                (90,078)
Volume 6

1839   **89,379**
                                                (90,078)
Volume 7. It includes the will of James Wood, D.D., Master of St. John's College, Cambridge, and the Dean of Ely, which was recorded in the PCC and proven at Chester; see page 86. A will was registered for Bolton Jackson of Baltimore, Maryland; see page 533.

1839   **89,380**
                                                (90,079)
Volume 8

1839–1840   **89,381**
                                                (90,079)
Volume 9

1840   **89,382**
                                                (90,080)
Volume 10

1840–1841   **89,383**
                                                (90,081)
Volume 11. It includes the will of Samuel Hulme, brewer of Radcliffe, which was dated August 1828 and proven in 1840; see page 239.

1840–1841   **89,384**
                                                (90,082)
Volume 12

1841   **89,385**
                                                (90,083)
Volume 13

1841–1842   **89,386**
                                                (90,084)
Volume 14. It includes the will of John Dickenson, Esq. of Devonshire Place, London, recorded in the PCC and proven at Chester; see page 731. An admon with will annexed will be found at the end of the film; see page 475.

1841–1842   **89,387**
                                                (90,085)
Volume 15

1841–1842   **89,388**
                                                (90,086)
Volume 16

1842–1843   **89,389**
                                                (90,087)
Volume 17

1842–1843   **89,390**
                                                (90,088)
Volume 18

1843–1844   **89,391**
                                                (90,089)
Volume 19

1843–1844   **89,392**
                                                (90,090)
Volume 20

1843–1844   **89,393**
(90,091)

Volume 21

1844   **89,394**
(90,092)

Volume 22

1844–1845   **89,395**
(90,092)

Volume 22 (cont.)

1844–1845   **89,396**
(90,093)

Volume 23

1845   **89,397**
Volume 24

1845–1846   **89,398**
Volume 25

1845–1846   **89,399**
Volume 26

1846–1847   **89,400**
Volume 27. It includes some admons with will annexed.

1846–1847   **89,401**
Volume 28. It includes some admons with will annexed.

1846–1847   **89,402**
Volume 29. It includes some admons with will annexed.

1847–1848   **89,403**
Volume 30. It includes some admons with will annexed.

1847   **89,404**
Volume 31. It contains a group of sixteen 1846 wills.

1847–1849   **89,405**
Volume 32

1847–1848   **89,406**
Volume 33. It includes some admons with will annexed.

1847–1848   **89,407**
Volume 34. It includes the will of Ellen Little dated 1854; see pages 189–190.

1848–1850   **89,408**
Volume 35. It includes some admons with will annexed.

1848–1849   **89,409**
Volume 36

1848–1851   **89,410**
Volume 37. It includes some admons with will annexed.

1849–1851   **89,411**
Volume 38

1849–1850   **89,412**
Volume 39

1849–1850   **89,413**
Volume 40. It includes two wills extracted from the registry of the PCC.

1850–1852   **89,414**
Volume 41. It includes the will of Thomas Day made in England but proved and registered in New York on 26 May 1851.

1850–1852   **89,415**
Volume 42

1850–1852   **89,416**
Volume 43

1851–1852   **89,417**
Volume 44

1851–1853   **89,418**
Volume 45

1852–1854   **89,419**
Volume 46

1852–1854   **89,420**
Volume 47

1852–1854   **89,421**
Volume 48

1852–1853   **89,422**
Volume 49. It includes the will of George Blake dated 10 July 1830; see pages 839–840.

1853–1854   **89,423**
Volume 50

1853–1854   **89,424**
Volume 51

1854–1855   **89,425**
Volume 52. It includes the will of William Goore, Esq. of Liverpool and West Derby, with a first grant in February 1830; and a second grant in 1854.

1854–1856   **89,426**
Volume 53. It has some incorrect pagination.

1854–1855   **89,427**
Volume 54

1854–1856   **89,428**
Volume 55

1855–1856	**89,429**
Volume 56	

1856	**89,430**
Volume 57	

1856–1857	**89,431**
Volume 58. It includes the will of Griffith Edwards dated 1851.	

1856–1857	**89,432**
Volume 59	

1856–1857	**89,433**
Volume 60	

1857–1858	**89,434**
Volume 61. It contains extracts of several wills, which were first proven in the PCC.	

1857–1858	**89,435**
Volume 62. It has some incorrect pagination.	

Infra Original Wills, Admons, and Inventories for the Consistory Court of Chester

---

1533–1589
Missing. Apparently infra probates were not recorded separately in this court until 1590 or none of the original records has survived. Check the supra probates described previously.

1590–1591,	**89,703**
1600 A–W,	
1602 A–Y	

This film contains only three documents for 1590–1591. The section for 1600 begins and ends with the same will and inventory of Grace Worsley, widow of Barton. Otherwise, the alphabetical sequence is regular except for an L entry, which appears before the last H. See the next note.

1592–1599,
1601, 1603
Missing. Either they never existed, are now lost, or may have been filed incorrectly with the supra series or perhaps even the infra and supra series for Cheshire. The act books or the repository where the originals are kept may have further information. See Camp's *Wills and Their Whereabouts*.

1604 A–Y	**89,704**

1605, 1608 A–Y	**89,705**

There is only one document for 1605; see the note for 1592–1599.

1606–1607
Missing. See the note for 1592–1599.

1608
See film 89,705 above.

1609 A–Y	**89,706**

1610 A–Y	**89,707**

1611
Missing. See the note for 1592–1599.

1612–1613 A–Y	**89,708**
1616, 1619 A–Y	

Each year has its own alphabetical sequence.

1614–1615
Missing. See the note for 1592–1599.

1616
See film 89,708 above.

1617–1618
Missing. See the note for 1592–1599.

1619
See film 89,708 above.

1620
Missing. See the note for 1592–1599.

1621, 1624,	**89,709**
1627–1628 A–Y	

Each year has its own alphabetical sequence.

1622–1626
Missing. See the note for 1592–1599. Part of 1624 will be found on film 89,709.

1627–1628
See film 89,709 above.

1629
Missing. See the note for 1592–1599.

1630–1631 A–Y	**89,710**
1633, 1635 A–Y	
1636–1637 A–Y	
1640–1641	

Each year has its own alphabetical sequence. There are only a few documents for 1640–1641; see the note for 1592–1599.

1632, 1634,
1638–1639
Missing. See the note for 1592–1599. See film 89,710 for 1633, 1635–1637.

1640–1641
See film 89,710.

1642–1659
Missing, due to the Civil War and Commonwealth. See the probate decision table for further instructions. Some infra records for 1642–1650 may have been filed with the supra series.

1660,   89,711
1661 A–W
There are only a few documents for 1660; see the note for 1592–1599.

1662
Missing. See the note for 1592–1599.

1663 A–Y   89,712

1664–1665 A–Y   89,713
Each year has its own alphabetical sequence.

1666 A–Y   89,714

1667 A–Y   89,715
Includes a W for 1668.

1668 A–Y   89,716
See the preceding film for another W.

1669–1670 A–Y   89,717
Each year has its own alphabetical sequence.

1671–1672 A–Y   89,718
Each year has its own alphabetical sequence.

1673–1674 A–Y   89,719
Each year has its own alphabetical sequence.

1675 A–Y   89,720

1676–1677 A–Y   89,721
Each year has its own alphabetical sequence.

1678–1679 A–Y   89,722
Each year has its own alphabetical sequence.

1680–1681 A–Y   89,723
Each year has its own alphabetical sequence.

1682–1683 A–Y   89,724
Each year has its own alphabetical sequence.

1684–1685 A–Y   89,725
Each year has its own alphabetical sequence.

1686 A–Y   89,726

1687 A–G   89,727

1687 G–T   89,728

1687 T–Y   89,729

1688 A–E   89,730

1688 E–Y   89,731

1689 A–L   89,732

1689 L–Y   89,733

1690 A–B   89,734

1690 B–R   89,735

1690 S–Y   89,736

1691 A–Y   89,737

1692 A–C   89,738

1692 C–L   89,739

1692 L–Y   89,740

1693 A–Y   89,741
See the next film for supplemental wills for this year.

1693 A–Y   89,742
The supplementary documents for this year were found at a later date and are indexed separately in both volumes 18 and 63 of the printed index, which see for further information.

1694 A–Y   89,743

1695 A–Y   89,744

1696 A–Y   89,745

1697 A–Y   89,746

1698 A–Y   89,747

1699 A–Y   89,748

1700 A–Y   89,749

1701–1702 A–Y   89,750
Each year has its own alphabetical sequence. For 1701 an A appears in the Bs; an H comes between T and W; an R appears in the Hs; and the order at the end of the Ss goes S, R, T, S, T before settling into alphabetical sequence again. For 1702 a Y appears in the Hs.

1703–1704 A–Y   89,751
Each year has its own alphabetical sequence.

1705–1706 A–Y   **89,752**
Each year has its own alphabetical sequence.

1707–1708 A–Y   **89,753**
Each year has its own alphabetical sequence.

1709–1710 A–Y   **89,754**
Each year has its own alphabetical sequence. For 1710 a
W appears about halfway through the Ss.

1711–1712 A–Y   **89,755**
Each year has its own alphabetical sequence.

1713–1714 A–Y   **89,756**
Each year has its own alphabetical sequence.

1715–1717 A–Y   **89,757**
Each year has its own alphabetical sequence.

1718–1719 A–Y   **89,758**
Each year has its own alphabetical sequence. For 1719
two Bs come between O and P, an F comes between G
and H; another F comes between S and T, and an M
appears after the first W.

1720–1721 A–Y   **89,759**
Each year has its own alphabetical sequence. For 1720 a
B comes after P, two Ds come between W and Y, an N
comes before R, and an S appears in the Hs.

1722–1728
Missing. See the note for 1592–1599.

1729–1730 A–B   **89,760**

1729–1730 B–L   **89,761**

1729–1730 L–Y   **89,762**
R comes after S. This film includes the admon for
Elizabeth Mayall of Ashton-under-Lyne, which was
involved in probate both in 1743 and 1744.

1731–1732 A–M   **89,763**

1731–1732 M–Y   **89,764**

1733–1734 A–L   **89,765**

1733–1734 L–Y   **89,766**

1735–1736 A–S   **89,767**

1735–1736 S–Y   **89,768**

1737–1738 A–Y   **89,769**

1739–1740 A–Y   **89,770**

1741–1742 A–Y   **89,771**

1743–1744 A–Y   **89,772**

1745–1746 A–Y   **89,773**

1747–1748 A–Y   **89,774**
Each year has its own alphabetical sequence.

1749–1750 A–Y   **89,775**
Each year has its own alphabetical sequence. For 1750 a
Q appears before the Ws.

1751–1752 A–Y   **89,776**
Each year has its own alphabetical sequence.

1753–1754 A–Y   **89,777**
Each year has its own alphabetical sequence.

1755–1757 A–Y   **89,778**
Each year has its own alphabetical sequence.

1758–1775
Missing. See the note for 1592–1599.

1776 A–Y   **89,779**

1777–1779 A–Y   **89,780**
Each year has its own alphabetical sequence.

1780–1781 A–Y   **89,781**
Each year has its own alphabetical sequence.

1782–1783 A–Y   **89,782**
Each year has its own alphabetical sequence; however,
there are not many documents for either of these years;
see the note for 1592–1599. For 1783 there are two As
among the Bs and an F appears in the Js.

1784 A–Y   **89,783**

1785 A–Y   **89,784**

1786 A–Y   **89,785**

1787 A–Y   **89,786**

1788 A–Y   **89,787**

1789 A–Y   **89,788**

1790 A–O   **89,789**

1790 O–Y   **89,790**

1791 A–H   **89,791**
The wills of John Gabbot, yeoman of Withnell in the
parish of Leyland; Hugh Green, mariner of Liverpool;
John Gill, mariner of Liverpool; Cunningham Glass,

mariner of Liverpool; Luke Grant, mariner of Liverpool; James Gafney, mariner of Liverpool; Abigail Gorton, widow of Bury; David Gravel, mariner of Liverpool; Edward Gurney, ship's steward of Liverpool; Samuel Gaskin, mariner of Liverpool; Martin Groat, mariner of Liverpool; and Martin Grote, mariner of Liverpool; plus an admon for Hannah Gladdi, widow of Liverpool, appear with a miscellaneous collection of infra documents on film 166,082, which is listed at the end of these infra original wills.

1791 H–Y   **89,792**
The will of Peter Klawson, mariner of Liverpool; the admons of Andrew Kane, Benjamin Kay, and Michael Killin, all mariners of Liverpool, and of James Knight, gentleman of Manchester; as well as the wills of John Kempster, shoemaker of Liverpool, John Kendrick, mariner of Liverpool, and John Kearns, mariner of Liverpool appear with a miscellaneous collection of infra documents on film 166,082, which is listed at the end of these infra original wills.

1792 A–C   **89,793**

1792 C–Y   **89,794**

1793 A–P   **89,795**

1793 P–Y   **89,796**

1794 A–Y   **89,797**

1795 A–K   **89,798**

1795 K–Y   **89,799**

1796 A–Y   **89,800**
An R appears among the Bs.

1797 A–F   **89,801**

1797 F–Y   **89,802**

1798 A–O   **89,803**

1798 O–Y   **89,804**

1799 A–G   **89,805**

1799 G–Y   **89,806**

1800 A–H   **89,807**

1800 H–O   **89,808**

1800 O–Y   **89,809**
The will of William Yeats, mariner of Liverpool, appears with a miscellaneous collection of supra and infra documents on film 166,083, which is listed at the end of the supra original wills.

1801 A–J   **89,810**

1801 J–R   **89,811**

1801 R–Z   **89,812**

1802 A–B   **89,813**

1802 B–H   **89,814**

1802 H–R   **89,815**

1802 R–Y   **89,816**

1803 A–L   **89,817**

1803 L–Z   **89,818**

1804 A–Y   **89,819**

1805 A–J   **89,820**

1805 K–Y   **89,821**
The will and admon of Elizabeth Needham, spinster of Manchester, and an admon, which is not listed in the printed index, for Fairhurst Nelson, cooper and mariner on the ship *Mary and Hannah*, whose next of kin was a brother Samuel Nelson, cabinetmaker of Liverpool, appear with a miscellaneous collection of infra documents on film 166,082, which is listed at the end of these infra original wills.

Probate records for eleven other persons will be found in the miscellaneous collection of supra and infra documents on film 166,083, which is listed at the end of the supra original wills. They are as follows: Joseph Noble, mariner of Liverpool, admon, will, and a note; Samuel Needham, plumber and glazier of Manchester, will and admon; John Needham, bachelor of Manchester, admon; Joseph Nelson, mariner of the ship *Commerce* of Liverpool, admon; John Oakes of Atherton, will; Hugh Owens, mariner of Liverpool, admon; James Ogden of Lowsides in Oldham, will; Thomas Ogden, joiner of Blackburn, will; Benjamin Nixon, cordwainer of Ardwick in Manchester, admon; Andries Neandee, mariner of Liverpool, will; and Robert Naulbury, mariner of Liverpool, admon.

1806 A–M   **89,822**
The will of George Greenhalgh, yeoman of Ainsworth, appears with a miscellaneous collection of supra and infra documents on film 166,083, which is listed at the end of the supra original wills.

1806 M–Y   **89,823**
The wills of Esther Stott, spinster of Salford, and Samuel Renshaw, whitster of Pilsworth in Middleton, appear with a miscellaneous collection of supra and infra documents

on film 166,083, which is listed at the end of the supra original wills.

1807 A–O   **89,824**
The will of James Halliwell, yeoman of Sharples in Bolton, and the admon of Joseph Goddard, cabinetmaker of Halifax, Yorks., appear with a miscellaneous collection of supra and infra documents on film 166,083, which is listed at the end of the supra original wills.

1807 O–Y   **89,825**
The will of William Smith, plaisterer and painter of Hampson Delph near Worsley, appears with a miscellaneous collection of supra and infra documents on film 166,083, which is listed at the end of the supra original wills.

1808 A–E   **89,826**

1808 E–Y   **89,827**
The will of John Whitehead of Rochdale appears with a miscellaneous collection of infra documents on film 166,082, which is listed at the end of these infra original wills.

The will of Mally Wilde, widow of Prestwich, is located in a similar collection on film 166,083, which is listed at the end of the supra original wills.

1809 A–Y   **89,828**
The admon of Abraham Mason, coalminer of Hollinwood in Oldham, and two wills and an admon for Thomas Melledew, yeoman of Middleton, appear with a miscellaneous collection of supra and infra documents on film 166,083, which is listed at the end of the supra original wills. The admon for John Carter, mariner of Liverpool, will be found with the supra documents on film 89,652.

1810 A–Y   **89,829**
The wills of James Cave, yeoman of Down Holland, Mary Lythgoe, widow of West Leigh, and Ellis Nutter, yeoman of Fence Gate in the Forest of Pendle; plus admons for William Robinson, laborer of Wray, and Mary Wrigley, spinster of Castleton in Rochdale, appear with a miscellaneous collection of supra and infra documents on film 166,083, which is listed at the end of the supra original wills.

1811 A–Y   **89,830**
The admon of Ann Thornton of Colne appears with a collection of supra and infra documents on film 166,083, which is listed at the end of the supra original wills.

1812 A–Y   **89,831**

1813 A–Y   **89,832**

1814 A–Y   **89,833**
Films 89,833 and 89,834 overlap, but it is not known if they cover exactly the same material. They are not in the same order and there may be information on one which is not on the other.

1814 C–W   **89,834**

1815 A–Y   **89,835**
Part of the Ts come before the Rs. The wills of Ann Meadows, widow of Netherton in Sephton, and David Morris, yeoman of Horwich, appear with a miscellaneous collection of supra and infra documents on film 166,083, which is listed at the end of the supra original wills.

1816 A–Y   **89,836**

1817 A–Y   **89,837**

1818 A–Y   **89,838**

1819 A–Y   **89,839**

1820 A–Y   **89,840**

1821 A–E   **89,841**

1821 E–Y   **89,842**

1822 A–Y   **89,843**

1823 A–Y   **89,844**

1824 A–W   **89,845**
The Es follow the Fs.

1825 A–Y   **89,846**

1826 A–R   **89,847**

1826 R–W   **89,848**

1827 A–H   **89,849**

1827 H–Y   **89,850**
The Ps come between N and O.

1828 A–Y   **89,851**

1829 A–Y   **89,852**

1830 A–M   **89,853**

1830 M–Y   **89,854**

1831 A–L   **89,855**

1831 L–Y	**89,856**

1832 A–Y	**89,857**

1833 A–L	**89,858**

1833 L–Y	**89,859**

A Q and V follow Y.

1834 A–M	**89,860**

Three admons for Betty Mills of Smallbridge in Rochdale appear with a miscellaneous collection of supra and infra documents on film 166,083, which is listed at the end of the supra original wills.

1834 N–Y	**89,861**

1835 A–Y	**89,862**

The will of Jesse Delap, widow of Toxteth Park, appears with a miscellaneous collection of supra and infra documents on film 166,083, which is listed at the end of the supra original wills.

1836 A–F	**89,863**

The will of Thomas Brown, mariner of Liverpool, appears with a miscellaneous collection of supra and infra documents on film 166,083, which is listed at the end of the supra original wills.

1836 F–W	**89,864**

An R and V appear between J and K. There is another V entry just before the end of the Ps.

1837 A–L	**89,865**

Probate records for five persons will be found in the miscellaneous collection of supra and infra documents on film 166,083, which is listed at the end of the supra original wills. They are as follows: John Hall, mariner of Liverpool, admon; John Hardey, yeoman of Flixton, will and admon; Jeremy Halliwell, weaver of Rumworth in Dean, will; Peter Jones, mariner of Liverpool, two admons; John Haworth the elder, cotton weaver of Whittle Le Woods, will.

1837 L–Z	**89,866**

Probate records for three persons will be found in the same collection as described in the preceding note. They are for: Edmund Rostrown, weaver of Whitworth in Rochdale, two admons; Robert Richardson, yeoman of Garston, will and two admons; and Elizabeth Tasker, widow of Liverpool, will.

1838 A–Z	**89,867**

An I comes after the Ls. The will and admon of James Millington, gentleman of Winwick, appears with a miscellaneous collection of supra and infra documents on film 166,083, which is listed at the end of the supra original wills.

1839 A–L	**89,868**

A G appears in the Cs. The will of James Cameron of Salford, and the admon of John Harding, gentleman of Newton, appear with a miscellaneous collection of supra and infra documents on film 166,083, which is listed at the end of the supra original wills.

1839 L–Z	**89,869**

1840 A–M	**89,870**

The will of Ellen Almond, widow of Southport in North Meols, appears with a miscellaneous collection of infra documents on film 166,082, which is listed at the end of these infra original wills.

1840 M–Z	**89,871**

1841 A–Z	**89,872**

1842 A–G	**89,873**

1842 G–Z	**89,874**

1843 A–O	**89,875**

1843 O–Z	**89,876**

A U appears in the Os.

1844 A–Z	**89,877**

An R will be found among the Ns. The admon of James Duckworth, beer seller of Musbury in Bury, appears with a miscellaneous collection of infra documents on film 166,082, which is listed at the end of these infra original wills.

1845 A–L	**89,878**

1845 L–Z	**89,879**

A U appears in the Ws.

1846 A–R	**89,880**

1846 R–Z	**89,881**

1847 A–Z	**89,882**

The will for a Rimmer is mistakenly identified as Kimmer and filed among the Ks. Another R appears just before the Ls.

1848 A–H	**89,883**

1848 H–P	**89,884**

1848 P–Z	**89,885**

1849 A–F	**89,886**

1849 F–Z	**89,887**

1850 A–H **89,888**

1850 H–T **89,889**

Some of the Ls come between H and J. The wills of Richard Pickering, yeoman of Lower Darwen in Blackburn, and Mary Houlton, widow of Newton Heath in Manchester, appear with a miscellaneous collection of infra documents on film 166,082, which is listed at the end of these infra original wills.

1850 T–Z **89,890**

1851 A–G **89,891**

1851 G–S **89,892**

1851 S–Z **89,893**

1852 A–G **89,894**

The admon of Ann Follitt, widow of Eccles, appears with a miscellaneous collection of infra documents on film 166,082, which is listed at the end of these infra original wills.

1852 G–Z **89,895**

Probate records for seven persons will be found in the miscellaneous collection of infra documents on film 166,082, which is listed at the end of these infra original wills. They are as follows: Ellen Percival, widow of Hulme in Manchester, admon; Thomas Porter, bricklayer of Bretherton in Croston, will; John Pickett, collier of Parr in Prescot, will; John Pritchard, joiner of Liverpool, will; Thomas Yeoman, painter of Little Woolton in Childwall, will; George Yates, corn dealer of Hulme in Manchester, admon; and William Prestwich, silk weaver of Audenshaw in Ashton under Lyne, admon.

1853 A–L **89,896**

1853 L–Z **89,897**

1854 A–G **89,898**

1854 G–Z **89,899**

1855 A–L **89,900**

The admon of Mary Ann Evans of Manchester, and the will with codicil of Samuel Brundrett, market gardener of Didsbury in Manchester, appear with a miscellaneous collection of infra documents on film 166,082, which is listed at the end of these infra original wills.

1855 L–Z **89,901**

An O will be found among the Rs. The admon of Sarah Nightingale, formerly the wife of a Haslam then of Richard Nightingale, weaver of Aspull, appears with a miscellaneous collection of supra and infra documents on film 166,083, which is listed at the end of the supra original wills.

1856 A–Z **89,902**

1857 A–V **89,903**

1857 V–Z **89,904**

1858 **89,905**

There are twelve to thirteen documents on this roll, and they are not in alphabetical order of any kind.

166,082

This film is a miscellaneous collection of thirty-eight infra documents, only one of which for the pre–1840 period was not in the printed indexes. Twenty-one of the documents are from the Gs and Ks of 1791. Two were probated in 1805; one each in 1808, 1840, and 1844; two each in 1850 and 1855. The remaining eight were for 1852 and include one F, five Ps, and two Ys. Each is listed in the stray-name index to this volume.

Supra Act Books for the Consistory Court of Chester

Index **90,094**

Books A–H, vols. 474–478. This film is a partial index to the supra act books, probably for 1690–1822. Since the act books are arranged chronologically, it is easier to look for the required date in the films that follow rather than try to match up an entry from this index.

1580–1581

Missing. See the caveats and the bill books listed in the miscellaneous section for possible information to bridge this gap. (Some of the early entries microfilmed under the category of caveats look suspiciously like act books.)

1582–1592 **166,149**

No book or volume numbers are given, but these do not seem to be caveats or bill books. They have the appearance of act books.

1593–1595

Missing. See the above note for 1580–1581.

1596–1617 **90,095**

Books 1–2, vols. 435–436. The entries jump from 18 September 1601 to 11 July 1608, then continue chronologically to 6 July 1609, and then revert to 22 September 1601. Volume 435 ends with 1 July 1608. Volume 436 begins with 20 December 1608, jumps back to June 1608, but by the third page it settles back into a chronological routine starting with 13 July 1609.

1617–1635 **90,096**

Books 3–4, vols. 437–438.

1635–1644,   **90,097**
1649
Book 5, vol. 439.

1645–1660
Except for two entries in 1649, this period is missing due
to the Interregnum and Commonwealth. See the probate
decision table for further instructions.

1661–1667   **90,097**
Book 6, vol. 440.

1667–1676   **90,098**
Books 7–8, vols. 441–442.

1676–1692   **90,099**
Books 9–10, vols. 443–444.

1693–1695   **90,100**
Book 11, vol. 445.

1695–1718
Missing. See the note above for 1580–1581.

1719–1723   **90,100**
Book 12, vol. 446.

1723–1727
Missing. See the note above for 1580–1581.

1728–1736   **90,100**
Book 13, vol. 447.

1736–1741   **90,101**
Book 14, vol. 448.

1741–1765
Missing. See the note above for 1580–1581.

1765–1777   **90,101**
Books 15–16, vols. 449–450.

1777–1793   **90,102**
Books 17–18, vols. 451–452.

1794–1803   **90,103**
Books 19–20, vols. 453–454.

1804–1811   **90,104**
Books 21–22, vols. 455–456.

1811–1819   **90,105**
Books 23–24, vols. 457–458. The act book entries start
on page 274. Pages 1–271 contain 105 registered copy
wills for 1701–1769, of which more than half are actually for 1721–1740. There is an index to these wills at
the start of the film, but it does not include those registered from 1741–1769. These remaining thirty wills are
arranged chronologically rather than alphabetically.

1819–1824   **90,106**
Book 25, vol. 459.

1824–1831   **90,107**
Books 26–27, vols. 460–461.

1831–1839   **90,108**
Books 28–29, vols. 462–463.

1839–1842   **90,109**
Book 30, vol. 464.

1842–1844   **90,110**
Book 31, vol. 465.

1844–1846   **90,111**
Book 32, vol. 466.

1846–1848   **90,112**
Book 33, vol. 467.

1848–1850   **90,113**
Book 34, vol. 468.

1850–1851   **90,114**
Book 35, vol. 469.

1851–1853   **90,115**
Book 36, vol. 470.

1853–1855   **90,116**
Book 37, vol. 471.

1855–1857   **90,117**
Books 38–39, vols. 472–473.

Infra Act Books for the
Consistory Court of Chester

1580–1660
Any entries before 1660 should have been recorded with
the supra series.

1660–1668   **90,121**
Volume 484. Starts with 1663, reverts to 1660–1663,
followed by an index for 1660–1668 which is arranged
by year and alphabetized. The act entries start again in
the following yearly order: 1663, 1666, 1667, 1663,
1662, and 1663.

1668–1729
Missing. See the caveats and the bill books listed in the
miscellaneous section for possible information to bridge
this gap.

1729–1740   **90,121**
Volume 485

1741–1765
Missing. See the note above for 1668–1729.

1765–1800   **90,121**
Volumes 486–488

1801–1826
Missing. See the note above for 1668–1729.

1826–1858   **90,122**
Volumes 489–490

---

*Miscellaneous: Abstracts, Documents,
and Select Indexes for
Probates Relating to Lancashire*

Some information from the Consistory Court of Chester
(see Cheshire for additional details) has been compiled
and partially published. Although not complete, searches
in this material may accelerate research or supplement
previous findings. It is presumed that the researcher
would compare any discoveries in printed abstracts with
the original records for other details and possible transcription errors.

1) 1580–1807 Caveat Books

These warning notices often contain information similar
to that of an act book; however, their coverage would be
restricted depending on what value another party might
place on delaying probate action. They could supplement
the act books or actual probate information and be used
as a substitute for the periods where either the supra or
infra act books are missing. In the case of this court, the
entries are frequently statistical accounts tied to a visitation. Their breakdown on film is as follows:

1580–1587   **395,070**
                                                  (item 1)
Books 1–4

1587–1602   **90,120**
Vol. 483. Despite the change from book to volume, these
seem to be part of the same records as found on films
395,069–395,072 and fit nicely the gap on film 395,070.
Two entries for 1603 are attached to the entries for 1592,
and one for 1602 appears among those for 1600.

1683–1705   **395,070**
Books 5–24. There are no entries for 1685, 1687–1689,
1692–1693, 1698.

1706–1730   **395,071**
Books 25–53. There are no entries for 1714–1715, 1717,
1726. Further entries for 1723–1725 appear on the next
film.

1733–1770   **395,072**
Books 54–76. There are no entries for 1754–1759. Book
56 contains an absolution from excommunication.

1723–1725   **395,072**
                                                  (last item)
Following Book 76 are several pages of supra and infra
entries for this time period, whereas the preceding entries
all seem to have been supra ones.

1799–1802,   **395,069**
1807
Vols. 1–2. These all seem to be infra entries. Volume 1
has two entries for 1799, one for 1800, two for 1801, one
for 1802, followed by another for 1800. Volume 2 seems
to be a thorough coverage for the year 1807 but goes
from September–December, followed by January–
August.

2) 1701–1826 Bill Books

These ledgers may have accompanied the act books.
Sometimes they give information comparable to act
books as in the sections for 1722–1727, 1778–1782, and
1789–1797. Otherwise, they tend to list mainly names
with columns of sums representing fees charged for probating or other diocesan services and expenditures of the
court. The overlapping time periods seem to be due to a
mixing of account books with day books. If so, the day
books are the ones most likely to give information similar to an act book. Their breakdown on film is as follows:

1701–1706,   **166,150**
1722–1727,
1725–1729

1737–1746,   **166,151**
1730–1752

1754–1759,   **166,152**
1756–1765

1771–1776,   **166,153**
1778–1782,
1777–1784

1789–1797   **166,154**

1791–1803,   **166,155**
1798–1803

1803–1808   **166,156**

1810–1812,   **166,157**
1811–1812

1813–1815,   **166,158**
1816–1818

1823–1824,	**166,159**
1824–1826	

3) 1521–1800 Probate Documents Used in Testamentary Suits

This is a large filmed collection of various documents gathered together as evidence in several thousand cases. It may contain some wills no longer found with the originals. The documents are filed alphabetically by the first two letters of the testator's surname.

FHL 942.7 B4Lc

The Lancashire & Cheshire Record Society published an index to this collection as follows: 1487–1620 (vol. 33, 3d part, also on film 823,508, 4th item and fiche 6,072,939), 1621–1700 (vol. 43, also on film 823,510, 4th item and fiche 6,072,949), and 1701–1800 (vol. 52, 2d part, also on film 823,512, 4th item). The filmed collection is outlined below.

1541–1620 A	**166,084**
1547–1620 B–C	**166,085**
1547–1620 D–F,	**166,086**
1539–1620 G	
1540–1620 H	**166,087**
1521–1620 I–L,	**166,088**
1525–1620 M–P	

Two Ls appear before I. The Ps are not arranged strictly alphabetically.

1541–1620 R–S	**166,089**
1532–1620 T–Y	**166,090**

The alphabetical order is not exact by letter and overall seems to be reversed, Y–T.

1621–1700 A–Bi	**166,091**
1621–1700 Bi–D	**166,092**

The alphabetical order is not exact.

1621–1700 E–G	**166,093**

E–G is not arranged strictly alphabetically.

1621–1700 H	**166,094**

The alphabetical order is not exact.

1621–1700 I–M	**166,095**

The alphabetical order is not always exact.

1621–1700 N–P	**166,096**

The Ps are not arranged strictly alphabetically.

1621–1700 R–S	**166,097**

The Rs are not arranged strictly alphabetically.

1621–1700 T–Y	**166,098**
1701–1800 A–B	**166,099**

The Bs are not arranged strictly alphabetically.

1701–1800 C–E	**166,100**
1701–1800 F–H	**166,101**

G comes before F and the alphabetical order within each letter is inexact.

1701–1800 I–K	**166,102**

The alphabetical order is not always exact.

1701–1800 L	**166,103**

The alphabetical order is not always exact.

1701–1800 M–P	**166,104**

The alphabetical order is inexact.

1701–1800 R–Y	**166,105**

The alphabetical order is not always exact.

4) 1600–1800s Abstracts of Deeds and Leases for Lancashire and Cheshire

93,629

The last segment of this typed copy contains extracts from 116 wills, which indicate land transfers. It is not known whether or not any of these are missing from the regular series of wills. These extracts are arranged in alphabetical order.

5) 1824–1857 Limited Administrations

These are specific instructions from the court issued in conjunction with the probating of a will limiting the authority of the executors or narrowing their supervision to a portion of the estate. Frequently the will or a copy is attached. Some of the wills may predate 1824. Each volume is preceded by an index.

1824–1833	**90,118**

Vol. 479. The first index at the start of volume 482 seems to be the original on which the index to volume 479 was based.

1833–1857	**90,119**

Vols. 480–482. Note the above explanation for the two indexes at the start of volume 482.

6) 1553–1810 Rochdale

Copies of Rochdale wills proved at Chester have been typed and arranged alphabetically as follows:

A–B	**1,594,544**
Volume 1	**(item 5)**
A–B	**1,594,564**
Volume 1 continues from page 330.	**(item 1)**
C	**1,594,564**
Volume 2	**(item 2)**
D–G	**1,594,564**
Volume 3	**(item 3)**
H	**1,594,564**
Volume 4	**(item 4)**
H	**1,594,565**
Volume 4 continues from page 85.	**(item 1)**
I–L	**1,594,565**
Volume 5	**(item 2)**
M–R	**1,594,565**
Volume 6	**(item 3)**
M–R	**1,545,500**
Volume 6 continues from page 335.	**(item 1)**
S	**1,545,500**
Volume 7. Pages 1–100 were refilmed at the end.	**(item 2)**
T–Z	**1,545,500**
Volume 8	**(item 3)**
T–Z	**1,545,501**
Volume 8 continues from page 450.	**(item 1)**

7) "Abstracts of Miscellaneous Leases, Wills, Deeds, etc. of Estates in Lancashire"

This is an earlier, more detailed listing of the contents of the CRO as published in its *Guide to the Lancashire Record Office*, 1962 (FHL Ref 942.72 A2L), particularly the sections entitled "Families and Estates" and "Solicitors' Accumulations." The filming took place in 1947. The films do not include a master index.

The most useful films for probates are 93,552–93,555. Film 93,554 contains a listing of forty-two wills, 1719–1890, and ends with fifteen pages of "Roman Catholic Wills Enrolled in the Lancashire County Record Office."

8) 1558–1823 *A History of Newton Chapelry in the Ancient Parish of Manchester*

**FHL 942.7
B4c n.s.
vols. 52–55**

These four volumes, published between 1904–1905 by the Chetham Society, include lists of wills for people from Newton, 1558–1823; Failsworth, 1577–1800; and Bradford. Failsworth and Bradford are townships within the chapelry of Newton.

9) *The Northern Genealogist*   **FHL 942 B2ng**

Abstracts for nine Lancashire wills proved at York and published in volume 1 of this periodical include: Isabella Gooddaie, widow of Thomas of Holme in Chageley (1603, p. 177); Richard Wade, yeoman of Hauton (1611, p. 177); George Smyth of Haberiam Eaves in Whalley (1611, p. 178); James Ridehalgh, yeoman of Gilclough, Great Marsden in Whalley (1674, p. 178); Richard Atherton, esquire of Atherton in Leigh (1730, p. 178); Thomas Sprowell, innkeeper of Todmorden in Rochdale (1730, p. 179); Thomas Massey, surgeon of Liverpool (1777, p. 233); Betty Hawcourt, widow of Manchester (1779, p. 233); Tyzack Trotter, merchant of Liverpool (1779, p. 233).

Two further abstracts appear in volume 2 as follows: Sir Robert Bindlose of Barwicke (1630 at York, p. 39) and Sir William Mallorie of Hoton (1411 at Richmond, p. 48).

Indexes for the Archdeaconry Court of Richmond

A few abstracts of documents relating to Richmond probates will be found in the miscellaneous section. Searches in these items and the stray-name index to this volume may reveal entries not found or easily found in the films arranged by deanery below.

The printed indexes should be more reliable than any known manuscript indexes. Pay special attention to the code letters indicating the deanery name by which the original records are filed:

> A for Amounderness
> F for Furness
> K for Kendal
> L for Lonsdale

Match the entries found with the corresponding year and alphabet in the subsequent sections for each deanery.

The printed indexes are oriented only to Lancashire. They do not include references to persons from Westmorland whose records were probated in Kendal or Lonsdale deaneries, nor that portion of Yorkshire covered by Lonsdale. Unfortunately, they are also incomplete for references to Lancashire of records probated in the Eastern Deaneries in Yorkshire.

If one needs to see the manuscript indexes, they will be listed at the start of the section for the Deanery of Lonsdale.

Consult Camp's *Wills and Their Whereabouts* for details of records not filmed.

The printed indexes are also available on microfilm or microfiche as indicated by the six- or seven-digit number below the call number.

1359–1858	FHL 942.7 B4Lc vol. 105 823,525 (item 2) & 6,073,011

Vol. 105 of the Lancashire & Cheshire Record Society. The appendix to this volume (pp. 126–143) is an index to Lancashire wills for both the Consistory of Cheshire and the Archdeaconry of Richmond, which were not recorded in any printed index as of 1953. The documents came from family records, Roman Catholic wills as required by the act of 1717, and others which surfaced after several sortings at different record offices. They are all housed at the Lancashire Record Office. More of these types of records may yet appear; hence, the value of including the act books in one's research in addition to the printed indexes.

1457–1680	FHL 942.7 B4Lc vol. 10 823,526 (item 3) & 6,072,916

Vol. 10 of the Lancashire & Cheshire Record Society. For the Commonwealth era, 1650–1660, see volume 4 of this same series as described under the section entitled "Indexes and Calendars" at the start of Lancashire. Entries in the printed index in italics refer to abstracts of some 2,279 wills for 1531–1652 missing from Richmond. These were found in the Towneley Manuscripts at the British Museum. Most of them are for the Deanery of Amounderness, but a list of eleven persons from Westmorland and Cumberland appears on page viii of the index and has been included in the stray-name index to this volume. See Camp's *Wills and Their Whereabouts* for further details.

The printed index also adds on pages ix–xi names where the probates were known to be lost and a list of some nineteen persons whose wills were abstracted and published in volume 26 of the Surtees Society. These nineteen are also listed in the stray-name index to this volume. Note the short addenda and errata bound with page 324 of the printed index.

1681–1748	FHL 942.7 B4Lc vol. 13 823,503 (item 4) & 6,072,919

Vol. 13 of the Lancashire & Cheshire Record Society.

1748–1792	FHL 942.7 B4Lc vol. 23 823,506 (item 2) & 6,072,929

Vol. 23 of the Lancashire & Cheshire Record Society. There is also an index to the probates of the manor of Halton, 1615–1790, on pages 139–144.

1793–1812	FHL 942.7 B4Lc vol. 66 823,516 (item 1) & 6,072,972

Vol. 66 of the Lancashire & Cheshire Record Society. The page after 105 purports to be a continuation of the index for Halton, 1793–1812. The entries for Halton actually start in 1794. More serious is the fact that the Vs are all from the deaneries of Amounderness and Furness and were printed out of sequence here.

1813–1837	FHL 942.7 B4Lc vol. 99 823,524 (item 1) & 6,073,005

Vol. 99 of the Lancashire & Cheshire Record Society. This volume includes one will from the manor of Halton for 1815. There is also a place index on pages 136–148 and a subject index (mainly of occupations) on pages 149–153.

1838–1858	FHL 942.7 B4Lc vol. 105 823,525 (item 2)

Vol. 105 of the Lancashire & Cheshire Record Society. As previously noted, the appendix is an index to wills from all over Lancashire, 1359–1858, not mentioned in any earlier printed index. There is also a place index on pages 144–159 and a subject index (mainly occupations) on pages 160–165.

Original Wills, Probate Bonds, Admons, and Inventories for the Archdeaconry Court of Richmond, Amounderness Deanery

---

Early–1660 A–Y	98,674

Box 1. The intent was to arrange these boxes chronologically, but boxes 1,2,3,5, and 6 are disorganized, with only an occasional grouping by year.

1661–1680 A   98,674
                                    (item 2)
Box 2. See the above note.

1681–1720 A   98,674
                                    (item 3)
Box 3. See the above note.

1721–1748 A   98,675
Box 4

1661–1664 B   98,675
                                    (item 2)
Box 5; see the above note. Some entries for 1664 are in
Box 6 and some for 1665 in Box 5.

1665–1669 B   98,675
                                    (item 3)
Box 6. See the note for Box 5.

1670–1675 B   98,675
                                    (item 4)
Box 7

1676–1696 B   98,676
Box 8 contains the records for 1676–1680.
Box 9 contains the records for 1681–1685.
Box 10 contains the records for 1686–1696.

1697–1720 B   98,677
Box 11 contains the records for 1697–1710.
Box 12 contains the records for 1711–1720.

1721–1740 B   98,678
Box 13 contains the records for 1721–1726.
Box 14 contains the records for 1727–1740.

1741–1748 B   98,679
Box 15

1661–1666 C   98,679
                                    (item 2)
Box 16

1667–1670 C   98,679
                                    (item 3)
Box 17

1671–1685 C   98,680
Box 18 contains the records for 1671–1677.
Box 19 contains the records for 1678–1685.

1686–1710 C   98,681
Box 20 contains the records for 1686–1694.
Box 21 contains the records for 1695–1710.

1711–1730 C   98,682
Box 22 contains the records for 1711–1720.
Box 23 contains the records for 1721–1730.

1731–1748 C   98,683
Box 24

1661–1673 D   98,683
                                    (item 2)
Box 25

1674–1690 D   98,683
                                    (item 3)
Box 26

1691–1710 D   98,684
Box 27

1711–1748 D   98,684
                                    (item 2)
Box 28

1661–1710 E   98,684
                                    (item 3)
Box 29

1711–1748 E   98,684
                                    (item 4)
Box 30

1661–1748 F   98,685
Box 31 contains the records for 1661–1680.
Box 32 contains the records for 1681–1700.
Box 33 contains the records for 1701–1720.
Box 34 contains the records for 1721–1748.

1661–1720 G   98,686
Box 35 contains the records for 1661–1670.
Box 36 contains the records for 1671–1690.
Box 37 contains the records for 1691–1720.

1721–1748 G   98,687
Box 38

1661–1666 H   98,691
Box 39

1667–1670 H   98,689
Box 40

1671–1677 H   98,690
Box 41

1678–1682 H   98,692
Box 42

1683–1690 H   98,688
Box 43

1691–1700 H   98,693
Box 44

1701–1710 H Box 45	**98,694**	**1681–1700 P** Box 64	**98,712**
1711–1720 H Box 46	**98,695**	**1701–1720 P** Box 65	**98,713**
1721–1730 H Box 47	**98,696**	**1721–1748 P** Box 66	**98,714**
1731–1748 H Box 48	**98,697**	**1661–1670 R** Box 67	**98,715**
1661–1690 I/J Box 49	**98,698**	**1671–1680 R** Box 68	**98,716**
1691–1748 I/J Box 50	**98,699**	**1681–1710 R** Box 69	**98,717**
1661–1680 K Box 51	**98,700**	**1711–1733 R** Box 70	**98,718**
1681–1748 K Box 52 contains the records for 1681–1720. Box 53 contains the records for 1721–1748.	**98,701**	**1733–1748 R** Box 70 (cont.)	**98,719**
1661–1680 L Box 54	**98,702**	**1661–1668 S** Box 71	**98,720**
1681–1710 L Box 55	**98,703**	**1669–1673 S** Box 72	**98,721**
1711–1748 L Box 56	**98,704**	**1674–1680 S** Box 73	**98,722**
1661–1680 M Box 57	**98,705**	**1681–1690 S** Box 74	**98,723**
1681–1720 M Box 58	**98,706**	**1691–1700 S** Box 75	**98,724**
1721–1748 M Box 59	**98,707**	**1701–1710 S** Box 76	**98,725**
1661–1710 N Box 60	**98,708**	**1711–1720 S** Box 77	**98,726**
1711–1748 N Box 61	**98,709**	**1721–1730 S** Box 78	**98,727**
1661–1748 O Box 61 (cont.)	**98,709** **(item 2)**	**1731–1748 S** Box 79	**98,728**
		1661–1670 T Box 80	**98,729**
1661–1670 P Box 62	**98,710**	**1671–1690 T** Box 81	**98,730**
1671–1680 P Box 63	**98,711**	**1691–1720 T** Box 82	**98,731**

1721–1728 T	**98,732**
1661–1748 U/V	

Box 83 starts out with Ts as described, then introduces a group of U/Vs intermingled with Ts, followed by another block of Ts. Some of the Ts for this period may appear on film 98,733.

1728–1748 T	**98,733**

Box 83 (cont.) may contain pre–1728 entries.

1661–1748 U/V
Misfiled. See film 98,732 above.

1661–1667 W Box 84	**98,734**
1668–1673 W Box 85	**98,735**
1674–1682 W Box 86	**98,736**
1682–1685 W Box 86 (cont.)	**98,737**
1686–1692 W Box 87	**98,738**
1692–1700 W Box 87 (cont.)	**98,739**
1701–1714 W Box 88	**98,740**
1715–1726 W Box 89	**98,741**
1727–1729 W Box 90	**98,742**
1729–1740 W Box 90 (cont.)	**98,743**
1741–1748 W Box 91	**98,744**
1661–1748 Y Box 91 (cont.)	**98,744** **(item 2)**
1748–1760 A	**99,342**
1748–1760 B	**99,342** **(item 2)**
1748–1760 C	**99,343**
1748–1760 D	**99,344**

1748–1760 E	**99,344** **(item 2)**
1748–1760 F	**99,344** **(item 3)**
1748–1760 G	**99,345**
1748–1753 H	**99,345** **(item 2)**
1748–1756 H	**99,239**

Not in strict chronological order and overlaps with the preceding film.

1756–1760 H	**99,240**
1748–1760 I–M	

The alphabetical groupings are well maintained in chronological order by year except for an M in 1756, which appears on the next film.

1748–1760 N–P	**99,241**
1748–1760 R–S	**99,242**
1748–1760 S–W	**99,243**
1748–1760 W–Y	**99,244**
1761–1770 A–B	**99,245**
1761–1770 B–C	**99,246**
1761–1770 D–H	**99,247**
1761–1770 H–J	**99,248**
1761–1770 K–P	**99,249**
1761–1770 R–S	**99,250**
1761–1770 S–Y	**99,251**
1771–1780 A–C	**99,252**
1771–1780 D–H	**99,253**
1771–1780 I–R	**99,254**
1771–1780 S–Y	**99,255**
1781–1790 A–C	**99,256**
1781–1790 D–H	**99,257**
1781–1790 I–P	**99,258**
1781–1790 R–Y	**99,259**

1791–1800 A	99,260		1811–1820 W–Y	99,288

V follows W.

1791–1800 B–C	99,261	

1821–1830 A–B	99,289

1791–1800 D–G   99,262

1821–1830 B   99,290

1791–1800 H–L   99,263

1821–1830 B–C   99,291

1791–1800 M–R   99,264

1821–1830 C   99,292

1791–1800 S–T   99,265
Ends with three Ws.

1821–1830 D–E   99,293

1791–1800 U–Y   99,266
See the preceding film for more Ws.

1821–1830 E–F   99,294

1801–1810 A   99,267

1821–1830 G–H   99,295

1801–1810 B–C   99,268

1821–1830 H   99,296

1801–1810 C–E   99,269

1821–1830 H–L   99,297

1801–1810 F–H   99,270

1821–1830 M–P   99,298

1801–1810 H   99,271

1821–1830 P–R   99,299

1801–1810 I–M   99,272

1821–1830 S   99,300

1801–1810 N–R   99,273

1821–1830 S–W   99,301

1801–1810 S   99,274

1821–1830 W–Y   99,302

1801–1810 S–T   99,275

1831–1840 A–B   99,303

1801–1810 W–Y   99,276

1831–1840 B–C   99,304

1811–1820 A–B   99,277

1831–1840 C–D   99,305

1811–1820 B–C   99,278

1831–1840 D–E   99,306

1811–1820 C   99,279

1831–1840 F   99,307

1811–1820 D–G   99,280

1831–1840 F–G   99,308

1811–1820 G   99,281

1831–1840 H–J   99,309

1811–1820 H   99,282

1831–1840 K–M   99,310

1811–1820 H–L   99,283

1831–1840 M–P   99,311

1811–1820 L–P   99,284
This film includes twenty pages of mathematical charts.

1831–1840 P–R   99,312

1811–1820 Q–S   99,285

1831–1840 S   99,313

1811–1820 S–T   99,286

1811–1820 T–W   99,287
There are no U/Vs on this film. See the next film for the Vs.

1831–1840 S–T   99,314
There is a document for S dated 1831 but not proven until 1856.

1831–1840 T–W   **99,315**
There are no U/Vs on this film. See the next film for the
Vs.

1831–1840 W–Y   **99,316**
V follows W.

1841–1850 A–B   **99,317**
There is a document for Thomas Banks dated 1842 but
not proven until 1859.

1841–1850 B–C   **99,318**

1841–1850 C–D   **99,319**

1841–1850 D–F   **99,320**

1841–1850 G   **99,321**

1841–1850 G–H   **99,322**

1841–1850 H–K   **99,323**

1841–1850 L–N   **99,324**

1841–1850 O–R   **99,325**

1841–1850 R–S   **99,326**

1841–1850 S   **99,327**

1841–1850 T–W   **99,328**

1841–1850 W   **99,329**

1851–1858 A–B   **99,330**

1851–1858 B–C   **99,331**

1851–1858 C   **99,332**

1851–1858 D–F   **99,333**

1851–1858 G–H   **99,334**

1851–1858 H–J   **99,335**

1851–1858 K–M   **99,336**

1851–1858 M–P   **99,337**

1851–1858 P–R   **99,338**

1851–1858 S   **99,339**
See film 99,314 for another S.

1851–1858 S–W   **99,340**

1851–1858 W–Y   **99,341**

*Registered Copy Wills for the
Archdeaconry Court of Richmond,
Amounderness Deanery*

1530–1858
Do not exist; see the original wills.

*Act Books for the
Archdeaconry Court of Richmond,
Amounderness Deanery*

All of the act books for Amounderness were filmed and
should be a source of additional information. They are
arranged as follows:

1530–1668
Do not exist.

1669–1671   **99,950**
                                                       (item 1)
Amounderness Act Book. The acts are in Latin. The
entries for 1669–1670 appear first followed by their
index, and then a similar arrangement for 1670–1671.

1672–1718
Do not exist, except for one entry for 1705, which see
below.

1705   **99,950**
                                                       (item 2)
At the beginning of this group of act entries for the other
four deaneries from 1712–1718 are two pages from an act
book for 1705 containing one item for Amounderness.

1719–1729   **99,950**
                                                       (item 4)
Amounderness Act Book. The acts are in Latin. There is
an index at the end of this section for this time period.

1730–1748   **99,951**
                                                       (item 1)
Amounderness Act Book. The acts are in Latin until
1733. The index at the end continues on to 1759. The
index is arranged alphabetically with each letter subdivided chronologically for all of the years treated.

1748–1815   **100,059**
Amounderness Act Book. The acts are divided into three
sections, each with its own index. First comes an index
for 1748–1759 arranged alphabetically, with each letter
subdivided chronologically for all of the years treated.
This is followed by the act entries. The second section
treats 1760–1798 in the same fashion, and the third does
the same for 1798–1815.

1815–1845   **100,060**

Amounderness Act Book. The acts are divided into two sections in the same manner as the preceding film. The first group covers 1815–1830, and the second is for 1830–1845. At the end of the first group is a reference to registers and terriers and a list of the chapels within the five deaneries.

1846–1857   **100,061**

Amounderness Act Book. The acts for 1846–1857 are arranged like the two preceding rolls of film.

Original Wills, Probate Bonds, Admons, and Inventories for the Archdeaconry Court of Richmond, Furness Deanery

---

1551–1748 A   **98,568**

Box 155 contains the records for 1551–1660.
Box 156 contains the records for 1661–1700.
Box 157 contains the records for 1701–1748.

1528–1615 B   **98,569**

Box 158

1616–1680 B   **98,570**

Box 159 contains the records for 1616–1660.
Box 160 contains the records for 1660–1680.

1681–1748 B   **98,571**

Box 161 contains the records for 1681–1700.
Box 162 contains the records for 1701–1720.
Box 163 contains the records for 1721–1748.

1544–1748 C   **98,572**

Box 164 contains the records for 1544–1660.
Box 165 contains the records for 1661–1700.
Box 166 contains the records for 1701–1748.

1562–1748 D   **98,573**

Box 167 contains the records for 1562–1680.
Box 168 contains the records for 1681–1748, but there are more Ds intermingled with the Es.

1570–1748 D–E   **98,573**
    (item 3)

Box 168 (cont.). There is an N at the start of the Es. Ds and Es are intermingled in the latter part.

1562–1748 F   **98,574**

Box 169 contains the records for 1562–1671.
Box 170 contains the records for 1671–1710.
Box 171 contains the records for 1711–1748.
The chronological order of these boxes is inexact. There are documents for 1674, 1678, and 1690 in Box 169.

1560–1748 G   **98,575**

Box 172 contains the records for 1560–1690.
Box 173 contains the records for 1691–1748.

1571–1748 H   **98,576**

Box 174 contains the records for 1571–1660.
Box 175 contains the records for 1661–1700.
Box 176 contains the records for 1701–1748.

1576–1748 I/J   **98,577**

Box 177

1563–1748 K   **98,578**

Box 178 contains the records for 1563–1660.
Box 179 contains the records for 1661–1690.
Box 180 contains the records for 1691–1748.

1575–1748 L   **98,579**

Box 181 contains the records for 1575–1700.
Box 182 contains the records for 1701–1748.

1559–1748 M   **98,579**
    (item 2)

Box 182 (cont.) contains the records for 1559–1660.
Box 183 contains the records for 1661–1700.
Box 184 contains the records for 1701–1748.

1570–1748 N   **98,579**
    (item 5)

Box 185 contains the records for 1570–1720.
A document for N appears on film 98,573.
Box 186 contains the records for 1721–1748.

1584–1748 O   **98,579**
    (item 6)

Box 186 (cont.)

1538–1748 P   **98,580**

Chronological order is inexact.
Box 187 contains the records for 1538–1660.
Box 188 contains the records for 1661–1700.
Box 189 contains the records for 1701–1748.

1574–1748 R   **98,581**

Box 190 contains the records for 1574–1660.
Box 191 contains the records for 1661–1700.
Box 192 contains the records for 1701–1748.

1547–1700 S   **98,582**

Box 193 contains the records for 1547–1660.
Box 194 contains the records for 1661–1680.
Box 195 contains the records for 1681–1700.

1701–1748 S   **98,583**

Box 196 contains the records for 1701–1720.
Box 197 contains the records for 1721–1748.

1550–1660 T   **98,584**

Box 198

1661–1700 T	**98,585**	**1821–1830 D–G**	**99,145**
Box 199			
1701–1748 T	**98,586**	**1821–1830 G–L**	**99,146**
1613–1748 U/V		**1821–1830 M–S**	**99,147**
Box 200			
		1821–1830 T–Y	**99,148**
1573–1660 W	**98,587**		
Box 201		**1831–1840 A–C**	**99,149**
1661–1748 W	**98,588**	**1831–1840 D–J**	**99,150**
Box 202 contains the records for 1661–1690.		**1831–1840 K–P**	**99,151**
Box 203 contains the records for 1691–1730.			
Box 204 contains the records for 1731–1748.		**1831–1840 R–Y**	**99,152**
1583–1748 Y	**98,588**	**1841–1850 A–B**	**99,153**
	(item 3)		
Box 204 (cont.)		**1841–1850 B–E**	**99,154**
1748–1760 A–C	**99,125**	**1841–1850 E–H**	**99,155**
1748–1760 D–J	**99,126**	**1841–1850 I–R**	**99,156**
1748–1760 K–R	**99,127**	**1841–1850 R–Y**	**99,157**
1748–1760 S–Y	**99,128**	**1851–1858 A–C**	**99,158**
1761–1770 A–F	**99,129**	**1851–1858 C–G**	**99,159**
1761–1770 G–P	**99,130**	**1851–1858 H–R**	**99,160**
1761–1770 R–Y	**99,131**	**1851–1858 S–W**	**99,161**
1771–1780 A–J	**99,132**		
1771–1780 K–Y	**99,133**		

Registered Copy Wills for the Archdeaconry Court of Richmond, Furness Deanery

1781–1790 A–L	**99,134**
1781–1790 M–W	**99,135**
1791–1800 A–H	**99,136**
1791–1800 I–Y	**99,137**

1528–1858
The situation for registered copy wills is the same as that for the Deanery of Lonsdale, which see for further information.

1801–1810 A–F	**99,138**
1801–1810 G–O	**99,139**

Act Books for the Archdeaconry Court of Richmond, Furness Deanery

1801–1810 P–Y	**99,140**
1811–1820 A–E	**99,141**

All of the act books for Furness were filmed and should be a source of additional information. They are arranged as follows:

1811–1820 F–O	**99,142**
1811–1820 P–W	**99,143**

1528–1711
Do not exist except for one entry for 1705, which is described below.

1821–1830 A–C	**99,144**

1712–1718 99,950
(item 2)

The acts for Copeland, Furness, Kendal, and Lonsdale deaneries are mixed together without an index, but in chronological order. Personal and place names, including an indication of deanery, appear in the left margin. The acts are in Latin. They include references to some marriage license bonds for 1705 and 1712–1715.

At the beginning of this group of act entries are two pages from an act book for 1705 containing one item for Furness. There are also references to caveats, which refer to contested estates, and to sequestrations, which involve property where there was no heir or claimant.

1719–1726 99,950
(item 3)
166,279

The acts for Copeland, Furness, Kendal, and Lonsdale are in turn rather mixed. There is a master index at the beginning. The actual entries for Furness appear on pages 82–113. The acts are in Latin. (The second film is an exact duplicate of the first film covering the years 1719–1726, but the second may be more readable.)

1727–1748 99,951
(item 2)

Furness Act Book. The acts are in Latin until 1733. The index at the end continues on to 1770. The index is arranged alphabetically with each letter subdivided chronologically for all of the years treated.

1748–1858 100,065

Furness Act Book. The acts are divided into four sections, each with its own index. First comes an index for 1748–1770 arranged alphabetically, with each letter subdivided chronologically for all of the years treated. This is followed by the act entries. The second section treats 1771–1798 in the same fashion. The third covers 1798–1838, but part of the As in the index follow the Cs, and there is a reference to registers and terriers at the end of this section of acts. The last section is for 1839–1858.

Calendars for the Archdeaconry Court of Richmond, Lonsdale Deanery

---

Since the printed indexes do not cover those portions of Lonsdale Deanery pertaining to Westmorland and Yorkshire, the filmed calendars will first be listed here. The filmed calendars stop in 1720. Hence, the act books will be outlined next as a substitute index for 1720–1857. The filmed calendars are arranged as follows:

1535–1720 A 98,557
(item 6)

This nineteenth-century manuscript begins with maps and a gazetteer for the eight deaneries. Next come the calendars, arranged alphabetically by the names of the five Western Deaneries, for the letter A, etc. Lonsdale will be the fifth deanery indexed in each case. Watch for L in the right margin to be certain that it is Lonsdale Deanery. An L, W, or Y notation below the entry refers to the county of residence: Lancashire, Westmorland, or Yorkshire.

The entries are listed in chronological order except for a few listed out of sequence after 1720 or on a supplement to be found either at the beginning or the end of that alphabetical portion for each deanery.

An indication to the types of probate is given first, followed by the date of probate, person's name and residence. If a will has been registered, the index will give the name of the register and page number. Cross-references to documents filed with the Eastern Deaneries are also provided. References to "Calendar W" usually refer to an item now lost.

All of the original records, regardless of type, were filed together in boxes after the pattern of this calendar. Match the index entry with the years and letters listed under the section entitled "Original Wills, Probate Bonds, Admons, and Inventories" to determine the microfilm call number.

Wills not located between 1697–1731 might be found in the section entitled "Registered Copy Wills." Items not filmed can be identified by consulting Camp's *Wills and Their Whereabouts*.

1543–1720 B 98,558
(item 5)

1531–1720 C 98,559
(item 5)

1566–1720 D 98,559
(item 10)

1550–1720 E 98,560
(item 5)

1537–1720 F 98,560
(item 10)

1480–1720 G 98,560
(item 15)

1532–1720 H 98,561
(item 5)

1551–1720 I/J 98,562
(item 5)

1541–1720 K 98,562
(item 10)

1549–1720 L	**98,562** **(item 15)**
1529–1720 M	**98,563** **(item 5)**
1469–1720 N	**98,563** **(item 10)**
1579–1720 O	**98,563** **(item 15)**
1549–1720 P	**98,563** **(item 20)**
1557 Q	**98,563** **(item 25)**

One entry, may refer to W.

1550–1720 R	**98,564** **(item 5)**
1533–1720 S	**98,565** **(item 5)**
1532–1720 T	**98,566** **(item 5)**
1551–1720 U/V	**98,566** **(item 10)**
1530–1720 W	**98,567** **(item 5)**
1530–1720 Y	**98,567** **(item 10)**

Act Books for the Archdeaconry Court of Richmond, Lonsdale Deanery

---

All of the act books for Lonsdale were filmed and can be used in lieu of any further indexes as well as a source of additional information. They are arranged as follows:

1712–1718	**99,950** **(item 2)**

The acts for Copeland, Furness, Kendal, and Lonsdale deaneries are mixed together without an index, but in chronological order. Personal and place names, including an indication of deanery, appear in the left margin. The acts are in Latin. They include references to some marriage license bonds for 1705 and 1712–1715.

At the beginning of this group of act entries are two pages from an act book for 1705 containing three items for Lonsdale. There are also references to caveats, which refer to contested estates, and to sequestrations, which involve property where there was no heir or claimant.

1719–1726	**99,950** **(item 3)** **166,279**

The acts for Copeland, Furness, Kendal, and Lonsdale are in turn rather mixed. There is a master index at the beginning. The actual entries for Lonsdale appear on pages 154–182. The acts are in Latin, but the index is sufficiently clear to find original documents without reading the act itself. (The second film is an exact duplicate of the first film covering the years 1719–1726, but the second may be more readable.)

1727–1748	**99,951** **(item 4)**

Lonsdale Act Book. The acts are in Latin until 1733. The index at the end continues on to 1775. The index is arranged alphabetically with each letter subdivided chronologically for all of the years treated. One could go directly from the index to the original probate; however, the act may provide additional information.

1748–1858	**100,068**

Lonsdale Act Book. The acts are divided into four sections, each with its own index. First comes an index for 1748–1775 arranged alphabetically, with each letter subdivided chronologically for all of the years treated. This is followed by the act entries. The second section treats 1776–1798 in the same fashion. The third covers 1798–1844. There is a reference to registers and terriers at the end of this section of acts. The last section is for 1845–1858.

Original Wills, Probate Bonds, Admons, and Inventories for the Archdeaconry Court of Richmond, Lonsdale Deanery

---

1535–1611 A Box 297	**98,820**
1611–1660 A Box 297 (cont.)	**98,821**
1661–1690 A Box 298	**98,822**
1691–1748 A Box 299	**98,823**
1543–1588 B Box 300	**98,824**
1588–1610 B Box 300 (cont.)	**98,825**
1611–1630 B Box 301	**98,826**

1631–1640 B Box 302	**98,827**		**1537–1660 F** Box 320	**98,846**
1641–1664 B Box 303	**98,828**		**1661–1700 F** Box 321	**98,847**
1665–1676 B Box 304	**98,829**		**1701–1748 F** Box 322	**98,848**
1677–1685 B Box 305	**98,830**		**1480–1620 G** Box 323	**98,849**
1685–1695 B Box 306	**98,831**		**1621–1670 G** Box 324	**98,850**
1696–1710 B Box 307	**98,832**		**1671–1700 G** Box 325	**98,851**
1711–1720 B Box 308	**98,833**		**1701–1748 G** Box 326	**98,852**
1720–1730 B Box 308 (cont.)	**98,834**		**1532–1615 H** Box 327	**98,853**
1731–1748 B Box 309	**98,835**		**1616–1660 H** Box 328	**98,854**
1531–1610 C Box 310	**98,836**		**1661–1680 H** Box 329	**98,855**
1611–1630 C Box 311	**98,837**		**1681–1700 H** Box 330	**98,856**
1631–1660 C Box 312	**98,838**		**1701–1703 H** Box 331	**98,857**
1661–1680 C Box 313	**98,839**		**1703–1730 H** Box 331 (cont.)	**98,858**
1681–1700 C Box 314	**98,840**		**1731–1748 H** Box 332	**98,859**
1701–1720 C Box 315 is arranged in the following order: 1707–1710, 1707, 1701–1706, 1711–1720.	**98,841**		**1551–1690 I/J** Box 333	**98,860**
			1691–1748 I/J Box 334	**98,861**
1721–1748 C Box 316	**98,842**		**1541–1748 K** Box 335	**98,862**
1566–1680 D Box 317	**98,843**		**1549–1660 L** Box 336	**98,863**
1681–1748 D Box 318	**98,844**		**1661–1700 L** Box 337	**98,864**
1550–1748 E Box 319	**98,845**		**1701–1748 L** Box 338	**98,865**

1529–1615 M Box 339	**98,866**	**1623–1635 S** Box 354 (cont.)	**98,882**
1616–1660 M Box 340	**98,867**	**1636–1670 S** Box 355	**98,883**
1661–1680 M Box 341	**98,868**	**1671–1700 S** Box 356	**98,884**
1681–1700 M Box 342	**98,869**	**1701–1721 S** Box 357	**98,885**
1701–1748 M Box 343	**98,870**	**1721–1748 S** Box 357 (cont.)	**98,886**
1552–1690 N Box 344	**98,871**	**1532–1610 T** Box 358	**98,887**
1691–1748 N Box 345	**98,872**	**1611–1621 T** Box 359	**98,888**
1579–1748 O Box 345 (cont.)	**98,872** **(item 2)**	**1621–1660 T** Box 359 (cont.)	**98,889**
1549–1625 P Box 346	**98,873**	**1661–1680 T** Box 360	**98,890**
1626–1652 P Box 347	**98,874**	**1681–1700 T** Box 361	**98,891**
1653–1660 Missing. See the probate decision table for instructions on the Commonwealth era.		**1701–1720 T** Box 362	**98,892**
1661–1700 P Box 348	**98,875**	**1721–1748 T** Box 363	**98,893**
1701–1748 P Box 349	**98,876**	**1551–1748 U/V** Box 364	**98,894**
1557 Q Missing, try under W.		**1530–1600 W** Box 364 (cont.)	**98,894** **(item 2)**
1550–1630 R Box 350	**98,877**	**1601–1630 W** Box 365	**98,895**
1631–1680 R Box 351	**98,878**	**1631–1660 W** Box 366	**98,896**
1681–1700 R Box 352	**98,879**	**1661–1670 W** Box 367	**98,897**
1701–1748 R Box 353	**98,880**	**1671–1680 W** Box 368	**98,898**
1533–1623 S Box 354	**98,881**	**1681–1690 W** Box 369	**98,899**

1691–1700 W Box 370	**98,900**	**1821–1830 A–B**	**99,061**
1701–1721 W Box 371	**98,901**	**1821–1830 B–K**	**99,062**
		1821–1830 L–R	**99,063**
1721–1730 W Box 371 (cont.)	**98,902**	**1821–1830 S–Y**	**99,064**
1731–1748 W Box 371 (cont.)	**98,903**	**1831–1840 A–B**	**99,065**
		1831–1840 B–J	**99,066**
1580–1748 Y Box 371 (cont.)	**98,903** **(item 2)**	**1831–1840 K–P**	**99,067**
		1831–1840 R–Y	**99,068**
1748–1760 A–E	**99,041**	**1841–1850 A–D**	**99,069**
1748–1760 F–K	**99,042**	**1841–1850 E–K**	**99,070**
1748–1760 L–S	**99,043**	**1841–1850 L–S**	**99,071**
1748–1760 T–W	**99,044**	**1841–1850 S–Y**	**99,072**
1761–1770 A–G	**99,045**	**1851–1858 A–F**	**99,073**
1761–1770 H–N	**99,046**	**1851–1858 G–L**	**99,074**
1761–1770 O–Y	**99,047**	**1851–1858 M–Y**	**99,075**
1771–1780 A–O	**99,048**		

1781–1790 A–G 99,050

1781–1790 H–Y 99,051

1791–1800 A–P 99,052

1771–1780 P–Y 99,049

Registered Copy Wills for the Archdeaconry Court of Richmond, Lonsdale Deanery

1791–1800 R–Y 99,053

1801–1810 A–F 99,054

1801–1810 G–N 99,055

1480–1696
Do not exist; see the original wills.

1801–1810 P–Y 99,056
U/V comes between W and Y.

1697–1706   **166,277**
The "Carr" register for the deaneries of Copeland, Kendal, Lonsdale, and Furness. The wills for the various deaneries are mixed together in fair chronological order. There is an index at the end arranged alphabetically, with each letter subdivided chronologically for all of the years treated. The index does not indicate the deanery; however, this information is provided in the manuscript index cited at the start of the description of Lonsdale's records. See the sections entitled "Calendars" and "Act Books." Further entries for 1697–1698 will be found on the next film.

1811–1820 A–B 99,057

1811–1820 B–K 99,058

1811–1820 L–R 99,059

1705–1731   **166,278**
The "Todd" register covering 1716–1717 for the same deaneries as the above entry comes first. Its index appears at the back of the next register, which follows it.

1811–1820 S–Z 99,060

The "Preston" register starts with some entries for 1697–1698, but it mainly goes from 1705 through the first half of the 1720s with a few entries continuing on to 1731. Apparently there is no overlap between the three registers. The index starts out like the one on the preceding film by first covering the As for 1705–1723. It then refers to a rider that indexes the As for the "Todd" register before moving on to do the same for the Bs.

1731–1809

Do not exist; see the original wills.

1810–1811

See Camp's *Wills and Their Whereabouts.*

1812–1858

Do not exist; see the original wills.

Miscellaneous: Notes, Abstracts, and Their Indexes from Probates Relating to Richmond

---

Searches in this material may accelerate research or supplement previous findings, but they should not supplant research in the original records. Compare any finds here with the originals.

1) 1542–1649   **FHL 942.7 B4c**
                                              & 824,020
                                              (item 3)

Publications of the Chetham Society, New Series. Vol. 28 contains abstracts for wills (51) of Cheshire and Lancashire proven between 1572–1696, with an appendix to abstracts of wills (108) proved at York or Richmond, 1542–1649. (See Cheshire for further details.)

2) 1442–1579   **FHL 942 B4s**
                                              & 994,031
                                              (item 7) &
                                              6,073,308

Publications of the Surtees Society. The Society began publishing materials concerning the northern counties in 1834. Research on any of the counties that make up the Province of York could benefit from examining the contents of this series. A master index will be found in volume 150.

Vol. 26 contains abstracts of probates (208) relating to the Archdeaconry of Richmond, 1442–1579. All of those which pertain to Lancashire are published on page x of volume 10 of the Lancashire & Cheshire Record Society and are briefly reproduced here: John Andrew, vicar of

Mellinge (1563); John Cowper of Aldingham (1543); Roger Dukdale of Garestang (1467); John Fawcet of Over Kellet (1537); Leonard Fell of Ulverstone (1542); Thomas Graistock of Garstang (1561); Ales Hadockes of Lancaster (1562); Chris. Hodgkinsonn of Preston (1570); Rich. Holme, clerk of Tatham (1576); Anne Kirkbye of Kirkbye Ireleth (1566); Henry Kyghley, esq. of Inskip (1567); Francis Morlay, esq. of Melling (1540); Roger Pele, parson of Dalton in Furness (1541–42); Thos. Premytt, priest of Litham (1564); Thos. Stanley, Lord Mountegle of Melling (1558); John Syngleton of St. Michael upon Wyre (1545); Ellen Toppeym of Woodplumpton (1556); John Townley of Ribchester (1562); and William Westbye, esq. of Molbrek (1556).

3) *The Northern Genealogist*   FHL 942 B2ng
Abstracts for two Lancashire wills from Richmond will be found in the volumes of this series as follows: volume 3, page 26 (also on film 994,073 item 10), Richard Chester of Lancaster (1462). Richard Cropper of Pulton (1565) on page 125 also appears in volume 4, page 42.

4) "Abstracts of Miscellaneous Leases, Wills, Deeds, etc. of Estates in Lancashire." These films are described in greater detail under the miscellaneous section for Lancashire.

Film 93,555 lists for the Archdeaconry of Richmond under "No. 10, Various" a series of admons between 1792–1825 that are not always found in the printed indexes. Among these with overseas connections are entries for Harry Piper, merchant of Alexandria, Virginia, 8 February 1800; and Isac Willasey of Kington, Surry, Jamaica, 26 November 1806.

Manorial Court of Halton

1615–1790   **FHL 942.7 B4Lc**
                                           vol. 23
                                           823,506
                                           (item 2)

Vol. 23 of the Lancashire & Cheshire Record Society, pages 139–144, contains the index to some 250 probates of this court. After 1790, documents were probated for only nine persons. Eight of these are indexed on the last page of volume 66 and one in the preface of volume 99 of this same series. These nine persons, with their date of probate given in parenthesis, were: Francis Fell (1794), Rev. Robt. Fletcher (1795), Rich. Hartley (1798), Robt. Leaper (1798), Thos. Cowperthwaite (1799), Chris. Walling (1800), Ed. Baines (1805), Thos. Armistead (1806), and Wm. Bradshaw, Lord of the Manor (1815).

1615–1815 A–G   **93,650**

Box 1. All original wills, some copy wills, admons, inventories, etc., were filed in two boxes. The intent was to file each letter of the alphabet in chronological order. That this did not always succeed can be seen in the example of a B inventory found on the next film.

1615–1815 H–W   **93,651**

Box 2 contains the inventory of Wm. Borwick, taken in 1716, filed with the Ws.

1615–1815   **93,652**

The first part is an index by letter of the alphabet and year of probate. The number refers to the page in the second part where a brief probate act will be found recorded in English.

1743–1806   **93,761**

The records are in chronological order. The volume closes with five pages of manorial court records for 1743–1747.

Part 5 Northumberland
Probate Jurisdictions and Microfilmed Records

Introduction

No map has been prepared for Northumberland, since most of this county came under the jurisdiction of the Consistory Court of Durham. See Durham for a full description of that court's records.

Although the Peculiar Court of Hexham and Hexhamshire belonged to the Archbishop of York, its records and the geographic area it covered will be described in the following section, as the peculiar court was limited geographically to Northumberland. The earliest records for Hexham and Hexhamshire are two original wills dated 1587 and 1593, which are available at the Borthwick Institute, York. Supposedly, the records of this court were merged after the Restoration with the records of the Prerogative Court of York.

The records for the Prebendal Court of Tockerington consist of one bundle of documents covering the years 1741–1744. They are at the Borthwick Institute. Probates for this court may be included in the microfilms for General Peculiars listed under Yorkshire.

The prebendal court was confined to the parish of Thockrington or Tockerington and its townships, such as Cary Coats, Little Bavington, and Sweethope.

Probate Decision Table for Northumberland

If the Research Subject Lived in One of These Jurisdictions:	Peculiar of Hexham and Hexhamshire	Peculiar of Thockrington, Tockerington	Episcopal Consistory of Durham	Anywhere in the County, 1651–1660
Search the probate records of these courts in the order shown below:				
Peculiar Court of the Archbishop of York in Hexham and Hexhamshire	1			
Prebendal Court of Tockerington (see General Peculiars, Yorkshire)		1		
Consistory Court of Durham (see Durham)	3	3	1	
Chancery Court of the Archbishop of York (see Yorkshire)	2	4	4	
Prerogative Court of the Archbishop of York (see Yorkshire)	4	5	2	
Court of the Dean and Chapter of York (see Yorkshire)	5	2	3	
Prerogative Court of the Archbishop of Canterbury (see London)	6	6	5	1
Court of Delegates, 1643–1857 (see London)	7	7	6	

Probate Records of the Peculiar Court of Hexham and Hexhamshire

This court consisted of three parishes in their entirety: Allendale, Hexham, and St. John Lee. Smaller units belonging to Allendale were Allenhead, Cotton, and Ninebanks. The chapelry of Whitley was part of Hexham Parish. Smaller units within St. John Lee were Anick, Anick Grange, Bingfield, Cocklaw, Fallowfield, Hallington, Portgate, Sandhoe, Wall, and West Acomb.

There are very few records for this court. Thorough searches should be made for the probates of persons living in this jurisdiction at any time in the superior courts of York, starting with those described in the miscellaneous section that follows.

Time Period	Film or Call No.
1593–1602	**99,955**

These are act books of probates, admons, and tuitions. They are indexed in volume 60 of the Yorkshire Archaeological Society Record Series in Appendix II, pages 184–188. (FHL 942.74 B4a and also film 402,541)

1676–1706	**252,674**
	(item 2) &
	1,068,873
	(item 11)

These are registered copy wills and inventories, but the source is not clearly indicated. The years are intermixed somewhat but do go earlier than the starting date of 1694 assigned to them by Anthony J. Camp in *Wills and Their Whereabouts*, 4th ed. (London: The author, 1974). They were indexed by J. C. Hodgson as described in the miscellaneous section that follows. There is also a modern typed index at the start of item 11 on film 1,068,873. At the end of the wills there is a section of formularies of oaths administered in the time of Charles II, including "The Oath of Allegiance," "The Oath of Supremacy," "The Oath Against Symonie," two other oaths in Latin, and other forms.

Miscellaneous: Notes, Abstracts, and Their Indexes from Probates Relating to Northumberland

1) The majority of these have already been outlined in the miscellaneous section for Durham, which see for further details. Pay particular attention to J. W. Robinson's index on film 574,951, which includes J. C. Hodgson's index to Northumberland wills; the card index to wills in the Newcastle City Archives on film 207,622; the printed index for 1540–1599; J. J. Howe's collection on film 90,796; the publications of the Surtees Society; and J. Raine's Eboracensia. To the latter, add the following:

1593–1602	**98,554**

Volume 2. This is listed as Raine's Hexhamshire and would appear to be based on the act books described earlier.

1687–1727	**98,554**

Volume 4. This series was extracted from the Dean and Chapter of York act books and also labeled "Hexhamshire," but it obviously contains references to other parts of Durham and Northumberland as well.

There are numerous references to Hexhamshire in the remaining volumes (5–12) of Raine's Eboracensia. All of the volumes were indexed by Robinson, and other indexes to them appear on film 252,673 and as the last item on film 98,555.

2) 1649–1660	**1,564,756**
	(item 7)

Commonwealth Wills, 1649–1660: for the counties of Northumberland and Durham, extracted from the index at Somerset House, London (1909).

3) Area Wills

Berwick-upon-Tweed. Some thirty-five admons with wills annexed, 1840–1893, as extracted by a local solicitor, are item 1 on film 252,774. Item 2 adds twenty-eight wills for 1832–1877.

Kirkhaugh. Abstracts of wills for this parish, 1663–1818, are printed alphabetically by year of probate in volumes 40, 41, and 43 of *The Publications of the Society of Antiquaries of Newcastle-upon-Tyne* (FHL 942.82 B2a, 4th series). Each volume is separately indexed. There are two corrections for volume 40 on page 304 of volume 43. These volumes have also been filmed as follows: A–K, pages 253–276 of volume 40 is item 6 of 1,426,020; L–R, pages 173–193 of volume 41 is item 7 of 1,426,020; and S–W, pages 275–304 of volume 43 is item 1 of 1,426,021.

Part 6   Nottinghamshire
Probate Jurisdictions and Microfilmed Records

Introduction

The pre–1858 probate situation in Nottinghamshire was complicated by the fact that the majority of the county came under the jurisdiction of the Archdeaconry of Nottingham. The documents in that archdeaconry were filed under the name of the deanery in which they originated and were sent to the Exchequer Court of York. The remainder of the county belonged to several peculiars. The records of some of the smaller peculiars were not microfilmed, are located elsewhere, or have never been found.

The Archdeaconry of Nottingham became part of the Diocese of Lincoln in 1839, but it continued to send its probate records to York until 1858. The original wills, admons, and inventories proven at the Exchequer Court of York were returned to Nottingham in 1972. The registered copy wills and separate indexes and act books are still housed in Yorkshire. The result is that a thorough search for probates in Nottinghamshire requires a search of all of the indexes described in this section for both the archdeaconry and the peculiars as well as the section in this volume for Yorkshire.

The earliest original wills for the archdeaconry date from the 1460s. The archdeaconry kept its own act books from 1705 to 1858. Supposedly, these act books refer to all entries in both the Exchequer and Prerogative Courts of York, but one might wish to double-check with the individual act books for each of these courts as well as consult them for the period before 1705. There are also a number of unproved wills from 1712 to 1857 that were never sent to York.

Of the peculiars, only the three largest have records earlier than the seventeenth century. The records for Edwinstowe, Rufford Abbey, Skegby and Teversal, and St. John of Jerusalem were not microfilmed. The original documents for Mansfield are on film from 1640 to 1857. Some forty wills dating from 1470 to 1541 have been printed for Southwell, and the microfilm collection for this court covers a mix of original documents and registered copy wills from 1506 to 1857. Note also the section for General Peculiars under Yorkshire.

Probate Decision Table for Nottinghamshire

If the Research Subject Lived in One of These Jurisdictions:	Manors of Edwinstowe, Rufford Abbey, Skegby and Teversal	Manors of Gringley-on-the-Hill or Bawtry and Mansfield	Peculiars of Apesthorpe and Bole	Peculiar of Kinoulton	Peculiar of Southwell	Dean and Chapter of York	Exchequer of York	Anywhere in the County, 1653–1660
Search the probate records of these courts in the order shown below:	LT. BLUE PURPLE	DK. GREEN ORANGE	BROWN ROYAL BLUE	MAROON	YELLOW	ROSE	LT. GREEN	
Manor Court Records (NO FILMS)	1							
Manor Court Records		1						
General Peculiars (see Yorkshire)			1					
Peculiar Court of Kinoulton				1				
Peculiar Court of Southwell					1			
Prerogative Court of the Archbishop of York (see Yorkshire)	2	2	3	2	2	2	1	
Court of the Dean and Chapter of York (see Yorkshire)	3	3	2	3	3	1	(vacancy) 2	
Chancery Court of the Archbishop of York (see Yorkshire)	4	4	4	4	4	3	3	
Prerogative Court of the Archbishop of Canterbury (see London)	5	5	5	5	5	4	4	1
Court of Delegates, 1643–1857 (see London)	6	6	6	6	6	5	5	

NOTE: It would also be wise to search the microfilms listed later in this section as an index to the peculiars of Nottingham from 1500–1858. Included in this card index are entries for the archdeaconry, as well as documents dated after 1858. To determine the deanery to which a parish in the archdeaconry belonged, consult FHL Ref 942.74 P2, pages 24–71; or film 100,081 (item 9).

Calendars and Indexes for the Archdeaconry of Nottingham

(Some abstracts or extracts of documents relating to Nottinghamshire probates will be found in the miscellaneous section. Searches in these items and the stray-name index to this volume may reveal entries not found in the calendars outlined below. Such materials are usually edited and may still be in Latin for the earlier periods.)

The printed indexes are also available on microfilm as indicated by the six-digit number below the call number.

Time Period	Film or Call No.

1389–1688
See the printed indexes described in the section for Yorkshire in this volume.

1688–1731   **FHL 942.52 S2**
823,672 (item 1)
This is a typescript of a volunteer project completed for the Family History Library in 1970. It is based on the act books of the Exchequer Court of York from 1 December 1688 to 30 April 1731. It is unclear whether or not the archdeaconry's own act books were doublechecked for the entries from 1705–1731. The index is arranged alphabetically by name and provides further columns for place, deanery, date, and type of document.

1731–1802
See the microfilmed manuscript indexes described under Yorkshire in this volume.

1803–1858 A–S   **1,526,547**

1803–1858 T–Y   **1,526,548**

1712–1857   **189,888**
(last item)
An index to the unproved wills.

Original Wills, Admons, and Inventories for the Archdeaconry of Nottingham

(The arrangement is alphabetical by year of probate. To determine the deanery, see the Note in the section entitled "Calendars and Indexes.")

1466–1601   **1,278,625**
(item 1)
Retford, Newark, Nottingham, and Bingham

1466–1610   **1,278,625**
(item 2)
Nottingham and Bingham

1611–1650   **1,278,626**
Nottingham and Bingham

1651–1690   **1,278,627**
Nottingham and Bingham, with a continuation for 1681–1690 on the next film.

1681–1690   **1,278,628**
(item 1)
Nottingham and Bingham, continued from the last film.

1691–1698   **1,278,628**
(item 2)
Nottingham and Bingham

1698–1710   **1,278,629**
(items 1–2)
Nottingham and Bingham

1711–1712   **1,278,629**
(item 3)
Nottingham and Bingham. 1712 appears first; 1711 follows out of order and continues on the next film.

1711, 1713–1722   **1,278,705**
Nottingham and Bingham

1722–1730   **1,278,706**
Nottingham and Bingham

1730–1740	1,278,707	**1821–1845**	1,278,796
Nottingham and Bingham		Retford	
1741–1753	1,278,708	**1845–1858**	1,278,822
Nottingham and Bingham			(items 1–2)
		Retford	
1754–1765	1,278,709	**1588–1640**	1,278,822
Nottingham and Bingham			(items 3–8)
		Newark	
1765–1773	1,278,710	**1641–1694**	1,278,823
Nottingham and Bingham		Newark	
1774–1782	1,278,746	**1694–1722**	1,278,824
Nottingham and Bingham		Newark	
1783–1792	1,278,747	**1723–1751**	1,278,825
Nottingham and Bingham		Newark	
1792–1802	1,278,748	**1752–1781**	1,278,826
Nottingham and Bingham. 1792 begins with Ro.		Newark	
1802–1810	1,278,749	**1782–1808**	1,278,860
Nottingham and Bingham. 1802 begins with Me.		Newark	
1810–1817	1,278,750	**1809–1845**	1,278,861
Nottingham and Bingham. 1810 begins with Ha.		Newark	
1817–1825	1,278,751	**1846–1858**	1,278,862
Nottingham and Bingham. 1817 begins with Re.		Newark	

1825–1833   1,278,752
Nottingham and Bingham. 1825 begins with Sm.

1834–1847   1,278,770
Nottingham and Bingham

1848–1858   1,278,771
Nottingham and Bingham

Unproved Wills for the Archdeaconry of Nottingham

1712–1857   189,826

1466–1647   1,278,772
Retford

This collection includes some 112 documents housed at Nottingham and apparently never sent to York since they were never probated. Many of them are for widows. Note the index listed in the section entitled "Calendars and Indexes." The wills are filed in fair chronological order.

1648–1694   1,278,773
Retford

1694–1715   1,278,774
Retford

Genealogical abstracts have been made for each of these documents matching their order on the film. These were bound in one volume under the call number FHL 942.52 S2a (also on film 897,347 item 4). Since there are so few wills, it is just as easy to go through the abstracts to find a missing will as it is to search the microfilmed index.

1715–1731   1,278,791
Retford. 1715 begins with Hi.

1732–1760   1,278,792
Retford

Six of the abstracts detail contacts outside of Nottinghamshire as follows:

1761–1784   1,278,793
Retford

1785–1804   1,278,794
Retford

#7—Francis Hooley, yeoman of Normanton near Plumptre, Notts., 1762, mentions a brother John in His Majesty's service in Germany.
#29—Thomas Smith, weaver of Eastwell, Leics., 1791.
#30—John Cooper, innkeeper of Pleasley, Derbys., 1794.

1805–1820   1,278,795
Retford

#32—Benjamin Pickard, seaman of Nottingham belonging to Maidstone Frigate, Captain Matthews, 1797.
#42—Thomas Hickling, boot and shoemaker of Market Place or Thornton Lane, Leics., 1821, who mentions Mary, the daughter of William Hickling, late of New York.
#99—Anne Rimington, wife of Robert Rimington, deceased, of Long Bennington, Lincs., 1856.

Registered Copy Wills for the Archdeaconry of Nottingham

1389–1858
See the registered copy wills described in the section for Yorkshire in this volume.

Indexes to Act Books for the Archdeaconry of Nottingham

1521–1705
See the act books listed in the section for Yorkshire in this volume for both the Exchequer and Prerogative Courts of York. Note that these records would have to be searched up to 1719 for the Deanery of Retford, and up to 1735 for Newark.

1705–1858   189,888
Vol. 16 of an index to the act books by deanery. One may wish to go from this index to the more complete one of volume 17 on the next film or directly to the act books. If the date of probate is known, it is not necessary to use either index. The index in volume 16 is sketchy, providing only an alphabetical listing of surnames by year in the following order:

1705–1861 for the Deanery of Nottingham. Intermingled with the entries for this deanery are those for the deaneries of Bingham, 1705–1734, and of Retford, 1719–1724.

1725–1857 for the Deanery of Retford; also see the above note under Nottingham for 1719–1724.

1735–1857 for the Deanery of Bingham; also see the above note under Nottingham for 1705–1734.

1735–1857 for the Deanery of Newark.

1705–1827   189,889
Vol. 17 is another index to the act books. It indicates whether the original probate was a will or admon, but it stops thirty years short of the index described above for

volume 16 and is only arranged chronologically. In the description provided below, the intervening pages are blank or missing.

1705–1827, Nottingham Deanery, pages 1–52. Probably the entries for Bingham, 1705–1734, and Retford, 1719–1724, are located here.

1735–1827, Bingham Deanery, pages 89–103. 1725–1827, Retford Deanery, pages 133–150. 1735–1827, Newark Deanery, pages 181–197.

Act Books for the Archdeaconry of Nottingham

(Arranged in chronological order with the surnames in the margin, written in Latin until 1733. To determine the deanery, see the Note in the section entitled "Calendars and Indexes.")

1705–1723   189,890 (item 1)
Vol. 1 of the act books contains entries for the deaneries of Nottingham and Bingham mixed together, followed by those for Retford, 1719–1724.

1723–1750   189,890 (item 2)
Vol. 2 is arranged the same as volume 1, and Retford covers 1725–1750.

1750–1792   189,891
Vol. 3 contains entries for Nottingham and Retford deaneries.

1792–1807   189,892
Vol. 4 contains entries for Nottingham and Retford deaneries.

1735–1769   189,893 (item 1)
Vol. 5 contains entries for the deaneries of Bingham and Newark mixed together; however, the acts for Bingham from 1735–1750 should be found on film 189,890 above.

1770–1810   189,893 (item 2)
Vol. 6 contains entries for Newark and Bingham deaneries.

1808–1828   189,894
Vol. 7 contains entries for Nottingham and Retford deaneries.

1811–1830   189,895
Vol. 8 contains entries for Bingham and Newark deaneries.

1830–1858   189,896
Vol. 9 for Bingham Deanery is followed by Vol. 10 for Newark Deanery.

1828–1858   **189,897**
Vol. 11 contains entries for Retford Deanery.

1828–1837   **189,898**
Vol. 12 contains entries for Nottingham Deanery.

1837–1847   **189,899**
Vol. 13 contains entries for Nottingham Deanery.

1847–1853   **189,900**
Vol. 14 contains entries for Nottingham Deanery.

1853–1858   **189,901**
Vol. 15 contains entries for Nottingham Deanery.

Indexes for the Peculiar Courts of Nottinghamshire

(Some further references to the probate records of the peculiars of Nottinghamshire will be found in the miscellaneous section. Consult Anthony J. Camp, *Wills and Their Whereabouts*, 4th ed. [London: The author, 1974] for other records of particularly the smaller peculiars, which may not have been filmed.)

1506–1857 A–G   **1,278,702**
          G–R   **1,278,703**
          R–Z, Misc.   **1,278,704**
This is an update of the same master index outlined in the next entry, which see. The update was done in 1987 and includes deaneries. For a guide to the codes used in the index, see *Guide to the Nottinghamshire County Records Office* (FHL Ref 942.52 A5k).

1500–1858 A–H   **543,624**
          H–W   **543,625**
          W–Z   **543,626**
This is a master card index to all of the peculiars, with some references to the deaneries of Nottingham, and some later than 1858. Each card includes name, residence, CRO file number, type of document, and date. It was filmed in 1970. The last roll of film also contains some unnamed miscellaneous documents, fragments, letters, bonds, and references to ecclesiastical matters.

Manorial Court of Gringley-on-the-Hill or Bawtry

1739–1855   **189,829**
                                                                      (item 2)
A manuscript index arranged chronologically by year and date of probate for the wills, 1739–1855, followed by admons, 1805–1855. It would be better to use the more complete card index listed above for the peculiar courts of Nottinghamshire.

1739,   **189,885**
1761–1855
The original probate documents are followed by a separate section consisting of admons for 1805–1855.

Genealogical abstracts have been made for each of these documents matching their order on the film. These were bound in one volume under the call number FHL 942.52/G3 S2g (also on film 599,737 item 2). To locate a missing will, go to this typescript that starts with an index of seventeen pages, then to the wills on pages 1–124, and finally to the admons on pages 125–141.

Peculiar Court of Kinoulton

1730–1765   **99,930**
                                                                      (item 1)
A manuscript calendar with entries comparable to an act book.

1767–1846   **189,829**
                                                                      (item 3)
A manuscript index first of wills, then admons for 1767–1825, and finally inventories for 1778–1846. It would be well to use the more complete card index listed above for the peculiar courts of Nottinghamshire.

1730–1765   **99,930**
                                                                      (item 1)
Original probate records. There are three additional probates not listed in the calendar: C for 1725, W for 1727, and G for 1728.

1758–1846   **189,886**
Original probate records. Genealogical abstracts have been made for each of these documents, which were bound in one volume under the call number FHL 942.52/K1 S2k (also on microfiche 6,026,297). To locate a missing will, go to this typescript which starts with an index of five pages, then to the wills for 1758–1846 on pages 1–28, to the admons for 1767–1826 on pages 29–39, and finally to the inventories and other court business on pages 40–42.

Original Probate Records and Abstracts for the Manorial Court of Mansfield

(Admons may be listed separately after 1711.)

1640–1857   **189,829**
                                                                      (item 1)
A manuscript index arranged roughly chronologically as follows: pages 1–44 for wills and admons from

1640–1738, pages 44–47 for the same but in no order for 1739–1793, pages 47–48 for admons from 1735–1749, pages 48–51 for wills from 1743–1793 (this group starts with 1748 and is not in exact order except for a fair series for 1745–49), pages 51–56 for another coverage from 1753–1792, pages 56–63 for wills from 1770–1812, pages 63–65 for admons from 1793–1812, pages 65–69 for wills from 1813–1823, pages 69–73 for admons from 1813–1857, pages 73–74 for another series of admons for 1712–1718, and pages 74–89 for wills from 1824–1857. It would be wise to use the more complete card index listed at the front of the section for the peculiar courts of Nottinghamshire.

1751–1857   **1,471,198**
                                                  (item 4)

Another index to the admons of this court will be found on the first seven pages of this film. Information provided is the name of the intestate, date proved, administrators, and names of sureties. Starting on page 8 is another index to wills, 1751–1857, arranged by the year in which the will was proven.

NOTE: Genealogical abstracts have been made for each of the original records matching their order on the films listed below. The call numbers for the abstracts are noted under the description of each film. To locate a missing will it is often easier to use the typescripts of these abstracts, which are indexed separately for 1640–1857 in two volumes identified as Abbott-Milner, Milner-Young and addenda under FHL 942.52/M1 S2m (also on film 962,617 items 1 and 2).

1580–1606
See the following section of registered copy wills for this court.

1607–1639
Missing.

1640–1651   **189,866**
The genealogical abstracts are on pages 1–97 of volume 1 of FHL 942.52/M1 S2m and item 3 of film 962,617.

1652–1658   **189,867**
The abstracts continue on pages 98–169 of the typescript volume described under film 189,866 above.

1659–1664   **189,868**
The genealogical abstracts are on pages 170–238 of volume 2 of FHL 942.52/M1 S2m and item 4 of film 962,617.

1665–1672   **189,869**
The abstracts continue on pages 239–366 of the typescript volume described under film 189,868 above.

1673–1679   **189,870**
The abstracts continue on pages 367–443 of the typescript volume described under film 189,868 above.

1680–1684   **189,871**
The abstracts continue on pages 444–539 of the typescript volume described under film 189,868 above.

1685–1690   **189,872**
The genealogical abstracts are on pages 540–612 of volume 3 of FHL 942.52/M1 S2m and item 1 of film 962,618. Pages 574–584 contain letters of attorney and land rights granted by the court from 1688–1689.

1691–1700   **189,873**
The abstracts continue on pages 613–721 of the typescript volume described under film 189,872 above.

1701–1711   **189,874**
The abstracts continue on pages 722–878 of the typescript volume described under film 189,872 above.

1712–1724   **189,875**
The genealogical abstracts are on pages 879–998 of volume 4 of FHL 942.52/M1 S2m and item 2 of film 962,618.

1725–1742   **189,876**
The abstracts continue on pages 999–1166 of the typescript volume described under film 189,875 above. See the next film for further entries for 1741–1742.

1741–1771   **189,877**
Chronological order is inexact; see the preceding film for other entries for 1741–1742. The genealogical abstracts are on pages 1167–1340 of volume 5 of FHL 942.52/M1 S2m and item 1 of film 962,619.

1772–1802   **189,878**
The abstracts continue on pages 1341–1483 of the typescript volume described under film 189,877 above.

1803–1823   **189,879**
Lacks an orderly arrangement. The genealogical abstracts are on pages 1484–1626 of volume 6 of FHL 942.52/M1 S2m and item 2 of film 962,619.

1824–1830   **189,880**
Lacks an orderly arrangement. The abstracts continue on pages 1627–1701 of the typescript volume described under film 189,879 above.

1831–1845   **189,881**
Lacks an orderly arrangement. The abstracts continue on pages 1702–1845 of the typescript volume described under film 189,879 above.

1846–1857   **189,882**
Lacks an orderly arrangement. The abstracts continue on pages 1846–1940 of the typescript volume described under film 189,879 above.

Registered Copy Wills for the Manorial Court of Mansfield

1580–1606   **1,471,198**
                                                                  (item 3)

Index at the back.

Original Admons for the Manorial Court of Mansfield

1640–1711
See the original probate records described in the section before last.

1712–1718   **189,883**
                                                                  (item 1)
Lacks an orderly arrangement. The genealogical abstracts are on pages 1941–1979 of volume 7 of FHL 942.52/M1 S2m and item 3 of film 962,619. Inventories are included.

1719–1734
See the original probate records described in the section before last.

1735–1749   **189,883**
                                                                  (item 2)
Lacks an orderly arrangement. The abstracts continue on pages 1980–2003 of the typescript volume described above under film 189,883 item 1.

1750–1792
See the original probate records described in the section before last.

1793–1857   **189,884**
Lacks an orderly arrangement. The abstracts continue on pages 2004–2129 of the typescript volume described above under film 189,883 item 1.

Indexes and Printed Records for the Peculiar Court of Southwell

1470–1547   **Microfiche**
                                                                  6,021,919
                                                                  card 12
The Historical Manuscripts Commission, Series 27, Twelfth Report provides indexes in Appendix IX to the enrolled wills, 1470–1542, on pages 541–542, and to volume 1 of the registered copy wills, 1538–1547, on pages 542–543.

1470–1541   **FHL 942 B4ca**
                                                                  vol. 48
The Camden Society printed forty of the enrolled wills in their New Series of 1891 (reprinted in volume 48 of the Royal Historical Society Publications, pages 96–145, in 1965). The majority are in Latin with a brief translation in the margin. All names mentioned in these wills will be found in their name index on pages 223–234.

1470–1600   **189,827**
                                                                  (item 1)
Manuscript Index. The entries before 1506 are to act books.

1601–1629   **189,827**
                                                                  (item 2)
Manuscript Index

1639–1726 A–G   **189,828**
                                                                  (item 1)
Manuscript Index

1639–1726 G–Y   **189,828**
                                                                  (item 2)
Manuscript Index

1680–1857   **189,828**
                                                                  (item 3)
Manuscript Index of Wills

1771–1857   **189,828**
                                                                  (item 4)
Manuscript Index of Admons

NOTE: The card index listed at the front of the section for the peculiar courts of Nottinghamshire is probably more complete than any of the manuscript indexes, but it may not include the registered copy wills. However, it is often easier to find a missing will by searching the typescripts of genealogical abstracts available for most of the films listed below.

Original Probate Records and Abstracts for the Peculiar Court of Southwell

1470–1505
Missing. See the enrolled wills mentioned above.

1506–1566   **189,830**
Arranged chronologically and alphabetically. There are no abstracts.

1567–1620
Not filmed. See the registered copy wills and admons for this court.

1621–1623   **189,834**

Arranged chronologically and alphabetically. The genealogical abstracts are found under FHL 942.52 S2so 1621–1631, part 1, and item 2 of film 908,156. The first five pages of the abstracts are unpaged and look like act entries, but they are entitled "Inventories and Administrations: 1621–1627." The wills for 1621 are in reverse alphabetical order from T–B on pages 1–13, for 1622 A–W on pages 14–30, and for 1623 A–C on pages 31–40.

1623–1625   **189,835**

The abstracts continue in the typescript volume (item 3 of film 908,156) described under film 189,834 above. The first five pages are for inventories, 1623–1625; followed by the wills for 1623 F–W on pages 1–15; 1624 B–W on pages 16–34; and 1625 L, A–J, then in reverse order W–M on pages 35–61.

1625–1627   **189,836**

The abstracts continue in the typescript volume (item 4 of film 908,156) described under film 189,834 above. The wills for 1625 include two more Ms, a K and J on pages 1–4. The wills for 1626 are found on pages 6–35 and for 1627 on pages 36–52. The order is inexact, but the abstracts should match the arrangement of the original documents on this film.

1627–1630   **189,837**

The genealogical abstracts are found under FHL 942.52 S2so 1621–1631, part 2, and item 1 of film 823,873. The first four pages are for inventories unaccompanied by wills or admons, 1627–1630. Pages 1–7 contain the wills for 1629 P–W; pages 8–27 the wills for 1630 A–I; pages 28–33 the wills for 1627 H–W; pages 33–40 the wills for 1627 in reverse order from C–A (see the preceding film for other entries for 1627); pages 41–69 the wills for 1628 B–W; pages 70–88 the wills for 1629 A–O; and finally an index of twenty-seven pages, which is repeated by its own carbon copy.

1630–1638   **189,838**

The genealogical abstracts are found under FHL 942.52 S2so 1630–1638 and item 2 of film 823,873. Indexed at the end, followed by a carbon copy of the same index.

1639

Not filmed. See the registered copy wills and admons for this court.

1640–1645   **189,840**

Arranged chronologically and alphabetically. The genealogical abstracts are found under FHL 942.52 S2s 1640–1641 and item 14 of film 538,120. There are numerous inventories and some twenty-two admons. There is only one entry for 1645.

1646–1648

Missing. The records for these years may be at the CRO or among the records for the PCY and the PCC.

1649–1652   **189,841**

Arranged chronologically and alphabetically. The abstracts continue in the typescript volume described under film 189,840 above. The year 1651 is missing; see the note for 1653–1659. Two entries for the Ms of 1650 will be found with 1652.

1653–1659

Missing, due to the Interregnum and Commonwealth. See the probate decision table for further instructions.

1660–1857

Not filmed. See the registered copy wills and admons for this court.

Registered Copy Wills for the Peculiar Court of Southwell

(See the admons for this court for further wills.)

1530–1566

Not filmed. See the original wills.

1567–1592   **189,831**

Vol. A contains both wills and admons, which are unindexed but in good chronological order by the date of probate. The genealogical abstracts are found in three volumes labeled FHL 942.52 S2s 1: 1567–1578, 2: 1578–1587, 3: 1587–1592. All three are also on film 908,507.

1592–1613   **189,832**

Vol. B contains both wills and admons. There is an index at the beginning for 1592–1594. The genealogical abstracts for the wills are in one volume, FHL 942.52 S2s 4: 1592–1613 and item 1 of film 908,372 and fiche 6,026,304. The abstracts for the admons are in another volume, FHL 942.52 S2sa, 1592–1613 and item 2 of film 908,372.

1613–1621   **189,833**

Vol. C contains mainly wills with some references to admons. It is unindexed. The genealogical abstracts are incomplete, but in one volume labeled FHL 942.52 S2s 5: 1613–*1639* and item 1 of film 908,156. They start with ten unnumbered pages entitled "Inventories and Admons, 1614–1618," followed by 158 short entries, many of which appear to be admons. Then come the wills through 1618.

1621–1631

The registry was not kept. See both the original wills and admons for this court.

1631–1639   **189,839**

This is a continuation of volume C on film 189,833. There are some admons. No genealogical abstracts were made of this film.

1639–1660
The registry was not kept. See both the original wills and admons for this court.

1660–1681   **189,842**
The volume number is unreadable. There is an index at the beginning. The genealogical abstracts are in FHL 942.52 S2s, 1660–1681 and item 2 of film 496,516. The pages are unnumbered, but the entries are arranged chronologically.

1681–1725   **189,843**
The volume number is unreadable. It starts with an index followed by admons for 1660–1670. Then come the wills for 1681–1725 with what appears to be a partial index at the end. There is a K for 1699 with the miscellaneous admons on film 189,865.

The abstracts for the admons and some tuition bonds are in FHL 942.52 S2sa, 1660–1670 and item 1 of film 547,571. The genealogical abstracts for the wills are in FHL 942.52 S2s,1681–1725 and on microfiche 6,026,304. They are arranged chronologically and include the will of Robert Gravely, gentleman of Knowsthorp, Yorks., dated 11 March 1699.

1726–1766   **189,844**
The volume number is unreadable. An index comes at the end. There are wills for D in 1740 and M, B, and E in 1744 with the miscellaneous admons on film 189,865. The abstracts are chronologically arranged in FHL 942.52 S2s, 1726–1766 and item 2 of film 547,571.

1766–1782   **189,845**
The volume number is unreadable. An index comes at the end. The abstracts are chronologically arranged in FHL 942.52 S2s, 1766–1782 and item 1 of film 547,572.

1782–1801   **189,846**
The volume number is unreadable. An index comes at the end. The genealogical abstracts are chronological but inexact. They start with a certificate for Robert White, son of Samuel White, yeoman of Cropwell Bishop, dated 13 November 1818. The abstracts are in FHL 942.52 S2s, 1782–1801 and item 2 of film 547,572.

1801–1811   **189,847**
This is Vol. 11 of the registered copy wills, but it contains a loose document at the first referring to a will registered at the Dean and Chapter of York for Elizabeth Parnell, spinster of Laneham, dated 10 July 1798 and granted to her nephew and sole executor, John Minnitt. Volume 11 is indexed at the end. The abstracts are in FHL 942.52 S2s, 1801–1811 and item 3 of film 547,572. The last four pages are a handwritten index.

1811–1822   **189,848**
The volume number is unreadable. An index comes at the end. The abstracts are in FHL 942.52 S2s,

1811–1822 and item 1 of film 547,573. The last six pages are a handwritten index. There is an entry for John Slack, farmer of Broxholme, Lincs., dated 1796 and proved 1811.

1822–1832   **189,849**
The volume number is unreadable. An index comes at the end. The abstracts are in FHL 942.52 S2s, 1822–1832 and item 2 of film 547,573. The last six pages are a handwritten index. There are entries for the will of Ambrose Higginbotham, farmer of Wishaw, Warws., dated 1810 and proved 1822; and Edward Peart, physician of Owston, Lincs., proved at the Archdeaconry of Stow before being entered here in 1825.

1832–1847   **189,850**
The volume number is unreadable. An index comes at the end. The abstracts are in FHL 942.52 S2s, 1832–1847 and item 1 of film 547,574. The last eight pages are a handwritten index.

1848–1857   **189,851**
The volume number is unreadable. An index comes at the end. There are admons as well. The abstracts are in FHL 942.52 S2s, 1848–1857 and item 2 of film 599,731. The last four pages are a handwritten index.

Admons for the Peculiar Court of Southwell

(Some admons will be found among the wills, both original and registered copies.)

1506–1617
See both the original and registered copy wills for this court.

1618–1620   **189,852**
The documents are mainly in chronological order and include some wills. The genealogical abstracts are in FHL 942.52 S2sa, 1618–1620 and item 2 of film 547,574.

1621–1635
See both the original and registered copy wills for this court.

1636–1642   **189,853**
The documents are mainly in chronological order and include a few wills. About halfway through the film appear some ten or eleven marriage bonds dating from 1588–1666. The bonds for people from outside of the jurisdiction of Southwell are included here: 28 April 1588—William Blythe, gent. of Wollaton & Oliffe Tomlinson;   21 July 1588—Stephan Brittan, clerk of Bennyngton, Lincs., & Mary Glascocke, wid., dau. of John Dankes of Hawton; 1 November 1589—William

Ballard the younger of Southwell & Alice Martyn of Newark; and 15 May 1666—William Warren, blacksmith of Norwell & Elizabeth Alcockes late of Newark on Trent.

Mixed with the bonds are several pages of bishop's transcripts as follows: Kirklington for 1642 (15 entries), South Muskham for 1627 (29 entries), and Ruddington for 1635 (48 entries). The abstracts are in FHL 942.52 S2sa, *1637*–1642 and item 3 of film 547,574. They do not include all of the above.

1642–1659
See the original wills for this court.

1660–1665,   189,854
1668–1670
The documents are mainly in chronological order and include at least one nuncupative will, perhaps others. See film 189,843 of the registered copy wills for more admons from 1660–1670. The abstracts are in FHL 942.52 S2sa, 1660–1669 and on microfiche 6,026,305. They start with an index of fifteen unnumbered pages.

1671–1685   189,855
The documents are mainly in chronological order. There are no entries for 1683. The abstracts are in FHL 942.52 S2sa, 1671–*1692* and item 1 on film 547,568. They start with an index of seventeen unnumbered pages.

1686–1692   189,856
The documents are mainly in chronological order. The entries for 1686 come after 1687. There are no entries for 1691. The abstracts are described under film 189,855. The abstracts end with the bond of George Chappell, gent. of Southwell, dated March 1695.

1693–1694
Missing; perhaps they were not filmed or are to be found among the registered copy wills.

1695–1857
In addition to the manuscript indexes mentioned at the start of the section for Southwell, there is a typescript volume that indexes the abstracts of admons from 1695–1857. See FHL 942.52 S2sa Index and also item 2 of film 547,568.

1695–1720   189,857
The documents are mainly in chronological order. See film 189,856 for another entry for 1695. The abstracts are in FHL 942.52 S2sa, 1695–*1722* and item 3 of film 547,568. For an index to them, see the preceding note for 1695–1857.

1721–1740   189,858
There is some confusion in the filing of the first two years; otherwise they are in chronological order. The abstracts are in FHL 942.52 S2sa, 1721–1740 and item 1 of film 547,569. See the index for 1695–1857 described above.

1741–1759   189,859
There is little order to the arrangement of these documents, but the typescript index to the abstracts mentioned above under 1695–1857 will help. See film 189,861 for one more entry for 1750 and two for 1758. The abstracts are in FHL 942.52 S2sa, 1741–*1780* and item 2 of film 547,569.

1760–1780   189,860
Two more marriage bonds for *1666* appear at the end of this film. See film 189,861 for sixteen more admons in this time period, and note the overlap with films 189,862 and 189,863. For the abstracts, see the note under film 189,859.

1750–1799   189,861
This is a short collection of documents in fair chronological order that more properly belong with the two preceding films and the succeeding two. The index to abstracts mentioned above for 1695–1857 helps to sort them out. The abstracts are in FHL 942.52 S2sa, *1772–1857*, pages 1164–1185 and item 1 of film 547,570.

1771–1784   189,862
These documents are first arranged A–W for 1771–1777, followed by 1778–1784. See films 189,860, 189,861, and 189,863 for additional entries for this time period. The abstracts are in FHL 942.52 S2sa, *1772–1857*, pages 1037–1108 for 1771–1777 and pages 1109–1163 for 1778–1784, and also appear in item 1 of film 547,570.

1771–1818   189,863
These documents are first arranged A–W for 1771–1793, followed by 1794–1818. See films 189,860, 189,861, and 189,862 for additional entries for this time period. The abstracts are in FHL 942.52 S2sa, *1772–1857*, pages 1186–1240 for 1771–1793 and pages 1241–1333 for 1794–1818, and also appear in item 1 of film 547,570.

1819–1834   189,864
Alphabetically arranged. The abstracts are in FHL 942.52 S2sa, *1772–1857*, pages 1335–1431 and item 1 of film 547,570.

1835–1857   189,865
                                                 (item 1)
Chronologically arranged. The abstracts are in FHL 942.52 S2sa, *1772–1857*, pages 1432–1541 and item 1 of film 547,570.

1619–1744   189,865
                                                 (item 2)
A miscellaneous collection of seven probate cases as follows:

1619 inventory of Elizabeth Sharpe, widow of Norwell. 1741 renunciation of Anne Burrow, widow of Leeds, Yorks., for the estate of her son-in-law Thomas Dixon, bookseller of Mansfield; his will is attached, also see the last item below. 1744 bond and inventory of Gervas Hutton of Mansfield. 1699 copy of a will enrolled in 1749 for Alice Kirkly, wife of Nathaniel Kirkly of East Markham. 1744 will and bond of Anne Man, widow of Mansfield. 1744 copy of the will of Alexander Burden, mayor of Nottingham. 1744 will and bond of George Ellis, maltster of Mansfield. 1741 bond and inventory for Thomas Dixon mentioned above.

Miscellaneous: Abstracts, Documents, and Select Indexes for Probates Relating to Nottinghamshire

---

Searches in this material may accelerate research or supplement previous findings but should not supplant research in the original documents.

1) 1827–1857   578,914
(items 1 & 2)

Wills, Requisitions and Commission Book from the CRO. This is a chronological listing of wills for persons from Nottinghamshire "proved in other courts, chiefly Canterbury, also Lichfield and elsewhere." There is an index at the end of items 1 and 2 of this film.

2) 1383–1616   **FHL 942 B4s**

The Publications of the Surtees Society. The Society began publishing materials concerning the northern counties in 1834. Research on any of the counties that make up the Province of York could benefit from examining the contents of this series. A master index is in volume 150.

Abstracts of some wills from the PCC concerning the northern counties, including Nottinghamshire, were published in volume 116 (1383–1558) and volume 121 (1555–1616). These two volumes have been microfilmed as items 5 and 6 of film 990,300. Likewise there may be something of interest for Nottinghamshire in the volumes of this series that are abstracts of some wills registered at York, especially the PCY. These include volume 4 (1316–1430), volume 30 (1426–1467), volume 45 (1395–1491), volume 53 (1484–1509), volume 79 (1509–1531), and volume 106 (1531–1551).

3) 1512–1568   **FHL 942.52 B4th**
vol. 22

Vol. 22 of the Thoroton Society Records Series entitled *Nottinghamshire Household Inventories*. It contains all the surviving inventories (118) for Southwell. Indexed in the back.

4) Early   **FHL 942.52 C4t**
vol. 22

Transactions of the Thoroton Society. Pages 80–112 are "Extracts from Wills Relating to the Parish Churches and Houses of Friars of Nottingham."

5) 1521–1801   **FHL 942 B2ng**
vol. 1

The Northern Genealogist printed some of the records for Edwinstowe on pages 20–24.

6) 1670–1710   **FHL 942.52 H2cl**

Vol. 1 of the Record Series of the Centre for Local History of the University of Nottingham. It contains the transcribed wills and inventories (31) for the parish of Clayworth.

Part 7 Westmorland
Probate Jurisdictions and Microfilmed Records

Introduction

Westmorland was almost evenly divided between the jurisdiction of the Consistory Court of Carlisle (see Cumberland for a full description of that court's records) and the jurisdictions of the Archdeaconry Court of Richmond and three manorial courts. Apparently, references to part of Westmorland belonging to the pre-Reformation Diocese of Lichfield and Coventry are unfounded.

The Archdeaconry of Richmond was part of the Diocese of York until 1541 and thereafter the Diocese of Chester. Evidently, the Diocese of Chester never exercised superior jurisdiction over Richmond in probate matters; rather, such business continued to be handled by the Prerogative Court of York. The probates granted by the Archdeaconry Court of Richmond were usually filed under the name of the deanery in which the testator resided.

Only the parish of Kirkby Lonsdale with its six chapelries (Barbon, Firbank, Hutton Roof, Killington, Mansergh, Middleton) and two townships (Casterton, Lupton) in the southeast corner of the county belonged to the Deanery of Lonsdale. Since this deanery overlapped the county borders of Lancashire and Yorkshire, and since traditionally and numerically its records are most frequently identified with Lancashire, the records for Lonsdale are described and listed in this volume under Lancashire. The remainder of the county of Westmorland covered by the Archdeaconry of Richmond belonged to the Deanery of Kendal, whose records are outlined below.

The earliest original will for the Deanery of Kendal was proven in 1476. Many of the original records for the 1500s and early 1600s are torn and/or water stained; in some cases only fragments survive. Some of the originals were lost (probably when the records were moved to a new repository in 1748) or misfiled, although a few of the lost ones for the deaneries of Copeland and Kendal were recovered. A list of eleven testators leaving wills between 1555 and 1603 has been published,[1] and the names are included in the index in this volume. Abstracts of these records were preserved by the British Museum along with the more numerous entries for the Deanery of Amounderness. (See Lancashire for further details.) References to "Calendar W" usually mean that the original has been lost or possibly filed with the Eastern Deaneries, which were in Yorkshire and are described under that county's section of this volume.

The registered copy wills for Kendal are sparse, and the act books are confined to the eighteenth and nineteenth centuries. Inventories rarely appear with the administration bonds after 1750 but still will be found frequently with the wills as late as 1770.

Of the three manorial courts, Ravenstonedale has by far the most records. The original wills, administrations, and inventories, 1670–1856, are all mixed together in rough chronological order by the initial letter of the surnames involved. There are no act books, but there are two items that could be used as substitute act books. The first is a "List of Bonds," 1767–1818, which are brief abstracts of both probate and administration bonds issued during that time period. The second is a register of

[1]Henry Fishwick, ed., *A List of the Lancashire Wills Proved within the Archdeaconry of Richmond, from A.D. 1457 to 1680; and of Abstracts of Lancashire Wills, from A.D. 1531 to 1652*, Lancashire & Cheshire Record Society, Vol. 10 (The Record Society, 1884), pp. viii–ix. See page 40 of this volume for Robinson and Benn; and page 147 for Atkinson, Barnes, Borwicke, Butcher, Cowperthwat, Jackson, Knype, Manwering, and Wilson.

all probate actions since 1670. The entries here are brief but might supply some additional information beyond that of the original documents.

The records for the Manorial Court of Temple Sowerby, 1575–1816, are arranged similarly. Likewise, there is a substitute act book entitled the "Schedule" that lists references to the original documents in chronological order from 1575 to 1801.

The few records for the Manorial Court of Docker, 1686–1770, were not available at the time of microfilming. They are now available at the Cumbria Record Office, Carlisle. No records for this court are on microfilm.

Probate Decision Table for Westmorland

If the Research Subject Lived in One of These Jurisdictions:	Manor of Docker	Manor of Ravenstone-dale	Manor of Temple Sowerby	Archdeaconry of Richmond	Episcopal Consistory of Carlisle	Anywhere in the County, 1653–1660
Search the probate records of these courts in the order shown below:	DK. BROWN	ROSE	LT. BLUE	GREEN	YELLOW	
Manor Court of Docker (NO FILMS)	1					
Manor Court of Ravenstonedale		1				
Manor Court of Temple Sowerby			1			
Archdeaconry Court of Richmond (Kendal Deanery—see Lancashire for Lonsdale Deanery)	2			1		
Archdeaconry Court of Richmond (Eastern Deaneries—see Yorkshire)	3			2		
Consistory Court of Carlisle (see Cumberland)	4	2	2	4	1	
Prerogative Court of the Archbishop of York (see Yorkshire)	5	3	3	3	2	
Court of the Dean and Chapter of York (see Yorkshire for vacancy jurisdiction)	6	4	4	5	3	
Chancery Court of the Archbishop of York (see Yorkshire)	7	5	5	6	4	
Prerogative Court of the Archbishop of Canterbury (see London)	8	6	6	7	5	1
Court of Delegates, 1643–1857 (see London)	9	7	7	8	6	

Calendars for the Archdeaconry Court of Richmond, Kendal Deanery

(A few abstracts of documents relating to Richmond probates, and Westmorland in general, will be found in the miscellaneous section. Searches in these items and the stray-name index to this volume may reveal entries not found or easily found in the films below.)

The filmed calendars stop in 1720. Hence, the act books will be outlined next as a substitute index for 1720–1857 (for which see the following section). The filmed calendars are arranged as follows:

Time Period	Film or Call No.
1536–1720 A	**98,557** **(item 5)**

This nineteenth-century manuscript begins with maps and a gazetteer for the eight deaneries. Next come the calendars, arranged alphabetically by the names of the five Western Deaneries, for the letter A. Kendal will be the fourth deanery indexed in each case. Watch for a K in the right margin to be certain that it is Kendal Deanery. A W or L notation below the entry refers to the county of residence: Westmorland or Lancashire.

The entries are in chronological order except for a few listed out of sequence after 1720 or on a supplement to be found either at the beginning or the end of that alphabetical portion for each deanery.

An indication to the types of probate is given first, followed by the date of probate, person's name and residence. If a will has been registered, the index will give the name of the register and page number. Cross-references to documents filed with the Eastern Deaneries are also provided. References to "Calendar W" usually indicate an item now lost.

All of the original records, regardless of type, were filed together in boxes after the pattern of this calendar. Match the index entry with the years and letters in the section entitled "Original Wills, Probate Bonds, Admons, and Inventories" to determine the microfilm call number.

Wills not located between 1697–1731 might be found among the registered copy wills. Items not filmed can be identified by consulting Anthony J. Camp, *Wills and Their Whereabouts,* 4th ed. (London: The author, 1974).

1531–1720 B	**98,558** **(item 4)**
1476–1720 C	**98,559** **(item 4)**
1546–1720 D	**98,559** **(item 9)**
1560–1720 E	**98,560** **(item 4)**
1530–1720 F	**98,560** **(item 9)**
1529–1720 G	**98,560** **(item 14)**
1542–1720 H	**98,561** **(item 4)**
1532–1720 I/J	**98,562** **(item 4)**
1533–1720 K	**98,562** **(item 9)**
1503–1720 L	**98,562** **(item 14)**
1530–1720 M	**98,563** **(item 4)**
1556–1720 N	**98,563** **(item 9)**
1559–1720 O	**98,563** **(item 14)**
1530–1720 P	**98,563** **(item 19)**
1599 Q	**98,563** **(item 24)**

One entry.

1530–1720 R	**98,564** **(item 4)**

1515–1720 S	**98,565**
	(item 4)
1554–1720 T	**98,566**
	(item 4)
1572–1720 U/V	**98,566**
	(item 9)
1531–1720 W	**98,567**
	(item 4)
1558–1720 Y	**98,567**
	(item 9)

Act Books for the Archdeaconry Court of Richmond, Kendal Deanery

All of the act books for Kendal were filmed and can be used in lieu of any further indexes as well as a source of additional information. They are arranged as follows:

1712–1718   **99,950**
                                                      (item 2)
The acts for Copeland, Furness, Kendal, and Lonsdale Deaneries are mixed together without an index but in chronological order. Personal and place names, including an indication of deanery, appear in the left margin. The acts are in Latin. They include references to some marriage license bonds for 1705 and 1712–1715.

At the beginning of this group of act entries are two pages from an act book for 1705 containing eight items for Kendal. There are also references to caveats, which refer to contested estates, and to sequestrations, which involve property where there was no heir or claimant.

1719–1726   **99,950**
                                                      (item 3)
                                                      166,279
The acts for Copeland, Furness, Kendal, and Lonsdale are in turn rather mixed. There is a master index at the beginning. The actual entries for Kendal appear on pages 114–153. The acts are in Latin, but the index is sufficiently clear that one can find original documents without reading the act itself. (The second film is an exact duplicate of the first film covering the years 1719–1726, but the second may be more readable.)

1727–1748   **99,951**
                                                      (item 3)
Kendal Act Book. The acts are in Latin until 1733. The index at the end continues on to 1762. The index is arranged alphabetically with each letter subdivided chronologically for all of the years treated. One could go directly from the index to the original probate; however, the act may provide additional information.

1748–1830   **100,066**
Kendal Act Book. The acts are divided into three sections, each with its own index. First comes an index for 1748–1762 arranged alphabetically, with each letter subdivided chronologically for all of the years treated; this is followed by the act entries. The second section treats 1763–1798 in the same fashion, and the third does the same for 1798–1830. At the end of the film is a list of parishes for which "registers and terriers" were missing through 1820. The earliest entry was for 1664. There is no indication as to what types of registers were meant.

1830–1857   **100,067**
Kendal Act Book

Original Wills, Probate Bonds, Admons, and Inventories for the Archdeaconry Court of Richmond, Kendal Deanery

1536–1630 A   **98,589**
Box 205

1631–1748 A   **98,590**
Box 206 contains the records for 1631–1680.
Box 207 contains the records for 1681–1710.
Box 208 contains the records for 1711–1748.
The film ends with an admon bond for 1753 for William Atkinson and a will proven in 1735 for John Archer, which was copied in 1753 for a Chancery suit.

1531–1590 B   **98,591**
Box 209

1591–1615 B   **98,592**
Box 210

1616–1625 B   **98,593**
Box 211

1626–1640 B   **98,594**
Box 212

1641–1660 B   **98,595**
Box 213

1661–1670 B   **98,595**
                                                      (item 2)
Box 214

1671–1690 B   **98,596**
Box 215 contains the records for 1671–1680.
Box 216 contains the records for 1681–1690.

1691–1710 B   **98,597**
Box 217 contains the records for 1691–1700.
Box 218 contains the records for 1701–1710.

1711–1726 B Box 219	**98,598**
1727–1748 B Box 220 contains the records for 1727–1740. Box 221 contains the records for 1741–1748.	**98,599**
1476–1620 C Box 222	**98,600**
1621–1660 C Box 223	**98,601**
1661–1680 C Box 224	**98,602**
1681–1700 C Box 225	**98,603**
1701–1730 C Box 226	**98,604**
1731–1748 C Box 227	**98,605**
1546–1625 D Box 228	**98,606**
1626–1670 D Box 229. Printed form for bonds appears about 1670 for a few years, then less frequently until rarely used.	**98,607**
1671–1710 D Box 230 contains the records for 1671–1690. Box 231 contains the records for 1691–1710.	**98,608**
1711–1748 D Box 232	**98,609**
1560–1748 E Box 233	**98,610**
1530–1660 F Box 234	**98,611**
1661–1710 F Box 235	**98,612**
1711–1748 F Box 236	**98,613**
1529–1630 G Box 237	**98,614**
1631–1680 G Box 238	**98,615**
1681–1710 G Box 239	**98,616**

1711–1748 G Box 240	**98,617**
1542–1604 H Box 241	**98,618**
1605–1630 H Box 242 contains a page from an ecclesiastical act book for May-June 1636, which is filed here with the probates of 1622. The inventory for James Hodgson of Crosthwaite, filed under 1626, could actually be dated 1676.	**98,619**
1631–1640 H Box 243	**98,620**
1641–1670 H Box 244	**98,621**
1671–1690 H Box 245. See film 98,619 for another possible entry for 1676.	**98,622**
1691–1700 H Box 246	**98,623**
1701–1720 H Box 247	**98,624**
1721–1730 H Box 248	**98,625**
1731–1748 H Box 249	**98,626**
1532–1630 I/J Box 250	**98,627**
1631–1660 I/J Box 251	**98,628**
1661–1700 I/J Box 252	**98,629**
1701–1748 I/J Box 253	**98,630**
1533–1660 K Box 254	**98,631**
1661–1748 K Box 255	**98,632**
1503–1620 L Box 256 has a document proven in 1615 and filed with 1616.	**98,633**
1621–1660 L Box 257	**98,634**

1661–1710 L   **98,635**
Box 258

1711–1748 L   **98,636**
Box 259

1530–1635 M   **98,637**
Box 260

1636–1660 M   **98,638**
Box 261

1661–1700 M   **98,639**
Box 262

1701–1748 M   **98,640**
Box 263

1556–1660 N   **98,641**
Box 264

1661–1700 N   **98,642**
Box 265

1701–1748 N   **98,643**
Box 266

1559–1748 O   **98,643**
                                (item 2)
Box 266 (cont.)

1530–1630 P   **98,644**
Box 267

1631–1660 P   **98,645**
Box 268

1661–1690 P   **98,646**
Box 269

1691–1720 P   **98,647**
Box 270

1721–1748 P   **98,648**
Box 271

1530–1625 Q/R   **98,649**
Box 272. This film starts with the only Q entry, which is for 1599, followed by the Rs for 1530–1625.

1626–1680 R   **98,650**
Box 273

1681–1720 R   **98,651**
Box 274

1721–1748 R   **98,652**
Box 275

1515–1590 S   **98,652**
                                (item 2)
Box 275 (cont.). The entry for 1515 and another for 1537 appear at the end of the film. An inventory and will for 1587 will be found at the start of film 98,654 below.

1591–1620 S   **98,653**
Box 276

1621–1641 S   **98,654**
Box 277. The first item on this film is an inventory and will for 1587. Then comes the normal sequence for 1621–1641.

1641–1652 S   **98,655**
Box 278

1656–1680 S   **98,656**
Box 279

1681–1700 S   **98,657**
Box 280

1701–1720 S   **98,658**
Box 281

1721–1730 S   **98,659**
Box 282

1731–1748 S   **98,660**
Box 283

1554–1635 T   **98,661**
Box 284

1636–1680 T   **98,662**
Box 285. A document proven in 1639 is filed with 1640.

1681–1700 T   **98,663**
Box 286

1702–1748 T   **98,664**
Box 287

1572–1748 U/V   **98,664**
                                (item 2)
Box 287 (cont.). The chronological sequence for this series is as follows: 1661–1664, 1721–1739, 1715 (one item), 1572–1647, 1709 (one item), and 1744 (one item).

1531–1590 W   **98,665**
Box 288 has a document proven in 1560 and filed with 1557.

1591–1615 W   **98,666**
Box 289

1616–1636 W   **98,667**
Box 290

1637–1670 W   **98,668**
Box 291. The documents from 1637–1650 could not be opened sufficiently for filming. Thus, this film actually starts with a series for 1651–1660. This is followed by a reference to a document proven in 1647, which was "sealed down" and could not be filmed. Then comes another section for 1643–1650, and finally the series for 1661–1670. There is a tuition bond dated 1672 for Thomas, the son of Thomas Wilson, filed with 1670.

1671–1680 W   **98,669**
Box 292. Note the reference to 1672 in the preceding film.

1681–1694 W   **98,670**
Box 293

1695–1710 W   **98,671**
Box 294

1711–1730 W   **98,672**
Box 295

1731–1748 W   **98,673**
Box 296

1558–1742 Y   **98,673**
                                 (item 2)
Box 296 (cont.)

1748–1760 A–C   **99,076**
An A admon for 1753 will be found on film 98,590 above.

1748–1760 D–H   **99,077**

1748–1760 J–P   **99,078**

1748–1760 P–W   **99,079**
The chronological sequence is inexact.

1748–1760 W   **99,080**

1761–1770 A–D   **99,081**

1761–1770 E–H   **99,082**

1761–1770 J–S   **99,083**

1761–1770 T–Y   **99,084**

1771–1780 A–F   **99,085**

1771–1780 G–N   **99,086**
The last three documents for N are out of sequence: 1778, 1780, and 1777.

1771–1780 P–Y   **99,087**

1781–1790 A–G   **99,088**

1781–1790 H–L   **99,089**
H, I, and J are mixed together.

1781–1790 L–Y   **99,090**

1791–1800 A–F   **99,091**

1791–1800 G–P   **99,092**

1791–1800 R–Y   **99,093**

1801–1810 A–E   **99,094**
The first C will, dated 1799, was written on the back of a broadside advertising the patent medicines and other wares of H. Walmsley, stationer of Lancaster.

1801–1810 F–K   **99,095**

1801–1810 L–R   **99,096**

1801–1810 S–Y   **99,097**

1811–1820 A–C   **99,098**

1811–1820 D–J   **99,099**

1811–1820 K–P   **99,100**

1811–1820 R–W   **99,101**

1811–1820 W–Y   **99,102**

1821–1830 A–B   **99,103**

1821–1830 B–F   **99,104**

1821–1830 G–L   **99,105**

1821–1830 M–R   **99,106**

1821–1830 S–W   **99,107**
The Ws end in 1829. See the next film.

1821–1830 W–Y   **99,108**
The Ws begin in 1829. At the start of the U/V series is a notice dated 1815 concerning the enclosure of the manor and township of Caton in the parish of Lancaster. There is a Y document for 1825 mixed in with the 1830s.

1831–1840 A–B   **99,109**
This film starts with a very long, bound will for Mrs. Harriot Carter proven in 1836. Then come the As for 1831–1840, followed by the Bs, which end in 1837. See the next film. There is a B document for 1834 filed in 1833.

1831–1840 B–F   **99,110**
The Bs start in 1837. Note the C entry on the preceding film.

1831–1840 G–J   **99,111**

1831–1840 K–O   **99,112**

1831–1840 P–S   **99,113**

1831–1840 T–Y   **99,114**
The Ws contain a document for 1843.

1841–1850 A–B   **99,115**

1841–1850 B–F   **99,116**

1841–1850 F–G   **99,117**

1841–1850 H–M   **99,118**

1841–1850 N–S   **99,119**

1841–1850 T–Y   **99,120**
There is a W document for 1843 found on film 99,114.

1851–1858 A–D   **99,121**
See the note for C on the next film.

1851–1858 E–J   **99,122**
In the Hs for 1854 is part of an undated will for Edward Clough of Preston.

1851–1858 K–R   **99,123**

1851–1858 S–Y   **99,124**

Registered Copy Wills for the Archdeaconry Court of Richmond, Kendal Deanery

---

1476–1696
Do not exist; see the original wills.

1697–1706   **166,277**
The "Carr" register for the deaneries of Copeland, Kendal, Lonsdale, and Furness. The wills for the various deaneries are mixed together in fair chronological order. There is an index at the end arranged alphabetically, with each letter subdivided chronologically for all the years treated. The index does not indicate the deanery; however, this information is provided in the manuscript index described at the start of Kendal's records in the section entitled "Calendars." Further entries for 1697–1698 will be found on the next film.

1705–1731   **166,278**
The "Todd" register covering 1716–1717 for the same deaneries as the above entry comes first. Its index appears at the back of the next register that follows.

The "Preston" register starts with some entries for 1697–1698, but it mainly goes from 1705 through the first half of the 1720s with a few entries continuing on to 1731. Apparently there is no overlap between the three registers. The index starts out like the one on the preceding film by first covering the As for 1705–1723. It then refers to a rider that indexes the As for the "Todd" register before moving on to do the same for the Bs.

1731–1809
Do not exist; see the original wills.

1810–1811
See Camp's *Wills and Their Whereabouts.*

1812–1858
Do not exist; see the original wills.

Indexes and Original Probate Records for the Manorial Court of Ravenstonedale

---

(A few abstracts of documents relating to this court might be found in the miscellaneous section.)

1670–1856 Index   **97,321**
This film begins with a nineteenth-century index to all documents in the time period covered. The names are arranged roughly alphabetically, and each entry provides the year of probate, name, residence, and type of probate.

1767–1818 Bonds   **97,321**
                                                         (item 2)
The index described above is followed by a "List of Bonds." These listings are brief abstracts of the key information to be found in both probate and administration bonds. They are listed in chronological order. Use the preceding index first. If it refers to a bond in this time period, check this section next and then search for the original bond and any accompanying documents as outlined below.

1670–1856 Register   **97,321**
                                                         (item 3)
Following the list of bonds is "A Register of all Probates of Wills, Administrations, and Tuitions." This register is in chronological order and has the same information as the index, except it does have the full date of probate. One might wish to double-check it with the index and the originals in the hope that a little extra information might be gleaned.

| 1670–1856 A–B | 97,321 |
| | (item 4) |

Box 1 contains the original documents for this portion of the alphabet filed roughly chronologically. They seem to be arranged in approximately the same order as the index.

| 1670–1856 B–F | 97,322 |

Box 1 (cont.)

| 1670–1856 F–H | 97,323 |

Box 2

| 1670–1856 H–O | 97,324 |

Box 2 (cont.). The only items for O appear toward the end of the Ms.

| 1670–1856 P–W | 97,325 |

Box 3

Indexes and Original Probate Records for the Manorial Court of Temple Sowerby

(A few abstracts of documents relating to this court might be found in the miscellaneous section.)

| 1575–1816 Index | 97,326 |

The index seems to have been made at the same time and in the same fashion as the one described for Ravenstonedale. Listings to the originals are in alphabetical order and give the year of probate, name, residence, and type of probate.

| 1575–1801 Schedule | 97,326 |
| | (item 2) |

This item is comparable to the register mentioned for Ravenstonedale. See the section for the Manorial Court of Ravenstonedale for further details.

| 1575–1816 A–Y | 97,326 |
| | (item 3) |

Box 4 (the previous three boxes refer to Ravenstonedale) contains the original documents filed in the same order as the index.

Miscellaneous: Abstracts and Select Indexes for Probates Relating to Westmorland

Searches in this material may accelerate research or supplement previous findings but should not supplant research in the original records. Compare any finds here with the originals.

| 1) 1383–1616 | FHL 942 B4s |

The Publications of the Surtees Society. The Society began publishing materials concerning the northern counties in 1834. Research on any of the counties that make up the Province of York could benefit from examining the contents of this series. A master index will be found in volume 150.

Abstracts of some wills from the PCC concerning the northern counties, including Westmorland, were published in volume 116 (1383–1558) and volume 121 (1555–1616). These two volumes have been microfilmed as items 5 and 6 of film 990,300. Likewise, there may be something of interest for Westmorland in the volumes of this series that are abstracts of some wills registered at York, especially the PCY. These include volume 4 (1316–1430), volume 30 (1426–1467), volume 45 (1395–1491), volume 53 (1484–1509), volume 79 (1509–1531), and volume 106 (1531–1551).

	also 994,031
	(item 7) &
	6,073,308

Abstracts of probates (208) relating to the Archdeaconry Court of Richmond (1442–1579) were published in volume 26. They may or may not refer to the deaneries of Kendal and Lonsdale.

| 2) Varies | FHL 942.8 P2i |

Index and Extracts of Cumbrians in Wills Proved at the Prerogative Court of Canterbury, 1984. Compiled by Jim Richardson and Ron Shaw and published by the Cumbria Family History Society. Only some of the items indexed have accompanying extracts.

3) 1457–1680	FHL 942.7 B4Lc
	vol. 10, p. viii
	also 823,526
	(item 3)

Vol. 10 of the Lancashire & Cheshire Record Society. It mentions nine probates housed at the British Museum for persons from Kendal Deanery. They are as follows: William Atkinson of Preston Richard (1571); John Barnes, husbandman of Burton (1591); Mabil Borwicke, widow of Troutbeck (1571); Anne Butcher of Everingshead (1585); Guy Cowperthwat of Kenlinger (1570); Edwine Jackson of Ambleside (1603); Christopher Knype of Crossebancke (1555); Katherin Manwering of Kendal (1569); and William Wilson of Kendal (1564).

| 4) 1609–1795 | FHL 942 B2ng |

The Northern Genealogist. There are a few scattered references in this publication to wills of Westmorland residents. The extracts of volume 1 concern wills proven at York for: Christopher Middleton of Deansbiginge (1603), James Bellingham of Over Levens (1680), Deborah Baynes of Appleby (1736), and Sir William Fleming of Rysdal (1736). Volume 3 provides information on a few more Richmond wills.

5) 1686–1738   **FHL 942.88 S2s**
                                                      also 476,216
                                                           (item 2)

Some Westmorland Wills, 1686–1738. This book was edited by John Somervell and published in Kendal in 1928. The information given refers to Quakers. There are eighty-one wills and inventories, plus other data from Quaker records.

6) Varies   **FHL 942.8 C4c**
Transactions of the Cumberland & Westmorland Antiquarian & Archaeological Society. An occasional probate will be found printed in both the 1st Series and the more numerous New Series of this publication. There are master indexes to volumes 1–12 and 13–25 of the New Series, which would be worth consulting for research on a particular person.

Part 8   Yorkshire
Probate Jurisdictions and Microfilmed Records

Introduction

Probate procedures in Yorkshire required numerous courts and officials to serve such a large geographic area with so many diverse jurisdictions. The unusual name of the prominent court during the Middle Ages reflects this situation: the Exchequer Court of the Archbishop of York, sometimes referred to as the Exchequer Court of the deans.

The Exchequer Court, along with the Chancery Court of the Archbishop of York and the Court of the Dean and Chapter of York, all have records dating from the fourteenth century. They were joined later in the sixteenth century by the Prerogative Court of the Archbishop of York (PCY) and a host of small peculiar courts, most of whose records also date from the sixteenth century.

To carry out its testamentary business, the Exchequer Court depended upon the services of four archdeaconries subdivided into seventeen deaneries. The act books reproduce these subdivisions, and the original records are usually grouped under the name of the deanery and by the date when the probate was proven. The "Deanery Book" (FHL Ref 942.74 P2, also items 2–4 on film 100,081) provides a listing of parishes and the deaneries to which they belong. (Item 6 on film 100,081 gives an even more detailed listing by villages not found in the typescript book.)

The microfilming done for the Exchequer and Prerogative Courts concentrates on the registered copy wills, 1389–1858, and act books, 1502–1858. The registered copies do not include inventories but should be accompanied by an entry like an act book before 1502. Original records were filmed to fill in missing portions of the register books and will include inventories from the late seventeenth through the late eighteenth centuries. Also filmed were original unproved wills known as *reinfecta* wills (see page 19 of item 1 of film 100,081) in York and a register of wills decreed out of court, 1778–1833.

The Prerogative Court held jurisdiction in cases of *bona notabilia* (property worth £5 or more) crossing ecclesiastical or county boundaries within the province. It appears that it even handled some cases normally reserved for the Prerogative Court of Canterbury. The records of the Prerogative Court of York are filed with those of the Exchequer Court, with the exception of the act books from at least 1624–1858. The earlier act books may be recorded with those for the Deanery of York City.

The Chancery Court of the Archbishop of York, sometimes confused with the Consistory Court, probated many of the wills of the clergy and was the main probate court when the archbishop made a visitation to a lower court, during which time the lower court was said to be inhibited or closed. The Chancery Court also acted as an appellate court. There are printed cause papers for the files of cases pertaining to appeals from 1527–1858.

The Dean and Chapter functioned as the main probate court during vacancies of the office of the archbishop. It also held peculiar jurisdiction over certain parishes, and the records of many other peculiar courts were filed with the records of this court. The records are separated into categories: the business of peculiar jurisdictions and that of the vacancies. The original records from the business of peculiar jurisdictions were rearranged in the last few years, and a modern listing of the contents was added. This new arrangement was filmed in 1989. There are also some filmed abstracts available from the Court Books of the Dean and Chapter.

The Archdeaconry of Richmond existed separately from the Exchequer Court with almost the same power as that of a diocese. Technically, it belonged to the Diocese of York until 1541 and thereafter the Diocese of Chester, but superior jurisdiction over Richmond in probate matters continued to be handled by the Prerogative Court. Richmond's records are also filed by deanery. Since most of the Deanery of Lonsdale was in Lancashire, the records for the Yorkshire parishes belonging to Lonsdale will be found listed under Lancashire.

The four Yorkshire parishes on the Lancashire border that were covered by Lonsdale were Bentham, Clapham, Sedbergh, and Thornton in Lonsdale. These parishes included the chapelries and townships of Chapel le Dale and Ingleton for Bentham; Austwick, Lawkland, and Newby for Clapham; and Dent, Dowbiggin, Garsdale, and Howgill for Sedbergh.

Most Yorkshire parishes pertaining to Richmond came under the three Eastern Deaneries of Richmond, Catterick, and Boroughbridge. Unfortunately, the original records for the Eastern Deaneries have not been filmed. The microfilms for Richmond consist of the manuscript calendars, 1410–1857; the act books; and the registered copy wills.

Microfilms of the peculiar courts are arranged under a general section as well as by separate entries under the name of the principal town in each jurisdiction. Both sections should be searched. (Item 1 of film 100,081 has a useful guide to this system written in 1914.) In the case of three peculiars, ancient ecclesiastical boundaries have been ignored in favor of geographical ones. The microfilms for the peculiar of Hexham are listed under Northumberland. Those for the peculiars of Allerton and Howden are here with Yorkshire, despite their theoretical alignment with Durham.

It should be noted that some microfilming has been done in the Registry of Deeds for the three Yorkshire ridings. Abstracts of wills concerning real estate were entered among the deeds from the start of the eighteenth century. Check the Family History Library Catalog for further details.

Probate Decision Table A for Yorkshire

If the Research Subject Lived in One of These Jurisdictions:	*Peculiars Not Inhibited*	*Peculiars Inhibited*	*Prebends of York*	*Peculiar of Beverley*	*Manors of Crossley, Bingley, and Pudsey*	*Peculiar of St. Leonard's Hospital, York*	*Peculiar of Howden*	*Peculiar of the Subdean of York*
Search the probate records of these courts in the order shown below:	WHITE CIRCLED IN RED	WHITE CIRCLED IN RED	WHITE CIRCLED IN NAVY	YELLOW	LT. BLUE	LT. ORANGE	PURPLE	WHITE CIRCLED IN BLUE (PRESTON)
Indicated Court (see Separate Peculiars for town name)	1	1	1					
Adjacent Courts	2	4	4			2		
Court of the Provost of St. John's Beverley				1				
Manorial Court Records					1			
Court of St. Leonard's Hospital, York						1		
Peculiar Court of Howden and Howdenshire							1	
Court of the Subdean of York								1
Consistory Court of Durham (see Durham)							2	
Prerogative Court of the Archbishop of York	3	3	3	2	2	3	3	3
Court of the Dean and Chapter of York	4	2	2	3	3	4	4	4
Chancery Court of the Archbishop of York	5	5	5	4	4	5	5	2
Prerogative Court of the Archbishop of Canterbury (see London)	6	6	6	5	5	6	6	5
Court of Delegates, 1643–1857 (see London)	7	7	7	6	6	7	7	6

Probate Decision Table B for Yorkshire

If the Research Subject Lived in One of These Jurisdictions:	Archdeacon of York or West Riding	Archdeacon of the East Riding	Succentor of York	Chancellor of York	Precentor of York	Dean of York	Dean and Chapter of York	Peculiar of the Archbishop in Ripon
Search the probate records of these courts in the order shown below:	**LT. GRAY (MEXBOROUGH)**	**PINK (MAPPLETON)**	**WHITE CIRCLED IN BROWN (TUNSTALL)**	**SALMON**	**DK. GRAY**	**DK. ORANGE**	**BROWN**	**BLUE-GREEN**
Court of the Archdeacon of York or West Riding	1							
Court of the Archdeacon of the East Riding		1						
Court of the Succentor of York			1					
Court of the Chancellor of York				1				
Court of the Precentor of York					1			
Court of the Dean of York						1		
Peculiar Court of the Archbishop in Ripon (NO RECORDS)								1
Prerogative Court of the Archbishop of York	3	3	3	3	3	3	2	2
Court of the Dean and Chapter of York	4	4	2	2	2	2	1	3
Chancery Court of the Archbishop of York	2	2	4	4	4	4	3	4
Prerogative Court of the Archbishop of Canterbury (see London)	5	5	5	5	5	5	4	5
Court of Delegates, 1643–1857 (see London)	6	6	6	6	6	6	5	6

Probate Decision Table C for Yorkshire

If the Research Subject Lived in One of These Jurisdictions:	Peculiar of Middleham	Peculiar of Allerton (before 1666)	Peculiar of Allerton (1666–1857)	Episcopal Consistory of Durham	Episcopal Consistory of Chester	Archdeaconry of Richmond	Exchequer of York	Anywhere in the County, 1653–1660
Search the probate records of these courts in the order shown below:	WHITE CIRCLED IN GOLD	WHITE CIRCLED IN DK. ORANGE	WHITE CIRCLED IN DK. ORANGE	WHITE CIRCLED IN PINK	WHITE CIRCLED IN PURPLE	YELLOW-GREEN	GREEN	
Royal Peculiar Court of Middleham	1							
Peculiar Court of Allerton and Allertonshire			1					
Consistory Court of Durham (see Durham)		1	2	1				
Consistory Court of Chester (see Lancashire)					1			
Archdeaconry Court of Richmond (Eastern Deaneries—see Lancashire for Lonsdale Deanery)	2					1		
Prerogative Court of the Archbishop of York	3	2	3	2	2	2	1	
Court of the Dean and Chapter of York		3	(vacancy) 4	(vacancy) 3	(vacancy) 3	(vacancy) 3	(vacancy) 2	
Chancery Court of the Archbishop of York		4	5	4	4	4	3	
Prerogative Court of the Archbishop of Canterbury (see London)	4	5	6	5	5	5	4	1
Court of Delegates, 1643–1857 (see London)	5	6	7	6	6	6	5	

	1554–1568	FHL 942.74 B4a
		vol. 14
		402,538 (item 3)
		599,867 (item 3)

Vol. 14 of the Record Series of the Yorkshire Archaeological Society. The appendix lists the admons in the Act Books, 1553–1568.

Indexes and Calendars for the Exchequer and Prerogative Courts of the Archbishop of York

(Some abstracts or extracts of documents relating to Yorkshire probates will be found in the miscellaneous section. Searches in these items and the stray-name index to this volume may reveal entries not found in the calendars outlined below. Such materials are usually edited and may still be in Latin for the earlier periods.)

1) The printed indexes are also available on microfilm where indicated by the six-digit number below the call number of the book. In many cases they were filmed twice.

Time Period	Film or Call No.

1389–1514   FHL 942.74 B4a
                                        vol. 6
                                        402,538 &
                                        599,724 (item 3)

Vol. 6 of the Record Series of the Yorkshire Archaeological Society. Included are admons and unregistered wills through 1502. Appendix I on pages 193–198 adds entries from the Act Books not found elsewhere for 1502–1514. The letter "s" before a name indicates that an abstract is available in the series published by the Surtees Society, which see in the miscellaneous section. There is an errata listing of three items for this volume on page 204, as well as two items for volume 4. See the next volume for further additions and corrections.

1514–1553   FHL 942.74 B4a
                                        vol. 11
                                        402,538 (item 2)
                                        599,725 (item 4)

Vol. 11 of the Record Series of the Yorkshire Archaeological Society. Appendix I on pages 209–243 refers to the admons in the Act Books for the same time period. An errata list for this volume appears on page 208, and pages 244–246 provide further additions and corrections to volume 6.

1554–1568   FHL 942.74 B4a
                                        vol. 14
                                        402,538 (item 3)
                                        599,867 (item 3)

Vol. 14 of the Record Series of the Yorkshire Archaeological Society. The appendix lists the admons in the Act Books, 1553–1568.

1568–1585   FHL 942.74 B4a
                                        vol. 19
                                        402,539 &
                                        599,868 (item 4)

Vol. 19 of the Record Series of the Yorkshire Archaeological Society. The appendix lists the admons in the Act Books, 1568–1585.

1585–1594   FHL 942.74 B4a
                                        vol. 22
                                        402,539 (item 2)
                                        547,181 (item 4)

Vol. 22 of the Record Series of the Yorkshire Archaeological Society. The appendix lists the admons in the Act Books, 1585–1594.

1594–1602   FHL 942.74 B4a
                                        vol. 24
                                        402,539 (item 3)
                                        599,869 (item 3)

Vol. 24 of the Record Series of the Yorkshire Archaeological Society. The appendix lists the admons in the Act Books, 1594–1602.

1603–1611   FHL 942.74 B4a
                                        vol. 26
                                        402,539 (item 4)
                                        599,870 (item 1)

Vol. 26 of the Record Series of the Yorkshire Archaeological Society. The appendix lists the admons in the Act Books, 1603–1611.

1612–1619   FHL 942.74 B4a
                                        vol. 28
                                        402,540 (item 1)
                                        599,870 (item 3)

Vol. 28 of the Record Series of the Yorkshire Archaeological Society. The appendix lists the admons in the Act Books, 1612–1619. Two items of errata are on page 227.

1620–1627   FHL 942.74 B4a
                                        vol. 32
                                        402,540 (item 2)
                                        599,871 (item 1)

Vol. 32 of the Record Series of the Yorkshire Archaeological Society. The appendix lists the admons in the Act Books, 1620–1627. There are five items of errata for this volume on page 183.

1627–1636   **FHL 942.74 B4a**
                                 vol. 35
                                 402,540 (item 3)
                                 599,871 (item 4)

Vol. 35 of the Record Series of the Yorkshire Archaeological Society. There are a few wills for 1637. The
appendix lists the admons in the Act Books, 1627–1652.
There are three items of errata facing the Preface. In volume 49, Appendix II refers to unregistered wills or probate acts of wills lost or destroyed for 1633–1634.

1636–1652   **FHL 942.74 B4a**
                                 vol. 4
                                 402,537 (item 2)
                                 599,724 (item 1)

Vol. 4 of the Record Series of the Yorkshire Archaeological Society. See the previous listing for the admons,
1627–1652, and perhaps some additional wills for 1637.
The alphabet is repeated in two-year groupings throughout the time period, with the exception of a Z for
1639–1640 that appears on page 201. There are three
items of errata on page vi, plus others in volume 6. See
the next listing for other entries between 1649–1652.

1649–1660   **FHL 942.74 B4a**
                                 vol. 1
                                 402,537 (item 1)
                                 599,723 (item 1)

Vol. 1 of the Record Series of the Yorkshire Archaeological Society. Pages 49–245 index the Yorkshire
wills proven in London during the Commonwealth
period, and pages 246–261 do the same for the admons.
There is a master index at the end of the volume.
Abstracts of some of these wills appear in volume 9,
which see in the miscellaneous section.

1660–1665   **FHL 942.74 B4a**
                                 vol. 49
                                 547,175

Vol. 49 of the Record Series of the Yorkshire Archaeological Society. Appendix I on pages 106–147 lists the
admons in the Act Books, 1660–1665. Two corrections
appear opposite page 1, and an omission is on page 104.

1666–1672   **FHL 942.74 B4a**
                                 vol. 60
                                 402,541 (item 1)

Vol. 60 of the Record Series of the Yorkshire Archaeological Society. Appendix I on pages 118–180 lists the
admons in the Act Books, 1666–1672.

1673–1680   **FHL 942.74 B4a**
                                 vol. 68
                                 402,541 (item 2)
                                 599,877 (item 2)

Vol. 68 of the Record Series of the Yorkshire Archaeological Society. Appendix I on pages 138–212 lists the
admons in the Act Books, 1673–1680.

1681–1688   **FHL 942.74 B4a**
                                 vol. 89
                                 402,541 (item 3)
                                 599,880 (item 5)

Vol. 89 of the Record Series of the Yorkshire Archaeological Society. No wills are registered here between
1685–April 1686; see the section for vacancy wills,
1683, 1686–1688, under the Court of the Dean and
Chapter of York. Appendix I on pages 75–142 lists the
admons in the Act Books, 1681–1686.

1688–1710 A–K   **FHL 942.74 S2y**
                                 908,171

A typescript calendar of the Exchequer Court *only*.
Compiled by the Family History Library based on its
microfilms of the Act Books. It does not include the
deaneries of Nottingham. For the Deanery of Holderness
with Hull, 1688–1705, see the entry for the Prerogative
Court below. Note also the next entry.

1688–1710 L–Z   **FHL 942.74 S2y**
                                 908,171 (item 2)

A continuation of the previous item, which see. NOTE:
There are also microfilmed calendars for *both* courts, but
to the registered copy wills only on film 99,445 (items
1–6).

1711–1731 A–H   **FHL 942.74 S2y**
                                 873,931

A typescript calendar of the Exchequer Court *only*.
Compiled by the Family History Library based on its
microfilms of the Act Books. It does not include the
deaneries of Nottingham. See the next entry.

1711–1731 I–Y   **FHL 942.74 S2y**
                                 873,931 (item 2)

A continuation of the previous item, which see. NOTE:
There are also microfilmed calendars for *both* courts, but
to the registered copy wills only on films 99,445 (items
7–9) and 99,446 (items 1–14).

1688–1731   **FHL 942.74 S2yp**
                                 990,061 (item 2)

A typescript calendar of the Prerogative Court and the
Deanery of Holderness with Hull in the Exchequer
Court. This is a second edition of a work compiled by
the Family History Library based on its microfilms of
the Act Books. (The first edition for the PCY only is
item 1 of film 924,746. Holderness for 1688–1705 is
item 3 of film 924,148.) See the previous four entries for
details on the Exchequer Court and films of calendars for
the registered copy wills of both courts.

2) The filmed calendars that follow group all documents
for both courts alphabetically by the first letter in the
surname under the year and month of probate. If no volume and folio numbers are given, then the dates of probate must be matched with those of the microfilmed

registered copy wills, many of which are not in chronological order, to find the entry.

1731 May–1737 May   **99,446**
                                           (item 15)

What appears to be the original, but smaller, version of this calendar is on film 98,924 item 6.

1737 Jun–1741 Mar   **99,446**
                                           (item 16)

What appears to be the original, but smaller, version of this calendar is on film 98,924 item 7.

1741 Mar–1745 Jul   **99,447**
                                           (item 1)

What appears to be the original, but smaller, version of this calendar is on film 98,924 item 8.

1745 Aug–1757 May   **99,447**
                                           (item 2)

1757 Jun–1770 Dec   **99,447**
                                           (item 3)

1771 Jan–1777 Jun   **99,448**
                                           (item 1)

1777 Jul–1785 May   **99,448**
                                           (item 2)

1785 Jun–1792 Dec   **99,448**
                                           (item 3)

1793 Jan–1799 Dec   **99,448**
                                           (item 4)

1800 Jan–1803 Dec   **99,449**
                                           (item 1)

1804 Jan–1809 May   **99,449**
                                           (item 2)

1809 Jun–1814 Aug   **99,449**
                                           (item 3)

1814 Sep–1819 Feb   **99,449**
                                           (item 4)

1819 Mar–1823 May   **99,450**
                                           (item 1)

1823 Jun–1826 Dec   **99,450**
                                           (item 2)

1827 Jan–1830 Oct   **99,450**
                                           (item 3)

1830 Nov–1834 Apr   **99,451**
                                           (item 1)

1834 May–1837 Jun   **99,451**
                                           (item 2)

1837 Jul–1840 Feb   **99,451**
                                           (item 3)

1840 Mar–1842 Aug   **99,451**
                                           (item 4)

1842 Sep–1845 May   **99,452**
                                           (item 1)

1845 Jun–1847 Jun   **99,452**
                                           (item 2)

1847 Jul–1849 Sep   **99,452**
                                           (item 3)

1849 Oct–1851 Nov   **99,452**
                                           (item 4)

1851 Dec–1853 Aug   **99,453**
                                           (item 1)

1853 Sep–1855 Jun   **99,453**
                                           (item 2)

1855 Jul–1857 Aug   **99,453**
                                           (item 3)

1857 Sep–1858 Jan   **99,453**
                                           (item 4)

Original Wills, Admons, and Inventories for the Exchequer and Prerogative Courts of the Archbishop of York

---

(The original documents are filed by the year and month of probate. Occasionally the films appear to be in rough alphabetical order, although that may be reverse alphabetical order.)

1389–1637

Not filmed. Use the registered copy wills. For details, consult Anthony J. Camp's *Wills and Their Whereabouts*, 4th ed. (London: The author, 1974).

1638 Jan–Mar   99,519

1638 Apr–Jul   99,520

1638 Aug   99,521

1638 Sep–1639 Jan   99,522

1639 Jan–Feb   99,523

1639 Mar–May	**99,524**
1639 May–Oct	**99,525**
A few inventories are spotted here.	
1639 Oct–Dec	**99,526**
1640 Jan–Apr	**99,527**
1640 Apr–Jul	**99,528**
1640 Jul–Dec	**99,529**
1641 Jan–May	**99,530**
1641 May–Sep	**99,531**
1641 Sep	**99,532**
1641 Oct–1642 May	**99,533**
1642 May	**99,534**
1642 Jun–Oct	**99,535**
1642 Oct–Dec	**99,536**
1643 Jan–Oct	**99,537**
1643 Oct–Dec	**99,538**
1644 Jan–Jul	**99,539**
1644 Aug–Oct	**99,540**
1644 Oct–Dec	**99,541**
1645 Jan–Apr	**99,542**
1645 Apr–Aug	**99,543**
1645 Sep–Oct	**99,544**
1645 Oct–1646 Mar	**99,545**
1646 Apr–Jun	**99,546**
1646 Jul	**99,547**
1646 Aug–Nov	**99,548**
1646 Nov–Dec	**99,549**
1647 Jan–Apr	**99,550**
1647 Apr–Jun	**99,551**
1647 Jul–Sep	**99,552**

1647 Oct–Dec	**99,553**
1648 Jan–May	**99,554**
1648 May	**99,555**
1648 Jun–Oct	**99,556**
1648 Oct–Dec	**99,558**
1649 Jan–Apr	**99,557**
1649 Apr–Jul	**99,559**
1649 Aug–Dec	**99,560**
1650 Jan–Apr	**99,561**
1650 May–Aug	**99,562**
1650 Sep–Dec	**99,563**
1651 Jan–Jul	**99,564**
1651 Aug–Dec	**99,565**
1652 Jan–Dec	**99,566**

1652–1659
Missing, due to the Commonwealth and Interregnum. Note the printed abstracts listed in the miscellaneous section, and see the probate decision tables for further instructions.

1660–1684
Not filmed. Use the registered copy wills. For details, consult Camp's *Wills and Their Whereabouts.*

1685 Jan–Apr	**99,591**
1685 May–Jul	**99,592**
1685 Aug–Oct	**99,593**
1685 Nov–Dec	**99,594**

1686–1687
Vacancy. See the Court of the Dean and Chapter of York.

1688–1690
Not filmed. See the note above for 1660–1684.

1691 Jan–Feb	**99,596**
1691 Feb–Mar	**99,597**
1691 Mar–Apr	**99,598**

1691 May	99,599	1694 Jun (cont.)	99,628
1691 Jun–Jul	99,600	1694 Jul–Aug	99,629
1691 Aug–Sep	99,601	1694 Sep–Oct	99,630
1691 Oct–Nov	99,602	1694 Nov–Dec	99,631
1691 Dec–1692 Jan	99,603	1695 Jan–Feb	99,632
1692 Feb–Mar	99,604	1695 Mar	99,633
1692 Mar	99,605	1695 Apr	99,634
1692 Apr	99,606	1695 May	99,635
1692 May	99,607	1695 Jun–Jul	99,636
1692 Jun–Jul	99,608	1695 Aug	99,637
1692 Jul	99,609	1695 Sep–Oct	99,638
1692 Aug–Sep	99,610	1695 Nov–Dec	99,639
1692 Oct–Dec	99,611	1696 Jan–Feb	99,640
1692 Dec	99,612	1696 Mar	99,641
1693 Jan	99,613	1696 Apr–May	99,642
1693 Jan–Feb	99,614	1696 Jun	99,643
1693 Mar	99,615	1696 Jul–Aug	99,644
1693 Mar–Apr	99,616	1696 Sep–Oct	99,645
1693 May	99,617	1696 Nov–Dec	99,646
1693 Jun–Jul	99,618		

1697–1699
Not filmed. Use the registered copy wills. For details, consult Camp's *Wills and Their Whereabouts*.

1693 Jul	99,619	1700 Jan–Feb	99,648
1693 Aug–Oct	99,620	1700 Mar–Apr	99,649
1693 Aug–Oct (cont.)	99,621	1700 May	99,650
1693 Nov–Dec	99,622	1700 Jun	99,651
1694 Jan–Feb	99,623	1700 Jul–Aug	99,652
1694 Mar	99,624	1700 Sep–Oct	99,653
1694 Apr	99,625	1700 Nov–Dec	99,654
1694 May	99,626	1701 Jan–Mar	99,655
1694 Jun	99,627		

1701 Apr–May	**99,656**
1701 Jun	**99,657**
1701 Jul–Aug	**99,658**
1701 Sep–Oct	**99,659**
1701 Nov–Dec	**99,660**
1702 Jan–Feb	**99,661**
1702 Mar–Apr	**99,662**
1702 May	**99,663**
1702 Jun	**99,664**
1702 Jul–Aug	**99,665**
1702 Sep–Oct	**99,666**
1702 Nov–Dec	**99,667**
1703 Jan–Feb	**99,668**
1703 Mar–Apr	**99,669**
1703 May–Jun	**99,670**
1703 Jul–Aug	**99,671**
1703 Sep–Nov	**99,672**
1703 Dec–1704 Jan	**99,673**
1704 Feb–Mar	**99,674**
1704 Apr–May	**99,675**
1704 Apr–Jun (cont.)	**99,676**
1704 Jul–Aug	**99,677**
1704 Sep–Oct	**99,678**
1704 Nov–Dec	**99,679**

1705–1858

Not filmed. Use the registered copy wills. For details, consult Camp's *Wills and Their Whereabouts*.

Unproved or Other Original Wills, Admons, and Inventories for the Exchequer and Prerogative Courts of the Archbishop of York

(The description of these documents on page 19 of item 1 of film 100,081 reports that there were several bundles marked A, B, and C, as well as three or four other bundles of wills and bonds that were never proven. As is noted below there are also two printed indexes to these records. The indexes are incomplete; thus, a thorough search should be made of the desired time period indicated.)

1640–1670	**FHL 942.74 B4a vol. 49 547,175**

Vol. 49 of the Record Series of the Yorkshire Archaeological Society. Appendix III on pages 164–166 indexes some of the wills from Bundles A and B.

1668–1741	**FHL 942.74 B4a vol. 89 402,541 (item 3) 599,880 (item 5)**

Vol. 89 of the Record Series of the Yorkshire Archaeological Society. Appendix II, part I on pages 143–145 lists further entries from Bundles A and B by deanery for 1668–1741 as well as from the PCY for 1679–1705.

1497–1700s	**99,949**

Item 1 is labeled miscellaneous. The earliest entry noted is 1497 for Robert and Isabelle Pinkenei or Pynkney. Most of the entries date from the late 1500s, with some for 1607–1661. Deaneries represented include Cleveland, Newark, Nottingham, Buckrose, Harthill, Ripon, Beverley, and Bulmer.

Item 3 lists in order by deanery entries for Holderness, mainly from the 1600s; Ryedale, from 1681–early 1700s; and Retford, mainly from the 1700s.

1650–early 1700s	**99,915**

Item 1 provides entries for supposedly the deaneries of Cleveland, Dickering, Nottingham, Craven, and Bulmer.

Item 2 has two documents dated 1637 and 1633, but most of the probates fit the time period described above. They are mainly from the PCY, with perhaps a few from the Dean and Chapter, and at the end is one for Ainsty dated 1699 and another for Buckrose in 1695. Over halfway through the film is a variety of documents gathered by the Dean and Chapter during a visitation to northwestern Lancashire in the late eighteenth century. These documents include: marriage licenses from

1767–1772 (eighteen), mainly for the parishes of Kirkby Irelyth and Dalton, but also Ulverston, Coulton, and Conigstone in Lancashire and Bowtell in Cumberland; a number of wills for the area of Kirkby Irelyth, 1769–1771; and bishop's transcripts for Kirkby Irelyth, 1766–1771, and Seathwaite, 1766–1769.

1650–early 1700s   **99,916**
Item 1 may be to Bundle A. It lists entries by deanery for Doncaster, Pontefract, City of York, and Harthill. One renunciation is included. There are numerous bonds.

Item 2 is for Bundles B and C.

1642–1744   **98,920**
Item 1 is not identified but contains fifteen original wills that may be *reinfecta*. Most are from the late 1600s.

1689–1849   **100,080**
The last item on this film is a series of original wills mainly from the nineteenth century. It is difficult to determine what they are. Several are marked "revoked," or did not name executors. At least one was contested. Among them are two documents for ordinations and appointments to curacies. The sixth entry includes receipts for property distributed by the executor of the estate of Ann Alice Morely, spinster, in 1824. Her will comes some eleven documents later. One of the revoked wills is for Thomas Thornton, private in the 1st Battalion of the 6th Regiment of Foot in Spain. His widow, Elizabeth Thornton, was still in Bradford in 1813.

Item 4 of this same film appears to be a caveat concerning the estate of John Raper, gentleman of Reeth in Grinton, Yorks., whose will was proven in 1806.

Item 5 is a large section of notices of probate grants that were valued a second time for the Inland Revenue Office. They range from 1805–1881 and give names, the probate registry, and date of probate.

Registered Copy Wills for the Exchequer and Prerogative Courts of the Archbishop of York

(In addition to the printed and filmed calendars, each volume of the registered copy wills may be separately indexed, either at the front or back of the film. The early volumes are in Latin. The names of the testators are often written in the margin. If the registered copy is hard to read, note the section for original wills or consult Camp's *Wills and Their Whereabouts* for further details.)

1389–1396   **99,454**
Volume 1, indexed.

1396–1464   **99,455**
Volume 2

1398–1465   **99,456**
Volume 3, indexed.

1465–1476   **99,457**
Volume 4

1476–1500   **99,458**
Volume 5

1501–1506   **99,459**
Volume 6

1507   **99,460**
Volume 7, indexed.

1508–1514   **99,460 (item 2)**
Volume 8, indexed.

1514–1530   **99,460 (item 3)**
Volume 9

1530–1531   **99,461**
Volume 10, indexed.

1531–1544   **99,462**
Volume 11

1531–1544   **99,463**
Volume 11 continues from folio number 403.

1544   **99,464**
Volume 12, indexed.

1544–1553   **99,465**
Volume 13

1544–1553   **99,466**
Volume 13 continues from folio number 140.

1544–1553   **99,467**
Volume 13 continues from folio number 753.

1554–1555   **99,468**
Volume 14

1555–1559   **99,469**
Volume 15

1555–1559   **99,470**
Volume 15 continues from folio number 181.

1559–1560   **99,471**
Volume 16

1561–1568 Volume 17	**99,472**	**1603–1605** Volume 29	**99,492**
1561–1568 Volume 17 continues from folio number 323.	**99,473**	**1603–1605** Volume 29 continues from folio number 219.	**99,493**
1568–1571 Volume 18, indexed at the end.	**99,474**	**1606–1608** Volume 30	**99,494**
1570–1575 Volume 19	**99,475**	**1606–1608** Volume 30 continues from folio number 580.	**99,495**
1570–1575 Volume 19 continues from folio number 426.	**99,476**	**1609–1611** Volume 31	**99,496**
1575–1576 Volume 20	**99,477**	**1609–1611** Volume 31 continues from folio number 331.	**99,497**
1576–1580 Volume 21	**99,478**	**1612–1613** Volume 32	**99,498**
1580–1585 Volume 22	**99,479**	**1614–1616** Volume 33	**99,499**
1580–1585 Volume 22 continues from folio number 580.	**99,480**	**1614–1616** Volume 33 continues from folio number 618.	**99,500**
1585–1588 Volume 23	**99,481**	**1616–1617** Volume 34	**99,501**
1585–1588 Volume 23 continues from folio number 440.	**99,482**	**1616–1617** Volume 34 continues from folio number 417.	**99,502**
1589–1591 Volume 24	**99,483**	**1618–1619** Volume 35	**99,503**
1591 Volume 24 continues from folio number 589.	**99,484**	**1620–1622** Volume 36	**99,504**
1591–1594 Volume 25	**99,485**	**1620–1622** Volume 36 continues from folio number 555.	**99,505**
1591–1594 Volume 25 continues from folio number 1155.	**99,486**	**1622–1623** Volume 37	**99,506**
1594–1597 Volume 26	**99,487**	**1622–1623** Volume 37 continues from folio number 308.	**99,507**
1597–1599 Volume 27	**99,488**	**1624–1625** Volume 38	**99,508**
1597–1599 Volume 27 continues from folio number 105.	**99,489**	**1624–1625** Volume 38 continues from folio number 252.	**99,509**
1599–1602 Volume 28	**99,490**	**1626–1627** Volume 39	**99,510**
1599–1602 Volume 28 continues from folio number 540.	**99,491**	**1626–1627** Volume 39 continues from folio number 183.	**99,511**

1627–1629	**99,512**
Volume 40	
1627–1629	**99,513**
Volume 40 continues from folio number 181.	
1630–1632	**99,514**
Volume 41	
1630–1632	**99,515**
Volume 41 continues from folio number 71.	
1630–1632	**99,516**
Volume 41 continues from folio number 548.	
1632–1633	**99,517**
Volume 42	

1633–1634
No wills seem to have been registered between 1 August 1633–31 July 1634. Note the description for volume 35 of the printed indexes in the section in this volume for "Indexes and Calendars." See Camp's *Wills and Their Whereabouts* for details of the originals for this period that have not been filmed.

1634–1637	**99,518**
Volume 42 continues from folio number 163.	

1638–1659
No wills were registered during this time period. See the preceding section for "Original Wills."

1660–1661	**99,567**
Volume 43	
1660–1661	**99,568**
Volume 43 continues from folio number 250.	
1661–1662	**99,569**
Volume 44	
1662–1663	**99,570**
Volume 45	
1663–1665	**99,571**
Volume 46	
1663–1665	**99,572**
Volume 46 continues from folio number 597.	
1665–1666	**99,573**
Volume 47	
1666–1667	**99,574**
Volume 48	
1666–1667	**99,575**
Volume 48 continues from folio number 66.	

1666–1667	**99,576**
Volume 48 continues from folio number 612.	
1667–1668	**99,577**
Volume 49	
1668–1669	**99,578**
Volume 50	
1669–1670	**99,579**
Volume 51	
1670–1671	**99,580**
Volume 52	
1671–1672	**99,581**
Volume 53	
1672–1673	**99,582**
Volume 54	
1673–1674	**99,583**
Volume 55	
1675	**99,584**
Volume 56	
1676–1677	**99,585**
Volume 57	
1676–1677	**99,586**
Volume 57 continues from folio number 368.	
1678–1680	**99,587**
Volume 58	
1678–1680	**99,588**
Volume 58 continues from folio number 189.	
1681–1682	**99,589**
Volume 59	
1683–1684	**99,590**
Volume 60	

1685–1688
No wills were registered from 1685 through April 1686, and there was a vacancy from April 1686 to December 1688. See the section for "Original Wills" for 1685, and the Court of the Dean and Chapter of York for the vacancy.

1688–1690	**99,595**
Volume 61	

1691–1696
No wills registered. See the section for "Original Wills."

1697–1699 Volume 62	**99,647**	**1727–1728** Volume 79 continues from folio number 400.	**99,698**
1700–1704 No wills registered. See the section for "Original Wills."		**1728–1729** Volume 80	**99,699**
1705–1706 Volume 63	**99,680**	**1729–1731** Volume 81	**99,700**
1707–1708 Volume 64	**99,681**	**1729–1731** Volume 81 continues from folio number 160.	**99,701**
1708–1709 Volume 65	**99,682**	**1731–1732** Volume 82	**99,702**
1709–1710 Volume 66	**99,683**	**1732–1734** Volume 83	**99,703**
1710–1711 Volume 67	**99,684**	**1735–1736** Volume 84	**99,704**
1712–1713 Volume 68	**99,685**	**1736–1739** Volume 85	**99,705**
1713–1714 Volume 69	**99,686**	**1738–1739** Volume 86	**99,706**
1714–1716 Volume 70	**99,687**	**1740–1741** Volume 87	**99,707**
1716–1717 Volume 71	**99,688**	**1741–1742** Volume 87 continues from folio number 290.	**99,708**
1717–1718 Volume 72	**99,689**	**1742–1743** Volume 88	**99,709**
1718–1719 Volume 73	**99,690**	**1744–1745** Volume 89	**99,710**
1719–1720 Volume 74	**99,691**	**1745–1748** Volume 90	**99,711**
1720–1721 Volume 75	**99,692**	**1746–1748** Volume 91	**99,712**
1721–1723 Volume 76	**99,693**	**1748–1749** Volumes 92 and 93	**99,713**
1721–1723 Volume 76 continues from folio number 521.	**99,694**	**1750–1751** Volume 94 covers 1750. Volume 95 covers 1751.	**99,714**
1723–1724 Volume 77	**99,695**	**1752** Volume 96	**99,715**
1724–1725 Volume 78	**99,696**	**1753** Volume 97	**99,716**
1725–1727 Volume 79	**99,697**		

1754 Volume 98	**99,717**
1755 Volume 99	**99,718**
1756–1757 Volume 100 covers 1756. Volume 101 covers 1757.	**99,719**
1758 Volume 102	**99,720**
1759 Volume 103	**99,721**
1760 Volume 104	**99,722**
1761 Volume 105	**99,723**
1761–1762 Volume 106	**99,724**
1763 Volume 107	**99,725**
1764 Volume 108	**99,726**
1765 Volume 109	**99,727**
1766 Volume 110	**99,728**
1767 Volume 111	**99,729**
1768–1769 Volume 112 covers 1768. Volume 113 covers 1769. A will that is unindexed appears at the end of this film on folio number 288 for Thomas Jackson of Raskelf proven February 1769.	**99,730**
1770 Volume 114. Some entries for April, May, and October follow December.	**99,731**
1771 Volume 115. Entries for May, March, August, and October occur between November and December.	**99,732**
1772 Volume 116	**99,733**
1773 Volume 117	**99,734**

1774 Volume 118	**99,735**
1775 Volume 119. Entries for May occur between September and October.	**99,736**
1776 Volume 120	**99,737**
1777 Volume 121	**99,738**
1778 Volume 122	**99,739**
1779 Volume 123	**99,740**
1780 Volume 124	**99,741**
1781 Volume 125	**99,742**
1782 Volume 126. January follows February. After August come December, October, September, and November in that order.	**99,743**
1783 Volume 127	**99,744**
1784 Volume 128	**99,745**
1785 Volume 129	**99,746**
1786 Volume 130	**99,747**
1787 Volume 131	**99,748**
1788 Volume 132	**99,749**
1789 Volume 133	**99,750**
1790 Volume 134	**99,751**
1791 Volume 135	**99,752**
1792 Volume 136	**99,753**

1793 **99,754**	**1810** **99,771**
Volume 137	Volume 154, indexed.

1794 **99,755**	**1811** **99,772**
Volume 138	Volume 155, indexed.

1795 **99,756**	**1812** **99,773**
Volume 139. A second sequence from January through December follows the first.	Volume 156, indexed.

1796 **99,757**	**1813** **99,774**
Volume 140. Two sequences from January through December occur.	Volume 157, indexed.

1797 **99,758**	**1814** **99,775**
Volume 141	Volume 158, indexed.

1798 **99,759**	**1814** **99,776**
Volume 142	Volume 158 continues from folio number 140.

1799 **99,760**	**1815** **99,777**
Volume 143. Four sequences from January through December occur.	Volume 159. Three sequences from January through December occur.

1800 **99,761**	**1815** **99,778**
Volume 144. Arranged January through September, then from January through December. Some entries for August and September might be located with May in the second sequence.	Volume 159 continues from folio number 610.

	1816 **99,779**
	Volume 160

1801 **99,762**	**1817** **99,780**
Volume 145	Volume 161

1802 **99,763**	**1818** **99,781**
Volume 146	Volume 162

1803 **99,764**	**1819** **99,782**
Volume 147. No chronological order until July, then proceeds through December.	Volume 163

1804 **99,765**	**1820** **99,783**
Volume 148. No chronological order until July, then proceeds through December.	Volume 164

1805 **99,766**	**1820** **99,784**
Volume 149	Volume 165. This appears to be roughly the second half of 1820, but in two sequences.

1806 **99,767**	**1821** **99,785**
Volume 150	Volume 166

1807 **99,768**	**1822** **99,786**
Volume 151. No chronological order until June. Ends with November.	Volume 167

	1823 **99,787**
	Volume 168 ends with March 1823.

1808 **99,769**	**1823** **99,788**
Volume 152	Volume 168 continues from folio number 130 with March–December.

1809 **99,770**	**1824** **99,789**
Volume 153, indexed.	Volume 169, Book 1 contains January–July.

1824   **99,790**
Volume 170, Book 2 or July–December.

1825   **99,791**
Volume 171, Book 1 or January–June.

1825   **99,792**
Volume 172, Book 2 or July–December.

1826   **99,793**
Volume 173, Book 1 or January–June.

1826   **99,794**
Volume 174, Book 2 or June–December.

1827   **99,795**
Volume 175, Book 1 or January–June.

1827   **99,796**
Volume 176, Book 2 or July–December.

1828   **99,797**
Volume 177, Book 1. The months are grouped in three sequences: January–June, January–December, and January–August.

1828   **99,798**
Volume 178, Book 2. The months are grouped in two sequences: August–December and another for January–December.

1829   **99,799**
Volume 179, Book 1 or January–June.

1829   **99,800**
Volume 180, Book 2 or July–December.

1830   **99,801**
Volume 181, Book 1 or January–June.

1830   **99,802**
Volume 182, Book 2 or July–December

1831   **99,803**
Volume 183, Book 1. The months are grouped in two sequences: January–December and September–December.

1831   **99,804**
Volume 184, Book 2. The months are grouped in three sequences: January–August, March–December, and July–December.

1832   **99,805**
Volume 185, Book 1 or January–June.

1832   **99,806**
Volume 186, Book 2 or July–December. There may be some intermingling of July and August.

1833   **99,807**
Volume 187, Book 1 or January–June. The wills are in alphabetical order by month.

1833   **99,808**
Volume 188, Book 2 or July–December. Alphabetical order by month.

1834   **99,809**
Volume 189, Book 1 or January–June. Alphabetical order by month.

1834   **99,810**
Volume 190, Book 2 or July–December. Alphabetical order by month.

1835   **99,811**
Volume 191, Book 1 or January–June. Alphabetical order by month.

1835   **99,812**
Volume 192, Book 2 or July–December. Alphabetical order by month.

1836   **99,813**
Volume 193, Book 1. The months are grouped in three sequences: January–April, February–April, and February–June.

1836   **99,814**
Volume 194, Book 2 or July–December.

1837   **99,815**
Volume 195, Book 1 or January–June.

1837   **99,816**
Volume 196, Book 2 or July–December.

1838   **99,817**
Volume 197, Book 1 or January–June.

1838   **99,818**
Volume 198, Book 2 or July–December.

1839   **99,819**
Volume 199, Book 1 or January–June.

1839   **99,820**
Volume 200, Book 2 or July–December.

1840   **99,821**
Volume 201, Book 1 or January–June.

1840   **99,822**
Volume 202, Book 2 or July–December.

1841   **99,823**
Volume 203, Book 1 or January–June.

1841   **99,824**
Volume 204, Book 2 or July–December.

1842   **99,825**
Volume 205, Book 1 or January–June.

1842   **99,826**
Volume 206, Book 2 or July–December.

1843   **99,827**
Volume 207, Book 1 or January–June.

1843   **99,828**
Volume 208, Book 2 or July–December.

1844   **99,829**
Volume 209, Book 1 or January–June.

1844   **99,830**
Volume 210, Book 2 or July–December.

1845   **99,831**
Volume 211, Book 1 or January–June.

1845   **99,832**
Volume 212, Book 2 or July–December.

1846   **99,833**
Volume 213, Book 1 or January–June.

1846   **99,834**
Volume 214, Book 2 or July–September. Indexed for
Books 2 and 3.

1846   **99,835**
Volume 215, Book 3 or October–December. See preceding volume for an index.

1847   **99,836**
Volume 216, Book 1 or January–March. Indexed by
month.

1847   **99,837**
Volume 216, Book 1 continues with March–June. See
the preceding film for an index.

1847   **99,838**
Volume 217, Book 2 or July–December. Indexed by
month.

1848   **99,839**
Volume 218, Book 1 or January–May.

1848   **99,840**
Volume 219, Book 2 or June–August. Indexed.

1848   **99,841**
Volume 219, Book 2 continues with August–December.
See the preceding film for an index.

1849   **99,842**
Volume 220, Book 1 for January. Index covers January–
June.

1849   **99,843**
Volume 220, Book 1 continues with January–June. See
the preceding film for an index.

1849   **99,844**
Volume 221, Book 2 for July–October. Index covers
July–December.

1849   **99,845**
Volume 221, Book 2 continues with October–December.
See the preceding film for an index.

1850   **99,846**
Volume 222, Book 1 for January–March. Index covers
January–June.

1850   **99,847**
Volume 222, Book 1 continues with March–June. See
the preceding film for an index.

1850   **99,848**
Volume 223, Book 2 for July.

1850   **99,849**
Volume 223, Book 2 continues with July–December.

1851   **99,850**
Volume 224, Book 1. Indexed through June.

1851   **99,851**
Volume 224, Book 1 continues. See preceding film for
an index.

1851   **99,852**
Volume 225, Book 2. Indexed through December.

1851   **99,853**
Volume 225, Book 2 continues. See preceding film for
an index.

1852   **99,854**
Volume 226, Book 1 for January–February. Index
covers January–December.

1852   **99,855**
Volume 226, Book 1 continues with February–June. See
preceding film for an index.

1852   **99,856**
Volume 227, Book 2 or July–December. See film 99,854
for an index.

1852   **99,857**
Volume 227, Book 2 continues with December. There is
one will for October at the end. See film 99,854 for an
index.

1853   **99,858**
Volume 228, Book 1 for January–April. Index covers January–June.

1853   **99,859**
Volume 228, Book 1 continues with April–June. See the preceding film for an index.

1853   **99,860**
Volume 229, Book 2 or July–September. Indexed.

1853   **99,861**
Volume 230, Book 3 or October–December. Indexed.

1854   **99,862**
Volume 231, Book 1 or January–March. Indexed.

1854   **99,863**
Volume 232, Book 2 or April–June. Indexed.

1854   **99,864**
Volume 233, Book 3 or July–September. Indexed.

1854   **99,865**
Volume 234, Book 4 or October–December. Indexed.

1855   **99,866**
Volume 235, Book 1 or January–March. Indexed.

1855   **99,867**
Volume 236, Book 2 or April–June. Indexed.

1855   **99,868**
Volume 237, Book 3 or July–September. Indexed.

1855   **99,869**
Volume 238, Book 4 or October–December. Indexed.

1856   **99,870**
Volume 239, Book 1

1856   **99,871**
Volume 240, Book 2

1856   **99,872**
Volume 241, Book 3

1856   **99,873**
Volume 242, Book 4. Indexed for October–December.

1857   **99,874**
Volume 243, Book 1 or January–March.

1857   **99,875**
Volume 244, Book 2 or April–June.

1857   **99,876**
Volume 245, Book 3 or July–September.

1857–1858   **99,877**
Volume 246, Book 4 for October–December 1857 and January 1858.

Act Books for the Exchequer Court of the Archbishop of York

The acts are in Latin until 1733, but the names in the margins are usually easily recognizable.

The deaneries are listed alphabetically by the four archdeaconries: 1) Archdeaconry of York or the West Riding: Christianity or City of York (hereafter referred to as just York), Ainsty, Craven with Ripon, Doncaster, Pontefract with Halifax; 2) Archdeaconry of the East Riding: Buckrose, Dickering, Harthill with Hull until 1688 (Beverley was not a deanery but may appear as such in the registers or more likely is included with Harthill), Holderness with Hull after 1688; 3) Archdeaconry of Cleveland: Bulmer, Cleveland, Ryedale; 4) Archdeaconry of Nottingham: Bingham, Newark, Nottingham, and Retford.

It is essential to determine what deanery a parish belongs to by checking the "Deanery Book" under FHL Ref 942.74 P2 or items 2–4 of film 100,081.

1502–1514   **99,979 &**
                                        991,208
Vol. 1 includes all of the deaneries in archdeaconry order starting with York, Nottingham, East Riding, and Cleveland. The starting and ending dates for each deanery are not clear. For Harthill, 1502–1505, see film 99,983 below. Where the act books have been filmed twice, usually the first film is larger and easier to read.

1514–1521   **99,979**
                                         (item 2),
                                          991,208
Vol. 2 includes all deaneries in archdeaconry order as follows: York, East Riding, Cleveland, and Nottingham. The deaneries of Bulmer, Newark, Nottingham, and Retford begin with 1515, and Newark ends with 1522.

1521–1544   **99,980 &**
                                        991,209
Vol. 3 includes all deaneries in archdeaconry order as follows: York, East Riding, Cleveland, and Nottingham. According to the spine of the original manuscript volume there are these exceptions to the time period stated above: York 1538–1542; Ainsty begins with 1537, Doncaster with 1523, Cleveland with 1522, Nottingham with 1522, and Newark with 1522; and Bingham 1522–1545. The first film should be easier to read.

1530–1531 **99,980**
1544–1545 **(item 2),**
991,209

Vol. 4 is a vacancy act book and more properly belongs to the Court of the Dean and Chapter of York. An exact duplicate appears as item 5 on film 99,955.

1544–1554 **99,981 &**
991,210

Vol. 5 includes all deaneries in the order described for volume 3 above. The first film should be easier to read.

1555–1558 **99,982 &**
991,211

Vol. 6 includes all deaneries in the order described for volume 3 above. There are entries for Doncaster on both sides of the section for Pontefract, and in the middle of the last group for Doncaster are more entries for Ainsty. Bingham ends with 1557. The first film should be easier to read.

1558–1568 **99,983 &**
991,212

Vol. 7 includes all deaneries in the order described for volume 3 above. The following ending dates differ from the time period listed above: Ainsty 1563, Pontefract 1565, Doncaster 1566, Craven with Ripon 1567, Harthill with Hull 1565, Holderness 1565, Dickering 1566, Bulmer 1565, and Cleveland 1566. Harthill includes entries for 1502–1505. Some of the entries for Newark appear halfway through Pontefract, and another portion for Newark comes between Nottingham and Bingham. The first film should be more readable.

1559–1561

Vacancy. See the separate act book for this period under the Court of the Dean and Chapter of York.

1563–1568 **99,983**
(item 2),
991,212

Vol. 8 continues from the ending dates itemized for the deaneries in volume 7 above in the order listed there through 1568.

1568–1570

Vacancy. See the Court of the Dean and Chapter of York.

1570–1575 **99,984 &**
991,213

Vol. 9 includes all deaneries in archdeaconry order as follows: York, East Riding, Cleveland, and Nottingham, with the exceptions that the Deanery of Buckrose comes between Ryedale and Cleveland, and Harthill continues from 1573–1575 at the end of the film. The first film should be more readable.

1575–1588 **99,985 &**
991,214

Vol. 10 includes the deaneries in the order mentioned for volume 9 above except that the deaneries of Bulmer and Ryedale appear between Dickering and Buckrose, and there are no entries here for Newark, Nottingham, and Bingham. The entries for York may go through 1589, but those for 1575 should be on the next film with Newark for 1583. The following deaneries have ending dates different from the time period described for this film: Ainsty 1579, Pontefract 1579, Doncaster 1580, Craven 1580, Harthill 1580, Holderness 1582, Dickering 1583, Bulmer 1582, Ryedale 1584, Cleveland 1583, and Retford 1576. The first film should be more readable.

1576–1588 **99,986**

Vol. 10 continues with the deaneries of Retford, Newark, Nottingham, and Bingham. Note the preceding film for Retford 1575–1576. There should be entries for York for 1575 here with those of Newark for 1583.

1579–1588 **99,987 &**
991,215

Vol. 11 continues from volume 10 for the deaneries of Ainsty, Pontefract, Doncaster, and Craven with Ripon.

1580–1588 **99,988 &**
991,216

Vol. 12 continues from volume 10 for the deaneries of Harthill, Holderness, Dickering, Bulmer, Ryedale, and Cleveland. The first film should be more readable.

1588–1596 **99,989 &**
991,217

Vol. 13 for the deaneries of Holderness, Buckrose, Bulmer, Dickering, Ryedale through 1597, Cleveland, Retford, Newark, Nottingham, and Bingham in that order. The first film should be more readable.

1588–1596 **99,990 &**
991,218

Vol. 14 for the deaneries of York (1588 may be on film 99,985), Ainsty, Pontefract, Doncaster (ends 1597), Craven, and Harthill. The first film should be more readable.

1597–1607 **99,991 &**
991,219

Vol. 15 for the deaneries of York, Ainsty (the first two deaneries continue on film 100,001), Pontefract (ends 1608 and continues on film 100,010), Doncaster (ends 1608 and continues on film 100,010), and Craven 1597–1598. Some of the entries of Pontefract for 1597 are with Ainsty for 1606. The first film should be more readable.

1597–1607 **99,992 &**
991,220

Vol. 15 continues with Craven. See the preceding film. Craven continues on film 100,001. The second film for volume 15, 991,220, actually continues from the preceding one with Pontefract, 1603–1608.

1597–1607   **99,993 &**
                                                                  991,221

Vol. 16 for the deaneries of Bulmer, Ryedale, Cleveland, and Nottingham with Bingham, Retford, and Newark.

1597–1607   **99,994 &**
                                                                  991,222

Vol. 17 for the deaneries of Harthill, Holderness, Dickering, and Buckrose.

1608–1623   **99,995 &**
                                                                  991,223

Vol. 18 for the deaneries of Bulmer (ends 1625 and continues on film 100,041), Ryedale (1608 only), Cleveland (see film 100,041), Nottingham with Bingham, Retford (ends 1624), and Newark. (The last three deaneries for the Archdeaconry of Nottingham continue on film 100,049.)

1608–1625   **99,996**

Vol. 18 continues with Ryedale through 1623 and completes the other deaneries itemized on the preceding film. Ryedale continues on film 100,041. In the second filming sequence, volume 18 is completely contained on film 991,223.

1608–1630   **99,997 &**
                                                                  991,224

Vol. 19 for Harthill and Holderness (through 1626).

1608–1630   **99,998 &**
                                                                  991,225

Vol. 19 continues with Holderness 1626–1629, Dickering (ends 1629), and Buckrose. Film 991,225 actually continues volume 19 from Holderness, 1618–1629.

1630–1645   **99,999**

Vol. 20 for the deaneries of Harthill, Holderness, the rest of Harthill, Buckrose, and Dickering.

1646–1669   **100,000**

Vol. 21 for Harthill (see film 100,032 for a continuation of this deanery), Holderness through 1675 (see film 100,038 for a continuation), Buckrose through 1678 (also continues on film 100,038), and Dickering (continues on film 100,032).

1608–1627   **100,001 &**
                                                                  991,226

Vol. 1A for the deaneries of York, Ainsty (ends 1626), and Craven 1607–1615. The second film, 991,226, contains only Ainsty.

1615–1624   **100,002 &**
                                                                  991,227

Vol. 1A continues for the Deanery of Craven with Ripon. See the preceding film. The second film, 991,227, contains Craven, 1607–1624, and York, 1608–1627.

1627–1641   **100,003**

Vol. 2A for the deaneries of York, starts 1630 (there appears to be a gap in the records of this deanery from 1628–1629), Ainsty, and Craven. (Craven starts in 1626 and apparently has a gap for 1625.) There are no entries for these three deaneries from 1642–1668. Craven continues on film 100,028.

1668–1686   **100,004**

Vol. 3A for the deaneries of York (ends 1684), and Ainsty. See the preceding film. Note the vacancy of 1683.

1685–1722   **100,004**
                                                                  (item 2)

Vol. 4A for the deaneries of York and Ainsty (ends 1712). Note the vacancy of 1686–1688.

1722–1751   **100,005**

Vol. 5A for the deaneries of Craven with Ripon (1738–1751) and York. See films 100,028–100,029 for Craven with Ripon, 1668–1737.

1752–1797   **100,005**
                                                                  (item 2)

Vol. 6A for the Deanery of York.

1798–1838   **100,006**

Vol. 7A for the Deanery of York.

1839–1858   **100,007**

Vol. 8A for the Deanery of York.

1713–1749   **100,007**
                                                                  (item 2)

Vol. 9A for the Deanery of Ainsty.

1750–1814   **100,008**

Vols. 10A–12A for the Deanery of Ainsty. Volume 10A covers 1750–1772, volume 11A covers 1773–1797, and volume 12A is 1798–1814.

1814–1858   **100,009**

Vols. 13A–15A for the Deanery of Ainsty. Volume 13A is 1814–1829, volume 14A is 1829–1842, and volume 15A is 1842–1858.

1608–1627   **100,010**

Vol. 1B for the deaneries of Pontefract with Halifax and Doncaster (the latter covers 1608–1617 and continues on the next film).

1618–1628 100,011
Vol. 1B continues for Doncaster.

1627–1640 100,012
Vol. 2B for Pontefract with Halifax and Doncaster.

1640–1667 100,013
Vol. 3B for Pontefract with Halifax and Doncaster. Doncaster continues on film 100,023.

1668–1705 100,014
Vols. 4B–5B for the Deanery of Pontefract with Halifax. Volume 4B covers 1668–1680, and volume 5B is 1680–1705.

1705–1731 100,015
Vols. 6B–7B for the Deanery of Pontefract with Halifax. Volume 6B covers 1705–1719, and volume 7B is 1719–1731.

1731–1751 100,016
Vols. 8B–9B for the deaneries of Pontefract with Halifax and Doncaster. Volume 8B covers 1731–1742 for just Pontefract with Halifax. Volume 9B is 1742–1751 for Pontefract with Halifax, and also includes 1740–1751 for the Deanery of Doncaster. For Doncaster from 1668–1739 see films 100,023–100,024.

1752–1778 100,017
Vols. 10B–11B for the Deanery of Pontefract with Halifax. Volume 10B covers 1752–1764, and volume 11B is 1764–1778.

1778–1801 100,018
Vols. 12B–13B for Pontefract with Halifax. Volume 12B covers 1778–1789, and volume 13B is 1789–1801.

1801–1817 100,019
Vols. 14B–15B for Pontefract with Halifax. Volume 14B is 1801–1809, and volume 15B is 1809–1817.

1817–1836 100,020
Vols. 16B–18B for Pontefract with Halifax. Volume 16B covers 1817–1824, volume 17B is 1825–1829, and volume 18B is 1829–1836.

1836–1848 100,021
Vols. 19B–20B for Pontefract with Halifax. Volume 19B is 1836–1841, and volume 20B is 1842–1848.

1848–1858 100,022
Vols. 21B–22B for Pontefract with Halifax. Volume 21B covers 1848–1854, and volume 22B is 1855–1858.

1668–1722 100,023
Vols. 23B–24B for the Deanery of Doncaster in continuation of film 100,013. Volume 23B covers 1668–1684, and volume 24B is 1685–1722.

1722–1768 100,024
Vols. 25B–26B for Doncaster. Volume 25B is 1722–1739. For 1740–1751 see film 100,016. Volume 26B is 1752–1768.

1769–1807 100,025
Vols. 27B–28B for Doncaster. Volume 27B is 1769–1789, and volume 28B is 1789–1807.

1807–1834 100,026
Vols. 29B–31B for the Deanery of Doncaster. Volume 29B covers 1807–1819, volume 30B is 1819–1826, and volume 31B is 1826–1834.

1834–1858 100,027
Vols. 32B–34B for Doncaster. Volume 32B is 1834–1842, volume 33B is 1842–1851, and volume 34B is 1851–1858.

1668–1721 100,028
Vols. 1C–2C for the Deanery of Craven with Ripon in continuation of film 100,003. Volume 1C covers 1668–1684, and volume 2C is 1684–1721.

1721–1778 100,029
Vols. 3C–4C for Craven with Ripon. Volume 3C covers 1721–1737. For 1738–1751 see film 100,005. Volume 4C is 1752–1778.

1779–1835 100,030
Vols. 5C–7C for Craven with Ripon. Volume 5C covers 1779–1800, volume 6C is 1800–1817, and volume 7C is 1818–1835.

1835–1858 100,031
Vol. 8C is the Deanery of Craven with Ripon.

1669–1723 100,032
Vols. 1D–2D for Dickering and Harthill. Volume 1D is Dickering 1669–1684 and Harthill 1670–1688 in continuation of film 100,000. Volume 2D is Dickering 1685–1719 and Harthill 1688–1723. NOTE: There is a typed index for Dickering, 1688–1710, under FHL 942.74 P22ch.

1719–1751 100,033
Vol. 3D for Dickering.

1724–1751 100,034
Vol. 4D is Buckrose 1741–1751 (see films 100,038 for 1679–1741 and 100,036 for 1752–1820) and Harthill 1724–1751.

1752–1858 100,035
Vols. 5D–8D for Harthill. Volume 5D is 1752–1786, volume 6D is 1787–1813, volume 7D is 1814–1839, and volume 8D covers 1839–1858.

1752–1820   **100,036**

Vols. 9D–11D for Dickering and Buckrose. Volume 9D is 1752–1778 for both deaneries. Volume 10D is 1778–1802 for both deaneries. Volume 11D is 1803–1820 for both deaneries.

1820–1858   **100,037**

Vols. 12D–13D for Dickering and Buckrose. Volume 12D is 1820–1840 for both deaneries. Volume 13D is 1840–1858 for both deaneries. It ends with 1857–1858 for the Deanery of Ryedale (see film 100,048).

1676–1741   **100,038**

Vols. 1E–2E for Holderness and Buckrose in continuation of film 100,000. Volume 1E is 1676–1705 for Holderness with Hull (note the typed index for Holderness, 1688–1705, listed in the section for "Indexes and Calendars" and on item 3 of film 924,148), and 1679–1741 for Buckrose. Volume 2E is 1705–1721 for Holderness with Hull. Buckrose continues on film 100,034.

1721–1779   **100,039**

Vols. 3E–4E for Holderness with Hull. Volume 3E covers 1721–1746, and volume 4E is 1746–1779.

1780–1858   **100,040**

Vols. 5E–8E for Holderness with Hull. Volume 5E is 1780–1804, volume 6E is 1805–1821, volume 7E is 1822–1839, and volume 8E covers 1839–1858.

1623–1668   **100,041**

Vols. 1F–2F for the Archdeaconry of Cleveland in continuation of films 99,995 and 99,996. Volume 1F is 1624–1641 for Bulmer, 1623–1641 for Ryedale, and 1624–1641 for Cleveland. Volume 2F finishes all three deaneries through 1668. There is a section for Bulmer 1666–1668 between Ryedale and Cleveland.

1669–1721   **100,042**

Vols. 3F–4F for the Archdeaconry of Cleveland. Volume 3F is 1669–1688 for Bulmer, 1669–1683 for Cleveland, and 1669–1689 for Ryedale. Volume 4F is Cleveland 1683–1697, 1700–1709. Then comes 1688–1698 for Bulmer followed by 1698–1700 for Cleveland, and then Bulmer again from 1699–1720. Last comes Ryedale for 1689–1721.

1709–1738   **100,043**

Vols. 5F–6F for the Archdeaconry of Cleveland. Volume 5F is 1709–1735 for Cleveland. Volume 6F is 1720–1738 for Bulmer and 1721–1738 for Ryedale.

1735–1764   **100,044**

Vols. 7F–8F for the Archdeaconry of Cleveland. Volume 7F is 1735–1748 for Cleveland, and 1739–1749 for both Ryedale and Bulmer. Volume 8F is 1749–1763 for Cleveland, and 1750–1764 for both Ryedale and Bulmer.

1763–1795   **100,045**

Vols. 9F–10F for the Archdeaconry of Cleveland. Volume 9F is 1764–1780 for both Bulmer and Ryedale, and 1763–1778 for Cleveland. Volume 10F is 1780–1790 for Bulmer and Ryedale, and 1779–1795 for Cleveland.

1791–1819   **100,046**

Vols. 11F–12F for the Archdeaconry of Cleveland. Volume 11F is 1791–1805 for Ryedale, 1795–1806 for Cleveland, and 1791–1806 for Bulmer. Volume 12F is 1806–1818 for Ryedale, 1806–1819 for Bulmer, and 1806–1818 for Cleveland.

1818–1847   **100,047**

Vols. 13F–15F for the Archdeaconry of Cleveland. Volume 13F is 1819–1825 for both Ryedale and Bulmer, and 1818–1825 for Cleveland. Volume 14F is 1825–1836 for Ryedale, Bulmer, and Cleveland. Volume 15F is 1836–1846 for Ryedale, 1836–1847 for Bulmer, and 1837–1847 for Cleveland.

1846–1858   **100,048**

Vol. 16F is 1848–1858 for Bulmer, 1846–1857 for Ryedale (see film 100,037 for 1857–1858), and 1847–1858 for Cleveland.

1623–1641   **100,049**

Vol. 1G for the Archdeaconry of Nottingham is a continuation of film 99,995. It covers 1623–1640 for Nottingham with Bingham, 1624–1641 for Retford, and 1624–1640 for Newark.

1641–1673   **100,050**

Vol. 2G for the Archdeaconry of Nottingham. All three deaneries begin in 1641, but Retford ends in 1672 and Newark in 1670.

1671–1701   **100,051**

Vol. 3G is 1674–1691 for Nottingham with Bingham, 1673–1696 for Retford, and 1671–1701 for Newark.

1691–1730   **100,052**

Vol. 4G is 1691–1714 for Nottingham with Bingham, 1697–1730 for Retford, and 1702–1719 for Newark.

1730–1751   **99,960**
                                                 (item 2)

The act book for Retford for this time period is filed with volume 7 of the act books for the Prerogative Court (PCY). See the following section in this volume. Retford continues below on film 100,056.

1714–1773   **100,053**

Vols. 5G–6G cover 1714–1738 for Nottingham with Bingham, 1720–1745 for Newark, and 1752–1773 for Nottingham with Bingham. See the next entry for Nottingham. Newark continues on film 100,057 below.

1739–1751   **99,960**
(item 3)

The act book for Nottingham with Bingham for this time period is filed with volume 7 of the PCY act books. See the preceding entry for 1752–1773.

1774–1824   **100,054**

Vols. 7G–8G for Nottingham with Bingham. Volume 7G is 1774–1802, and volume 8G covers 1803–1824.

1825–1858   **100,055**

Vols. 9G–10G for Nottingham with Bingham. Volume 9G is 1825–1839, and volume 10G covers 1839–1858.

1752–1825   **100,056**

Vols. 11G–12G for Retford in continuation of item 2 of film 99,960 above. Volume 11G is 1752–1799, and volume 12G covers 1800–1825.

1746–1858   **100,057**

Vols. 13G–15G for Retford and Newark. Volume 13G is 1825–1858 for Retford. Volume 14G is 1746–1812 for Newark in continuation of film 100,053 above. Volume 15G is 1812–1858 for Newark.

Act Books for the Prerogative Court of the Archbishop of York

---

The acts are in Latin until 1733, but the names in the margins are usually easily recognizable.

Early–1623

PCY act books for the earliest periods are part of the Deanery of the City of York, which see in the preceding section on the Exchequer Court.

1624–1644   **99,957**

Vol. 1 of PCY act books.

1645–1652   **99,957**
1660–1678   **(item 2)**

Vol. 2 of PCY act books. No entries are recorded here from 1652–1660 due to the Commonwealth and Interregnum periods.

1679–1717   **99,958**

Vols. 3–4 of PCY act books. Volume 3 is 1679–1705, and volume 4 covers 1706–1717. Abstracts from the act books for 1679–1685 were published in *The Northern Genealogist* (FHL 942 B2ng vol. 2, pp. 13–16, 53–56, 187–190; vol. 3, pp. 44–47, 75–78, 116–123, 173–176; and vol. 4, pp. 19–21 and 85–88).

1718–1743   **99,959**

Vols. 5–6 of PCY act books. Volume 5 is 1718–1730, and volume 6 covers 1731–1743.

1743–1751   **99,960**

Vol. 7 of PCY act books. This film includes the deanery act books for Retford, 1730–1751, and for Nottingham with Bingham, 1739–1751.

1752–1763   **99,961**

Vol. 8 of PCY act books.

1763–1772   **99,962**

Vol. 9 of PCY act books.

1772–1793   **99,963**

Vols. 10–11 of PCY act books. Volume 10 is 1772–1782, and volume 11 covers 1782–1793.

1793–1805   **99,964**

Vols. 12–13 of PCY act books. Volume 12 is 1793–1800, and volume 13 covers 1800–1805.

1806–1813   **99,965**

Vols. 14–15 of PCY act books. Volume 14 is 1806–1810, and volume 15 covers 1810–1813.

1814–1820   **99,966**

Vols. 16–17 of PCY act books. Volume 16 is 1814–1817, and volume 17 covers 1817–1820.

1820–1825   **99,967**

Vols. 18–20 of PCY act books. Volume 18 is 1820–1821, volume 19 is 1821–1823, and volume 20 covers 1823–1825.

1825–1828   **99,968**

Vols. 21–22 of PCY act books. Volume 21 is 1825–1826, and volume 22 covers 1826–1828.

1828–1833   **99,969**

Vols. 23–25 of PCY act books. Volume 23 is 1828–1829, volume 24 is 1829–1831, and volume 25 covers 1831–1833.

1833–1837   **99,970**

Vols. 26–27 of PCY act books. Volume 26 is 1833–1835, and volume 27 covers 1835–1837.

1837–1840   **99,971**

Vols. 28–29 of PCY act books. Volume 28 is 1837–1839, and volume 29 covers 1839–1840.

1840–1843   **99,972**

Vols. 30–31 of PCY act books. Volume 30 is 1840–1842, and volume 31 covers 1842–1843.

1843–1845   **99,973**

Vol. 32 of PCY act books.

1845–1848   **99,974**

Vols. 33–34 of PCY act books. Volume 33 is 1845–1846, and volume 34 covers 1846–1848.

1848–1851   **99,975**
Vols. 35–36 of PCY act books. Volume 35 is 1848–
1850, and volume 36 covers 1850–1851.

1851–1854   **99,976**
Vols. 37–38 of PCY act books. Volume 37 is 1851–
1852, and volume 38 covers 1853–1854.

1854–1856   **99,977**
Vols. 39–40 of PCY act books. Volume 39 is 1854–
1855, and volume 40 covers 1855–1856.

1857–1858   **99,978**
Vol. 41 of PCY act books.

Other Registers for the Exchequer and Prerogative Courts of the Archbishop of York

---

1592–1638   **99,956 &**
                                                  991,228
                                                  (item 2)
Register of Caveats and Curations. This volume starts
with a manuscript index. The entries are arranged like an
act book, and include tuitions. Hence, it would be of
value for research involving guardianship and contested
estates.

1778–1833   **98,920**
                                                    (item 2),
                                                    991,228
                                                    (item 1)
Register of Wills Decreed Out of Court. Act book entries
only.

COURT BOOKS

These registers appear to be a portion of the Abstract
Books for all courts or possibly the Proctors' Abstract
Books. They include testamentary matters, excommunications, and other business of an ecclesiastical court.
They refer to the "libel" or document that initiates the
cause papers. See the miscellaneous section for more on
cause papers.

The registers are arranged chronologically by legal term;
that is, roughly quarterly. They are worth gleaning, as
will be seen in the example for 1823 below.

1820–1822   **100,082**
                                                    (item 2)

1822–1825   **100,082**
                                                    (item 3)
Starts with two pages for 1842–1843. Details of a renun-
ciation were entered for the Exchequer Court on 5
August 1823 concerning the will of Anne Waterton,

widow, formerly of Adwick le Street, Yorks., afterward
Demerara in the West Indies, but late of New York
where a codicil to the will was added in 1821.

1825–1829   **100,082**
                                                    (item 4)
Ends with documents dated 1836, 1835, and 1838.

1829–1834   **100,083**

1834–1839   **100,083**
                                                    (item 2)

1839–1847   **100,083**
                                                    (item 3)

1845–1852   **100,083**
                                                    (item 4)

Indexes and Calendars for the Chancery Court of the Archbishop of York

---

There is some confusion between the Chancery Court
and the Consistory Court. Since the Consistory Court of
York left no known probate records, it is presumed that
any references to it under the subject of probates refer
instead to the Chancery Court.

Apparently there are no registered copy wills or surviving act books for the Chancery Court of York. However,
see the miscellaneous section for printed wills of the
clergy and for cause papers where an appeal was made,
both of which were matters of special interest to this
court.

1) The printed indexes may also be available on
microfilm.

1427–1658   **FHL 942.74 B4a**
                                               vol. 73, part 1
                                               599,878 (item 1)
Vol. 73 of the Record Series of the Yorkshire Archaeological Society. This index to the originals is known to
be incomplete. The earliest references may be to
Exchequer Court wills. The index is useful for searching
film 99,373 and may prove helpful with other films in
the early periods.

1316–1822   **FHL 942.74 B4a**
                                               vol. 93 &
                                               599,881 (item 4)
Vol. 93 of the Record Series of the Yorkshire Archaeological Society. This is not an index to original documents; rather, it is an index to references of probates
enrolled along with all other ecclesiastical matters in the

individual registers of each archbishop. These are not registered copy wills or act books of the Chancery Court, but the dates of probate should assist in finding the document filed among the original records for this court.

1823–1824

No wills were proved in the Chancery Court.

1825–1857   FHL 942.74 B2bo
                                 vol. 1

Vol. 1 of the Borthwick Institute *Bulletin*. The index is on pages 39–42. This is a further index to probates in the "Archbishops' Registers."

2) The filmed indexes are to manuscript calendars. The first part is divided into two categories, one for wills of the clergy and the other for laymen. The printed indexes outlined above also should be used and may assist where there is a gap in the filmed calendars from 1725–1808. If not, the original documents for that period are filed chronologically by year and are not all that numerous; thus, they are fairly easy to peruse.

1660–1713   98,924

Vol. 31 A. The first part is a calendar for clergymen, 1660–1710. Item 2 adds seventeen additional entries, all but two of which have been inserted in the first part.

1660–1714   98,924
                                 (item 3)

A calendar for probates of laymen proven during visitations. This is followed by a list of omissions. The alphabetical order is not strict, and other years are entered besides those of the visitation periods.

1713–1724   98,924
                                 (item 4)

Vol. 34. A and B of this calendar are missing.

1808–1858   98,924
                                 (item 5)

Despite the title, the earliest entry in this calendar is for 1809. The calendar is arranged chronologically by the first letter of each surname.

Original Wills, Admons, and Inventories for the Chancery Court of the Archbishop of York

---

(Starting with film 99,376, the originals are usually in chronological order by the year of probate.)

1427–1578   99,373

There is no order to these documents. Many are for clergymen. The printed indexes are helpful. Anthony J. Camp reports that many of the early documents may be

probates of the Exchequer Court, but this will be difficult to determine on film. See film 991,207 below.

Early–1737   99,374

There is no order to these documents. About one fourth of the way through are two documents for the 1500s, and there is another for 1590 toward the very end of the film. At about the midway point is one for the 1400s. Otherwise these documents cover from 1643–1737, with the majority being for 1719–1737. Of the fifty-five documents for the 1600s, thirty-seven are for the visitation years of 1667, 1674, 1682, 1684–1685, 1693, and 1697–1698. There may be a correlation with the filmed calendar in the preceding section, item 3 of 98,924. See the next film.

Early–1742   99,375

This film follows the pattern of the preceding one. There are four documents for the 1500s, including one toward the end of the film for 1575. The rest of the coverage is for 1648–1742, with the majority being for 1719–1742. Again, thirty-one of the forty-eight documents for the 1600s match with the same visitation years as mentioned on the previous film, plus the visitations of 1662 and 1690.

1535–1599   991,207

These are additional documents mentioned by Camp as having been found since the collection for 1427–1658 was compiled. The documents have been restored, and each group of them is introduced by a modern addition of the archivist.

The wills are in good chronological order through 1579. After that date there is a group for 1586–1589 followed by another for 1580–1582. The sequence then reverts to 1579 and proceeds in correct order through 1599.

After the group for 1599 come a series for Durham Vacancy, 1552/3 and 1587 (two documents); Chester Vacancy, 1560–1561 (five documents); the Royal Visitation of 1559 (one document); and the visitations of 1563 (one), 1567 (seven), and 1571/2–1599 (thirty-five—two for Chester, ten for York, two for Carlisle, one more for York, and twenty more for Chester, labeled as the Visitation of 1578 but each will indicates that it was a vacancy).

Starting with the group of wills for 1586/7–1589, the probate idents are often written on the backside of copies of marriage licenses issued in the eighteenth century. These date from 1713–1754, with most of them being for the period from 1718–1744. The following places in Yorkshire are represented: Adel, Arncliffe, Atwick, Barnoldswick, Batley, Bempton, Bridlington, Burnsall, Coley, Folkton, Giggleswick, Gisburn, Halifax, Hexham, Horton, Hull, Hutton Buscel, Keighley, Kettlewell, Kilburn, Kildwick, Kirkby Malzeard,

Leathley, Malton, Marton, Ripon, Scarborough, Skipton, Waddington. It is presumed that these licenses are archived elsewhere, and only those that refer to places outside of Yorkshire will be noted here:

In the wills for 1591–1591/2 is one for 17 December 1744 for John Haighton of Chaigley, Lancs., and Ellen Cottam of Skipton. With 1593–1593/4 is one for 5 November 1743 for James Sayer of Sunderland, Durham, and Catherine Brown, widow of Scarborough. With 1597–1597/8 is one for 10 July 1735 for John Taylor of Waddington and Mary Edmundson of Whaley, Lancs. With 1598–1598/9 are two: one for 4 January 1713 for Robert Chappell of Crowle, Lincs., and Ann Santon of Hull, and the other for 24 August 1718 for Francis Brailsford of Heath in Derby and Mary Scott of Birstall.

1580–1606   **99,376**
See the preceding film. This film ends with a will written in 1606 but proven in 1608 for John Scarth, clerk of Crathorne.

1607–1615   **99,377**

1616–1620   **99,378**

1621–1627   **99,379**

1628–1634   **99,380**

1635–1638   **99,381**

1639–1642   **99,382**

1643–1660   **99,383**
See also films 99,374 and 99,375.

1661–1665   **99,384**
See also films 99,374 and 99,375.

1666–1667   **99,385**
See also films 99,374 and 99,375.

1668–1673   **99,386**
See also films 99,374 and 99,375.

1674–1677   **99,387**
See also films 99,374 and 99,375.

1678–1682   **99,388**
See also films 99,374 and 99,375.

1683–1688   **99,389**
See also films 99,374 and 99,375.

1689–1692   **99,390**
See also films 99,374 and 99,375.

1693–1699   **99,391**
See also films 99,374 and 99,375.

1700–1712   **99,392**
See also films 99,374 and 99,375.

1713–1718   **99,393**
See also films 99,374 and 99,375.

1719–1730   **99,394**
See also films 99,374 and 99,375.

1731–1750   **99,395**
See also films 99,374 and 99,375.

1751–1769   **99,396**

1770–1775   **99,397**

1776–1789   **99,398**
See the next film for at least one other entry for 1781.

1790–1806   **99,399**
Starts with an entry for 1781.

1807–1845   **99,400**
There was a vacancy from 1807–1808. See the Court of the Dean and Chapter of York.

1846–1857
Not filmed. See the Dean and Chapter of York for the vacancy of 1847. For details on all of these years, consult Camp's *Wills and Their Whereabouts*.

Indexes and Calendars for the Court of the Dean and Chapter of York

---

What follows pertains to the peculiar jurisdiction of the Dean and Chapter of York as well as its involvement with other peculiars in Yorkshire in general. The vacancy jurisdiction of the Dean and Chapter of York will be listed in a separate section to follow this one.

1) The printed index to wills and bonds, not inventories, is incomplete. It does include indexes to registered copy wills and one act book, both of which will be described with their respective microfilms. It might be used in conjunction with the filmed index, 1383–1858, listed below to match an inventory with a registered will.

1524–1724   **FHL 942.74 B4a**
vol. 38 &
599,872 (item 2)
Vol. 38 of the Record Series of the Yorkshire Archaeological Society. The index appears as an appendix to this volume.

2) The filmed calendars follow:

1383–1858	**1,648,257**
	(item 3)

A modern typescript listing of original probate records filmed in 1989. It should be used in place of the other filmed calendars that follow, except in the case of the vacancy jurisdiction. The entries are in alphabetical order and then by date. Each indentifies exactly the type of original documents available.

1438–1728	**98,916**
	(item 4)

This is described as a calendar to General Peculiars as well. It is by year and the initial letter of the surnames. The short calendars for 1723 and 1723–1725, items 3 and 10 of film 100,080, may belong to this court.

1650–1756	**98,922**
	(item 3)

Item 3 begins with an index for the vacancy of 1686–1688. The regular calendar for the Dean and Chapter is part of the same volume and starts on page 41 for 1650–1680. The portion for 1681–1756 begins on page 68.

1757–1858	**98,922**
	(item 2)

Original Wills, Admons, and Inventories for the Court of the Dean and Chapter of York

---

First Group

(This first grouping of films refers to the new arrangement of original documents filmed in 1989. It supersedes anything that follows for the Dean and Chapter except for the Vacancy Jurisdiction and any films identified as registered copy wills or act books. This filming represents a slight reduction compared to the older one, but it is still quite readable. If unreadable or the desired document cannot be found, then consult the older filming.

Each document is preceded by a modern identification page that gives name, residence, date, and type of document. If the will has also been registered, a reference to the volume and folio numbers should be provided as well. The documents are arranged by year in alphabetical order.)

1383–1553	**1,647,858**
1554–1579	**1,647,859**
1580–1602	**1,647,860**
1603–1629	**1,647,861**
1630–1657	**1,647,862**
1660–1664	**1,648,010**
1665–1671	**1,648,011**
1672–1679	**1,648,012**
1679–1685	**1,648,013**
1686–1695	**1,648,014**
1696–1707	**1,648,015**
1708–1722	**1,648,016**
1723–1734	**1,648,017**
1735–1746	**1,648,018**
1747–1761	**1,648,200**
1762–1773	**1,648,201**
1774–1783	**1,648,202**
1784–1796	**1,648,253**
1797–1807	**1,648,254**
1808–1819	**1,648,255**
1820–1840	**1,648,256**
1841–1858	**1,648,257**

Second Group

(This second grouping of films is the older one replaced by the previous grouping, which see. The records in the older group are by initial letter of the surname in alphabetical order, but the surnames are not filed in any exact order and the time period covered on each film is difficult to determine. Supposedly, most of these records date mainly from 1660. Note that there are other parts or films for bonds and inventories in the older group besides those found here, and that some wills are located with them.)

Early–1739 A	**98,926**
Box 1	

Early–1739 A	**98,927**

Box 1, cont. There is no apparent order, but these documents seem to run mainly from the 1670s forward.

Early–1739 B Box 1	**98,928**	**Early–1739 I & J**	**98,949**
Early–1739 B Box 2	**98,929**	**Early–1739 I & J**	**98,950**
Early–1739 B Box 2, cont.	**98,930**	**Early–1739 K**	**98,951**
Early–1739 B Box 3	**98,931**	**Early–1739 L** Boxes 1 and 2	**98,952**

Early–1739 B   **98,932**
Box 4

Early–1739 L   **98,953**
Box 3

Early–1739 C   **98,933**
Box 1

Early–1739 M   **98,954**
Box 1

Early–1739 C   **98,934**
Box 2

Early–1739 M   **98,955**
Box 2

Early–1739 C   **98,935**
Box 3

Early–1739 M   **98,956**
This box is labeled simply M and seems to cover mainly 1531–1612.

Early–1739 C   **98,936**
Box 4

Early–1739 M   **98,957**
This box appears to be a continuation of the preceding one and covers mainly 1613–1728.

Early–1739 D   **98,937**

Early–1739 N   **98,958**
Boxes 1 and 2. Box 1 supposedly covers 1638–1689. The latest document noted was for 1681. Box 2 starts with 1681 but seems to be mainly eighteenth century.

Early–1739 D   **98,938**
Box 1

Early–1739 E   **98,939**
Boxes 1 and 2

Early–1739 N   **98,959**
This box is labeled simply N. There are documents here dated 1661, 1680, 1698, and 1724, but most are pre-1640.

Early–1739 F   **98,940**
Boxes 1 and 2

Early–1739 F   **98,941**
Boxes 1 and 2, cont.

Early–1739 O   **98,960**
This box is labeled simply O.

Early–1739 G   **98,942**
Box 1

Early–1739 P   **98,961**
Box 1

Early–1739 G   **98,943**
Box 2

Early–1739 P   **98,962**
Box 2

Early–1739 G   **98,944**
Box 3

Early–1739 P   **98,963**
This box is labeled simply P.

Early–1739 H   **98,945**
Box 1

Early–1739 R   **98,964**
Box 1 seems to cover mainly from the 1500s through the late 1600s.

Early–1739 H   **98,946**
Box 2

Early–1739 H   **98,947**
Box 3

Early–1739 R   **98,965**
Box 2 seems to cover mainly from the early 1600s through 1739.

Early–1739 H   **98,948**
Box 4

Early–1739 R   **98,966**
This box is labeled R, "Old Wills etc.," and contains documents dated as early as 1529 and as late as 1719.

Early–1739 S 98,967
Box 1 is mainly the early period, but at least one document is dated 1716. See the note for film 98,970.

Early–1739 S 98,968
Box 2 is 1680–1739, but note the preceding film and those that follow for S.

Early–1739 S 98,969
Box 2A is a continuation of the preceding one, which see.

Early–1739 S 98,970
This box is labeled S, "Old Wills etc. three Bundles." In the main the documents date from 1541–1724, but toward the end of the film is a long inventory for John Stubbes, barber of Gotheromgate, dated 1450/51. There are at least another thirty readable wills for S, 1653–1691 (most are for 1660–1675) among the inventories on film 98,999.

Early–1739 S 98,971
A continuation of the preceding film, which see. This bundle contains mainly documents from 1551–1692. However, there are inventories for Thomas Symson, parson of York taken in 1491, and for John Scarle in 1403; and the film ends with that of John de Scardeburgh taken in 1395. The latter does not appear in the new arrangement of original documents outlined at the start of this section.

Early–1739 S 98,972
Box S–A covers at least 1554–1724. See the note under film 98,970.

Early–1739 T 98,973
Box 1 carries the label of 1669–1684 but documents were noted dated 1624 and 1693, and there is at least one from the fifteenth century.

Early–1739 T 98,974
Box 2 covers 1677–1739.

Early–1739 T 98,975
This box is simply called "Old Wills T." Documents were noted for 1557–1739. The contents of the box are continued on the next film.

Early–1739 T 98,976
Documents were noted dated from 1540 through at least 1732.

1573–1672 U & V 98,977
(item 1)
It would appear that there are none for this portion of the alphabet from 1673–1739.

Early–1739 W 98,978
Box 1 covers mainly 1619–1683.

Early–1739 W 98,979
Box 2 is mainly 1680–1739 but noted in passing are documents for 1562, 1660, 1663, and 1667.

Early–1739 W 98,980
Box 2A is 1679–1739.

Early–1739 W 98,981
This box is labeled simply W and contains documents from 1517–1717.

Early–1739 W 98,982
Box W–A is mainly 1553–1717, but there appears to be at least one document from the fifteenth century.

Early–1739 Y 98,977
(item 2)
There are three portions to this coverage. The first is early, the second mainly 1680–1737, and the last appears to be 1551–1679.

1739–1748 98,983
From this point onward there is no attempt at alphabetical arrangement, but the filing does seem to be roughly chronological by the date proved. There is an admon out of sequence here for 1737 for William Middleton of Kirkby Irelyth, Lancs.

1749–1751 98,984
Lacks order and continues on the next film.

1750–1758 98,985
Continues from the previous film, in fair order but by year only. There is a will proven in 1722 for Isabell Lunn, widow of the City of York.

1759–1766 98,986
Lacks order.

1767–1773 98,987
From this point on the documents are ordered by year of probate.

1774–1781 98,988

1782–1788 98,989

1789–1796 98,990

1797–1802 98,991

1803–1809 98,992

1810–1817 98,993

1818–1827 98,994

1828–1839 98,995

1840–1857 98,996

Registered Copy Wills for the Court of the Dean and Chapter of York

1321–1553   **FHL 942.74 B4a**
                                              vol. 38 &
                                  599,872 (item 2)
Vol. 38 of the Record Series of the Yorkshire Archaeological Society is a printed index to the first four volumes
of registered copy wills, 1321–1553, and also to one act
book, 1559–1636. Volume 60, pages 189–190, of this
same series (also available on film 402,541) indexes the
wills registered in the Chapter Act Books and other
records kept in the Zouche Chapel for 1336–1429.

1321–1493   **1,545,163**
                                                   (item 1)
Vol. L2/4

1493–1543   **1,545,163**
                                                   (item 2)
Vol. L2/5A

1543–1558
This volume has not yet been filmed. See the section for
"Original Wills."

1547–1553   **1,545,163**
                                                   (item 3)
The first seven pages form an act book, 1545/6–1553.
They are followed by five blank pages and then the regis-
tered copy wills.

1557–1638   **99,878**
Vol. 5 has its own index.

1639–1808
Not registered. See the section for "Original Wills."

1809–1825   **99,879**
Vols. 1 and 2. Volume 1 is 1809–1817 and is indexed.
Volume 2 is 1818–1825 and is indexed. Both volumes
are also arranged chronologically.

1825–1858   **99,880**
Vols. 3 and 4. Volume 3 is 1825–1840. The index continues on page 550. Volume 4 is 1840–1858.

Probate and Administration Bonds for the Court of the Dean and Chapter of York

(In the following collection, each obligation and condition has been numbered in the lower center portion of the
document at a later date. The filmed calendar indexes
them by initial letter of the surname and refers to these
document numbers. Bonds also will be found among the
original wills and the inventories. All of these documents
also should be in the new arrangement of "Original
Wills" outlined at the start of this section for the Dean
and Chapter.)

1588–1630   **98,922**
                                                   (item 1)
The filmed calendar.

1588–1630   **100,074**
Documents 1–400. Includes a few inventories.

1588–1630   **100,075**
Documents 401–694

1588–1630   **100,076**
Documents continue for 694–800.196

1588–1630   **100,077**
Documents 801–1040

1588–1630   **100,078**
Documents continue for 1040–1200.

1588–1630   **100,079**
Documents 1201–1378

Inventories and Wills Difficult to Read for the Court of the Dean and Chapter of York

(Both wills and bonds may be found among these inventories. Most of these documents should be listed in the
filmed index, 1383–1858, mentioned at the start of the
section for "Indexes and Calendars" for the Dean and
Chapter. They will be easier to find in the new arrangement described under "Original Wills." Some exceptions
are noted below.)

1500s–1625   **98,997**
All inventories except for two bonds and one will for
William Coupland of Newthorpe, Yorks., proven in
1676. Toward the end of the film are documents for 1681
and 1687.

1547–1667   **98,998**
Mostly inventories. There are five bonds for 1698, three
for 1699, and thirteen wills, only two of which are fairly
easy to read. These two are for George Mordinge, yeoman of Helperthroppe, proven in 1615; and for John
Hodgson of Stillington, proven in 1664.

1490–1720   **98,999**
Box A of inventories, bonds, and wills. Only one of the
wills is unreadable. Most of the wills (around thirty) are
for the letter S between 1653–1691, including William

Soleby, yeoman of Laneham, Notts., proven in 1672 or 1675; Richard Shemill, laborer of Anston, Yorks., proven in 1669 (not in the new arrangement); William Simpson of Great Driffield, proven in 1676; and Robert Squire of Waghen, Yorks., proven in 1671 (not in the new arrangement). Also included are seven bonds, a will for C proven in 1660, and a will for T proven in 1670. About three fourths of the way through the film is the will of John Hall of Stokton, proven in 1490 (not in the new arrangement). Near the end of the film is the will of Richard Holmes of Eastdrayton, Notts., plus a tuition bond proven in 1587 (not in the new arrangement).

1500–1714   99,000
Mainly wills, many labeled imperfect or illegible, but there are a number that are legible. Among them are wills for C 1666, S 1672, C 1660, S 1673, S 1660, B 1643, T 1592, F 1531, W 1560, S 1597, T 1597, P 1674, J 1547, D 1583, B 1559, W 1615, S 1595, D 1629, D 1616, F 1531, M 1646, C 1530, T 1591, B 1571, Y 1616, T 1686, B 1664, B 1677, R 1686, W 1670, B 1660, H 1660, H 1672, and F 1753. About three fourths of the way through the film is an accounting by Anne Cave, widow, of how the estate of Christopher Cave was handled in 1618 (not in the new arrangement). The film ends with a document dated 1604 that refers to William Elwick of Misterton, Notts. (not in the new arrangement).

1400–1701   99,001
These are all inventories except for one will. There is no order to them, but they are legible. The will is for John Woodburn, husbandman of Kirkby Ireleth, Lancs., proven in 1680.

1400–1701   99,002
(Continued.) No wills.

1429–1695   99,003
There are several bonds but only two wills. Halfway through the film is a will for B, proven in 1531. Near the end of the film is a will for F, proven in 1660 as a vacancy will.

1488–1691   99,004
These are inventories except for two administration bonds.

Act Books and Other Registers for the Court of the Dean and Chapter of York

---

1) Probate Act Books and Abstract Book

1545/6–1553   1,545,163
(item 3)
Vol. M2/3B. The first seven pages contain some seventeen acts; registered copy wills make up the rest of the volume.

1559–1636   1,545,163
(item 4)
Vol. L1/1A of these act books is indexed in volume 38 of the Record Series of the Yorkshire Archaeological Society (FHL 942.74 B4a and item 2 of film 599,872).

1665–1673   1,545,163
(item 5)
Vol. L1/1B consists of two parts, both covering the same time period. The first is a probate act book that contains marriage licenses as well. The second is a register of citations.

1774–1847   100,082
Item 1 of this film is an abstract book from the court books of the Dean and Chapter. The register contains testamentary business, excommunications, and other business of the ecclesiastical court. It is arranged chronologically by legal term, that is, roughly quarterly.

2) Chapter Act Books
The wills in Chapter Act Books, 1346–1429, are indexed in volume 60 of the Record Series of the Yorkshire Archaeological Society (FHL 942.74 B4a and film 402,541). There may not be any wills in Chapter Act Books after 1546, but all such filmed act books are outlined here.

1345–1353   1,545,163
(item 7)
Vol. H1/1

1343–1558   1,545,164
(items 1–9)
Vols. H1/2–3, L2/3A, H2/1–3, H3/1–3. Item 1 is volume H1/2 for 1343–1370. Item 2 is volume H1/3 for 1352–1386. Item 3 is volume H2/1 for 1401–1435. Item 4 is volume L2/3A for 1410–1427, including visitations. Item 5 is volume H2/2 for 1468–1480. Item 6 is volume H2/3 for 1427–1504. Item 7 is volume H3/1 for 1504–1543. Item 8 is volume H3/2 for 1507–1508. Item 9 is volume H3/3 for 1543–1558. Items 6,7, and 9 are partially indexed.

1565–1634   1,655,697
Vol. H4

1634–1701   1,545,165
(item 1)
Vol. H5, partly indexed.

1701–1830   1,545,166
(items 1–6)
Vols. H6–7, H9/1–3, H10/1. Item 1 is volume H6 for 1701–1728. Item 2 is volume H7 for 1728–1747. Item 3 is volume H9/1 for 1747–1756. Item 4 is volume H9/2 for 1756–1771. Item 5 is volume H9/3 for 1784–1807. Item 6 is volume H10/1 for 1807–1830.

1830–1890   **1,545,168**
                                                              (items 1–3)
Vols. H10/2, H11/1–2. Item 1 is volume H10/2 for
1830–1842. Item 2 is volume H11/1 for 1842–1873. Item
3 is volume H11/2 for 1873–1890.

1890–1936   **1,545,170**
                                                              (items 1–2)
Vols. H11/3–4. Item 1 is volume H11/3 for 1890–1914,
and item 2 is volume H11/4 for 1914–1936.

Indexes and Calendars for the Vacancy Jurisdiction of the Court of the Dean and Chapter of York

(These records are included in the calendars of the
Exchequer and Prerogative Courts from 1743, and references also may be found there for the earlier periods.)

1) Printed Index

1683,   **FHL 942.74 B4a**
1686–1688   **vol. 89 &**
                                                              402,541 (item 3)
                                                              599,880 (item 5)
Vol. 89 of the Record Series of the Yorkshire Archaeo-
logical Society. Appendix II, Part II on pages 146–165 is
an index to the registered copy wills. (None is registered
after April 1686.) Appendix III, pages 166–168, adds an
index to the act books for admons and wills that were not
registered. (There are no entries in the act books after
April 1686.) Appendix IV, pages 169–208, is an index to
the original records. Appendix V, pages 209–210, adds a
list of documents no longer extant.

2) Filmed Calendars

1686–1688   **98,922**
                                                              (item 3)
Indexed alphabetically by the initial letter of each surname and then the month from March 1686–March
1687. The first index goes through page 22. On page 23,
the index begins again but by month and then by letter
from March 1687–June 1688. There are no entries for
1683 here, but there is an act book.

1776–1777   **98,916**
                                                              (item 3)
This is a manuscript volume including calendars to cer-
tain peculiar courts. The list of vacancy wills for this
time period is on pages 103–110. See the next film.

1807–1808,   **98,922**
1847   **(item 4)**
The wills for 1807–1808 are listed by letter and the
month of probate. There is another calendar for this time
period on item 3 of film 98,916 on pages 111–131. The
entries for 1847 continue on pages 133–152 of that film.

Original Wills, Admons, and Inventories for the Vacancy Jurisdiction of the Court of the Dean and Chapter of York

(The records are filed by the year and month of probate.)

Pre–1683
See the section of the same title for the Exchequer and
Prerogative Courts of York.

1683 Volume A	**99,005**
1683 Volume B	**99,006**
1683 Volume B, cont.	**99,007**
1683 Volume C	**99,008**
1686 Jan	**99,009**
1686 Feb	**99,010**
1686 Mar	**99,011**
1686 Apr	**99,012**
1686 May	**99,013**
1686 Jun	**99,014**
1686 Jun, cont.	**99,015**
1686 Jul	**99,016**
1686 Aug	**99,017**
1686 Sep	**99,018**
1686 Oct	**99,019**
1686 Nov	**99,020**
1686 Dec	**99,021**
1687 Jan	**99,022**
1687 Feb	**99,023**
1687 Mar	**99,024**
1687 Apr	**99,025**

1687 May 99,026

1687 Jun 99,027

1687 Jul–Aug 99,028

1687 Sep–Oct 99,029

1687 Nov–Dec 99,030
January–March 1688 may be mixed in with the records of this film or the next.

1688 Apr 99,031
See the note for the preceding film.

1688 May 99,032

1688 Jun 99,033
Either there are no records for July–December 1688 (see the printed index above), or they are filed with the Exchequer and Prerogative Courts of York.

1724 May 99,034

1724 Jun 99,035

1743, 1761
See the records of the Exchequer and Prerogative Courts of York.

1776–1777 99,036
The records are for December 1776 and January 1777.

1807 Nov 99,037

1807 Dec 99,038
1808 Jan
The records for these two months are mixed together.

1847 99,039
The records are in alphabetical order. They include October–November but are mainly December 1847.

1847 99,040
The records are in alphabetical order. They include more entries for October, one each for August and March, but they are mainly November 1847.

Registered Copy Wills for the Vacancy Jurisdiction of the Court of the Dean and Chapter of York

---

(Only the following volume was filmed. See the section for "Original Wills" for the rest.)

1724 99,881
Volume 1 is unindexed.

Act Books for the Vacancy Jurisdiction of the Court of the Dean and Chapter of York

---

1530–1531, 99,980
1544–1545 (item 2)
These are listed as volume 4 of the Exchequer Act Books with which they are filed, but they are vacancy act books filed by deanery. The vacancies were from November 1530–December 1531 and September 1544–January 1545. They also appear on film 991,209, and there is a further partial copy of them on item 5 of film 99,955.

1559–1561 98,923
In chronological order.

1568–1570 98,923
(item 2)
In chronological order. An index starts on folio 7, or fourteen pages into the volume.

1683, 1686 98,922
(item 3)
This is a bound manuscript volume containing other information as described elsewhere. The act book of 1686 begins on page 103, and the act book for 1683 follows it.

Indexes and Calendars for the Consistory Court of the Commissary of the Archdeaconry of Richmond, Eastern Deaneries

---

1) Printed Index

1474–1617 A–G FHL 942 B2ng
vol. 3
The printed index is a supplement to volume 2 of *The Northern Genealogist* and is numbered as pages 1–48, but it will be found bound at the back of volume 3. It only indexes the surnames A–G and may be incomplete. It does include both original and registered copy wills. Volumes 1–3 of the registered copy wills are referred to as the cross (+) volume. Of volumes A–G, the surnames A, E, and G were not available for indexing and apparently have been lost. The title page claims that the index starts in 1588; however, the registered copy wills include some from the fifteenth century.

2) Filmed Calendars

1410–1610 A 98,904
Volume 1 includes references to court cases.

1410–1610 B 98,905
Volume 2 covers Ba–Bk.
Volume 3 covers Bl–Bz.

1410–1610 C–F   **98,906**
Volume 4 is Ca–Cot.
Volume 5 is Cou–D.
Volume 6 is E–F.

1410–1610 G–L   **98,907**
Volume 7 is G–Hat.
Volume 8 is Hau–Hz.
Volume 9 is I/J–K.
Volume 10 is L.

1410–1610 M–R   **98,908**
Volume 11 is Ma–Ml.
Volume 12 is Mo–O.
Volume 13 is P–Q.
Volume 14 is R.

1410–1610 S–Z   **98,909**
Volume 15 is Sa–Sl.
Volume 16 is Sm–Sy.
Volume 17 is T.
Volume 18 is U/V–Wh.
Volume 19 is Wi–Z.

1611–1700 A–K   **98,910**
This period is covered by three volumes labeled A–B,
C–F, and G–K.

1611–1700 L–Y   **98,911**
This period is covered by three volumes labeled L–P,
R–S, and T–Y.

1503–1699   **98,913**
This bound manuscript volume has been given the reference 19A. It is an older version of the above and should
be incorporated into the preceding calendars in its
entirety. A note adds that wills for Knaresborough
proven in the archdeaconry before 1640 are included.

1700–1826   **98,912**
This is a bound manuscript volume containing several
items. The first is an index to probates for A–Y. Most of
the letters come to an end in this item between
1812–1823, with the exceptions of E that goes through
1825, G and N through 1826, and O through 1825.

Opposite to Y is a list of nine unproved wills for various
letters between 1770–1800. Then comes a list of terriers
by parish and date, followed by another index of parishes
with the names of pew holders from 1720. Then follows
a list of "The Names of the Towns, Villages, etc. within
the Deaneries of Amounderness, Lonsdale, Furness,
Kendale, and Coupland."

Finally, there is the rest of the probate index: A
1813–1825, B 1815–1826, C 1821–1825 (one more after
Y), D 1820–1826, F 1822–1825, H 1815–1823 (the rest
of H plus I/J are after Y), K 1820–1825, L 1818–1826, M

1809–1825, P 1816–1826, S 1810–1826, R 1813–1825,
T 1814–1826, W 1817–1826, Y 1818–1825, one more C
for 1826, H 1823–1826, and I/J 1824–1826.

1826–1857   **98,912**
                                                    (item 2)
Another manuscript volume. The probate index continues on without a break into copies of thirty-three marriage licenses issued between 21 September 1822–12
April 1823. Two Quakers are mentioned. The entries that
refer to places outside of Yorkshire are listed below.

21 September 1822—Robert Harding of High Conis-
cliffe, Durham (christened at Gainford, Durham) and
Elizabeth Brown of Manfield, Yorks.
7 October 1822—William Todd of St. James Clerkenwell,
London (christened at Brignall, Yorks.) and Elizabeth
Middleton of Startforth (christened at Rokeby, Yorks.).
15 November 1822—Walker Thompson, a Quaker of
Newcastle upon Tyne, Northumberland, and Mary
Knowles of Low Row, Grinton, Yorks.
13 December 1822—Anthony Steele of Barnard Castle,
Durham, and Frances Hardy of Barningham, Yorks.
8 January 1823—Henry Hirst of Colne, Lancs., and
Mary Wardman of Ripley, Yorks.
25 February 1823—George Peacock of Blackwell,
Darlington, Durham, and Susan Sykes of Richmond.

Original Records for the Consistory Court of the Commissary of the Archdeaconry of Richmond, Eastern Deaneries

---

1521–1857
The original records for the three Eastern Deaneries of
Richmond, Catterick, and Boroughbridge have not been
filmed. See the registered copy wills and the abstracts
outlined in the miscellaneous section. Consult Camp's
Wills and Their Whereabouts.

Registered Copy Wills of the Consistory Court of the Commissary of the Archdeaconry of Richmond, Eastern Deaneries

---

(The coverage of the registered wills is spotty and should
not replace the use of original documents. Abstracts of
some of the wills are noted in the miscellaneous section.
The early registers consist of volumes labeled 1–3, formerly referred to as the cross (+) volume, and A–G. It
would appear that volumes A, E, and G have been lost.)

1474–1485,   **98,914**
1503, 1529–1551
Vols. 1–3 may include some wills for the Western
Deaneries. The film title adds volume A, but no entries

could be found for it. The film starts with volume 3 for 1529–1551. Next is volume 1 that covers 1474–1485, not 1490. Although no entries beyond 1485 were noted, there are earlier ones: at least one for 1420 and another for 1427. Then come the fragments for 1503 that make up volume 2. About halfway through the film are three or four inventories dated 1590.

1552–1585   **98,915**
Vols. B–D, and F. First comes volume B with the wills for 1564–1573. This is followed by volume C for 1552–1564, which starts with an index to the wills for the same time period and ends with three other indexes. The first appears to be for admons, 1529–1573, followed by two for wills for 1552–1564 and 1552–1573.

The last item on the film contains volume D, 1573–1579, and volume F, 1580–1585. There is no break between the two. Volume D starts with three indexes: the first is for wills, 1573–1579; the second for admons, 1570–1579; and the third for wills, 1570–1573. After the wills comes another index to wills for 1573–1579, followed by the wills of volume F.

1586–1719
There are none; consult the originals.

1720–1731   **98,921**
An index is at the end, but only A–M survives of it.

1732–1782
There are none; consult the originals.

1783–1791   **99,881**
                                                       (item 2)
The first will in this volume is dated 1783 and the last is dated 1788. It appears that all of the wills were proved between 1790–1791. A partial index starts on folio 309. It does not include the twelve wills on folios 156–185 and 306.

1792–1857
There are none; consult the originals.

Act Books and Other Registers for the Consistory Court of the Commissary of the Archdeaconry of Richmond, Eastern Deaneries

1663–1664   **99,953**
Despite what appears on the spine of this manuscript volume, only the probate act book for the Eastern Deaneries from December 1663–December 1664 was filmed. It does include one marriage license on folio 9 for 6 February 1663, for Thomas Hugginson of East Witton and Grace Atkinson of Hornby.

1665–1679
Nothing available.

1680–1694   **99,952**
                                                       (item 2)
This is a journal or minute book showing the accounts of fees paid by individuals for a marriage license or testamentary matter. Like an act book, it also gives the names, residences, and a short reference to the business involved. It is referenced as volume 21A. A note dated 1870 adds, "concerning Western business also, in contentious matters." Some marriage licenses will be found here, although most of it deals with probates.

1695–1706
Nothing available.

1707–1714,   **99,952**
1746   **(item 1)**
Another journal or minute book like the one described above, although the references to marriage licenses seem more numerous.

1715–1735
Nothing available.

1736–1741   **99,953**
                                                       (item 2)
Act Book

1742–1743
Nothing available.

1744–1746   **99,954**
A volume broken into five sets of act books. It does include a summation of fees charged. There are no marriage licenses. Note the entries for 1746 on item 1 of film 99,952 above.

1747–1765
Nothing available.

1766–1771   **99,954**
This second act book continues the volume mentioned above without a break between the two parts. At the end is a one-page summary listing official fees.

1772–1776
Nothing available.

1777–1806   **99,954**
Part 3 in continuation of the volume mentioned above without a break between it and part 2. Fees are no longer recorded. Part 3 covers 1777–1792 and continues without a break into part 4, or 1792–1800. Part 5, 1801–1806, continues in turn without breaking with part 4. Starting with 1792 in part 3, the entries are in alphabetical order.

1807–1808
Nothing available.

1809–1830   **99,954**
                                                          (item 2)
Another volume of act books, arranged chronologically.

1830–1854   **99,954**
                                                          (item 3)
The last act book, arranged chronologically.

Original Records for the General Peculiars in Yorkshire

The records of the peculiar courts in Yorkshire are filed under two broad designations: General Peculiars and Separate Peculiars. Check the Separate Peculiars first for the name of the principal town of that peculiar in alphabetical order. If nothing is found there or the time period of interest is lacking, then try the General Peculiars found here. Search next the records of the Court of the Dean and Chapter of York.

1438–1728   **98,916**
                                                          (item 4)
A filmed calendar to both the Court of the Dean and Chapter of York and the General Peculiars. It is by year and the initial letter of the surname.

1707–1858   **98,916**
                                                          (item 2)
A filmed calendar arranged on pages 1–22 by the initial letter of the surnames from 1707–1729. This portion does not overlap with the calendar on item 4 listed above. The second portion of the calendar starts on page 23 and is 1730–1858. It is chronological and gives in columns the surname, year, given name and residence, type of probate, and the approximate worth of the estate in pounds.

1663–1709   **99,949**
                                                          (item 2)
A list of *reinfecta* wills for peculiars found in the Prerogative Office. The list is not in any order but only contains thirty-four names. The original documents to which it refers follow the list, but again without order.

1660–1696   **99,401**
Box 1 of original documents. There is no order to them. The title of the film claims a time coverage from 1680–1696, but there are four documents that are very difficult to date that must be from the 1500s or earlier. There is also a document for each of the years of 1607, 1641, and 1654. Years that are represented by five or more documents are 1660, 1661, 1663, 1666, 1668, 1669, 1670, 1676, and 1681.

1660–1701   **99,402**
Box 2 of original documents. There is no order to them. The title of the film claims a time coverage from 1680–1696, but there are two documents that are very difficult to date that must be from the 1500s or earlier. There is also a document for each of the years of 1558, 1559, 1608, 1650, 1658, and 1701. Years that are represented by five or more documents are 1660, 1661, 1664, 1665, 1668, 1669, 1670, and 1677.

1707–1712   **99,403**
The first seventy-two documents on this film are original probates. There is no order to them but the six-year period outlined is covered, although the film title refers to 1708–1711.

1712–1717	**99,404**
1718–1721	**99,405**
1722–1725	**99,406**
1726–1729	**99,407**
1730–1736	**99,408**
1737–1743	**99,409**
1744–1751	**99,410**
1752–1758	**99,411**
1759–1765	**99,412**
1766–1771	**99,413**
1772–1777	**99,414**
1778–1784	**99,415**
1785–1790	**99,416**
1791–1798	**99,417**
1799–1807	**99,418**
1808–1817	**99,419**
1818–1825	**99,420**
1826–1835	**99,421**
1836–1858	**99,422**

Original Records for the Separate Peculiars in Yorkshire

(See the introductory note for peculiar courts in the previous section. The Separate Peculiars are arranged first alphabetically by town and then by rough chronological order therein.)

ACOMB

1456–1837   **FHL 942.74 B2bo**
vol. 2

Vol. 2 of the Borthwick Institute *Bulletin* provides a printed index on pages 161–168.

1709–1837   **98,916**
(item 5)

A filmed calendar. Use the printed index listed above.

1709–1837   **99,928**
(item 2)

The original records for Acomb are filed in two sections: 1709–1770 and 1771–1837. There is no order to either section. The break between items 1 and 2 on this film is difficult to discern.

ALDBROUGH

A township in the parish of St. John Stanwick in the North Riding. No original records have been filmed for this court. See the General Peculiars and Camp's *Wills and Their Whereabouts*. A printed index is available as follows:

1610–1700   **FHL 942.74 B4a**
vol. 60 &
402,541

Vol. 60 of the Record Series of the Yorkshire Archaeological Society provides a printed index to this court in Appendix II on page 181.

ALLERTON AND ALLERTONSHIRE

Allerton is a Durham peculiar situated entirely within the geographic boundaries of Yorkshire. More inventories for 1670–1750 will be found in the last item listed for this court.

1666–1845   **90,984**
(item 1)

Filmed calendar to wills and admons.

1666–1668   **90,984**
(item 2)

Original wills.

1670–1671   **90,998**
(item 1)

Original wills, admons, and inventories arranged in rough chronological order.

1671–1674   **91,000**

Original wills, admons, and inventories. There is only one will, and that is dated 1670 for an M.

1675–1679   **90,984**
(item 4)

Original wills, admons, and inventories.

1680–1681   **91,012**
(item 1)

Original wills, probate bonds, and inventories.

1680–1684   **91,012**
(item 2)

Original admons and inventories.

1682

Another will with a bond and inventory will be found on item 2 of film 91,034 below.

1685–1689   **91,019**

Original wills, admons, and inventories. The wills come first, followed by three sections for bonds and admons.

1691–1696   **91,035**
(item 3)

Original wills, bonds, and inventories. There are also some renunciations.

1691–1695   **91,040**
(item 1)

Original admons and inventories.

1697–1699   **91,035**
(item 2)

Original wills, bonds, inventories, and renunciations.

1696–1699   **90,984**
(item 5)

Original admons and inventories.

1700–1706   **91,034**
(item 3)

Original wills, bonds, and inventories.

1700–1709   **91,034**
(item 2)

After the will for 1682 come the admons for 1700–1709, plus a tuition bond for 1702.

1710–1719   **90,984**
(item 7)

Original wills and renunciations.

1720–1729   **90,985**
(item 2)

Original wills arranged chronologically. There is another will, P for 1723, among the inventories outlined at the end of this list.

1710–1739   **90,984**
(item 6)

Original probate and admon bonds. A further section for bonds starting with 1710 appears below. A guardianship bond, L for 1722, is among the inventories outlined at the end of this list.

1740–1758   **90,985**
                                                           (item 3)

Original wills and bonds in chronological order. The bonds appear as separate items on this film and will be itemized after the wills. Note the additional inventories outlined at the end of this list.

1760–1774   **90,985**
                                                           (item 5)

Original wills in chronological order.

1775–1838,   **90,985**
1845   **(item 7)**
Original wills in chronological order.

1710–1773   **90,985**
                                                           (item 1)

Original admons.

1740–1775   **90,985**
                                                           (item 4)

Original bonds in chronological order.

1775–1810   **90,985**
                                                           (item 6)

Original probate and admon bonds in reverse chronological order.

1670–1750   **90,984**
                                                           (item 3)

Original inventories.

ALNE AND TOLLERTON

(Not inhibited.)

1601–1858   **98,916**
                                                           (item 6)
Filmed calendar to wills and admons. Arranged by year. The last entry is for 1856.

1601–1670   **99,936**
Original records for Alne and Tollerton.

1671–1689   **99,937**
Original records, cont.

1690–1729   **99,938**
Original records, cont.

1730–1770   **99,939**
Original records, cont.

1770–1856   **99,940**
Original records, cont.

ALTOFTS IN NORMANTON

No records have been filmed for this manorial court. Consult Camp, *Wills and Their Whereabouts*. A printed index is available as follows:

1622–1677   **FHL 942 B2ng**
                                                              vol. 1

Vol. 1 of *The Northern Genealogist*, page 130.

AMPLEFORTH

Ampleforth was a prebendal court.

1661–1827   **98,916**
                                                           (items 3–4)
Filmed calendar to wills and admons. Ampleforth's calendar appears as pages 7–11 of the bound manuscript volume that is item 3 on this film. There is another manuscript listing of it in the bound volume that makes up item 4 between pages 52 and 53 of the calendar for the Court of the Dean and Chapter of York. There is yet another listing for 1661–1706 only on page 61 of the same volume.

1661–1827   **99,443**
Original records for Ampleforth.

APESTHORPE

No records have been filmed for this prebendal court in Nottinghamshire. See the General Peculiars and consult Camp, *Wills and Their Whereabouts*.

ARKENGARTHDALE

Some records for this manorial court were probated at Richmond, which see. Not inhibited.

1698–1812   **98,917**
                                                           (item 14)
A filmed calendar for this manorial court. The filmed title gives the years 1726–1808, but the coverage is as indicated above.

1698–1812   **FHL 942 B2ng**
No original records have been filmed for the Manorial Court of Arkengarthdale, but abstracts to all of the wills A–M are in *The Northern Genealogist*. A–H is found on pages 93–102 and 116–131 of volume IV (also item 11 of film 994,073). H continues on pages 24–29 of volume V, and I–M is on pages 93–96 of volume VI.

ASKHAM BRYAN

(Not inhibited.)

1710–1799   **99,928**
                                                           (item 1)

The original records for this manorial court are in the following order: an act book for 1772–1799, a list of fourteen wills and inventories with one dated 1686 and the rest from 1757–1799 followed by the actual documents, a calendar for 1710–1759, the original wills for

1710–1757 in the same order as numbered in the calendar, and admons and inventories for 1715–1759 as ordered in the calendar.

BARMBY MOOR

A prebendal court. After 1736 see York, Court of the Dean of, found near the end of this section.

1668–1736   **98,916
(item 4)**

This filmed calendar appears on page 62 of the calendar for the Court of the Dean and Chapter. Another version of it for 1670–1708 is joined to the calendar for the Court of the Dean of York as item 6 on film 100,080.

1668–1736   **99,927
(item 2)**

The original records are introduced by yet another calendar, 1670–1736. There is not much of a break between items 1 and 2 on this film. There is no order to these records.

NOTE: A marriage license for Barmby Moor dated 1727 appears at the end of film 99,403.

BARNOLDSWICK

(Not inhibited.)

1660–1794   **FHL 942 B2ng
98,917
(item 13)**

The calendar for this manorial court has been printed on pages 113–114 of volume I of *The Northern Genealogist*, and the manuscript calendar has been filmed.

1660–1794   **FHL 942.74 B4a
vol. 118 &
599,886**

No original records for Barnoldswick have been filmed, but abstracts of all of the documents appear on pages 53–81 of volume 118 of the Record Series of the Yorkshire Archaeological Society.

BATLEY

(Not inhibited.)

1391–1768   **FHL 942.74/B3 H2s
943,475**

Abstracts of selected wills for the Manorial Court of Batley were printed in a history of the parish published in 1894, pages 294–411. An index and further abstracts, 1651–1694, will be found in volume 74 of the Record Series of the Yorkshire Archaeological Society (FHL 942.74 B4a and item 2 of film 599,878).

1601–1698   **1,239,233**

Transcripts of the wills, bonds, and inventories. This film starts with an index but the records are in alphabetical order.

BEEFORD

(Not inhibited.) No original records have been filmed for this manorial court. Consult Camp, *Wills and Their Whereabouts*. A printed index is available as follows:

1586–1786   **FHL 942.74 B4a
vol. 68 &
599,877
(item 2)**

Vol. 68 of the Record Series of the Yorkshire Archaeological Society provides a printed index in Appendix II, pages 213–216.

BENINGBROUGH

See Newton-on-Ouse.

BEVERLEY

In the city of Beverley, probate jurisdiction was exercised in the sixteenth century by the Provost of the Collegiate Church of St. John.

1539–1552   **FHL 942.74 B4a
vol. 60 &
402,541**

A printed index is in volume 60 of the Record Series of the Yorkshire Archaeological Society, Appendix II, pages 182–184.

1539–1552   **98,920
(item 3)**

Registered copy wills of Beverley. See the preceding entry for an index.

BILTON

No records have been filmed for the Prebendal Court of Bilton. See the General Peculiars and Camp, *Wills and Their Whereabouts*.

BINGLEY

See Crossley.

BISHOP WILTON

(Not inhibited.)

1616–1858   **98,917
(item 4)**

A filmed calendar arranged alphabetically. There are no entries later than 1842. The calendar is followed by an act book, 1712–1721, that includes marriage licenses. This in turn is followed by another calendar, 1722–1842, in chronological order.

1616–1760   **99,441**

Original records. Two other wills for this court are with a miscellaneous collection on item 12 of film 100,080. They are for Mary Sanderson, widow of Benjamin Sanderson, proven in 1728; and Robert Turner, yeoman, proven in 1732.

1761–1842   **99,442**

Original records, cont., of Bishop Wilton.

BOLE

No records have been filmed for the Prebendal Court of Bole in Nottinghamshire. See the General Peculiars and Camp, *Wills and Their Whereabouts*.

BUGTHORPE

1669–1831   **98,916**
                                                     (item 3)

A filmed calendar for this prebendal court appears on pages 15–21 of a bound manuscript volume. Another version, 1669–1739, is found on page 63 of item 4 of the same film.

1669–1831   **99,440**

Original records.

BURTON SALMON

See Wistow.

COTTINGLEY

See Crossley.

CRAIKE

See the Consistory Court of Durham for time periods before 1837. Afterward, see the Exchequer Court of York.

CROSSLEY

(Not inhibited.) The Court of the Knights of St. John of Jerusalem in the manors of Crossley, Bingley, and Pudsey.

1585–1804   **98,917**
                                                     (items 1–2)

Item 1 is a filmed calendar, 1599–1804. It is followed by another calendar, 1585–1700, on item 2. There is also a printed index for 1580–1676 on pages 33–34 of volume I of *The Northern Genealogist* (FHL 942 B2ng).

1599–1804   **99,912**

Original records arranged by the initial letter of each surname.

1600–1645   **FHL 942.74/B1 B4b**
                                                     vol. 1

The wills were printed in full along with the inventories and abstracts of the bonds in the "Local Record Series" of the Bradford Historical & Antiquarian Society.

DRIFFIELD

See York, Court of the Precentor of, found near the end of this section.

DUNNINGTON

No records have been filmed for this prebendal court. See the General Peculiars and Camp, *Wills and Their Whereabouts*.

ELLOUGHTON

See Wetwang.

FENTON

1617–1854   **98,916**
                                                     (item 3)

A filmed calendar for this prebendal court is on pages 23–53 of a bound manuscript volume.

1617–1854 A–B   **99,428**

Original records of Fenton are filed by the initial letter of each surname.

1617–1854 C–F   **99,429**

Original records, cont.

1617–1854 G–K   **99,430**

Original records, cont. K is mixed with H.

1617–1854 L–R   **99,431**

Original records, cont.

1617–1854 S   **99,432**

Original records, cont.

1617–1854 T–W   **99,433**

Original records, cont. NOTE: A marriage license for Sherburn in this court dated 1744 appears toward the end of film 99,403.

FRIDAYTHORPE

No records have been filmed for this prebendal court. See Wetwang, as well as the General Peculiars and Camp, *Wills and Their Whereabouts*.

GIVENDALE

No records have been filmed for this prebendal court. See York, Court of the Dean of, found near the end of this section, and Camp's book as cited in the preceding entry.

GOODMANHAM

See York, the Dean and Chapter; Fridaythorpe; and Wetwang.

GRINDAL

No records have been filmed for this prebendal court. See the General Peculiars and Camp's book cited under Fridaythorpe above.

HESLINGTON

See Ampleforth.

HIGH WORSALL

See Allerton.

HOLME

| 1663–1703 | 98,916 (item 4) |

The filmed calendar for this prebendal court appears on page 64 of a bound manuscript volume.

| 1663–1703 | 99,439 (item 1) |

The original records for the thirty-one persons named in the calendar of this court are on the same film as those of Langtoft (item 2), but there is no break between the two groups of records. There is no order to either set of records.

Holme begins with documents for ten different persons, followed by another calendar to this court but labeled "Withernwick from 1663 to 1703," and then the rest of the wills. The last will for Holme is for Maxwell in 1675, followed by one for Johnson in 1679 to begin Langtoft.

HOWDEN AND HOWDENSHIRE

Howden is a Durham peculiar situated entirely within the geographic boundaries of Yorkshire.

| 1598–1624 | 99,941 (item 1) |

This group of documents starts with a calendar to fifty-six wills found in the Prerogative Office. The calendar is followed by a mix of original and copy wills but in no particular order.

To access the remainder of the original records listed below, it will first be necessary to consult the act books.

| 1622–1857 | 99,955 (item 2) |

The act books are in three volumes on this film, and cover respectively 1622–1642, 1660–1735, and 1736–1857.

| 1660–1672 | 99,423 |

The original records for Howden are filed by the year of probate.

| 1673–1685 | 99,424 |

Original records, cont.

| 1686–1700 | 99,425 |

Original records, cont.

| 1700–1710 | 99,426 |

Original records, cont.

| 1711–1720 | 99,427 |

Original records, cont.

| 1721–1730 | 99,941 (item 2) |

Original records, cont.

| 1731–1750 | 99,942 |

Original records, cont.

| 1751–1770 | 99,943 |

Original records, cont.

| 1771–1790 | 99,944 |

Original records, cont.

| 1791–1810 | 99,945 |

Original records, cont.

| 1811–1820 | 99,946 |

Original records, cont.

| 1821–1840 | 99,947 |

Original records, cont.

| 1841–1857 | 99,948 |

Original records, cont.

HULL

The Corporation of Kingston-upon-Hull processed some probates for its citizens.

| 1309–1425 | FHL 942 B2ng |

A printed index to thirty-six wills is on pages 181–183 of volume II of *The Northern Genealogist*.

1303–1791 **FHL 942.74/H1 A5ki**

The guide to the City of Hull's archives published in 1951 provides further information on its civic wills. Start with the index in the back of this volume by checking under the subject of wills and then personal names.

HUNSINGORE

(Not inhibited.)

1607–1839 **98,917**
(item 9)

A filmed calendar of the probates of this manorial court. No original records of this court have been filmed. Consult Camp, *Wills and Their Whereabouts.*

HUSTHWAITE

1661–1842 **98,916**
(item 3)

A filmed calendar for this prebendal court appears on pages 55–59 of a bound manuscript volume.

1661–1842 **99,925**
Original records of Husthwaite.

KINGSTON-UPON-HULL

See Hull.

KNARESBOROUGH

Knaresborough was an honour court, meaning a manorial court that presided over several other manors. It was not inhibited, but wills for this area may be found under several other jurisdictions, including prebendal jurisdiction for Knaresborough in the sixteenth century. See Camp, *Wills and Their Whereabouts,* for details. Except for the calendar, no original records have been filmed, but there are printed indexes and extracts from wills enrolled in the manorial court rolls as follows:

1640–1858 **98,917**
(items 7–8)

A filmed calendar of two bound manuscript volumes. Item 8 begins in 1708.

1640–1858 **942 B4s**
vol. 110

A printed index to the originals appears in volume 110 of the publications of the Surtees Society.

1507–1668 **942 B4s**
vols. 104, 110

The publications of the Surtees Society provide brief extracts from all of the enrolled probates of Knaresborough. Volume 104 covers 1507–1604 and volume 110, 1607–1668. Both volumes are indexed.

LANGTOFT

1647–1738 **98,916**
(item 4)

The filmed calendar for this prebendal court appears on page 65 of a bound manuscript volume.

1647–1738 **99,439**
(item 2)

The original records for the forty-three persons named in the calendar of this court are on the same film as those for Holme (item 1), but there is no break between the two groups.

Langtoft begins with documents for 1679, 1676, and 1678 followed by what appears to be the same calendar as outlined above. The calendar is divided into two parts, 1647–1699 and 1702–1738. There is little order, but the rest of the documents for 1647–1699, except one for 1703, are grouped together. The last group for 1702–1738 starts with a will for 1724.

LAUGHTON EN LE MORTHEN

See York, Court of the Chancellor of, found near the end of this section.

LINTON-ON-OUSE

(Not inhibited.)

1710–1735 **98,916**
(item 1)

The filmed calendar of this manorial court is the first page of a bound volume on this film.

1710–1735 **99,930**
(item 2)

Original records.

MAPPLETON

See York, Court of the Archdeacon of the East Riding of, found near the end of this section.

MARSDEN

(Not inhibited.)

1654–1855 **98,917**
(item 12)

The filmed calendar of the manorial court is a bound manuscript volume at the end of this film. A printed index will be found on pages 102–107 and 168–171 of volume II of *The Northern Genealogist* (FHL 942 B2ng). Also see film 99,914 below.

1654–1834 **99,913**
Original records.

1834–1855   **99,914**

The original records for Marsden continue. At the end of the film is another version of the calendar mentioned above.

MASHAM

1572–1858   **98,918**
                              (items 1–2)

Item 1 is a filmed calendar from a manuscript volume giving an index to the wills on pages 1–67 for 1572–1849, pages 69–90 to admons for 1710–1856, and pages 95–98 to wills for 1850–1858. Item 2 adds the index to the admons for 1614–1709. Another filmed calendar for 1609–1707 is on page 66 of item 4 of film 98,916. See also the printed indexes that follow and film 99,929 below.

A partial index for Masham is printed in *The Northern Genealogist* (FHL 942 B2ng) for what appears to be 1549–1751, but to A–Row only. A–B is on pages 132–136 of volume IV (also item 11 of film 994,073). Volume V adds B–C on pages 30–32, C–F on pages 103–105, and F–H on pages 153–156. Volume VI gives H–M on pages 16–22 and M–R on pages 86–89.

1609–1707   **99,929**
                                 (item 2)

Original wills, admons, and inventories of Masham. There is no break between the records of the first court on this film and Masham. The first court ends with a will for the parish of Mappleton dated 1822, and Masham begins with a bond dated 1694. The film ends with two manuscript calendars for this same time coverage. There is no order to the first calendar, but the second is chronological. The originals of some of the registered copy wills have apparently been lost.

1576–1654   **98,918**
                              (items 3–5)

Registered copy wills of Masham. Item 3 is an index to Register Book No. 1, 1576–1654. Item 4 is an index to Register Book No. 2, 1634–1699, that was not filmed. Item 5 is Register Book No. 1. The register appears to be a combination of act entries and copy wills. The first will is recorded on page 62. The act book entries take up pages 1–61 and then are scattered throughout the register. They may cover 1583–1604.

MEXBOROUGH

See York, Court of the Archdeacon or the West Riding of, found near the end of this section.

MIDDLEHAM

The original wills of the Court of the Royal Peculiar and Deanery of the Collegiate Church have not been filmed. Search also the Archdeaconry of Richmond. Consult Camp, *Wills and Their Whereabouts*.

1722–1854   **98,916**
                                 (item 7)

The filmed calendar for Middleham is in a manuscript volume that refers first to an earlier list of documents before 1611 that are now lost. Then comes a short list for 1637–1640, followed by the calendar for 1722–1854.

1789–1851   **98,916**
                                 (item 9)

The act book for Middleham is mislabeled as "Surrogate Deeds." It includes marriage licenses of which the pre-1837 entries referring to areas outside of Yorkshire are listed here.

29 January 1791—Wm Strahan of Blackburn, Lancs., and Esther Hoyle of Middleham.
27 May 1793—Geo. Wilson of Middleham and Frances Ramsay of St. James, Westminster.
8 December 1803—William Ludley of Grantham, Lincs., and Eliz. Walker of Middleham.
31 December 1808—John Kell of Stockton upon Tees, Durham, and Barbara Walton of Middleham.
22 May 1828—John Blackburn of Walton le Dale in Blackburn, Lancs., and Ann Sturdy of Middleham.
18 February 1833—Wm Gibson of Stockton upon Tees, Durham, and Fanny Hanby of Middleham.
30 July 1833—William Raine of Stockton upon Tees, Durham, and Agnes Bowman of Middleham.
25 November 1833—Joseph Gawkroger of Chatham in Clitheroe, Lancs., and Frances Hebden of Middleham.

An admon was also noted for John Leeming who died intestate in Salford, Lancs., in 1806. It was granted 26 November 1825 to the widow, Mary Leeming.

MONK FRYSTON

See Wistow.

NEWTON-ON-OUSE

This manorial court was not inhibited, but its wills were proved before the Reformation at York, the Peculiar Court of St. Leonard's Hospital, which see near the end of this section.

1682–1812   **99,930**
                                 (items 3–5)

The original records for Newton-on-Ouse are filed by year of probate but in reverse chronological order in three groupings: 1682–1700, 1701–1746, and 1752–1812.

NORTH GRIMSTON

See Langtoft.

NORTH NEWBALD

1633–1734   **98,916**
                                               (item 4)

The filmed calendar for this prebendal court appears on page 69 of a bound manuscript volume. See also the next entry.

1633–1734   **99,927**
                                               (item 3)

Original records. There is little break between the records of North Newbald and those preceding it for Wadworth and Barmby Moor. The first document on this film for North Newbald is dated 1728. There is no order. Another calendar comes last of all.

NOTE: Nine marriage licenses for North Newbald, 1697–1729, appear toward the end of film 99,403.

OSBALDWICK

This prebendal court covered part of the parish by the same name. See also the Prebendal Court of Strensall.

1631–1739   **98,916**
                                               (item 4)

The filmed calendar is on page 70(A) of a bound manuscript volume. See also the next entry.

1631–1739   **99,444**
                                               (item 2)

Original records of Osbaldwick. There is a calendar at the end.

OVERTON

See Shipton.

PRESTON

See York, Court of the Subdean of, found near the end of this section.

PUDSEY

See Crossley.

RAVENFIELD

See York, Court of the Archdeacon or the West Riding of, found near the end of this section.

RICCALL

1690–1833   **98,916**
                                               (item 3)

The filmed calendar for this prebendal court is on pages 63–77 of a bound manuscript volume.

1690–1833   **99,931**
Original records.

SALTON

No records for this court have been filmed. See the General Peculiars and Camp, *Wills and Their Whereabouts.*

SELBY

1681–1858   **98,916**
                                               (items 8, 10)

The filmed calendar appears as a bound manuscript volume in item 10. Item 8 is another volume containing a calendar for 1681–1714, an act book for 1715–1726, and a calendar for 1727–1788. The act book includes marriage licenses. Also note the printed abstracts in the following entry.

1635–1710   **FHL 942.74 B4a**
                                                vol. 47 &
                                                 599,873

Vol. 47 of the Record Series of the Yorkshire Archaeological Society purports to be abstracts of all the probates (695) in alphabetical order of this court. This is not the case as will be noted on film 99,921 below. The marriage licenses are also printed in this volume, 1664–1726.

1635–1710 A–G   **99,917**
Original records of Selby. Another A and three Bs appear on film 99,921.

1635–1710 H–P   **99,918**
Original records, cont. Two Hs, a K and P appear on film 99,921.

1635–1710 R–S   **99,919**
Original records, cont. An R and three more Ss are on film 99,921.

1634–1710 T–Z   **99,920**
Original records, cont. Four Ts and five Ws are on film 99,921.

1681–1731   **99,921**
Original records, cont. They are in chronological order from this point. There are some seventeen documents for 1681–1710 that are not in the abstracts mentioned above.

1732–1751   **99,922**
Original records, cont.

1752–1787   **99,923**
Original records, cont.

1788–1858   **99,924**
Original records, cont.

SHIPTON

No known records survive for this manorial court. Search the adjacent courts.

SILSDEN

(Not inhibited.)

1588–1809   **98,917**
                                                  (items 10–11)
The filmed calendars for this manorial court are volume A on item 10 for 1588–1737 and volume B on item 11 for 1611–1809. The period 1588–1737 is also in print on pages 37–38 and 110–112 of volume I of *The Northern Genealogist* (FHL 942 B2ng).

No original records have been filmed. See Camp, *Wills and Their Whereabouts.*

SNAITH

(Not inhibited.)

1568–1858   **98,919**
                                                  (items 1–2)
The filmed calendars are in two volumes, 1568–1719 on item 1 and 1715–1858 on item 2.

1568–1586   **99,882**
Snaith original wills and inventories.

1568–1586   **99,883**
Original wills and inventories, cont.

1587–1591   **99,884**
Original wills and inventories, cont.

1587–1591   **99,885**
Original wills and inventories, cont.

1592–1597   **99,886**
Original wills and inventories, cont.

1592–1597   **99,887**
Original wills and inventories, cont.

1598–1604   **99,888**
Original wills and inventories, cont. Another for 1604 is on film 99,890.

1598–1604   **99,889**
Original wills and inventories, cont.

1605–1610   **99,890**
Original wills and inventories, cont. They are in rough chronological order. A will for 1604 is located here.

1611–1614   **99,891**
Original wills and inventories, cont.

1615–1620   **99,892**
Original wills and inventories, cont. There is an inventory dated 1616 for Elizabeth Sykes of Cowicke among the bonds on film 100,072 that is not listed in the calendar.

1621–1627   **99,893**
Original wills and inventories, cont.

1628–1634   **99,894**
Original wills and inventories, cont.

1635–1640   **99,895**
Original wills and inventories, cont.

1641–1646   **99,896**
Original wills and inventories, cont.

1647–1649   **99,897**
Original wills and inventories, cont.

1650–1658   **99,898**
Original wills and inventories, cont.

1659–1665   **99,899**
Original wills and inventories, cont.

1666–1682   **99,900**
Original wills and inventories, cont.

1683–1693   **99,901**
Original wills and inventories, cont.

1694–1706   **99,902**
Original wills and inventories, cont.

1707–1722   **99,903**
Original wills and inventories, cont.

1723–1728   **99,904**
Original wills and inventories, cont.

1729–1738   **99,905**
Original wills and inventories, cont.

1739–1754   **99,906**
Original wills and inventories, cont.

1755–1774   **99,907**
Original wills and inventories, cont.

1775–1784   **99,908**
Original wills and inventories, cont.

1785–1804   **99,909**
Original wills and inventories, cont.

1805–1824   **99,910**
Original wills and inventories, cont.

1825–1858   **99,911**
Original wills and inventories, cont.

1612–1694   **98,918**
                                                 (item 6)
Snaith registered copy wills.

1587–1694   **100,069**
Snaith original probate and admon bonds. There are
many tuition bonds. Most of the bonds on this film date
from 1587–1605.

1580–1699   **100,070**
Snaith bonds, cont.

1679–1683   **100,071**
Snaith bonds, cont.

1581–1683   **100,072**
Box A of Snaith bonds. It is a mix of probate, admon,
and tuition bonds. An inventory for 1616 is located here.

1590–1668   **100,073**
Snaith bonds, cont. The majority are for the 1660s.

1596–1858   **100,058**
Snaith act books. Volume 3 covers 1596–1628, volume 4
is 1715–1749, and volume 5 is 1755–1858.

SOUTH CAVE

1687–1858   **98,917**
                                                 (item 3)
The filmed calendar is a manuscript volume. There is
one entry for 1579 and none after 1843. Other wills for
the pre-Reformation period might be found with York,
Peculiar Court of St. Leonard's Hospital, at the end of
this section.

1579–1780   **99,436**
Original records.

1781–1843   **99,437**
Original records, cont.

STILLINGTON

No records for this prebendal court have been filmed.
See the General Peculiars and Camp, *Wills and Their
Whereabouts*.

STOCKTON ON THE FOREST

See Bugthorpe.

STRENSALL

1640–1739   **98,916**
                                                 (item 4)
The filmed calendar of this prebendal court is found on
pages 70(B)–72 of a bound manuscript volume.

1640,   **99,438**
1668–1739
Original records.

TEMPLE NEWSAM

(Not inhibited.) No original probates of this manorial
court have been filmed.

1612–1701   **98,917**
                                                 (item 6)
The filmed calendar is a bound manuscript volume. A
printed index is on pages 34–37 of volume I of *The
Northern Genealogist* (FHL 942 B2ng).

1612–1701   **FHL 942 B4t**
                                               vol. 33 &
                                                  98,917
                                                 (item 5)
                                                 599,922
                                                 (item 3)
Printed abstracts of all documents are alphabetically
arranged on pages 241–282 of volume 33 of this publication of the Thoresby Society.

TOCKERINGTON

No records have been filmed for this prebendal court
located in Northumberland. See the General Peculiars.

TUNSTALL

See York, Court of the Succentor of, found near the end
of this section.

ULLESKELF

No records have been filmed for the prebendal court. See
Wetwang; the General Peculiars; and Camp, *Wills and
Their Whereabouts*.

WADWORTH

1708–1760   **98,916**
                                                 (item 4)
The filmed calendar is on pages 80–81 of a bound
manuscript volume. See the next entry.

1708–1760   **99,927**
                                                 (item 1)
Original records of Wadworth start with two more ver-
sions of the calendar. There is no break on the film
between items 1 and 2, which is for the court of Barmby
Moor.

WARMFIELD WITH HEATH

There are apparently no original records for this manorial court.

1613,	**FHL 942 B2ng**
1642–1691	**vol. I**

See the printed index on page 129 of volume I of *The Northern Genealogist*. Note the reference to abstracts in Camp, *Wills and Their Whereabouts*.

WARTHILL

1681–1837　　　　　　　　　　　　**98,916**
　　　　　　　　　　　　　　　　　(item 3)
A filmed calendar for this prebendal court appears on pages 79–80 of a bound manuscript volume.

1681–1837　　　　　　　　　　　　**99,444**
　　　　　　　　　　　　　　　　　(item 1)
Original records.

WEIGHTON

1660–1856　　　　　　　　　　　　**98,916**
　　　　　　　　　　　　　　　　　(item 3)
A filmed calendar for this prebendal court appears on pages 83–101 of a bound manuscript volume.

1660–1690　　　　　　　　　　　　**99,933**
Original records.

1691–1730　　　　　　　　　　　　**99,934**
Original records, cont.

1731–1856　　　　　　　　　　　　**99,935**
Original records, cont. NOTE: Two marriage licenses for 1695 will be found toward the end of film 99,403.

WESTERDALE

Apparently there are no surviving original records for this manorial court. A list to some of them, 1669–1765, and abstracts to wills entered in the manor court rolls of Westerdale, 1550–1575, are on pages 46–66 in volume 74 of the Record Series of the Yorkshire Archaeological Society (FHL 942.74 B4a and item 2 of film 599,878).

WETWANG

1658–1709　　　　　　　　　　　　**98,916**
　　　　　　　　　　　　　　　　　(item 4)
A filmed calendar for this prebendal court appears on pages 78–79 of a bound manuscript volume. Wills for the 1500s might be found with Beverley. See also the entry below.

1658–1709　　　　　　　　　　　　**99,926**
Original records. Another copy of the calendar is at the end of the film.

NOTE: Right after the section for probates, 1707–1712, for the General Peculiars on film 99,403 comes a variety of different documents from the jurisdiction of Wetwang. Included are the bishop's transcripts of Elloughton for 1704, five accusations of fornication in 1706, and four marriage licenses for Fridaythorpe and Kirkby Wharfe as well as Wetwang dated 1663–1706.

WISTOW

1617–1707　　　　　　　　　　　　**98,916**
　　　　　　　　　　　　　　　　　(item 4)
A filmed calendar for the prebendal court is on pages 73–75 of a bound manuscript volume.

1617–1707　　　　　　　　　　　　**99,932**
Original records.

WITHERNWICK

See Holme.

YORK, COURT OF THE ARCHDEACON OF THE EAST RIDING OF

1571–1682,　　　　　　　　　　　　**99,929**
1701–1849　　　　　　　　　　　　**(item 1)**
Original records. There is no break between items 1 and 2 on this film. Item 1 ends with a will from Mappleton for 1822.

YORK, COURT OF THE ARCHDEACON OR THE WEST RIDING OF

1662–1740,　　　　　　　　　　　　**98,916**
1760–1839　　　　　　　　　　　　**(item 4)**
The filmed calendar is on page 68.

1662–1740,　　　　　　　　　　　　**99,434**
1760–1839
Original records.

YORK, COURT OF THE CHANCELLOR OF

No records of this court have been filmed. See the General Peculiars and Camp, *Wills and Their Whereabouts*.

YORK, COURT OF THE DEAN OF

1) Calendars, Printed Indexes, and Act Books

1531–1708,　　　　　　　　　　　　**100,080**
1735–1741　　　　　　　　　　　　**(items 6 & 9)**
The filmed calendar on item 6 includes at least one entry for 1710. Item 9 covers 1735–1741.

1604–1722   **FHL 942.74 B4a**
                                 vol. 73 &
                                 599,878
                                 (item 1)

Part II, pages 31–80, of volume 73 of the Record Series of the Yorkshire Archaeological Society is a printed index to the act books for the time period specified.

1722–1858

See the end of the third act book in the next entry.

1604–1722   **98,925**

There are three volumes of act books, and they appear in order on this film. Volume 1 covers 1604–1651. Volume 2 repeats entries in volume 1 for 1618–1629 and then covers 1660–1683. Volume 3 is 1684–1722, but starting on page 96 is a calendar for this court from 1722–1858. The act entries in all three volumes are indexed, 1604–1722, as indicated above.

2) Original Records of the Court of the Dean of York

There is little or no order until a fair chronological sequence begins in the eighteenth century.

1530–1672   **99,346**
                                             (item 1)

Original records. Most of the documents in item 1 end in 1660, but there is an ident for K dated 1672 that appears actually to be 1662, an S for 1670, and a C for 1710.

1662   **99,346**
                                             (item 2)

Original records. Note the preceding entry.

1662–1667   **99,347**

Original records, cont. Note item 1 of film 99,346.

1668–1671   **99,348**

Original records, cont. Note item 1 of film 99,346.

1672–1676   **99,349**

Original records, cont. Note item 1 of film 99,346.

1677–1680   **99,350**

Original records, cont.

1681   **99,351**

Original records, cont.

1682–1688   **99,352**

Original records, cont.

1689–1697   **99,353**

Original records, cont.

1698–1704   **99,354**

Original records, cont.

1705–1712   **99,355**

Original records, cont. Note item 1 of film 99,346.

1713–1719   **99,356**

Original records, cont.

1720–1726   **99,357**

Original records, cont.

1727–1734   **99,358**

Original records, cont.

1735–1740   **99,359**

Original records, cont.

1741–1750   **99,360**

Original records, cont.

1751–1760   **99,361**

Original records, cont.

1761–1767   **99,362**

Original records, cont.

1768–1775   **99,363**

Original records, cont.

1776–1783   **99,364**

Original records, cont.

1784–1790   **99,365**

Original records, cont.

1791–1796   **99,366**

Original records, cont.

1797–1802   **99,367**

Original records, cont.

1803–1810   **99,368**

Original records, cont.

1811–1817   **99,369**

Original records, cont.

1818–1827   **99,370**

Original records, cont.

1828–1838   **99,371**

Original records, cont.

1839–1857   **99,372**

Original records, cont.

YORK, COURT OF THE PRECENTOR OF

No original records were filmed for this court, except four wills from Great Driffield between 1601–1638 and one from Little Ouseburn for 1633 that are found on item 12 of film 100,080.

See the General Peculiars and Camp's book as outlined above for the Court of the Chancellor of York.

YORK, COURT OF THE SUBDEAN OF

1676–1729 **98,916**
(item 4)

The filmed calendar is pages 76–77 of a bound manuscript volume. Other smaller portions of the calendar appear on film 100,080: 1712–1729 (item 2), 1700–1710 (item 7), 1676–1699 (item 8), and 1676–1699 (item 11).

1676–1729 **99,435**
Original records.

YORK, COURT OF THE SUCCENTOR OF

No records have been filmed for this court. See the General Peculiars and Camp, *Wills and Their Whereabouts*.

YORK, PECULIAR COURT OF ST. LEONARD'S HOSPITAL

1410–1533 **FHL 942.74 B4a**
vol. 60 &
402,541

The printed index to the registered copy wills is on pages 191–193 of Appendix II of volume 60 of the Record Series of the Yorkshire Archaeological Society.

1410–1533 **1,545,163**
(item 6)
The registered copy wills are found in volume M2/6E.

Miscellaneous: Special Collections and Abstracts for Yorkshire

---

Searches in these materials may facilitate a particular kind of research or the finding of a specific individual, but they should not supplant research in the original documents.

1) 1527–1883 **FHL 942.74 B4b**
vol. 9

Vol. 9 of the Texts and Calendars of the Borthwick Institute is *Ecclesiastical Cause Papers at York: Files Transmitted on Appeal, 1500–1883* by W. J. Sheils. Cause papers are files of appeals from the lower courts within the Province of York. Many of these files concern testamentary business.

2) 1805–1881 **100,080**
(item 5)

Notices of Probate Grants valued a second time for the Inland Revenue Office. The notices provide name, probate registry, date of probate, and the amount of the valuation.

3) 1316–1616 **FHL 942 B4s**

The Publications of the Surtees Society. The Society began publishing materials concerning the northern counties in 1834. Research on any of the counties that make up the Province of York could benefit from examining the contents of this series. A master index is in volume 150.

Abstracts of some wills from the PCC referring to the northern counties are in volume 116 (1383–1558) and volume 121 (1555–1616). These two volumes are also items 5 and 6 of film 990,300.

Further abstracts from wills registered at York, especially the PCY, are in volume 4 (1316–1430) also on fiche 6,073,286; volume 30 (1426–1467) and fiche 6,073,312; volume 45 (1395–1491) and fiche 6,073,327; volume 53 (1484–1509) and fiche 6,073,335; volume 79 (1509–1531) and fiche 6,073,361; and volume 106 (1531–1551) and fiche 6,073,388. A small "s" by an entry in the printed calendars for the Exchequer and Prerogative Courts of York refers to these abstracts.

Volume 26 (also item 7 on film 994,031) contains copies of 208 wills and inventories from Richmond for 1442–1579, some of which are from the Eastern Deaneries.

4) 1648–1660, **FHL 942.74 B4a**
1542–1689 **vols. 9 & 134**

The Record Series of the Yorkshire Archaeological Society. Volume 9 (also item 2 of film 599,725) is abstracts of some of the wills (251) for Yorkshire proven at London during the Commonwealth period. Volume 134 adds the complete text of forty-seven inventories in the possession of the society for 1542–1689.

5) Wills of the Clergy

Vol. 10 of the Borthwick Texts and Calendars (FHL 942.74 B4b) contains abstracts of sixty-one wills for the clergy of York Minster, 1520–1600, edited by Claire Cross. Volume 15 adds the city clergy.

Abstracts of some of the wills of the clergy of Richmond for 1438–1587, mainly from the North Riding, are found on pages 25–28, 109–112, and 124–129 of volume III of *The Northern Genealogist* (FHL 942 B2ng). They continue for 1564–1602 on pages 41–48 of volume IV (also item 11 on film 994,073). There are two more on pages 1–2 of volume VI.

6) Area Wills

Abbotside. Abstracts from Richmond for probates of the townships of High and Low Abbotside, 1552–1688, are in volume 130 of the Record Series of the Yorkshire Archaeological Society (FHL 942.74 B4a and film 599,888).

Barwick in Elmet. Wills for this parish, 1419–1748, were published by G. D. Lumb (FHL 942.74/B13 V26ba).

Bradford. Wills were published in *The Bradford Antiquary* (FHL 942.74 B2B) for 1392–1460 on pages 201–203 of volume 1 and 1466–1543 on pages 19–22, 169–172, 218–220, and 247–250 of volume 2.

Halifax. For 1348–1559, see the two volumes of *Halifax Wills* by J. W. Clay and E. W. Crossley (FHL 942.74/H7 S2cLa and item 3 of film 845,445).

Leeds and surrounding area. Extracts from the registered copy wills of the Exchequer Court for Leeds, Pontefract, Wakefield, and other places appear in the volumes of the Thoresby Society (FHL 942 B4t) under the title of "Testamenta Leodiensia." They are in volume 2 (also item 1 of film 599,915) for 1391–1494, volume 4 (item 3 of 599,915) for 1496–1524, volume 9 (item 4 of 599,916) for 1514–1531, volume 11 (98,498) for 1531–1537, volume 15 (599,918) for 1537–1559, volume 19 (item 2 of 98,497) for 1539–1553, and volume 27 (98,495 and 599,921) for 1553–1561. More wills for Leeds and district from the late 1300s–1552 are in volume 22 (599,920) and volume 24 (item 2 of 599,920). Early Pontefract wills are in volume 26 (item 3 of 599,920). Wills for Rothwell, Saxton, Sherburn in Elmet, Swillington, Thorner, Whitkirk, and Woodkirk for the late 1300s–1554 are in volume 33 (item 3 of 599,922).

Sheffield. Abstracts of supposedly all wills proved at York prior to 1554 were published by T. Walter Hall under the title of "A Catalogue of the Ancient Charters" (FHL 942.74/S1 R2h) in 1913. Three years later, Mr. Hall published the abstracts for 1554–1560 under "A Descriptive Catalogue" (FHL 942.74 A5hai).

7) Stray Wills

The section entitled "Waifs and Strays" in each volume of *The Northern Genealogist* (FHL 942 B2ng) is worth going through for people recorded outside of their home county. Listed here are the entries from these sections referring to the Americas.

Volume 1, page 131 is an abstract of a will proven in 1767 for James Bean, planter of Hanover in Jamaica and of Aldbrough, Yorks. On page 242 is an abstract of a will proven in 1777 (volume 121 of the registered copy wills of the Exchequer Court, folio 360) for Joseph Kershaw, yeoman of Halifax, mentioning his sons in South Carolina. Page 243 adds the index entry only of a will proven in 1781 for William Sanderson, mariner of Hull who died in America.

Volume 2, page 32 refers to an admon dated 1690 in the York City Act Book for Beatrice Green of York who died in Virginia. Page 67 provides an abstract from the registered copy wills in 1784 (vol. 128, folio 160) for Edith Haslehurst, widow late of St. James, Cornwall and Jamaica, now of West Retford, Notts. An abstract is on page 69 for the will of Katherine Rawson, spinster of Newark, Notts., proven in 1768 (vol. 112, folio 240), who mentions her nephew, Samuel Peet, physician of Virginia. There is an index entry only on page 135 to the will of James Cort of Lancaster and of Trinidad that was proven in December 1802.

Volume 3, page 82 adds the abstracts of two wills proven at York (vol. 98, folios 292 and 313). The first was proven in 1754 for William Pullen, merchant of London and Jamaica. The second, proven in 1795, is for Richard Ware, sailmaker formerly of New Jersey, late of Hull, now of Whitby, Yorks.

8) Miscellaneous Wills

See William Paver's small volume of abstracts of wills "of noble and ancient families" of York published in 1830 on microfiche 6,053,047.

Holworthy's *Yorkshire Wills*. A reproduction of the original Books 1 and 2 at the Society of Genealogists filmed in 1965 on microfilm 476,993 (item 3).

SELECTED BIBLIOGRAPHY

Bouwens, B. G. *Wills and Their Whereabouts*. 2d ed. with alterations and corrections by Helen Thacker. London: Society of Genealogists, 1951.

Camp, Anthony J. *Wills and Their Whereabouts*. 4th ed. London: The author, 1974.

Earwaker, J. P., ed. *An Index to the Wills and Inventories Now Preserved in the Court of Probate, at Chester, from A.D. 1545 to 1620*. Manchester: The Record Society, 1879.

Gardner, David E., and Smith, Frank. *Genealogical Research in England and Wales*. Vol. 2. Salt Lake City: Bookcraft Publishers, 1959.

Genealogical Society of Utah. Research Papers, Series A, Nos. 7–48. *Pre–1858 English Probate Jurisdictions*. Salt Lake City, 1968.

Gibson, J. S. W. *Wills and Where to Find Them*. Extra vol. of the British Record Society. Chichester: Phillimore & Company, 1974.

Humphery-Smith, Cecil R., ed. *The Phillimore Atlas and Index of Parish Registers*. Chichester: Phillimore & Company, 1984.

Jones, B. C. "Lancashire Probate Records." *Transactions of the Historic Society of Lancashire and Cheshire*. Vol. 104. Liverpool, 1953. Pages 61–73.

Smith, David M. *A Guide to the Archive Collections in the Borthwick Institute of Historical Research*. Vol. 1. University of York: Borthwick Texts and Calendars, 1973.

Webb, C. C. *A Guide to Genealogical Sources in the Borthwick Institute of Historical Research*. University of York: Borthwick Institute of Historical Research, 1981.

GLOSSARY

(Cross-references are indicated by words in CAPITAL letters.)

Accompt
Archaic form of ACCOUNT, computation, or reckoning.

Account
A report to the court after the terms of the PROBATE have been carried out by the EXECUTOR or administrator. Sometimes the report will be filed with the other original records pertaining to a given case.

Act Book
Brief notations of the official business enacted by a court are entered daily in a register book. Separate act books for probates begin to appear during the Tudor period. They are more complete than a CALENDAR and may contain information not found in the PROBATE.

Administration
A PROBATE commissioning the next of kin or principal creditor to be the administrator of the property when one dies INTESTATE or without a valid will. The actual Letters of Administration do not survive but the ADMINISTRATION BOND does. Administration-with-Will-annexed refers to the issuance of Letters of Administration in cases of RENUNCIATION or where a competent EXECUTOR is unavailable. In this situation, the will may be filed separately or with the administration bonds.

Administration Bond
Those appointed to administer an estate by Letters of ADMINISTRATION were always bonded or legally bound in a set format to pay a stipulated amount if they failed to be honest and faithful in their task. The amount of the bond was usually double that of the estate's value and is stated in the first paragraph. The first paragraph of the bond is known as the obligation and is typically indented. It was written in Latin before 1733. The names of the administrators appear in the first two lines of the obligation, and the date in the last line. The second paragraph or condition of the bond comes out to the margin and is always in English. The first two lines of the condition identify the principal administrator and his/her relationship to the deceased.

Admon
The most common abbreviation for ADMINISTRATION.

Archdeaconry
A geographic unit of the Church of England just below that of the DIOCESE. It is presided over by an archdeacon and consists of several RURAL DEANERIES. Many archdeaconries held the right of PROBATE.

Assignation
A term normally used in an ACT BOOK to indicate an assignment to execute or administer the property, or have that right reassigned to a new EXECUTOR or administrator.

Bishop's Transcripts.

A contemporary copy of the christenings, marriages, and burials of a parish made by the parish minister to be sent to his bishop each year.

Bona Notabilia

Property worth £5 or more. There was no court fee for an estate worth less. If there should be *bona notabilia* involving more than one jurisdiction, then normally the higher court claimed the right of probate.

Calendar

A manuscript listing of TESTATORs and INTESTATEs kept by a court. Typically, it is arranged chronologically and by the initial letter of the surname. There is an omission rate of 5 percent or higher. Printed indexes depend upon ACT BOOKs for completeness.

Cathedral

A church representing the official seat or see of a bishop or archbishop and from which he supervises the management of the DIOCESE or PROVINCE. The day-to-day affairs of the cathedral are handled by a body of clergymen known as the Chapter under the direction of one of their number, the DEAN.

Caveat

A legal warning to a court not to proceed further with the probating of an estate until the private party responsible for the caveat is notified and has a chance to be heard.

Chancery

An ecclesiastical appellate court used only in the Province of York. The chancellor was a functionary of the archbishop of York and as such also held PECULIAR probate rights. This chancery should not be confused with the civil Court of Chancery in London.

Codicil

A postscript to a will by which the TESTATOR makes an addition or modification of the will at a later date.

Commissary

A court commissioned to function in a certain portion of a DIOCESE. Its jurisdiction is comparable to that of an ARCHDEACONRY.

Comp

See ACCOMPT.

Condition

See ADMINISTRATION BOND.

Consistory

The bishop's court presiding over the whole DIOCESE. The term is often preceded by the medieval designation for bishop, episcopal: episcopal consistory.

CRO

A common abbreviation for county record office or the depository for official records in each county.

Curation
Guardianship over older minors where the male orphan was usually between the ages of fourteen to twenty, and the female from twelve to twenty. See also TUITION.

Curon
An abbreviation for CURATION.

Day Book
Another way of referring to the ACT BOOK.

Dean
A clergyman who presides over the governing body of a CATHEDRAL, the Chapter. The dean may have separate PECULIAR probate rights beyond those of the DEAN AND CHAPTER.

Dean and Chapter
The governing body of a CATHEDRAL. Their probate rights included functioning as a PECULIAR court, serving as a superior court over certain other probate courts, and fulfilling the role of a bishop's or archbishop's court during a VACANCY in those positions. Other staff of the Chapter of the Archbishop of York who governed PECULIAR probate courts included the Chancellor, Precentor, Subdean, and Succentor.

Deanery
A simpler way of referring to RURAL DEANERY, not to be confused with the DEAN.

Diocese
A geographic unit of the Church of England just below that of the PROVINCE. It is presided over by a bishop and consists of several ARCHDEACONRIES. The diocese always held the right of PROBATE. There were twenty-two dioceses in England in 1797.

Exchequer
The unusual ecclesiastical usage of this term is confined to York where it referred to probate jurisdiction for the DIOCESE of York. PROBATEs within the Exchequer were normally granted by the RURAL DEANERIES.

Executor
The person(s) nominated by a TESTATOR to carry out the provisions of the will. Executrix refers to a woman.

Feoffee
See TRUSTEE.

FHL
Abbreviation used in this work to refer to the call number of a book or microfilm in the possession of the Family History Library of The Church of Jesus Christ of Latter-day Saints in Salt Lake City, Utah.

Folio
Several pages ranging from two to sixteen. Accordingly, a folio number may appear on every other page or less frequently depending on each situation. The reference in probate records is typically to a folio number, not to a page number.

Hiatus
A gap in the probate records caused when the court is INHIBITED or during a VACANCY.

Idents
A term used in this work to refer to a smaller page often found before an original will (usually the back of the folded probate document itself) that briefly identifies the deceased by name, residence, date the will was proved, and perhaps other identifiers.

Infra
In the Consistory Court of Chester, property worth less than £40 was probated by the RURAL DEANERY and filed separately at the CONSISTORY level.

Inhibited
During a VACANCY or VISITATION, a court might be inhibited or closed for several months. The result was a HIATUS or gap in the records as a superior or designated court assumed the probate business of the lower court during the inhibition.

Intestate
A person who dies without a will or whose will is invalid for some reason. In such cases, a court may issue Letters of ADMINISTRATION.

Inventory
A listing of the personal property of the deceased with its appraised value. Detailed inventories for most of the courts in the Province of York are available from about 1529 to 1780.

ML
Abbreviation for marriage license or one of the ways to seek permission to marry. The accompanying bond and even the allegation that there were no lawful impediments are sometimes found among the probate records.

Monition
A summons from a superior court requesting that a lower court send it certain documents.

Nuncupative
A will declared orally in the presence of three witnesses and written after the death of the TESTATOR. It was recorded in the ACT BOOK. The actual record may be filed with the ADMINISTRATION BONDs.

Obligation
See ADMINISTRATION BOND.

Overseer
Person appointed by the TESTATOR to supervise and advise the EXECUTOR.

PCC
Abbreviation for PREROGATIVE COURT OF CANTERBURY.

PCY
Abbreviation for PREROGATIVE COURT OF YORK.

Peculiar

A geographic unit of the Church of England before 1846, usually a parish or several parishes combined, that was always exempt from the control of the Rural Dean and Archdeacon and sometimes the Bishop and Archbishop. Hence, a peculiar tries to assume the rights normally reserved for the jurisdictions from which it is exempt.

PPR

See PRINCIPAL PROBATE REGISTRY.

Prebend, Prebendary

The office and title of a priest on the staff of a CATHEDRAL. The prebendary might preside over a PECULIAR, in which case it is referred to as a prebendal court.

Precentor

See DEAN AND CHAPTER.

Prerogative Court of Canterbury

The probate court of the PROVINCE of Canterbury. As such it took precedence over all other probate courts in England and Wales. It claimed superior jurisdiction when the property of the TESTATOR lay in two different DIOCESEs within the Province or crossed provincial boundaries. The wills of anyone dying outside of England and Wales who still held property there should have been probated in the PCC. Original jurisdiction was also available and widely employed by anyone seeking the security offered by the highest probate court in the land. Its London location made it even more attractive to many of the commercial and upper classes.

Prerogative Court of York

The probate court of the PROVINCE of York. It claimed superior jurisdiction when the property of the deceased lay in two different DIOCESEs within the Province. Despite the rights of the PREROGATIVE COURT OF CANTERBURY, the PCY often handled cases for anyone who died in that province or had property there, including those who died abroad.

Principal Probate Registry

Wills became civil documents in 1858. Since that date a copy of all English and Welsh wills is found, along with a master index, at the PPR, Somerset House, London.

Probate

The proving of a will by a court or the granting of official approval for the EXECUTOR or administrator to proceed to distribute the property of the deceased. Such authorization is known as the act of probate and may appear as a short paragraph at the bottom or reverse side of the will. It will always be in Latin before 1733. Any type of document associated with this process comes under the meaning of the general term of probate.

Probate Bond

The EXECUTOR may have been bonded to guarantee fidelity. The bond is similar to that of an ADMINISTRATION BOND but is referred to as a Probate or Testamentary Bond. The two types of bonds are filed with the original wills, or in a section for bonds, or sometimes separately by the type of bond.

Province

The highest geographic unit of the Church of England. It is presided over by an archbishop and consists of many DIOCESEs. Prior to 1920 there were only two provinces, the Province of Canterbury and the Province of York. Canterbury is superior to York. The Province of York is smaller in size, covering the eight northern counties from Cheshire, Yorkshire, and Nottinghamshire north to the Scottish border. In addition, York included the Isle of Man. Reflecting their status, the names of the probate courts of the two provinces start with the title, PREROGATIVE.

Registered Copy Will

After the act of PROBATE and for an additional fee, a proven will might be copied in its entirety into the official registers of the court. The registered copy wills are prominently displayed in large bound volumes and are usually consulted first in any visit to a probate depository. The drawbacks of using registered copy wills are the lack of signatures, possible copying errors, the possibility of a will being unregistered, and the lack of other PROBATE records that might have been with the original. There is also a chance of finding an UNPROVED will among the originals. Hence, the value of continuing to search the original records as well as any registered copies.

Reinfecta

A term used in the EXCHEQUER and PREROGATIVE COURT OF YORK to indicate an UNPROVED will.

Renunciation

Repudiation of the right of, or refusal to be, an EXECUTOR or administrator. There may be a separate document as well as an entry in the ACT BOOK.

Rpt

An abbreviation appearing particularly in the CALENDARs of the EXCHEQUER and PREROGATIVE COURT OF YORK to indicate that there is no accompanying INVENTORY. It stands for "respited," and it may also be indicated by an r or rp.

Rural Deanery

A geographic unit of the Church of England just below the ARCHDEACONRY. It is presided over by the Rural Dean and consists of about twelve to twenty parishes. It is usually referred to as a deanery but should not be confused with the jurisdiction of a DEAN. The Rural Dean was often called upon to handle probate matters but would not keep any probate records unless the deanery was also a PECULIAR.

Subdean

See DEAN AND CHAPTER.

Succentor

See DEAN AND CHAPTER.

Supra

In the Consistory Court of Chester, property worth £40 or more was probated in the consistory court and filed separately from the INFRA probates.

Testament

A testament has the appearance of a will but was limited in the Middle Ages to personal property. When it became legal to leave real estate via probate action in 1540, a single document emerged that was to become more commonly known as the "last will and testament."

Testator

The person who dictates or writes a will.

Trustee

It was common for a TESTATOR to put certain portions of the property into a trusteeship for future use of the heirs, or to generate interest to increase the value of the estate and provide an intermediate bequest to live on for the wife or minor children. In such cases, trustees would be nominated in addition to the EXECUTOR. Testators prior to 1540, when it was illegal to devise real estate through probate, might circumvent the law by putting land into a trusteeship and naming trustees or FEOFEES in the will to care for the property and supervise the transferral of the annual income, and eventually the land, to the heirs.

Tuition

Guardianship over younger minors where males were under the age of fourteen and females under the age of twelve. See also CURATION.

Tuon

An abbreviation for TUITION.

Unproved

Some wills were left with a court for safekeeping but were never PROBATEd. The family apparently distributed the property without bothering to notify the court, or perhaps did not know of the will's existence. Many courts have a section of unproved wills among their original records. In York, an unproved will is referred to as *REINFECTA*.

Vacancy

The interval of time between the leaving of a bishop or archbishop and the arrival of the successor. During such a period, the probate rights belonging to the office were assumed by the DEAN AND CHAPTER. See also HIATUS and INHIBITED.

Visitation

The time during which the officials of a lower court were called to report to a higher court. The lower court was said to be INHIBITED, and any probate business initiated during that time would be handled by the higher court or its representative.

WD

Abbreviation for will dated. The TESTATOR would still be alive at that time.

WP

Abbreviation for will proven or probated. The TESTATOR would now be deceased.

INDEX

[The asterisk (*) refers to names published by J. P. Earwaker; for explanation see page 1 of this volume. The dagger (†) refers to names compiled by Mrs. A. N. V. Turner; for explanation see page 27 of this volume.]

Adderton, James of Penreth: will, 1726, **40**

Alcockes, Elizabeth late of Newark on Trent: marriage license bond, 1666, **137**

Alexander, Elizabeth of Smardale, Westmorland: will, 1685, **39**

Allcock, Jane of Wilmslow, Ches.: will, 1733, **82**

Allen, Thomas of Cambridge: admon, 1647, **1***

Allen, Thomas of Stanhope Bridge: bond, 1768, **63**

Almond, Ellen, widow of Southport in North Meols: will, 1840, **103**

America, **200**
> see also Graham, Harrison, Hill, Jackson, Nanson, Nicholson, Pegg, Raincock, Smith

Andrew, George of Mottram: inventory, 1718, **21**

Andrew, John, vicar of Mellinge: will, 1563, **122**

Archer, John: will, 1735, copied for Chancery suit, 1753, **142**

Arderne, James, Dean of Chester: will, 1691, **82**

Arderne, Robert of Munster, Ireland: inventory, 1635, **1***

Armistead, Thos. of Halton, 1806, **122**

Armstrong, John of Gateshead: bond, 1770, **63**

Ashcroft, Henry of Preston: inventory, 1607, **76**

Ashcroft, James of Aughton: will, 1783, **86**

Ashton, Margaret: will, 1692, **20**

Ashton, William of West Indies and London: will, 1817, **90**

Atherton, Richard of Leigh: will, 1730, **108**

Atkinson, Francis of East Indies: admon, 1766, **27†**

Atkinson, Grace of Hornby: marriage license bond, 1663, **185**

Atkinson, James of Brampton and ship "The Captain": will, 1736, **27†**

Atkinson, William of Preston Richard: will, 1571, **147**

Atkinson, William: admon, 1753, **142**

Baines, Ed. of Halton, 1805, **122**

Baldwin, Miles of Foldridgehey: will, 1597, **75**

Ballard, William the younger of Southwell: marriage license bond, 1589, **137**

Balmer, Thomas of Jamaica: will, 1799, **27†**

Baltimore, **96**

Banks, Joseph, Lieutenant in 35th Regiment: admon, 1777 and 1782, **27†**

Banks, Thomas: will, 1859, **114**

Barbados, **17**
> see also West Indies

Barlow, John of Little Hulton: will, 1801, **87**

Barmby Moor, Yorks.
marriage license bond, 1727, **189**

Barnes, Amos of New Castle-on-Tyne: bond, 1803, **64**

Barnes, John of Burton: will, 1591, **147**

Barwick, William: will, 1669, **38**

Barwise, John of Wigton and Newfoundland: admon, 1839, **27†**

Bate, Abram of Leyland: will, 1727, **83**

Bateman, James of Old Withington: will, 1618, **19**

Batwell, Ann: copy of will from Prerogative Court of Ireland, 1757, **54**

Baty, James of New York: admon, 1809, **27†**

Bayly, Hugh: will, 1672, **38**

Baynes, Deborah of Appleby: will, 1736, **147**

Beachem, John: will, 1672, **38**

Bean, James of Jamaica and Aldbrough, Yorks.: will, 1767, **200**

Beck, John of East Indies: admon, 1829, **27†**

Bell, David of N. British Dragoons: admon, 1800, **27†**

Bell, Edmond of Denton: assignation, 1685, **39**

Bellingham, James of Over Levens: will, 1680, **147**

Benn, Elizabeth of St. Bees: will, 1592, **40**

Bennett, Ann of Tranmere: will, 1834 and 1842, **22**

Bennion, Mary of Ince: admon, 1721, **21**

Benson, George of Lyth, Westmorland: will, 1628, **1***

Benson, Thomas of Stanwix: will, 1727, **41**

Bentlie, Richard of Cumberbach: will, 1716, **21**

Beswick, George of Mottram: will, 1698, **20**

Bindlose, Sir Robert of Barwicke: will, 1630, **108**

Bird, Thomas: will, 1687, **39**

Birkbeck, Thomas of Barnard Castle: inventory, 1753, **62**

Birkenhead, Elizabeth, widow of Manley: will, 1622, **8**

Bishop Wilton, Yorks.
marriage license bonds, 1712–1721, **190**

Bishop's transcripts
Elloughton, 1704, **197**
Kirkby Irelyth, Lancs., 1766–1771, **160**
Kirklington, Notts., 1642, **137**
Ruddington, Notts., 1635, **137**
Seathwaite, Lancs., 1766–1769, **160**
South Muskham, Notts., 1627, **137**
St. John, Newcastle-upon-Tyne: marriages, 1748, **63**

Blackburn, John of Walton le Dale, Lancs.: marriage license bond, 1828, **193**

Blake, George: will, 1830, **97**

Blinston, Robert of Beaumaris, Anglesey: will, 1614, **1***

Irwen, Thomas of Aldston: will, 1779, **41**

Irwin, William, soldier of Guadeloupe: admon, 1796, **27†**

Isle of Man
see Cratchley

Jack, William: will, 1664, **37**

Jackson, Bolton of Baltimore, Maryland: will, 1839, **96**

Jackson, Edwine of Ambleside: will, 1603, **147**

Jackson, John of America: will, 1830, **27†**

Jackson, Joseph, Army captain: admon, 1777, **27†**

Jackson, Richard: will, 1671, **38**

Jackson, Thomas of Raskelf: will, 1769, **164**

Jackson, William: admon, 1775, **14**

Jamaica, **64, 122, 200**
see also West Indies

James, John of Knells: will, 1664, **37**

Jennyon, Dorothy of Newton: inventory, 1710, **20**

Jersey
see Bunting

Jones, Peter, mariner of Liverpool: admon, 1837, **103**

Judson, Henry: will, 1671, **38**

Judson, William of Hilton, Westmorland: will, 1664, **37**

Kane, Andrew, mariner of Liverpool: admon, 1791, **101**

Kay, Benjamin, mariner of Liverpool: admon, 1791, **101**

Kearns, John, mariner of Liverpool: will, 1791, **101**

Kell, John of Stockton upon Tees, Durham: marriage license bond, 1808, **193**

Kempster, John of Liverpool: will, 1791, **101**

Kendrick, John, mariner of Liverpool: will, 1791, **101**

Kent, **13, 131**
see also Dodd, Mayne

Kerr, Charles of Weymouth and 1st Regiment of Dragoons, 1822, **27†**

Kershaw, Joseph of Halifax: will, 1777, mentions his sons in South Carolina, **200**

Killin, Michael, mariner of Liverpool: admon, 1791, **101**

Kinsey, Peter of Nether Peover: will, 1721, **21**

Kirkby Irelyth, Lancs.
bishop's transcripts, 1766–1771, **160**
marriage licenses, 1767–1772, **160**

Kirkby, Joseph of Barbados: will, 1819, **27†**

Kirkbye, Anne of Kirkbye Ireleth: will, 1566, **122**

Kirklington, Notts.
bishop's transcripts, 1642, **137**

Kirkly, Alice of East Markham: will, 1699 and 1749, as wife of Nathaniel Kirkly, **138**

Klawson, Peter, mariner of Liverpool: will, 1791, **101**

Knight, James of Manchester: admon, 1791, **101**

Knowles, Mary of Low Row, Grinton, Yorks.: marriage license bond, 1822, **184**

Knype, Christopher of Crossebancke: will, 1555, **147**

Knyveton, Sir William of Mercaston, Derbys.: inventory, 1632, **1***

Kyghley, Henry of Inskip: will, 1567, **122**

Lake, Edward of Dublin: will, 1646, **1***

Lancashire
see Marriage license bonds

Langford, Jane of Withington: inventory, 1670, **79**

Langhbourne, Hew of Dufton: inventory, 1585, **31**

Langhorne, John, **31**

Langton, John of Cockermouth: will, 1777, **41**

Lawrie, Adam O., Marine Lieutenant: admon, 1814, **27†**

Lawson, John: will, 1664, **37**

Le Cocq, Peter of Guernsey and Liverpool: will, 1799, written in Boston, Massachusetts, in 1797, **87**

Leaper, Robt. of Halton, 1798, **122**

Ledsham, George of London: will, 1606, **1***

Leeming, John, died in Salford, Lancs.: admon, 1825, to Mary Leeming, widow of Middleham, **193**

Leicestershire, **130, 131**

Leigh, Agnes, widow of Ashton in Winwick: will, 1589–1591 [printed index mistakenly shows Agnes Wright], **75**

Leigh, Matthew of London: will, 1622, **1***

Lincolnshire, **131, 136, 176, 193**

Lingard, Anne of Mottram Andrew: admon, 1682, **20**

Lister, John: will, 1671, **38**

Little, Ellen: will, 1854, **97**

Littler, John: will, 1741–1742, **21**

Lloyd, Agnes of Beaumaris, Anglesey: will, 1606, **1***

London, **82, 90, 96, 184, 200**
Westminster, **193**
see also Bradshaw, Broomfield, Colbie, Done, Eaton, Erdswick, Farrer, Fitton, French, Hodges, Holmes, Ingham, Ledsham, Leigh, Markall, Phillips, Richmond, Rode, Yate

Lowe, Margaret of Bloarfield, Staffs.: will, 1603, **1***

Ludley, William of Grantham, Lincs.: marriage license bond, 1803, **193**

Lumley, Thomas of Corbridge, Northumb.: bond, 1771, **63**

Lunn, Isabell, widow of the City of York: will, 1722, **179**

Lythgoe, Mary, widow of West Leigh: will, 1810, **102**

Maddocks, Richard: will, 1661, **9**

Magnay, Fisher of Madras: will, 1857, **27†**

Makenzie, Roderick, captain of the "London": will, 1812, **27†**

Malbon, Thomas of Congleton: will, 1779, **26**

Mallorie, Sir William of Hoton: will, 1411, **108**

Malone, Patrick of Dublin: will, 1587, **1***

Man, Anne, widow of Mansfield: will, 1744, **138**

Manwering, Katherin of Kendall: will, 1569, **147**

Markall, Margaret of London: inventory, 1641, **1***

Marriage license bonds
1713–1754, used as idents in the Chancery Court of York, **175**
Barmby Moor, 1727, **189**
Bishop Wilton, 1712–1721, **190**
Dalton, Lancs., 1767–1772, **160**
Dean and Chapter of York, 1665–1673, **181**
1767–1772, **159**
Durham, 1589, **60**
Extracts in Howe's Collection, 1732–1735, **67**
Fenton, 1744, **190**
Kirkby Irelyth, Lancs., 1767–1772, **160**
Middleham, 1789–1851, **193**
North Newbald, 1697–1729, **194**
Richmond
1680–1694, **185**
1705, 1712–1715, **117**
1707–1714, **185**
1822–1823, **184**
Selby, 1715–1726, **194**
Southwell, Notts., 1588–1666, **136**
Weighton, 1695, **197**
Wetwang, 1663–1706, **197**

Martyn, Alice of Newark: marriage license bond, 1589, **137**

Mason, Abraham of Hollinwood in Oldham: admon, 1809, **102**

Mason, Allan of Jamaica: will, 1804, **27†**